§ FAMILY LIKENESS

FAMILY LIKENESS

SEX, MARRIAGE,
AND INCEST FROM
JANE AUSTEN TO
VIRGINIA WOOLF

MARY JEAN CORBETT

CORNELL UNIVERSITY PRESS
Ithaca and London

First published 2008 by Cornell University Press

Printed in the United States of America

Library of Congress Cataloging-in-Publication Data

Corbett, Mary Jean, 1962–
    Family likeness : sex, marriage, and incest from Jane
Austen to Virginia Woolf / Mary Jean Corbett.
        p. cm.
    Includes bibliographical references and index.
    ISBN 978–0–8014–4707–5 (cloth : alk. paper)
    1. English fiction—19th century—History and
criticism. 2. English fiction—Women authors—History
and criticism. 3. Family in literature. 4. Austen, Jane,
1775–1817—Criticism and interpretation. 5. Brontë,
Charlotte, 1816–1855—Criticism and interpretation.
6. Woolf, Virginia, 1882–1941—Criticism and
interpretation. 7. Sex in literature. 8. Marriage in
literature. 9. Incest in literature. I. Title.

    PR868.F29C67 2008
    823'.809—dc22

2008019568

Cornell University Press strives to use environmentally
responsible suppliers and materials to the fullest extent
possible in the publishing of its books. Such materials
include vegetable-based, low-VOC inks and acid-free
papers that are recycled, totally chlorine-free, or partly
composed of nonwood fibers. For further information,
visit our website at www.cornellpress.cornell.edu.

Cloth printing   10 9 8 7 6 5 4 3 2 1

✍ CONTENTS

Preface and Acknowledgments   *vii*

1. Making and Breaking the Rules:
   An Introduction   1

2. "Cousins in Love, &c." in
   Jane Austen   30

3. Husband, Wife, and Sister:
   Making and Unmaking the
   Early Victorian Family   57

4. Orphan Stories: Adoption and
   Affinity in Charlotte Brontë   86

5. Intercrossing, Interbreeding,
   and *The Mill on the Floss*   115

6. Fictive Kinship and Natural
   Affinities in *Wives and Daughters*   144

7. Virginia Woolf and
   Victorian "Incests"   174

Conclusion   *201*

Notes   *211*

Bibliography   *243*

Index   *259*

✍ PREFACE AND ACKNOWLEDGMENTS

> Family likeness has often a deep sadness in it. Nature, that great tragic dramatist, knits us together by bone and muscle, and divides us by the subtler web of our brains; blends yearning and repulsion; and ties us by our heart-strings to the beings that jar us at every movement.
>
> —George Eliot, *Adam Bede,* 1859

This book argues that potential or actual marriage between women and men within nineteenth-century families—whether involving cousins, in-laws, or figurative adoptees—represents a compelling alternative to the romance between strangers that most critics have taken to be the paradigm for the heterosexual marriage plot. It identifies a cultural tendency toward forging relationships with familial and familiar figures that testifies not only to the perceived perils of intimacy with strangers but also to the ambivalent attractions, for women in particular, of remaining within known or knowable first-family structures that may include sustained and sustaining relations with other women. An increasing focus in the late nineteenth century on the profit and danger of intrafamilial alliance, I suggest, produced an uneasy tension between marrying "in" and marrying "out." By century's end, a restrictive definition of incest emerged in the wake of sociological writing about working-class domestic life and early anthropological writing about the origins of heterosexual marriage and the civilized family: a class- and race-specific set of representations, inflected by gender, successfully differentiated that "savage" practice from the ordinary sexual and marital arrangements of English middle-class families. These arguments set the stage for close readings of works of fiction, in which notions of incest figure very differently, by the most celebrated women writers of the nineteenth century—Jane Austen, Emily and Charlotte Brontë, George Eliot, and Elizabeth Gaskell—as well as of lesser-known but no less instructive works by Harriet Martineau and Felicia Skene, with a final turn to the writings of Virginia Woolf.

My choice of authors and the focus of each individual chapter aim to be representative of a broad range of possible textual sites and interpretive approaches. But I have, for example, limited my scope to women's writing—specifically prose fiction—perhaps seeming to imply that neither male writers nor male and female poets of the period were implicated in the dynamics I explore. This is not at all the case: a more comprehensive project would no doubt discuss novels by Charles Dickens, Wilkie Collins, Anthony Trollope, and Thomas Hardy and take a long, hard look at both Elizabeth Barrett Browning's *Aurora Leigh* (1856) and Alfred, Lord Tennyson's *In Memoriam* (1850). So, too, some readers may be jarred by the jump from Gaskell, in the 1860s, to the modernist Woolf; they will recognize that the preoccupations of such figures as Dinah Mulock Craik, Margaret Oliphant, Mary Elizabeth Braddon, and multiple "New Women" writers of the 1880s and 1890s—particularly the partnership of Michael Field, who were aunt and niece—might warrant inclusion here. These omissions represent the limits of my scholarly competence as well as those of the time and space available to me. By concentrating only on prose works by women writers, I do, however, hope to indicate how and why their investment in family matters and family affections warrants separate, extended treatment.

These limits aside, my emphasis on the persistence of the first (or "birth") family in women's fictional representations may also perplex some readers in that it challenges the focus on the second (or "conjugal") family that informs so much current literary and historical analysis. For example, in a powerful and elegant book, Helena Michie has described Victorian "conjugality" as the psychic and social movement away from the ties that constitute the family of origin toward the exclusivity and isolation of the married couple.[1] Much as I admire the subtlety and verve of her argument, this project implies, against that grain, that there may be as much continuity as discontinuity between these formations. In making a case for attending to the ongoing importance of first-family bonds in domestic fiction, I am also mindful of Ruth Perry's comprehensive and persuasive study of how women lost economic and social power as sisters and daughters over the course of the eighteenth century, making marriage to men, whether strangers or familiars, that much more important as a matter of sheer survival.[2] As I see it, however, even though the practical economic value of first-family ties may diminish in the nineteenth century, their affective dimension actually intensifies. To be sure, domestic fiction primarily foregrounds middle-class women's emotional rather than economic vulnerability to the risks of taking family relationships, especially intragenerational relations to brothers and cousins, as a central paradigm for adult heterosexual eroticism. But the writings (like the lives) of Austen, the Brontës, Eliot, Gaskell, Woolf, and others also honor women's ongoing investment in first-family relationships, their passionate commitment to siblings or cousins of both sexes even in face of the unequal social and economic status of women and men more generally. To reread this body of work with family as well as marriage in mind opens up new perspectives on both.

I thus undertake a series of readings of nineteenth-century fiction by women in relation to key discourses shaping the representation of nineteenth-century families: legal and political debates about what constitutes legitimate marriage, scientific and lay inquiry into the dynamics of breeding and the mechanisms of variation, and the emergence of incest in anthropological writing and urban reportage as that which distinguishes civilization from savagery. Studying the changing forms of the family construct over the course of this period and analyzing the disparate means of making families that women's fiction explores, I argue that the particular contexts in which intrafamilial bonds were figured continue, in some discrete ways, to shape their meanings for us in the present. Along these lines, I begin by tracing the emergence of the modern understanding of incest in the late nineteenth century, locating it within a cultural formation that represents sex and marriage within the bourgeois family as a strategy for maintaining class and race homogeneity. Class and race exclusions naturalize what we have learned to call "endogamy" for cultural elites while distinguishing it from the incests perpetrated by culture's others, indicating the historical variability and contingency of both the prohibitions on incest and the practices deemed incestuous. Here I consider the implications of rethinking incest as a class and racial formation and initiate the critique of anthropological models of marriage-as-exchange developed later in the book. I look at Emily Brontë's *Wuthering Heights* (1847), famously dependent for its very structure on the reproductive traffic between two families, as a representation of the shifting meanings and configurations of family itself. Incorporating a figure for difference within the family in the form of an adoptee, Brontë's novel exposes a variety of ways in which kinship, far from being given or fixed, is historically created and culturally contested.

Turning back to the beginning of the nineteenth century, I analyze intrafamilial unions in Austen's fiction, historicizing cousin-marriage as a practice with multiple meanings and effects within her oeuvre. Exploring family formations in her novels, I argue that neither the language nor the practice of family has a single, fixed shape. Resolutely subordinated in most current criticism to the "exogamous" marriage plot and construed as figuratively or even literally incestuous, the strand of Austen's fiction that represents marriage within the family in positive terms leads me to conclude that marital ties need not displace a commitment to family but might instead strengthen it; that marrying within the family, for women, may be less risky than marrying outside it; and that Austen's interest lies especially in the marital options that create the most agency for her female characters. While all of her novels conclude with at least one marriage and the constitution of a second family, the happiest endings, as many readers have observed, feature marriages that reinforce sisterly ties. In *Mansfield Park* (1814), Fanny Price's position—a sister to her male cousins, but not to her female ones; a modest heroine who (immodestly) gives her heart away—enables her to secure a permanent position within an "endogamous" but hardly anomalous Mansfield family.

Sibling relationships provide the central focus in chapter 3, which explores the controversy surrounding marriage with a deceased wife's sister. The legal prohibition in 1835 of what had previously been a fairly unremarkable social practice inspired a campaign to overturn the ban, setting off a cultural debate about affinal marriage that lasted for almost seventy-five years. During the 1840s and 1850s, the middle-class men who opposed the law disputed the charge of incest leveled at such marriages, representing the dead wife's sister simply as an "affine." By their logic, taking a "stranger in blood" into the house as a second wife to raise one's orphaned children would be much less preferable to keeping the dead wife's sister in the family; in pamphlets, essays, and public testimony, they emphasized the threat of difference that a new, unknown wife portends. Drawing on these and other texts from the period but focusing in particular on Martineau's *Deerbrook* (1839) and Skene's *The Inheritance of Evil* (1849), I consider what wives and sisters, whose voices were largely excluded from the public debate, might have had at stake in this controversy, the tensions and continuities between first and second families it highlights, and the opportunities for redrawing the lines of familial membership it affords. Each novel represents a conflicted triangular bond between a husband and two sisters, giving voice to women's and men's desires for something in excess of, or in addition to, conjugal love.

In reading the fiction of Charlotte Brontë, I take up that most contested concept in the deceased wife's sister debate—"affinity"—as a lens for exploring adoption, a pervasive (though extralegal) practice of forging familial relationships. Both a means of constructing family and an analogue for marriage itself, adoption figures broadly in Brontë's work, demonstrating the exclusions on which the constitution of the family depends and the familial terms in which the adoptee's romantic relationships take shape. Plots that center on cross-racial adoption in her early unpublished writings, the juvenilia, set in an imaginary African colony expose the fractures within a highly intermarried imperial family, signifying the limits of solidarity while also articulating a racialized basis for family membership. In *Jane Eyre* (1847) and *Villette* (1853), Brontë recasts the drama of the female English orphan as a search for affinities, both biological and spiritual, foregrounding the complex internal dynamics of familial politics as shaped primarily by gendered rather than racialized asymmetries of power and privilege. Jane's plot in particular, overdetermined by the rivalries and hostilities of her parents' generation, hinges on constituting equitable intragenerational relationships that will undo the harm of earlier family settlements; her access to colonial wealth enables her to escape the lure of cousin-marriage, even as she, like Lucy Snowe in *Villette,* chooses a man whom she partially identifies as (nonbiological) kin. The orphan who begins her journey with only a father in heaven comes to have relations aplenty by novel's end; I partially locate the implications of Jane's triumph in relation to the emergent anthropological fictions of adoption, family, and marriage that her own narrative anticipates.

Amid increasing concern about the mating of like with like *or* unlike, the late nineteenth century saw a new emphasis on the biocultural consequences of human reproductive practices. Incest and miscegenation were the twinned horrors at the center of this emerging discourse of the family. Proximity and distance, sameness and difference came to represent particular and, at times, analogous risks. I take up these issues in relation to the biological making of family ties in *The Mill on the Floss* (1860). Like her contemporaries, Eliot was consumed by questions of inheritance, seeking ways to measure and assess the influence of environment, to determine what was inherited and passed down and what was not, and to trace the effects of contact among different peoples in forwarding or retarding individual (and cultural) development. I illustrate the connections across a range of discourses that problematize the (re)production of human families: politicizing "interbreeding" and "intercrossing" in terms of class and race, analysts characterize the risks of sex and marriage with either intimates or strangers in oddly similar ways. By situating *The Mill on the Floss* in relation to writings by Darwin and Lewes in which these issues are fully canvassed, I argue that Eliot's early historicism and particularly her conception of the individual were shaped in large part by the new racialized fictions of heredity.

Mined of late for its Darwinian resonances, Elizabeth Gaskell's unfinished novel *Wives and Daughters* (1864–66) consciously draws on and revises the conceptions of the family and motives for marriage that I analyze in its predecessors. Its Austenesque heroine, young Molly Gibson, inhabits a provincial landscape comparable to Martineau's Deerbrook. She becomes "like a daughter" to a local gentry couple, who, in Gaskell's deliberate echoing of *Mansfield Park,* disqualifies her from marrying either of their sons. During her absence from home, Molly's widowed father marries a "stranger" to impose order on his household: the second marriage brings Molly a stepmother whom she cannot love and a stepsister with whom she falls in love at first sight. When the stepsister becomes engaged to the Hamley son whom Molly prefers, the wavering line between brotherly affection and romantic attachment breaks down even as the sisterly bond is compromised. Gaskell's blended family raises all kinds of questions about the very status of family. Does a family derive from blood, from law, from affinity in the Brontëan sense? Is a blended family analogous to a biological one? Or is analogy itself something of a master figure we can use to think about the fictions of kinship? Drawing on the plots and patterns of earlier texts, *Wives and Daughters* decenters the biological basis for family ties even as it explicitly locates the formation of homosocial ties and heterosexual love within the familial paradigms of women's fiction.

I conclude the book with the life and work of Virginia Woolf, whose experience of late Victorian family life crucially shaped her continuous revisions of the past. Whereas most scholars discuss Woolf's experience of incest in terms of trauma, I contextualize it within nineteenth-century discourses of sex and marriage that marked the cultural landscape of Woolf's childhood, including the debate over marrying a deceased wife's sister, the construction of incest as a "savage" practice, and the discourse of child sexual abuse, which began to emerge in the 1880s. In a wide-ranging project, Woolf situates the Victorian family as the institution that, more intimately than any other, produced and reproduced the class, racial, sexual, and gendered dynamics of late imperial English culture. In her fictional writings—particularly the unfinished hybrid text, *The Pargiters* (1932–33)—Woolf reinscribed some of the assumptions she sought to critique, thus undermining some of her more radical claims, even as the limited range of discourses available to her constrained her efforts. When she represents stranger molestation or identifies sexual abuse with working-class life, Woolf remains within the class/race frameworks of her time. But in *The Years* (1937), she also represents the potential for developing new social arrangements among siblings and cousins who suffer the psychic wounds inflicted within the upper-middle-class Victorian household but still strive to imagine ways of "living differently." For all of Woolf's ambivalence about family life, this novel honors the affective and political power of inter- and intragenerational familial relationships and their role in forming the new order, to which *The Years* recurrently alludes. And in that effort, to which I return in a brief conclusion, I suggest that we can find hopeful models for rethinking "family" in our own time.

What began as a promise to myself to draft just one essay in a month's respite from other responsibilities grew into a full-scale project, which no doubt still bears the marks of its wholly accidental birth. Perhaps that lack of premeditation is what made writing this book such a pleasure. I do know that the institutions and individuals that supported its development also deserve quite a bit of the credit for the happiness that writing it afforded me. The past and present leadership of both the Department of English and the College of Arts and Sciences at Miami University has underwritten my scholarly pursuits in a variety of ways, including extended leave time and generous travel funding; I am most grateful to the university for the support of the John W. Steube Endowed Professorship, which made completing the book that much more imperative and possible. In addition to evincing warm enthusiasm for the project almost from the moment it landed on his desk, Peter J. Potter of Cornell University Press chose two exceptional readers for it, Margaret Homans and Kathy Alexis Psomiades, whose clear and candid criticisms of the manuscript have, I hope, enriched its final form. I have been fortunate indeed to have such people in my corner.

I have also been lucky enough to belong to an extended group of wonderful colleagues: Christine Krueger, Barbara Leckie, Teresa Mangum, Elsie Michie, Susan Morgan, Ellen Rosenman, Anca Vlasopolos, and many, many other members of the Interdisciplinary Nineteenth-Century Studies Association provided the first audiences for the ideas in this book, offering both intellectual support and enduring friendship to someone who is, like everyone, forever in need of both. Of this group, I must single out Deborah Denenholz Morse, who read nearly every word, for making valuable suggestions and always cheering me on—just as Regenia Gagnier and Rob Polhemus generously continue to do. Laura Mandell, Lori Merish, and Lynn Voskuil read the earliest efforts with a critical eye and helped me find my footing. Much later on, Madelyn Detloff, Ira Livingston, Kelly Mays, and Denise McCoskey persuaded me that I was on the right path. I am extremely grateful for their contributions.

In greater Boston, where this book really took hold, Kelly Hager, John Plotz, and Leah Price provided occasions for exchange that deepened my thinking and kept me working. Thanks to them and to all my colleagues and coconspirators at both ends of the steep hill at Brandeis University; they gave me a home away from my habitual one that I will always remember with affection. Without Lucy Norvell, Nedra Reynolds, and Mary Rutkowski, those three happy years in the northeast (and all the years that preceded and followed them) would have been much the poorer. In Cincinnati, Madelyn Detloff, Katie Johnson, Denise McCoskey, Tim Melley, and Kate Ronald have seen me through the book's final phase in style and with love. My life continues to be enriched by my old Stanford friends—Shay Brawn, Alex Chasin, Ira Livingston, and Kelly Mays—each one of whom, on any given day, can still amuse, console, challenge, and inspire me; I am more deeply indebted to them for their enduring love and goodness than I can easily say. I am also grateful beyond words to my family—including siblings, nieces, nephews, aunts, cousins, even cousins-in-law—for their encouragement and support. That so many of my kin are also my friends is one of our most meaningful achievements.

Several chapters of the book include material published elsewhere. Portions of chapters 1 and 3 first appeared in "Husband, Wife, and Sister: Making and Remaking the Early Victorian Family," *Victorian Literature and Culture* 35 (2007): 1–19. An earlier version of chapter 2 was published as "'Cousins in Love &c.' in Jane Austen," *Tulsa Studies in Women's Literature* 23 (2004): 237–59. Shorter versions of chapters 4 and 5, respectively, have appeared in edited collections: "'The Crossing o' Breeds' in *The Mill on the Floss*," in *Victorian Animal Dreams*, ed. Deborah Denenholz Morse and Martin Danahay (Aldershot, U.K.: Ashgate Publishing, 2007), 121–43; and "Orphan Stories: Charlotte Brontë's Racial Fictions of Adoption," in *Other Mothers*, ed. Ellen Rosenman and Claudia Klaver (Columbus: Ohio State University Press, forthcoming in 2008). I gratefully acknowledge the permission of these journals and publishers to reprint this revised material.

❧ FAMILY LIKENESS

🍎 CHAPTER 1

Making and Breaking the Rules: An Introduction

What, indeed, is marriage itself but a restriction of promiscuous intercourse?

—William Page Wood, *A Vindication of Law Prohibiting Marriage with a Deceased Wife's Sister*, 1861

"There are rules that apply to most people," says my father, "and there are people who are outside of those rules. People who are—"
   "How can you know that you—that we—are exceptions?"
   "I just do," he says. "You'll have to trust me."

—Kathryn Harrison, *The Kiss*, 1997

The great interdiction of incest is an invention of the intellectuals.

—Michel Foucault, "Sexual Choice, Sexual Act: Foucault and Homosexuality," 1982

Between the summer of 1907 and the spring of 1908, Virginia Stephen (later Woolf) composed a family memoir called "Reminiscences." While I will return to it at the end of this book, its final chapter is especially significant for my immediate purposes in that it provides a glimpse of the historical shift in the meanings of incest in its representation of one upper-middle-class Victorian family experience. "Reminiscences" tells of the aftermath of the death of Stella Duckworth Hills in 1897; the intimate relationship that developed thereafter between Jack Hills and his sister-in-law, Vanessa Stephen (later Bell); and the disapproval that that relationship incurred among some family members, especially George Duckworth, the Stephen sisters' half-brother. Representing Vanessa as "bound" to Jack "by a kind of instinctive fidelity, which admitted of no question," Virginia Stephen identified their shared grief at Stella's death after just three months of marriage as "the starting point of much quicker and more fervent feelings," feelings that took on quite dramatic importance.[1]

1

Significantly, "Reminiscences" only obliquely explains George's objection to this relationship, replicating, perhaps somewhat parodically at a distance of ten years, the aura of scandal surrounding the affair. As Jack and Vanessa draw closer together, Vanessa and Virginia draw a little apart to consider the situation:

> We . . . walked alone when we could, and discussed the state of the dif-
> ferent parties, and how they threatened to meet in conflict over her
> body. So far they did not more than threaten; but a man, or woman, of
> the world, George, for example or Kitty Maxse, might already foretell
> the supreme struggle of the future. Decency at present forbade open
> speech, but no doubt the suspicion was alive, and made itself felt in
> an unrest and intensity of feeling on George's part which we saw, but
> failed as yet to interpret. ("Reminiscences," 57)

As narrated here, the situation sounds dire: "conflict over [Vanessa's] body" promises to break out between Jack and George; allied with "Society," George and Kitty (a prototype for Clarissa Dalloway) embody the coercive forces of convention. Virginia thus implies that the "conflict" has a worldly and not just domestic dimension, setting up the "supreme struggle" on Vanessa's part against a doubled power. With "open speech" forbidden by "decency," a "suspicion" clearly aroused but not expressed, and an "unrest and intensity of feeling on George's part" that the sisters could perceive but not "interpret," the violation of a standard is everywhere suggested but nowhere named.

In their obscurity, these references still elude some readers today, who likewise neither name nor analyze the source of all the trouble.[2] Yet the proximate cause of George's opposition to the relationship between Vanessa and Jack would have been very clear to their contemporaries. For in 1907, as Virginia Stephen began to write the memoir, both Houses of Parliament finally passed the Deceased Wife's Sister's Marriage Act after many years of debate, legalizing a union that was still prohibited by English law in the last decade of the nineteenth century on the grounds that it constituted incest. Had they chosen to continue the relationship that began in 1897, that is, Vanessa and Jack could not have been legally married in England for another ten years (not that they could have known that); even had they gone abroad to marry, as some couples did, their marriage would not have been recognized in England. For in marrying Stella, Jack had gained not just a wife but also several sisters, none of whom under English law he could ever marry—no matter that, as Virginia puts it, Vanessa was "the natural person to be with him" after his wife's death, expressing a sentiment that, as we shall see, resonated with the rhetoric deployed by those marriage-law activists who sought to overturn the ban ("Reminiscences," 56).

In opposing the relationship, George no doubt acted in accord with his perception of the rightness of social and, for some late Victorians, religious conventions protecting the sanctity of domestic life. Although advocates for its repeal had repeatedly ridiculed the prohibition, others defended its crucial role in securing what one parliamentary supporter of the law called "the unrestrained and peculiarly affectionate intercourse which ought to exist for the happiness of families between the closest and nearest relations."[3] That her half-brother would have subscribed to this public convention for the conduct of private life is surely the case; that Virginia Woolf did not, we can discern from her work. One biographer surmises that the outrage of Aunt Milvain in *Night and Day* (1919) at Katharine Hilbery's condoning her cousin Cassandra Otway's liaison with William Rodney while Katharine and William are still ostensibly engaged to one another owes something to the familial disapproval over Vanessa's relationship with Jack.[4] More directly, Peter Walsh of *Mrs. Dalloway* (1925) deems it "incredible" that even so recently as the 1890s, Richard Dalloway had "seriously and solemnly" pronounced that "no decent man ought to let his wife visit a deceased wife's sister" who had formed an inappropriate liaison with her brother(-in-law).[5] Juxtaposing this remark with Richard Dalloway's earlier cameo appearance in *The Voyage Out* (1915), in which his alarming kiss initiates Rachel Vinrace into the potential violence of heterosexual desire, we can see just how Woolf persistently reworked such materials over time, forging a critique of a masculine double standard that indicted the arbiters of a respectability that can only appear as such by perpetuating what may look to us like the most astonishing hypocrisy.

In the abbreviated description of George Duckworth in "Reminiscences," Virginia Stephen sketches the terms by which he will reappear in later memoirs. "Under the name of unselfishness he allowed himself to commit acts which a cleverer man would have called tyrannical; and, profoundly believing in the purity of his love, he behaved little better than a brute"—but "at the moment," she concludes, George's position "seemed perfectly accountable; he was the simple domestic creature, of deep feeling, who...was setting himself to do all he could to be mother and sister and brother to us in one" ("Reminiscences," 58). Over a decade later, Woolf would echo and amplify those words in the conclusion to "22 Hyde Park Gate": "Yes, the old ladies of Kensington and Belgravia never knew that George Duckworth was not only father and mother, brother and sister to those poor Stephen girls; he was their lover also."[6] Between the first memoir and the second, much had changed, including the law: by the time Virginia Stephen left off writing "Reminiscences," George's "brutality" might almost have qualified as a criminal offense. For it was in 1908 that the Punishment of Incest Act criminalized sexual intercourse between parents and children, siblings of full or half blood, and grandfathers and granddaughters.

"For half a century," incest had not been subject to criminal penalty because the authors of the Matrimonial Causes Act of 1857, which created the new divorce courts, had "failed to make any provision" against them.[7] Although this omission may have been "sheer inadvertence," Sybil Wolfram speculates that the lack of criminal penalty protected those "persons at the time"—brothers- and sisters-in-law who defied the law by marrying abroad or in parishes where their affinal relationship to one another was not known—"with a strong interest in going free if they committed incest."[8] If this "rather obvious gap" in the criminal law tacitly condoned incest between relations by marriage, then it also turned a blind eye to incest between relations by blood. For long years treated in exactly the same way under English law and on the same footing in the eyes of the Anglican church, affinity (a relationship by marriage) and consanguinity (a relationship by blood) were formally distinguished from one another only with the legislation of 1907 and 1908.[9] Although there is no evidence to suggest that anyone had this goal in mind, lifting the prohibition on affinal incest effectively enabled the institution of legal penalties for consanguineal incest. With this legislation, then, the cultural meaning of Vanessa's past relationship with Jack changed. So, too, would George's prior sexual abuse of both Vanessa and Virginia appear in a different light: "the purity of his love" for his "closest and nearest relations" could be given, to our way of thinking, a more accurate name.

Along these lines, this book aims to recover what can be recovered of the history of incest as nineteenth-century middle-class people knew it, lived it, argued over it, and redefined it, for themselves and for us. I believe that in order for incest to be perceived now as, in the words of Judith Butler, "a sexual irregularity that is terrifying, repulsive, unthinkable in the ways that other departures from normative exogamic heterosexuality are"—as, in effect, both unnatural and uncultural—a series of strategic differentiations in the meanings of the word and the practices associated with it had to occur.[10] None of the other changes explored in this book is quite so dramatic as the legislation of 1907 and 1908, when one form of incest was abolished, while another, defined as occurring only between "blood" relations, was established. But my examples here should go some way toward demonstrating the magnitude of the major cultural shift in attitudes to sex and marriage within the family over the course of the nineteenth century.

If today we may be inclined to interpret the affirmation of "the unrestrained and peculiarly affectionate intercourse which ought to exist for the happiness of families between the closest and nearest relations" as an ideological warrant for intrafamilial sexual abuse, then we ought, first, to find out who those "closest and nearest relations" were from a nineteenth-century perspective. Which marriage practices among them were culturally accepted and encouraged? Which others were prohibited or penalized? What combinations of biologically related or unrelated persons constituted "the family"—and how firmly established was the idea of "biological relation" itself? What differences did marriage make not just to the individuals but also to the families that it joined together? How did families that did not fit the emergent nuclear norm—husband, wife, and (biological) children—negotiate their differences (or similarities) of descent in relation to adoption or remarriage? Did familial ties between same-sex and cross-sex siblings provide models for the romantic and marital paradigms that disrupted or reaffirmed those ties? And what roles did emergent or dominant norms of race and class—mechanisms of inclusion and exclusion—play in shaping marriage and family and their attendant meanings over the course of the period? These questions will preoccupy me throughout, just as they did those women whose written remains this book considers, and I address some of them in a reading of Emily Brontë's *Wuthering Heights* at the end of this chapter. In order to pursue them, however, I must clear some ground: by examining the discourse on incest as a social evil as it took shape in the nineteenth century, I hope to indicate its relationship to the middle-class incest, like marriage with a deceased wife's sister (hereafter MDWS), which forms my primary topic.

In an argument to which I return below, Ellen Pollak locates the emergence of an "incestuous notion of human subjectivity" in the late eighteenth century premised on class and race borders and boundaries that variously include and exclude "others"; most critics and historians agree that this subjectivity becomes dominant thereafter.[11] In this chapter, I suggest that it does so in part by normalizing "the unrestrained and peculiarly affectionate intercourse" of middle-class domesticity as against the differently "unrestrained" practices of the working classes and "savage" tribes—sometimes conflated—that constituted a major focus of early anthropology. For if "sexuality is originally, historically bourgeois," as Michel Foucault famously argued in the first volume of *The History of Sexuality,* then we can read the middle-class discourse on working-class and "primitive" incest as part of the cultural production of "class sexualities," one of the "shifts and transpositions" of the deployment of sexuality that "induces specific class"—and race—"effects."[12] As Elizabeth Wilson writes in a late-twentieth-century U.S. context, "suspicions that others engage in incestuous practices have long been part of the arsenal of moral prejudice that has been used to justify the social and political hegemony of the white middle class," whose ideology "implies that incest occurs more frequently in other classes or racial groups because these groups are morally inferior and are unable to restrain their animal impulses."[13] This ideological formation, generated in the nineteenth century, may provide another clue as to why there were no criminal penalties for incest in England between 1857 and 1908. I trace its development to the collaborative fantasies that took shape between the 1840s and the 1880s, especially by attending to what Rosemary Jann describes as "the crucial role played by sexual conduct in...attempts to construct the boundary that demarcates the fully human from the animal and to chart the progress of civilization."[14] The depiction of incest as a "savage" practice—rather than, say, a violation of nature or custom in which the "civilized" themselves might engage—installed at the heart of this discourse a particular class and racial bias that has had a decided effect on how incest is perceived even today. By analyzing the late-nineteenth-century discourse on incestuous "others," we can begin to outline the very different terms on which women writers from Austen to Woolf constructed their representations of sex and marriage within middle-class families.

For his contemporaries, the most shocking claim in the Reverend Andrew Mearns's pamphlet *The Bitter Cry of Outcast London* (1883) was his matter-of-fact statement that among the overcrowded rooms of South London, "incest is common."[15] Not for the first time, "the character of the London poor," as Daniel Bivona and Roger B. Henkle remark, "broke into public consciousness as if it were a *discovery*."[16] Closely questioned by the members of the Royal Commission on the Housing of the Working Classes, convened in 1884, Mearns and a slew of other witnesses were pressed to define their terms. How much incest had they observed or heard about? How "common" was it? Who engaged in it? Some responded by testifying to the difficulty of speaking publicly about incest, as one of those "nameless abominations which could only be set forth," the journalist George Sims wrote in 1889, "were we contributing to the *Lancet*."[17] In his testimony before the Royal Commission, the longtime factory and housing reformer Lord Shaftesbury "refused for propriety's sake to mention all the things he knew to exist"; yet he gave examples of children "endeavouring to have sexual connection," aping the behavior of adults with whom they shared a single room or bed.[18]

Twenty years earlier, however, in a speech to Parliament, Shaftesbury had seen fit to transgress the code of propriety in arguing that overcrowded housing in urban centers produced sexual depravity: "There were not only adults of both sexes living in the same room, but adult sons sleeping with their mothers, and brothers and sisters very commonly sleeping in the same bed. He was stating what he knew to be the truth when he said that incestuous crime was frightfully common—common to the greatest possible extent."[19] And twenty years before that, the correspondents on whose intelligence Edwin Chadwick relied in his *Report on the Sanitary Condition of the Labouring Population of Great Britain* (1842) remarked that from "a moral point of view," the "promiscuous mixture of sexes in sleeping-rooms" makes it "impossible to keep up even the common decencies of life."[20] "How they lie down to rest, how they sleep, how they can preserve common decency, how unutterable horrors are avoided, is beyond all conception," for "in the houses of the working classes, brothers and sisters, and lodgers of both sexes, are found occupying the same sleeping-room with the parents, and consequences occur which humanity shudders to contemplate": "These habits," Chadwick determined, "lead to the abandonment of all the conveniences and decencies of life,... which is destructive to the morality as well as the health of large classes of both sexes."[21] In Benjamin Disraeli's *Sybil* (1845), Walter Gerard makes a similar assertion: "There are great bodies of the working classes of this country nearer the condition of brutes than they have been at any time since the Conquest.... Incest and infanticide are as common among them as among the lower animals."[22]

Fully four decades before the sensational explosion of concern about incest among the working classes in the 1880s, then, early Victorian investigators were already describing it as "common" to working-class domestic life. Characterizing their human subjects as little better than "the lower animals" or "brutes," Judith R. Walkowitz argues, "urban explorers adapted the language of imperialism to evoke features of their own cities."[23] No doubt fueled by the spectacular publicity generated through such new media outlets as W. T. Stead's *Pall Mall Gazette,* the specific and polemical focus on incest as an effect of "overcrowded" housing and a putative cause of working-class degeneration did not, however, become a subject of intense public interest until the 1880s. Under what conditions did these ideas reemerge, and what gave them their new currency?

With multiple meanings in the nineteenth century, incest included a different set of perceived transgressions than we associate with the term today: as the historian Polly Morris writes, "The legal definition of incest bore very little relation to what we now think of as an intrafamilial sexual crime."[24] Although Chadwick and Shaftesbury located incest in what William Acton called the "promiscuous herding" of working-class men and women, the broadest public discussion of incest before the 1880s actually took place on the mainly middle-class terrain of the MDWS debate, as I explore below and again in chapter 3.[25] Assisted by the biologization of "the family," the continuous effort to repeal the MDWS prohibition did manage, by 1908, to narrow what counted as incest to include sex between "blood" relatives only, thus leaving in-laws, step-relations, and adoptive kin out of the question entirely. Yet even late in the nineteenth century, the claim that widowers who sought to marry their sisters(-in-law) were innocent of incestuous desire still met with fervent opposition: "On this issue," said the Duke of Argyll in the Lords debate on the bill in 1896, "men's instincts are utterly corrupt,... except when under the influence of religion and tradition, they resort to practices ruinous to their race and lower than any that are practiced by the beast."[26] Such rhetoric implicitly links the desire for in-law marriage to other forms of sexual corruption, although we can also see how the very idea of "instincts" takes on class- and race-based associations.

Alongside the persistent perception that where overcrowding is, there incest shall be, an emergent anthropological discourse of savagery began to present the practice not as an effect of an underlying cause but as a defining feature of the permanent residuum. "Victorian anthropologists' fascination with the sexual practices of primitive peoples," Seth Koven remarks, "closely mirrored social reformers' own obsession with working-class sexual promiscuity as a root cause of overpopulation, demoralization, and poverty."[27] Linking primitives at home and abroad and vacillating on the question of causation, this double perspective reshaped the dominant associations of incest. The separation of "civilized" from "savage," "culture" from "nature," self-disciplined "restraint" from self-indulgent "instinct" ultimately worked to distinguish middle-class kin-marriage from working-class depravity and indecency.

Indeed, to some people it was absolutely necessary to separate the two in promoting middle-class men's interests. In the fourth and final volume of *London Labour and the London Poor* (1861), for example, Bracebridge Hemyng undertook a study of "Prostitution in London" that enumerated the different categories of women—street-walkers, dress-lodgers, soldiers' women, "ladies of intrigue"—who had sex with men to whom they were not legally married. "The last head in our classification is 'Cohabitant Prostitutes,' " Hemyng writes, further subdividing that group into "those whose paramours" cannot afford or do not believe in marriage; those women who, should they (re)marry, would lose an income; and, finally, "those who have married a relative forbidden by law":

> We know that people will occasionally marry a deceased wife's sister, notwithstanding the anathemas of mother church are sure to be hurled at them. Yet ecclesiastical terrors may have weight with a man who has

conceived an affection for a sister-in-law, for whom he will have to undergo so many penalties.

Perhaps parliamentary agitation may soon legitimatize [*sic*] these connections, and abolish this heading from our category of Cohabitant Prostitution.[28]

Whether with or without benefit of clergy, a widower and his sister(-in-law) enter into a relationship unrecognized by the state and anathematized by the Anglican church, which maintains that because holy marriage makes man and wife "one flesh," a wife's sister is taboo to her brother-by-marriage. In cohabiting, the unsanctioned couple replicates the form of the man's first marriage, with the second sister filling the empty place of the first in a union that struck many contemporaries as fitting and meet, for reasons I examine more closely in chapter 3. Invoking "parliamentary agitation" in a sympathetic tone, Hemyng's commentary demonstrates the contingency of the category of "prostitute" on legal and religious institutions: repeal the ban, and "cohabitant prostitutes" suddenly become legitimate wives. But the real emphasis of this short discussion, as of so much MDWS material, falls on the situation of men, who either resist or succumb to "ecclesiastical terrors," suffering "many penalties," all the while in the grip of "an affection for a sister-in-law" that they cannot give up.

We may speculate that Hemyng treads lightly on the matter of MDWS— even as he deems any women who are party to it prostitutes—because such illicit unions were identified primarily with middle-class men. If indeed it were "a great hardship that any respectable portion of the community should be placed in a position where their domestic feelings are at war with their law," then at least a portion of that "hardship" would reside in the social and legal taint—"pernicious, in a public view, as exhibiting avowed disobedience to law"—attached to marriages of this sort.[29] Those who agitated for repeal of the ban argued that such unions stem from necessity and secure the comforts of family life to all. The evidence they mustered aimed to demonstrate that such marriages spring from honorable motives (among the middle classes) and from convenience and suitability (among the working classes); refuting the latter argument, one supporter of the ban asserted instead that "if the moral statistics of our millions could be exposed, it would be found that the real explanation of this problem was, while the middle classes married, those below them cohabited."[30] Yoking the lot of working people to their own in order to refute the claim that they were legislating on the basis of class interest, advocates of repeal also focused on the immorality of cohabitation without marriage, not the perceived taint of incest, as the real threat to working- and middle-class respectability.

Appointed in the 1840s at the urging of opponents of the prohibition on such marriages in order to inquire into their frequency, a Royal Commission declared that men and women of all classes entered into them, even in the absence of much hard evidence to that effect. "Of the marriages thus ascertained to have been contracted, very few were between persons in the poorer classes," its *First Report* admitted while also stating that "we have reason to conclude that such marriages are at least as frequent in those classes as in any other, and perhaps even much more so" (*First Report* ix). With verified incidents of MDWS among working people numbering only forty of the nearly 1,400 cases documented by a team of solicitors, the assertion that MDWS was "at least as frequent" among the poor as among the middle classes relied largely on rhetoric rather than statistics to establish that working-class widowers and their respectable upper-class counterparts differed very little in their aims and desires.

Arguing for repeal, the barrister Thomas Campbell Foster conjured an image of the typical bereaved working-class household, meant to approximate a middle-class norm:

> Amongst the lower classes such marriages are very common, from this fact chiefly[,] that on the death of the wife of a labouring man he has no one whatever to take care of his house, and usually a sister of his wife is the first person called in to take charge of the children and to look after his household affairs. A few weeks' residence in the house of a poor man, where there are not those means of living apart which exist in larger houses, brings them into very intimate connexion. There are but, perhaps, two rooms in the house; they live together with great familiarity, and usually the parties have, at the expiration of a month or two, endeavoured to marry. (*First Report* 2)

Because working people have smaller homes with fewer rooms than members of the middle class, "overcrowding" encourages the sexual contact that Foster terms "intimate connexion," but to their credit, working people do not wait very long, just "a month or two," before "endeavour[ing] to marry." In support of his case, Foster noted that the state of the law actively promoted immorality among the poor in denying marriage to those who, failing to legalize their bond, "have afterwards lived together in open cohabitation" of the kind that Hemyng also noticed, a condition rarely glimpsed among those in the higher classes who had greater power to evade the law, for instance by traveling elsewhere to be married (*First Report* 2). The main thrust of his remarks, however, is that working-class men face the same issues as middle-class men. For the middle-class widower is also reported to have "no one whatever to take care of his house," to rely on the sister(-in-law)'s help with the orphaned children, to live on terms of "great familiarity" with the lost wife's sister, to strive against the temptation such familiarity breeds, and, finally, to seek her hand in legitimate marriage. This rhetorical construction represented all widowers of whatever class position as subject to the same needs and desires: they all wanted wives, and widowers with children especially wanted their wives' sisters.

While MDWS discourse in the 1840s downplayed the charge of incest by constructing a cross-class vision of virtuous widowers seeking respectable marriage, urban investigators who penetrated working-class homes had a different story to tell, one in which the overcrowded conditions of tenement life produced acts of incestuous adultery that did not even require the death of first wives as an antecedent.[31] Numerous supporters of the ban argued that permitting a man to marry first one, then another sister would create trouble for the living: for if a man knew that he could marry the second should the first die, what would stop him from pursuing his sister-in-law in his wife's lifetime? "If...a man be really permitted by the law to marry his deceased wife's sister," wrote one parodist of this position under the alias "A Woman of England," "their domestic peace would be gone for ever, for...husbands, in such a case, would always be making love to their unmarried sisters-in-law, or the sisters-in-law to the husbands."[32] "Here are some pretty promising materials," wrote another pamphleteer, "for a romance of murder and adultery from which English married life has hitherto been considered free," at least among the middle classes, for analysts of working-class housing were a good deal less sanguine on this point.[33] One of Chadwick's investigators claimed to "have met with instances of a man, his wife, and his wife's sister, sleeping in the same bed together," citing "at least half-a-dozen cases in Manchester in which that has been regularly practiced."[34] While Hemyng characterized MDWS as "cohabitant prostitution," a prostitute in Hull told a Chadwick informant that "overcrowding" had been the proximate cause of her "fall": "She had lodged with a married sister, and slept in the same bed with her and her husband; that hence improper intercourse took place, and from that she gradually became more and more depraved."[35] Acton's treatise on prostitution made the same point: "The promiscuous herding of the sexes (no other word is applicable) through the want of sufficient house accommodation" was producing "that indifference to modesty" that made it but "a short step to illicit commerce."[36] If MDWS itself qualified in Hemyng's analysis as a form of prostitution, then a man's having sex with a living wife's sister could be construed as the cause of another.

Regarding housing reform rhetoric, Anthony Wohl observes that "overcrowding" constituted "the central evil around which all the others associated with working-class living grouped themselves"—but only from a middle-class perspective: "Among the working classes there were many complaints about high rents and sanitary conditions, but almost none concerning the lack of room space."[37] Middle-class reformers like Chadwick, however, characterized working-class housing as "destructive to the morality as well as the health of large classes of both sexes," thus mobilizing the imagery of sickness so that small "dwellings inhabited by entire families" were said to promote "not only the spread of contagious diseases...but incest as well."[38] Michael Mason notes the inferential logic by which social investigators made the leap from ideologically charged assumptions about privacy and proximity to unspeakable acts: "High densities of unmarried individuals in beds or bedrooms were alleged, and the reader then invited to draw the supposedly inevitable conclusion about sexual outcomes. Only occasionally was evidence produced that the worst had happened."[39] In a middle-class context, of course, such "evidence" would have been even more difficult to come by, since those homes were not subject to the forces of surveillance. "Private hotels and houses let to the upper and middle classes do not come within the provisions" that permitted common lodging-house inspections by the 1880s; school inspectors, police officers, and clergymen would never examine the homes of the affluent in search of unspeakable crimes.[40]

By designating "overcrowding" as the key cause of intrafamilial sex, housing reformers implied that the remedy for the one evil was the remedy for the other. This claim implicitly rearticulated heterosexual incest as a practice that middle-class homes, with children segregated by sex and sleeping apart from their parents, effectively prevented. "The practice of separating parents and children—the architectural practice of providing rooms in which that is even possible—is largely a work of the industrial revolution," notes Ian Hacking.[41] But that "those means of living apart which exist in larger houses" were not available to poorer people helped to secure the distinction between middle-class privacy, said to prevent incest, and working-class "promiscuous herding," alleged to encourage it. "The definition of what it means to be a bourgeois family was as much 'architectural' as anything else": at a time when working-class housing was being destroyed to make room for roads and railways, when the population of London was rising even as "slum" housing was aggressively being cleared (and not replaced), the material means of constituting a proper family in middle-class eyes was moving ever more out of reach for many.[42] As Foucault argued, "An entire politics for the protection of children or the placing of 'endangered' minors under guardianship" was generated from these circumstances, which "had as its partial objective their withdrawal from families that were suspected—through lack of space, dubious proximity, a history of debauchery, antisocial 'primitive-ness,' or degenerescence—of practicing incest" (*History of Sexuality* 129).

Over the course of the century such middle-class incests as MDWS and cousin-marriage came to appear, in contrast with the "habits" of the work-ing classes, as potentially positive strategies for preserving bourgeois morality and health. Thus even as Alfred Henry Huth, in *The Marriage of Near Kin* (1875), enumerated the evils of both race-mixture with and incest among "primitive" peoples, he simultaneously advocated in-marriage among white elites. "It is for many reasons commendable to marry a relative, for here one can exercise some *selection,*" evoking all of the post-Darwinian associations of that word, "since a man generally knows the state of health and the disposi-tion of members of his own family"; "in mankind, at least, a cross is always a dangerous thing."[43] If the biological wisdom of cousin-marriage—albeit not incest by English civil or canon law—was increasingly debated after 1860 regarding its effects on the offspring of such unions, then the social wisdom of this form of kin-marriage among elites was rarely in doubt. As I suggest below, cousin-marriage may have functioned as a form of what Ann Laura Stoler has termed "white endogamy"—a mechanism for constraining part-ner choice that also entails, in the words of Claude Lévi-Strauss, "the refusal to recognize the possibility of marriage beyond the limits of the human community," a denial of "the social existence of other people."[44] Construing it in this light enables us to rethink the meanings of sex or marriage with those culturally defined by class and race as one's own kind and the prohibi-tion on trafficking with those who are not. So in Trollope's *The Way We Live Now* (1875), when Lady Pomona Longestaffe tells her desperate daughter Georgiana that marrying the Jewish Mr. Brehgert "can't be possible. It's unnatural. It's worse than your wife's sister," she is articulating the unequal status of two taboos—one against incest, the other against miscegenation or mixture—that often work together, forbidding some choices, inciting others, marking and policing racial and cultural boundaries.[45] As Butler observes in a present-day context, "There must be exogamy. But there must be a limit to exogamy." Heterosexual marriage may not transgress "a certain racial self-understanding"—in this case, that (English) Jews are not really English—so that "the taboo against miscegenation limits the exogamy that the incest taboo mandates" (*Undoing* 122). As I further explore below, reading incest and miscegenation prohibitions together, as related formations, clarifies the different circumstances in which one or the other is solicited or proscribed, and to what ends.

Incest has a particular valence when it is posited as an endemic feature of the working classes, increasingly differentiated as a breed apart. One of the effects produced by the application of "the regime of sexuality...to the lower classes" lies in its constitution of working-class incest as a social threat that potentially perpetrates the reproduction and circulation of bad blood, with what is inherited or transmitted through and by this medium bearing both socioeconomic and biological import (*History of Sexuality* 129). In this configuration, the bodily fluids exchanged and recombined in sex, reproductive or not, may carry life or death for the individual, the family, the race, the class, the nation, and the empire. The belief that blood could carry "promises" or "menaces" informs a wide range of Victorian discourses after 1860, occupying the very center of discussions about human sexual reproduction, incest and miscegenation, endogamy and exogamy, interbreeding and crossbreeding (*History of Sexuality* 124). Incest is represented among the working classes, however, only as a social threat: with the absence of an effective taboo signifying the regressive status of the urban horde, late Victorians were able to disavow some incests as "savage" practices—the stuff of "primitive cultures" (in anthropology) and the developmentally backward (in urban sociology)—by identifying one of incest's perceived outcomes, interbreeding among an already degraded population, as cause for panic.

Representing working-class people as comparable to savages past and present, domestic and foreign, worked to secure the status of middle-class sexual morality. Closely reading the work of John F. McLennan and Herbert Spencer, Anita Levy writes, "Nineteenth-century anthropology constituted the other within a disciplinary structure based on modern middle-class norms of heterosexual monogamy," with one virtue of the latter understood as, in the words of the first epigraph above, its "restriction of promiscuous intercourse."[46] "Restrictions upon marriage were not a mark of a despotic period," asserted one speaker in the 1869 Commons debate on the latest MDWS bill, "but rather of a state of civilization and refinement; and to remove the restrictions that had been thought necessary for ages would be a step backwards into barbarism."[47] An early biographer of Matthew Arnold characterized his subject's opinion on the necessity of the MDWS ban in the same vein: "The sacredness of marriage, and the customs that regulate it, were triumphs of culture which had been won, painfully and with effort, from the unbridled promiscuity of primitive life," with such "triumphs" representing a distinctive advance over the "unbridled promiscuity" of even England's own "primitive" past.[48] Sounding much like the parliamentary advocates of the MDWS prohibition, some of whom were doubtless influenced by his own writings, McLennan asserts that "any regulated relation of the sexes is an advance on promiscuity."[49] Demonstrated not just by the cross-cultural findings of armchair anthropologists on sex and marriage among aboriginal Australians and native North Americans but also by more than four decades' worth of domestic urban reportage, the survival of primitive promiscuity into the present suggested that only "painfully and with effort" would those "triumphs" be maintained, being "a cultural achievement that only certain civilizations— and certain classes—had proved capable of attaining by learning to control their 'natural' impulses."[50] The practice of incest at home thereby signified a permanent crisis in the social body, an index of the persistence of savagery at the dark heart of civilization.

Incest as we know it emerges, then, as a sign of under- or even anti-development, enabling its disavowal by class/race elites and its displacement onto others. In *Primitive Marriage* (1865), McLennan wrote that "savages are unrestrained by any sense of delicacy from a copartnery in sexual enjoyments; and, indeed, in the civilized state, the sin of great cities shows that there are no natural restraints sufficient to hold men back from grosser copartneries": "A survey of the facts of primitive life...exclude[s] the notion that the law originated in any innate or primary feeling against marriage with kinsfolk," so the presence of "the law" marks an advance over its nonexistence among those who cannot and do not exercise restraint in their own pursuit of "sexual enjoyments."[51] In a subsequent essay, he further attacked the notion of a natural, instinctual aversion to incest (as would Charles Darwin), pointing to "the lowest strata" of contemporary London, "to a large extent...the direct representatives of those who formed the lowest strata in the earliest times":

> Let us take the case of London to illustrate our meaning. In that centre of arts, sciences, industries, and intelligence, are predatory bands, leading the life of the lowest nomads....nearly as low in their habits as the jackals of Calcutta. The city might be made to furnish illustrations of the progress of the family in every phase, from the lowest incestuous combinations of kindred to the highest group based on solemn monogamous marriage. It contains classes that know not marriage, classes approximating to marriage through habits of settled concubinage, and classes for whom promiscuity is an open, unabashed organization.[52]

"Incestuous combinations" among the lowest, "monogamous marriage" among the highest: the history of "the progress of the family" may be captured on the synchronic axis of the metropolis, even as that "lowest strata" diachronically persists with slight variation, interbreeding its members—who "have always existed, and were presumably lower formerly than they now are"—as a permanent core of resistance to law or morality.[53] The practice of incest becomes a key sociological sign of developmental backwardness among the London poor just at the moment at which it also emerges in anthropology to differentiate nature from culture, promiscuity from monogamy, securing the latter as the highest form of the "restriction of promiscuous intercourse" on which civilization depends. Here we find incest doubly distanced from middle-class contexts.

From a Foucauldian perspective, what keeps bourgeois families on the right side of "the law" is the persistence of the deployment of alliance. Defending the MDWS prohibition in 1873, the Lord Chancellor pointed to "the brutal passions of some of the lowest order . . . capable of overleaping even the natural barriers which exist between parent and child—between brother and sister."[54] If few evolutionary anthropologists or scientists of the time would have asserted that those barriers were "natural," the first volume of *The History of Sexuality* suggests that they were naturalized as part of the bourgeois family's self-conception. Its incorporation of "the ancient prohibitions of consanguine marriages" characterizes the deployment of alliance as "a system of rules defining the permitted and forbidden"; "to marry a close relative" is, not coincidentally, the very first interdiction that Foucault cites—but how "close," and what constitutes that closeness, is open to question and varies by context (*History of Sexuality* 41, 106, 39). Mobilized in early modern Europe in a contest over economic and political power, incest prohibitions pitted aristocratic prerogative against ecclesiastical authority: as Pollak summarizes their import, "the regulation of marriage and its politics in the history of the West has had everything to do with property and its transmission" (*Incest* 46).[55] With the fixed laws that govern "the permitted and forbidden" under an aristocratic regime, Foucault juxtaposes the "mobile, polymorphous, and contingent techniques of power" associated with the deployment of sexuality; these unsettle the "homeostasis of the social body" that the deployment of alliance works to maintain (*History of Sexuality* 106, 107). Taking its first and primary form among the bourgeoisie, the deployment of sexuality modified the older practices by which aristocratic wealth was transmitted: "the body that produces" and reproduces becomes the locus for the "numerous and subtle relays" by which sexuality operates (*History of Sexuality* 106, 107). Poised at "the interchange of sexuality and alliance," the site where the two deployments coincide, the bourgeois family managed incitement and prohibition, transgression and taboo, at its very core (*History of Sexuality* 108).

Although critics often overlook the point, it is crucial to my argument that we fully grasp the trajectory of Foucault's thinking: that "it was *around and on the basis of* the deployment of alliance that the deployment of sexuality was constructed" and not that the latter entirely displaced the former

(*History of Sexuality* 107, emphasis added). "The deployment of sexuality is 'superimposed,' it does not 'supplant' the deployment of alliance, but is constructed out of the latter, imbuing it with a new tactic of power"; Stoler further argues that "the family is the site of this convergence" (*Race* 38). As Vikki Bell notes, "both deployments" exist "within one temporality"; moreover, the incest taboo—"clearly discursive"—constrains the unchecked transgression of all proprieties that sexuality might perform.[56] It is thus what Butler terms a "productive constraint."[57] In one respect, then, prohibiting incest means fending off the full power of sexuality, which would otherwise scandalously flout the rules and laws that maintain the primacy of the forces associated with alliance. And in this light, we may interpret the middle-class perception of the "brutal" indifference of the working class to the "rules" governing "the permitted and forbidden" as a sign of cultural differentiation, an indicator of just how far removed from middle-class propriety, as exemplified in "solemn monogamous marriage," this group was made out to be.

Foucault intervenes in our thinking about incest by resituating its prohibition as a problem or impediment for the deployment of sexuality, particularly in its "original" bourgeois form, rather than as the most transparent sign of its efficacy. For the purposes of my project, however, his theses require modification on several fronts. To be sure, the "rules" that Foucault associates with alliance have their permutations in the English context. Henry VIII had rewritten the laws of the Roman Catholic Church to legitimate or invalidate several of his many unions; these laws were subsequently abolished or reinstated by Mary Tudor and Elizabeth I. Not all consanguineous marriages were prohibited in England—those between first cousins, for instance; while some affinal marriages—those with a dead wife's sister or a dead husband's brother—were.[58] These sixteenth-century examples provide one very obvious historical instance of the broader claim that "the incest taboo exists not for its own sake, as an arbitrary and absolute injunction, but contingently," owing, for example, to "its instrumentality in preserving the continuity of the male estate" (*Incest* 50). The nineteenth-century materials considered here stage and restage the debate over the naturalness of incest and the provenance of the taboo according to particular contingencies of their own.

Moreover, although I subscribe to the tenet that "the family is the interchange of sexuality and alliance," the incests that particularly preoccupied the nineteenth-century English middle classes (leaving Victorian pornography out of the equation) and found public expression in political and scientific debate as well as literary and anthropological fictions were primarily intragenerational. Building on the work of Craig Owens, Eve Kosofsky Sedgwick usefully suggests that "the turn-of-the-century Freudian recasting of the (supposedly universal) incest taboo—from being, as anthropologists describe it, a prohibition that chiefly involves avuncular and sibling-in-law relations, to being, in the Oedipal, a prohibition of directly cross-generational relations between parent and child"—has had "obfuscatory consequences for modern understandings of sexuality."[59] When Foucault invokes psychoanalysis as the emergent discipline that "rediscovered the law of alliance, the involved workings of marriage and kinship, and incest at the heart of this sexuality, as the principle of its formation and the key to its intelligibility," he generates a crucial insight that enables us to reexamine relationships within nineteenth-century families in those terms (*History of Sexuality* 113). But I am less interested in reproducing the psychoanalytic Oedipal norm "that one would find the *parents-children* relationship at the root of everyone's sexuality" and more intent on considering the residual impact of alliance—in its focus on delimiting or expanding the boundaries of kinship through marriage and reproduction—on sexuality (*History of Sexuality* 113, emphasis added). Rereading middle-class incests with an eye to how they were shaped by shifting constructions of family relations, in siblingship and cousinhood, enables us to articulate different perspectives on both the hegemonic construction of incest as intergenerational and heterosexual and the somewhat static and circumscribed image of "the bourgeois family" that Foucault creates.

As I have already suggested, middle-class incests also figure and are figured by race and class exclusions in ways that Stoler's rereading of Foucault best illustrates. Rather than dismiss Foucault as indifferent to empire, Stoler makes a careful genealogy of his thinking about the discourses of race and class, which she rightly calls "overlapping and interchangeable" rather than fully distinct from one another (*Race* 127). She argues that "the racial lexicons of the nineteenth century," operative at home and abroad, "have complex colonial etymologies through which . . . aristocratic discourses on 'purity of blood' were replayed and transformed" (*Race* 52).[60] Recognizing the coexistence of alliance and sexuality within the bourgeois family, she also suggests that "the tension between [them] as *distinct* organizing principles of power may configure differently when the issue of racism is centrally posed"—as it does, I believe, when we look specifically at incest as a racialized formation that traverses both deployments (*Race* 47, emphasis in original). From this perspective, we may say that the deployment of alliance itself contains features of an older racial formation; the Victorian preoccupation with "blood" condenses matters of both class and race with European and colonial determinants. While the metropolitan bourgeois family is not racially marked in Foucault's analysis, the rules that constrain it are profoundly racialized, as were the older aristocratic ones. Viewed in this context, the deployment of sexuality maintains the deployment of alliance's investment in incest: it is both a figure and a practice that contains "a racial politics of exclusion at its core" (*Race* 93). The incitement to incest that Foucault locates in the bourgeois family may thus also be understood as a mechanism for maintaining race and class homogeneity, albeit always as a fictive norm.[61]

Reconceiving nineteenth-century middle-class incests in these ways also enables us to revise our analysis of marriage-and-family fictions, a project to which Pollak's *Incest and the English Novel, 1684–1814* makes a significant theoretical contribution. "If one contingency affecting the status of in-marriage is the desire for extended kin groups," she writes, then "another is the fear of diluting national, ethnic, or racial purity by failing to preserve the integrity of geographic and cultural boundaries" (*Incest* 55). In her reading of eighteenth-century materials, the "incestuous notion of human subjectivity," in which one finds sexual satisfaction only with kin, contains within it, may even be based on, racialized borders and boundaries that exclude "others." As becomes more and more evident in a domestic middle-class context over the course of the nineteenth century, such a formation indeed "provides the soil and sustaining ground for naturalized notions of racial purity" by making the preference for sameness, anathema to some, seem very natural to others (*Incest* 187). For this reason, one of Pollak's conclusions—that "discourses of incest...as they were constituted in the early nineteenth century were always already inflected by racial thinking"—forms a key assumption of my study, which begins where hers ends, at *Mansfield Park*, and works within a similar theoretical framework (*Incest* 182).

Understanding that the role and place of incest requires simultaneous attention to discourses of miscegenation is especially useful in rethinking the models we deploy. For example, when Lévi-Strauss casts incest as the "direct opposite" of "inter-racial sexual relations," with the two united only by their shared status as "the most powerful inducements to horror," not only does he fail to notice that incest sometimes *is* miscegenation—a point readily apparent to those who study nineteenth-century U.S. literature as well as to any reader of Faulkner—but he also elides the mutual construction of these two categories (as in the Trollope example cited above), their historical imbrication, and their changing meanings over time and across context.[62] By contrast, Pollak casts cousin-marriage in *Mansfield Park* as a prophylactic against the metaphorical contaminations of both metropolitan otherness and colonial exploitation in Antigua. Linking eighteenth-century arguments against slavery and for kin-marriage to a single source in the discourse of English liberty, Pollak suggests that white men granted to black men the right to join "the traffic in women" even as they advocated easing bans on kin-marriage in a subtle inducement to traffic only in women defined as one's own kind (*Incest* 175–79).[63] Fascinating as this argument is, however, it requires modification in a later historical context. By the 1830s, when "the historically and ideologically convergent discourses" that called for an end to the twinned oppressions of slavery and marriage bans had been pried apart, the argument for repealing the prohibition on affinal marriage clearly itself relied on an exclusionary logic (*Incest* 178). Men of "the respectable classes" would choose a sister(-in-law) as a second wife because a man prefers a woman who is known intimately in her domestic circumstances over a "stranger" whose character, habits, and family history cannot be so readily determined. Indeed, the threat of the "stranger" to domestic security may be read as shorthand for a shifting corpus of class, race, and ethnic others with whom white middle-class men choose not to traffic.

The achievement of abolition and, subsequently, emancipation did not forestall the emergence of a viciously hierarchical "family of man" in which many men and most women were denied full personhood on the basis of race, class, ethnicity, or gender; indeed, one might say that even as the abolitionist movement makes all men brothers, white Englishmen of property collectively become something on the order of the eldest brother. In this respect, the agitation by nineteenth-century middle-class men for marital access to their dead wives' sisters may constitute "miscegenation anxiety"— or else invoke that anxiety only in order to make a more persuasive case. So, too, with the controversy among scientists as to the effects of interbreeding and the simultaneous emergence of a related debate among the early anthropologists as to the origin and meaning of the taboo on close kin: these may indicate that "incest anxiety" motivated the drive to distinguish "civilized" from "savage" marital and sexual practices or else mark the effort to expand control over the circulation and reproduction of otherness. During the course of the nineteenth century, we can indeed observe a narrowing and stratifying tendency of distinguishing legitimate and permissible practices for elites from the promiscuous attachments of degraded or degenerate others. But rather than posit either form of "anxiety" as an autonomous agent, we should keep open the possibility that fears about both racial intermixture and consanguineous sex were strategically mobilized to keep some men and women in their proper places.[64]

Although the circumstances of the nineteenth century require specific historical analysis, Pollak's theoretical framework, in which taboos on incest and miscegenation are mutually constitutive, is extremely useful for nineteenth-century studies insofar as it problematizes the model of heterosexual "exogamous" exchange that has shaped two generations of feminist theory and criticism. Informed especially by Butler's work on gender, sexuality, and kinship, historicist feminists with theoretical leanings have turned a critical eye on the psychoanalytic and anthropological fictions that still govern the production of a particular set of stories about the past. Pollak rightly argues that "modernity's dominant theoretical formulations about incest and incestuous desire are themselves rooted in the Enlightenment"; that they "helped to shape the discourses of the human sciences in the nineteenth century"; and that they "continue to dominate many Western theoretical formulations at the turn of the twenty-first century" including feminist ones (*Incest* 3). So the stories that readers, writers, and intellectuals tell about "the Victorian family," for instance—not just a major object of analysis for "the discourses of the human sciences in the nineteenth century" but among that century's most enduring products—frequently fail to interrogate their dependence on assumptions or beliefs naturalized or invented by readers, writers, and intellectuals of that era.

I think it is time to change the theoretical and historical lens through which we look at scholarly artifacts like "the Victorian family" or "the marriage plot" by defamiliarizing both the objects of analysis and the theoretical tools we have used to construct them. For example, in reading a summary of the central tenets of Gayle Rubin's classic essay, "The Traffic in Women" (1975), I am struck by how completely Rubin's terms, as summarized by Carolyn Dever, continue to define current scholarly understanding of the sex/gender arrangements of the nineteenth century: "Social organization is based on an incest taboo, specifically on the requirement of exogamy; the incest taboo is enforced through the control and exchange of women's bodies.... This kinship requires not only heterosexuality of its subjects but heterosexuality aimed monogamously and exogamously, outside the immediate family context."[65] The theoretical model from which this summary derives, which relies on concepts invented in the nineteenth century, might well have some descriptive purchase on the culture that generated those concepts. But just as surely as ideas of exogamy, monogamy, or heterosexuality need historicizing, so, too, do the other sexual and reproductive arrangements of the nineteenth century, frequently crowded out of the dominant narrative now normatively referred to as "normative," bear rethinking.

What if we challenge the assumed link between the incest taboo and the rules of exogamy, as the anthropologist Annette Weiner suggests, and acknowledge the ongoing importance of the (biological or adoptive) sibling tie, the "strategic role sibling intimacy has played in human history," as differently experienced by brothers and sisters?[66] Or entertain Sharon Marcus's provocative thesis that "female marriage, gender mobility, and women's erotic

fantasies about women were at the heart of normative institutions and discourses, even for those who made a religion of the family, marriage, and
sexual difference" in the Victorian period?[67] Or pursue the possibility, following Kathy Alexis Psomiades on the late-century invention of heterosexuality, that "bonds between women and feminine sexual agency...are
absolutely necessary to imagining feminine and masculine sexuality as alike
structured around the question of the gender of object choice"?[68] By doing
so, we could both historicize and re-theorize the intersecting elements of
the family-sex-marriage triad, making space within it for alternatives to the
dominant story of the exogamous heterosexual plot, the triumph of companionate marriage, and the installation of the nuclear family as a hegemonic
institution. We could, in other words, historicize the emergence of the norm,
as well as the resistances to it, and begin to chart its revision, even its potential
dissolution, in our own moment.

This project contributes to that larger one in ways that should become
clear over its course, but I want to give a specific example of how it aims
to problematize familiar material. I have already mentioned that one strand
of the opposition to the MDWS ban articulated a resistance to trafficking with strangers, a resistance that flew in the face of "exogamous" marriage as normalized by both (some) canonical domestic fiction and, perhaps
more importantly, our collective critical story about it. Marriage outside the
immediate limits of "the family" has been understood as the norm because it
expands patriarchal economic and social power; resistance to that norm may
thus reveal the presence of some barrier to exchange, some decided preference for staying within the constitutive limits of the group, or both. As Jean
Walton persuasively argues in a useful reformulation of Lévi-Strauss that
draws on Butler's work, whereas "endogamy is elaborated as a prohibition
on interracial marriage," in some circumstances "kinship is also elaborated
through systems of endogamy, that is, the imperative to marry *within* a given
social group."[69] If cross-racial or cross-class sex might be said to expand the
human community by redrawing the lines that define both humanness and
community, then a ban on inter-group relations sets limits to the homosocial bonding among men that constitutes one motive for exchange, thus
jamming the traffic in women. Phrased somewhat differently, the incitement to "endogamy"—whether in-marriage to a second sister or to a first
cousin—short-circuits exchange in favor of keeping a sister or a cousin in
the family, as Weiner suggests, rather than trading her out for someone or
something else.[70]

Thus, marrying *within* the family may not actually operate on the model
of exchange that we have constituted as the norm; at the very least, the fact of

intrafamilial marriage should bring us to reconsider the conceptual use-value of "exchange" as a way of thinking about nineteenth-century marriage. Much as I agree with Psomiades's important critique of "the notion that women circulate in heterosexual exchange in the same way that commodities circulate in capitalist exchange," I believe that we also need to distinguish among the different forms of heterosexual coupling that we encounter in anthropological, literary, and scientific fictions so as to specify the particular ways in which marriage within the family complicates the exchange model even before the rise of contract-based arguments for women's emancipation in the 1860s.[71] Moreover, an overly general use of terms such as *exogamy* and *endogamy* begs the question of how we define the groups within which or outside of which exchanges putatively take place. Once we understand incest as a racialized figure and a class practice, for example, we have to rethink the meanings of sex or marriage with one's own kind, and even who may be constituted as "one's own." Taking "the family" as a metonym for the race—as diverse Victorian disciplines and discourses were inclined to do—provides one means of marking the outer limits of what counts as human and who belongs to that family; within that framework, reconceiving endogamy as a form of race and class exclusion *and* inclusion is a contextually specific rather than universalizing use of the term. But it is also an appropriation of the term for our own descriptive and analytical purposes, not to be confused with what Victorian thinkers might have meant by it and not to be treated as a transcendent truth.

Adam Kuper notes that early anthropologists—like other writers of historical fiction and academic scholarship—"constructed mirror images of their own society" and "of some particular interpretation of their times" in their depictions of "the distant past."[72] Thus, at the origin of the terms *endogamy* and *exogamy* in McLennan's *Primitive Marriage,* we can see, for example, that he defines the former—"the rule which declares the union of persons of the same blood to be incest"—as the absence of exchange (*Primitive Marriage* 22n1). Within an endogamous tribe, McLennan argues, "there can be neither barter nor sale—neither the selling nor the buying of wives. On a marriage between two of its members, there is no foreign interest to be consulted or satisfied," and wives are not procured by force or theft (*Primitive Marriage* 22). "It is different," he continues, "if we conceive a number of such tribes aggregated in a political union": "While formerly the members of each could only marry among themselves, the members of all have acquired the right of intermarrying with one another," so in "inter-tribal marriages," which constitute an instance of exogamy, "there is room and a necessity for compensation. Such a marriage must be a subject of bargain, a matter of sale and purchase" (*Primitive Marriage* 22–23). Although the gendered asymmetry of power between men and "wives" persists in both formations, the lack of what McLennan calls a "foreign interest" in endogamy and the presence of terms such as *bargain, sale,* and *purchase* in his description of exogamy suggest the operation in McLennan's own times of different formative fictions within the Victorian heterosexual economy; if we put aside the consideration of exchange as *the* key figure for nineteenth-century marriage, we may become better attuned to the alternative currents that contest its primacy.

Practices such as MDWS and cousin-marriage may indicate a refusal or inability to look beyond the (racialized) limits of the family for a partner or enact a resistance to exchange, a phenomenon that Weiner terms "keeping-while-giving, a process that simultaneously affirms the historical strength of one's natal group as it authenticates its difference vis-à-vis others."[73] At the same time, to rejoin the Foucauldian analysis, the deployments of alliance and sexuality incite a proliferation of limits within the racialized family, inventing distinctions and degrees, producing the permissible and the impermissible. To the canonical horror of marriage or sex within the family—institutionalized in what today may appear to be the laughable proscription of marriage to a sister of the deceased wife—we may juxtapose the data of nineteenth-century fiction and poetry: all those cousin-marriages, all those vaguely suspect brother/sister bonds, all those subtle inducements to remain safely within the "endogamous" fold. At a very minimum, the incitement to marriage within the (white European) family prohibits, even as it acknowledges the possibility of, class/race intermixture. I contend that in these and other forms, incest, understood as "white endogamy," shadows the official narrative of exogamy as the mechanism whereby dominant groups maintain a fixed social order and increase their own social and economic power. The incitement to incest, the stimulation of sexual desire within the family, throws a wrench into the works of "exogamous" exchange, which has been so fundamental to feminist thinking about marriage and kinship, insofar as it locates those within the family as providing desire's true site and source of satisfaction: why should one ever look anywhere else?

Rereading nineteenth-century middle-class incests in terms of class and race thus entails rethinking the critical frameworks we adopt in approaching some very familiar texts of the period; I close this chapter by attending briefly to one important example. Leo Bersani has characterized *Wuthering Heights*—the *locus classicus* for discussions of incest in canonical Victorian fiction—as "an ingenious exercise in creating family ties and resemblances," whereby "everyone is finally related to everyone else, and in a sense, repeated in everyone else," through what J. Hillis Miller terms the reduction of all signs "to the same image."[74] Most readers of the novel use the language of siblingship, implicitly adopted by both Bersani and Miller, to describe the first-generation bond between Heathcliff and Catherine, as in William R. Goetz's claim that "Heathcliff's adoptive place in the family turns him into a brother of Catherine" and Joseph Allen Boone's observation that "their adult passion will retain this sense of a brother-sister relationship."[75] Even more pointedly, Boone jointly observes with Deborah E. Nord that "generations of readers"—driven to account for the patriarch's "unnatural" favoring of the adoptee over his own "natural" son, Hindley—"have hypothesized that the homeless waif whom Mr. Earnshaw brings back to the Heights from his Liverpool trip is his illegitimate son, hence Catherine's *actual* brother," as if a man might not prefer a biologically unrelated child to his own biological kin.[76] Despite this presumptive readerly drive to anchor relationships in blood connection, the bar to marriage between Heathcliff and Catherine nowhere registers in the text as incest: however sibling-like their bond may appear to critics, it is clearly not on the ground of their already being brother and sister, either by blood or informal adoption, that they do not marry. It is rather in Heathcliff's difference from the Earnshaws and the Lintons, articulated primarily in terms of race and class divisions that coincide with shifting formations of "the family" that an impediment to his forming a second family with the first Catherine lies.

The perceived prohibition on brother-sister incest, that is, might also be recognized as a taboo on miscegenation. Heathcliff's ambiguous status—his "extrafamilial origin," in Elsie B. Michie's term; his position as "racial and linguistic outsider," as Susan Meyer describes him—indeed marks him as an "*unrelated* intruder," to use Bersani's term, who must be exorcised from the novel in order for the plot of sameness to flourish.[77] That Catherine claims identity with him, however, while Mr. Earnshaw adopts him without asserting a blood tie establishes this child of "a different race and class"—either "a gift from God" or "from the devil," in Mrs. Earnshaw's words—as, at the very least, a member of the Earnshaw household.[78] Those who live at the Heights at the moment of Heathcliff's arrival "are not differentiated according to biological or genetic relationship. . . . Rather, the household is organized according to the older notion of kinship, when no word existed that meant 'only kin' within a household," when servants, apprentices, lodgers, and other related or unrelated people shared space and resources.[79] Ellen Dean, for example, describes herself as "almost always at Wuthering Heights" before she went to live at the Grange; as she nurses Hareton, so her mother once nursed Hindley (*WH* 28). She thinks of herself as Hindley's "foster sister" who "excused his behaviour more readily than a stranger would"; when she hears the news of his death, she "wept as for a blood relation" (*WH* 51, 144).[80] Ellen is, by these lights, a member of the family, even if that family might look "primitive" by mid–nineteenth-century standards; within that family, the adoptee, too, has a place. But Heathcliff's most crucial function in the novel is to indicate that "the boundaries between inside and outside the family, and hence between exogamy and endogamy, are shifting terms," a point that becomes especially apparent in the movement from the first to the second generation.[81]

Named (or renamed) for "a son who died in childhood," perhaps even for an elder son whose death had made Hindley the heir presumptive, "from the very beginning," Heathcliff "bred bad feeling in the house" (*WH* 30).[82] Hindley subsequently repays his rival for usurping "his father's affections and his privileges" by engineering "his degradation": "He drove him from their company to the servants, deprived him of the instructions of the curate, and insisted that he should labour out of doors instead," reclassifying Heathcliff as a servant who lacks full membership in the family (*WH* 31, 36). Edgar Linton's remark to Catherine upon Heathcliff's return after three years' absence indicates the consequences of Hindley's action: "The whole household need not witness the sight of your welcoming a runaway servant as a brother" (*WH* 75). Even Catherine herself, aiming to rationalize her decision to marry Edgar, recognizes that Hindley's intervention (along with her own protracted exposure to Grange luxury) has precipitated such a divide that "it would degrade me to marry Heathcliff now" (*WH* 63). Choosing Edgar over Heathcliff—marrying outside the family in one sense, but within it, in terms of class and race—aligns Catherine with the security and status we would now identify as the mark of white privilege.

Ultimately, neither Hindley's actions nor Edgar's remonstrances efficiently undermines the bond between Catherine and Heathcliff. The more aggressively they insist on classifying Heathcliff as a servant, the more assiduously she defends and claims him as a "friend": as Leonore Davidoff notes, "Just as the word *family* encompassed non-relatives, *friend* also referred to kin."[83] So the absence of a (knowable) biological relationship between Heathcliff and the Earnshaws does not exclude him from membership in the Heights family, even though his perceived class and racial difference, partially figured through the trope of adoption, to which I return in chapters 4 and 6, makes him an easy mark for Hindley's and Edgar's efforts to redefine his status. The novel most strongly resists a narrowly biological conception of "the family" in representing the first generation at the (in)famous moment when Catherine announces that Heathcliff is "more myself than I am" (*WH* 63).

Here she asserts a metaphysical unity that outweighs the presumed power of blood ties: she makes a claim of affinity, a word that denotes both a naturalized "inclination or attraction" and a "relation by marriage" (*OED*), thus suggesting the way in which adoptive relations are conceived along the lines of other family-making fictions. Catherine announces an identity with this "foreign" figure on a ground other than common blood or parentage, an identity forged in, but not reducible to, the shared context of their common upbringing.

This spiritual or psychic affinity coexists with signs of Heathcliff's difference, both those imposed from without and those borne within. Marked from the outset by race/class indeterminacy, the adoptee provokes or occasions an array of responses and outcomes, with his power to disrupt familial arrangements not fully apparent until he becomes a parent himself. In the household but not one of the family, Heathcliff oscillates between kin and servant, friend and stranger, owner and owned, even as his presence helps to precipitate firmer distinctions between those terms. Although both Hindley and Edgar insist that he does not belong, Heathcliff forces his way back in by marrying Isabella, successfully using the instruments of law and power to gather Linton and Earnshaw property in his own hands. Motivated by revenge, he orchestrates the first marriage of the second generation, with Linton Heathcliff bearing none of the affinity to the second Catherine that his father bore to the first, as their radically different versions of a heavenly day make clear (*WH* 189–90). From one point of view, this first first-cousin marriage is decidedly endogamous: Catherine weds her dying father's sister's son, a strategy for conserving the patrilineal heritage that Heathcliff notably manages to subvert to his own ends. From another angle, however, this marriage also looks exogamous, as the reproductive union between Heathcliff and Isabella in the first generation has altered the Linton family line by introducing difference into the mix.

By contrast with his cousin—who combines "the Earnshaws' handsome dark eyes" with "the Lintons' fair skin" in a pleasing mix of distinct qualities, showing a "spirit...high, though not rough" and a "capacity for intense attachments" that recalls both her father and mother—Linton Heathcliff embodies elements that do not blend (*WH* 146). Whereas the biological offspring of Linton and Earnshaw harmoniously merges aspects of both, Heathcliff and Isabella's son is the doomed-to-die hybrid that some of George Eliot's contemporaries, as I explore in chapter 5, would deem the inevitable product of racial intercrossing. Heathcliff's difference from Isabella, Nancy Armstrong observes, "makes them too exogamous for anything permanent to come of that admixture."[84] In keeping with the extreme but

by no means marginal thinking of the racial theory of the day, Brontë imagines the offspring of two varying "types" as "a pale, delicate, effeminate
boy" whose "sickly peevishness" indicates a sterile disposition (*WH* 155). If
Heathcliff's incorporation into the (white) community by means of adoption spawns both affinity and antagonism, then the fate of his son suggests a
biological limit to the father's miscegenating influence.

Stigmatizing cousin-marriage as "claustrophobic inbreeding" in a way that
most of Brontë's contemporaries absolutely would not have, Bersani argues
that the novel exposes "the familial strategies for transforming life into an
uninterrupted version of the same": "Only familial relations," he reflects,
"realize the ideal of a nontransforming union. I am at one with someone
else who is not really another; he is—in his very substance, in his blood—a
repetition of myself."[85] Conceived in this light, the projected union between
Catherine and Hareton at novel's end casts the newly nuclear family as a civil,
social, and affective structure that recognizes (some) kin as appropriate marriage partners, reifying the familiar/familial and expelling difference, while
the prior alliance between Catherine and Linton, albeit also a kin-union, fails
because of the difference that Linton embodies as the son of two very different parents. Yet kinship is multiply articulated in *Wuthering Heights:* as a
matter of biological relation, to be sure, but also constructed through both
adoption and marriage, which situate difference within the family. Even if
the "nontransforming union" of the second Cathy and Hareton is predicated
on the expulsion of Heathcliff and the death of Linton, the adoption of
Bersani's "unrelated intruder" has transformed the contours and composition
of the family that gave him ambivalent shelter and that he in turn profoundly
altered. For Bersani, the "nontransforming union" signified by marriage
within the family appears to rule out mixture in its emphasis on the purity of
sameness and shared blood. Heathcliff seems to make up no part of "the family" because Bersani, like most contemporary literary critics, implicitly defines
the nineteenth-century family mostly in terms of blood relation. But part
of what changes between the first and second generation is that the ground
for the "nontransforming union" has itself shifted: from the felt metaphysical
oneness of Catherine and Heathcliff—"Whatever souls are made of, his and
mine are the same"—to the biologically and socially grounded affinity of the
second Catherine for Hareton—"You are my cousin, and you shall own me"
(*WH* 62, 237). And part of the difference between Heathcliff and Hareton
depends on the first being of unknown and unknowable blood, while the
second is of "the ancient stock" (*WH* 254).

Through its ambiguous representation of the adoptee, *Wuthering Heights*
critiques the reproduction of sameness. Simultaneously, however, it deploys

a discourse of racial difference that poses the question of who belongs to "the family" in the loaded terms of blood, terms that were not yet hegemonic in 1847 but would become increasingly so. If kinship provides "the very structure of the narrative," the narrative also structures how and what we read as kinship—a point as relevant to the study of Jane Austen's fiction as it is to the works of Eliot or Elizabeth Gaskell.[86] Even as *Wuthering Heights* relies on "the importation of the nonfamiliar to set in motion its own plot," it redefines the scope and limits of "the familiar" over the course of the novel, in ways that correspond with and even anticipate a broader cultural tendency.[87] With "the family" deployed as a chief metaphor for imagining both "the nation" and "the race," the meanings of sex and marriage with one's own kind and with "others" undergo a profound shift. The instability of all of these terms, by which I mean their openness to historical change, constitutes the most enduring message of *Wuthering Heights* and provides a fitting entrée to the shifting meanings of family, marriage, and incest to which I now turn.

✿ CHAPTER 2

"Cousins in Love, &c." in Jane Austen

> "It is better to know as little as possible of the defects of the person with whom you are to pass your life."
>
> —Jane Austen, *Pride and Prejudice*, 1813

> "Ah! there is nothing like staying at home, for real comfort."
>
> —Jane Austen, *Emma*, 1816

Beyond the gothic terrors that Catherine Morland imagines in the closed-off chambers and curious cabinets of *Northanger Abbey* (1818), a more mundane mystery awaits solution, one that she cannot so readily gloss with reference to her reading. Announcing to Henry "that when he next went to Woodston, they would take him by surprize there some day or other, and eat their mutton with him," General Tilney explicitly tells his son "not to put yourself at all out of your way."[1] When the general proceeds to name the day, Henry expedites his departure from Northanger so that all will be ready for the visit. His response totally baffles Catherine, who makes remarks at which "Henry only smiled": "But how can you think of such a thing, after what the General said? when he so particularly desired you not to give yourself any trouble, because *any thing* would do" (*NA* 183, emphasis in original). Catherine's reflections on these puzzling events pose a central epistemological problem of the novel, indeed of Austen's entire body of work:

> He went; and, it being at any time a much simpler operation to Catherine to doubt her own judgment than Henry's, she was very soon obliged to give him credit for being right, however disagreeable to her his going. But the inexplicability of the General's conduct dwelt much on her thoughts. That he was very particular in his eating, she

had, by her own unassisted observation, already discovered; but why he should say one thing so positively, and mean another all the while, was most unaccountable! How were people, at that rate, to be understood? Who but Henry could have been aware of what his father was at? (*NA* 184)

Saying one thing but meaning another, the general defies Catherine's understanding, leading her to doubt the powers of "her own unassisted observation." As Henry earlier comments, Catherine does tend to judge "the motive of other people's actions" by her own, which makes her particularly likely to be imposed upon (*NA* 118). Yet Henry's ability to interpret his father's double talk is not really a matter of the superior discernment in all things with which Catherine credits him. It is rather a function of being his father's son, of knowing his father's linguistic ways as only he can; it is a product of his experience of Tilney domestic life—to which Catherine, as a stranger to the family, has no access. Like Anne Elliot in *Persuasion* (1818), who recognizes that "all that sounded extravagant or irrational" in the schemes of her father and sister "might have no origin but in the language of the relators," Henry merely demonstrates his experiential grasp on family knowledge that remains screened from public view in being so very well "aware of what his father was at."[2]

Such opacity represents a formidable impediment for strangers, even for those who might be somewhat more discerning than Catherine about the language and motives of others. Her dilemma, then, is not so much that her powers of observation are particularly limited as that she cannot judge the ways of other families by reference to the Morland circle: "Her own family were plain matter-of-fact people.... They were not in the habit therefore of telling lies to increase their importance, or of asserting at one moment what they would contradict the next" (*NA* 60). In contrast to Morland transparency, on which Catherine can rely to reveal the true state of things, other families' talk may deceive her. In the intimacies she forges with the Thorpes and the Tilneys—the two families that seek to attach her through marriage—Catherine's linguistic trials represent the perils of courtship, the experiential medium through which she will pass from the clarity and simplicity of her own family language into the potential ambiguity and obfuscation of another.

Northanger Abbey expresses the trials of courtship as a problem of language more directly than most of Jane Austen's novels, but such an emphasis is hardly unique to it: we need only think of *Emma*'s misreading of Mr. Elton's charade or the alphabets game she plays with Frank Churchill that so discomfits both Jane Fairfax and Mr. Knightley to register how critical a part words can play in concealing things. Generally speaking, Austen associates such hazards with strangers rather than with a heroine's "own family"; this association of language with concealment suggests the risk that inheres in conversational traffic beyond the domestic circle. Yet most Austen protagonists must engage in that traffic, must take part in a "drama of vulnerability" as a prerequisite to making their matches.[3] Not knowing others well enough to know what they mean by what they say, heroines as different as Catherine Morland and Emma Woodhouse each navigate an uncertain course made more difficult by their lack of familiarity, or "familiality," with various pretended or real suitors. In *Pride and Prejudice,* for example, Elizabeth Bennet's fraught encounters with strangers ultimately refine her ability to discern false from true representations and so enable her to establish the basis for forming a new family and a new family language of her own. She inhabits a plot in which she, like Catherine, learns to judge "the motive of other people's actions" according to a new standard. What makes this plot "successful," however, still rests on the mixed experience of familiality: Darcy comes to see Elizabeth and Jane as able to transcend their familial context and thus as capable of being incorporated into his, while Elizabeth can only situate Darcy within his proper milieu after she visits his ancestral home and speaks to the longtime housekeeper. His knowledge of her family and of its difference in status from his own forms the impediment; her belated access to knowledge of his domestic life builds the bridge to a better understanding. Indeed, Catherine Morland's seemingly naïve question—"How were people, at that rate, to be understood?"—resonates for almost all the major female figures in Austen's work. A suspicion of strangers can be overcome, with time, talk, and trouble, if the attraction to them proves more compelling than the risks they pose. But with the notable exception of *Persuasion,* in which the heroine's chief regret is that she brings to her marriage so few worthy friends—a term so capacious as to include a range of kin relations—the tendency in Austen's fiction toward one's "own family" has its comforts, too.

The two examples of projected cousin-marriage in *Pride and Prejudice* stand in stark contrast to the love match that forms its core narrative. To cement an already existing family alliance, Lady Catherine plans for her nephew and her daughter to "unite the two estates": by "the wishes of both sisters," the maternal cousins "are destined for each other by the voice of every member of their respective houses."[4] And she also shapes the other cousin-marriage subplot by offering the obsequious Mr. Collins some "particular advice and recommendation" concerning matrimony (*PP* 71). Aping the marriage strategy of her class, he decides on one of the Bennet sisters—distant cousins on the father's side, girls that his patroness would consider "not brought up high" (*PP* 71). In each case, it falls to Elizabeth to articulate and enact the principle of individual choice: she resists coercion by denying both Collins's appeal to the interests of her family and Lady Catherine's representation of Darcy's duty to the interests of *his* family. In both cases, the directive to marry a cousin figures a surpassable constraint.

The novel's characterization of cousin-marriage normalizes what literary critics, loosely following the anthropologists, call exogamy or, more simply for our purposes, marrying outside the family. This consummate form of the heterosexual plot culminates in "the ideal marriage [that] would combine and reconcile" difference as resemblance.[5] Reading her fiction as consistently Burkean, Tony Tanner argues that in Austen "everything tends towards the achieving of satisfactory marriages—which is exactly how such a society secures its own continuity."[6] To factor gender into the class discourse that *Pride and Prejudice* and its critics more or less explicitly deploy, we can add, with Clara Tuite, that the heroine is appropriated by the ruling class and married to an exemplar of landed manhood so as to vindicate "the upward social mobility of the lower-gentry or upper middle-class female within the marriage market," thus making for a modicum of gradual social change.[7] The genteel but penurious Elizabeth captures the well-to-do but pompous Darcy only at first by her fine eyes; it is more particularly her wit, her intelligence, and even her insults that make him eager to explain himself, after she rejects his verbal proposal, in written language that challenges the interpretations she had previously drawn under the influence of Wickham's eloquence and self-assured bearing. Material disparities of situation between the protagonists give way to a "deeper" similarity: in its "reliance on the figure of sexual exchange," Nancy Armstrong has famously argued, "the novel redistributes authority between Darcy and Elizabeth," transforming "all social differences into gender differences and gender differences into qualities of mind."[8] The "differences" between two strangers ultimately resolve themselves into an underlying sameness, as two become one even before the wedding night.

To be sure, the other marriage subplots illuminate the particular virtues of this union: both the prudent marriage, such as Charlotte Lucas's merger with Mr. Collins, and the status-seeking marriage, which Caroline Bingley hopes to bring about, cast into sharper relief the action involving unrelated strangers who fall in love over time and connect previously unconnected families. But like the projected cousin-marriages, these are made to look insufficient: only the fate of the central couple exemplifies, as Tuite has put it, "the naturalizing function of Austen's marriage plots and heterosexual romance," accomplishing the cultural work of presenting a particular form of love that conquers almost all differences as the norm (*Romantic Austen* 17). Joined by Darcy's sister Georgiana, the happy foursome produced by the marriages of two sisters to a pair of best friends forms the core of a new second family; by contrast, the "endogamous" plot of cousin-marriage in *Pride and Prejudice* is especially discredited. The very minimizing of the cousin's affective appeal works to align marriage within the family with the bad old days of unlimited aristocratic power.

Elsewhere in Austen, intrafamilial union takes on almost sinister overtones, as in the story Colonel Brandon tells in *Sense and Sensibility* (1811) of his thwarted love for his cousin Eliza. Adhering more closely than even Lady Catherine's scheme to the aristocratic paradigm, "in which a woman married her father's brother's son" so as to keep "her estate in her father's family," this subplot typifies the use of cousin-marriage as a means of consolidating the family fortune in men's hands by constraining a woman's power to choose.[9] Brandon describes Eliza as "one of my nearest relations, an orphan from her infancy, and under the guardianship of my father": while it is certainly possible that she is a maternal cousin, it seems more than likely, because of the disposition of the guardianship, that she is actually a rich relation on the father's side.[10] Married "against her inclination" to Brandon's older brother, Eliza's ruin directly follows, not through incestuous adultery with Brandon— a possibility first raised by the rumor that the second Eliza "is his natural daughter," then denied by Brandon himself—but via extramarital sex with other (presumably unrelated) men (*SS* 178, 57). Without the prerogative to choose the cousin we can infer she favors, Eliza exerts her own will only in breaking her marriage vows; deprived of her fortune by her marriage, she lacks even the economic power to support herself and her child.

While Brandon's narrative does not so much indict cousin-marriage per se as marriage to the *wrong* cousin, its gothic overtones imply that this match perpetuates feminine imprisonment for patriarchal interests, that it is "tainted by social ambition," as Ruth Perry describes the general run of "paternal firstcousin marriages" in Austen's fiction, "and the venial desire for accumulation of wealth."[11] Tellingly, in relating the sequel of the second Eliza's unhappy fate, it is not only the original injury to his cousin or the cruelty practiced on the child of his "unfortunate sister" but also the damage Willoughby has inflicted on him on which Brandon dwells: Willoughby "had . . . done that, which no man who *can* feel for another, would do" (*SS* 180, 182, emphasis in original). If "endogamous economics" rather than incestuous erotics dictates the impediment between the first Eliza and Brandon (as is true, from a different angle, for Fanny and Edmund during much of *Mansfield Park*), then it is still also the case that both mother and daughter figure largely in Brandon's imagination as men's property, to be disposed of in marriage, damaged by seduction, or put away by adultery.[12] "Happy had it been," Brandon sententiously concludes, "if she had not lived to overcome those regrets which the remembrance of me occasioned" (SS 179).

With its class and status motives laid bare, cousin-marriage—even its mere prospect—is either decidedly unattractive or downright destructive in these two novels, especially but not exclusively for women, because it ostensibly subordinates individual desire to family interest, as if those two principles were inevitably and irrevocably opposed. By contrast, Mansfield Park radically departs from this model. Admitting the idea of making strangers into suitable marriage partners, it gives full play to the charms of Mary and Henry Crawford and, in the end, just as fully discards them. The ultimate turn to marriage within the family "preserves the inviolability of Mansfield and excludes the risks attendant on" intercourse with strangers, in Glenda A. Hudson's words, by reforming the family from within; the cousin-union of Fanny and Edmund, Tanner further suggests, becomes "essential to the maintaining of the 'house' because so many of its actual blood descendants go to the bad."[13] Within this framework, Fanny Price achieves "upward social mobility," as Elizabeth Bennet does, but not exclusively through marriage: it is by leaving her birth family in the first place—by undergoing her own trials of estrangement on the road to familiality—that she gains her opportunity to marry into the Mansfield family of which, not incidentally, she has already become an integral part.

Considering cousin-marriage a regressive practice, those who seek to position Austen's fiction as more radical than conservative, more feminist than patriarchal, look askance at Fanny and Edmund's union, conferring an ideological slant on both the exclusion of the sexy Crawfords and the incorporation of the modest cousin as daughter and wife. As Claudia L. Johnson forcefully argues, "The language of disease permeates Mansfield Park, and the problem is not with perniciously 'new' people like the Crawfords...the problem is within the great house itself."[14] Subsequent commentators identify this metaphorical "disease" with various strands of the novel, especially as figured by the Bertram slave-owning interest in Antigua and by "the infection of acting," but Johnson herself specifies its nature rather differently.[15] Invoking Burke not to suggest Austen's allegiance to the fiction of the national family, she argues instead that Austen aims "to turn conservative myth sour" by illustrating how "Burkean models of parental authority go awry in Mansfield Park" (Jane Austen 97, 99).[16] The novel levels its charge not so much at metropolitan strangers as at fathers and the disease that breeds and is bred by their exclusion of others: the "*paternal* affection" of Sir Thomas Bertram and the prurience of Mr. Price are not "exempt from an aura of erotic implication" (*Jane Austen* 118, emphasis in original). Most generally, Johnson argues that "the principals in *Mansfield Park* gather together in a tighter knot of consanguinity because the larger world outside has always proved more than they could manage": Fanny and Edmund's marriage thus "savors of incest" (*Jane Austen* 119, 116). According to this line of thinking, the problem with Mansfield, especially by contrast with the "successful" cross-class union presented in *Pride and Prejudice,* lies less in its elimination of strangers than in its overly familial preference for kin. *Mansfield Park* exposes the incestuous insularity of the Bertrams, who cling to resemblance rather than embrace difference. Above all else, Johnson locates incest as the disease of the family at Mansfield, which the novel diagnoses without curing: "Because familial love... appears to be the only legitimate arena for strong feelings... it is prone to incestuous permutations" (*Jane Austen* 117). In making that claim, she extends the critique of cousin-marriage present in other Austen fictions to its logical conclusion. While Tanner and Armstrong view the production of resemblance as the work of the exogamous marriage plot, Johnson sees Austen as critiquing sameness as the basis for marriage and family life.

The terms and concepts that structure these critical arguments all bear further discussion. Rather than assume from the outset that either form of marriage carries a determinate ideological valence, we can simply note that a preference for marriage within the family, not only in *Mansfield Park,* provides an alternative to the cross-class marriage plot that *Pride and Prejudice* exemplifies. We should also recognize that it is not because they are blood kin that Elizabeth passes up Collins or Darcy passes on Miss DeBourgh: in early nineteenth-century England, cousin-marriage was perfectly legal, and to link Edmund and Fanny's marriage with incest is to misname it. Moreover, marriage could function as a means of either creating or solidifying bonds; marrying "out" and marrying "in" had different, sometimes class-specific purposes. Finally, to use the very singular term *family* is to fail to notice the plurality of kin-groups—from the narrowly nuclear unit of the John Dashwoods in *Sense and Sensibility* to the somewhat extended patriarchal ménage of *Mansfield Park* to the Hartfield-Donwell-Randalls triad of friends related by long cohabitation as well as marriage in *Emma*—that the term described at the turn of the nineteenth century. I posit that cousin-marriage, which has since become regarded as an anomalous and stigmatized form of what we now call heterosexual union, once held its place alongside the "exogamous" plot of romantic love and, further, that conceptions of incest, like configurations of family or household, have differed quite dramatically over time. Perhaps most importantly, as Perry has argued, "a kinship system that privileges consanguineal rather than affinal connection" may be "conservative with regard to class, mobility, and social change," yet potentially affords greater agency and opportunity to women (*Novel Relations* 123n40). In short, marriage within the family in Austen's fiction, particularly but not exclusively in *Mansfield Park,* offers an important variant on the now-dominant form of the heterosexual norm: strangers may be both entertained and entertaining, but they are finally put aside in favor of a home alliance that keeps others at a distance. Although this plot may disadvantage some female characters, like the first Eliza, it also creates advantages for others, for example Fanny Price.[17]

As I suggest in chapter 1, historicizing this form of marriage means both rethinking the conventional romance plot, with its emphasis on making familiars by coupling strangers, and revising our use of the terms "endogamy" and "exogamy"; although Johnson does not use these terms, they clearly underlie her argument about the novel, that marrying "in" rather than "out" is a symptom of the "disease" that she sees Austen diagnosing. In their place, I adopt the less loaded phrases "outside the family" and "within the family," even as I show that "the family" is not itself a fixed or singular unit in Austen's fiction. More broadly, I believe that in revisiting what now appears "unnatural," we can see that a family union offered as viable a road to marriage in Austen's time as the romance-between-strangers plot that has come to dominate our understanding of heterosexual courtship in nineteenth-century fiction. Here my project joins with that of Sharon Marcus, who argues that a sedimented, indeed hegemonic, view of heterosexual marriage prevents us from "seeing the diverse forms family and marriage took during the very period that witnessed their consolidation as vectors of power and social coherence."[18] In trying to reconstruct some of that diversity, we may also come to see that, in the case of *Mansfield Park,* marriage within the family arguably offers the heroine her best opportunity to reconcile individual desire and family interest: by the end of the novel, they are one and the same.

Few passages from *Mansfield Park* are so often quoted as the narratorial effusion precipitated by Fanny and William's joyful reunion:

> An advantage this, a strengthener of love, in which even the conjugal tie is beneath the fraternal. Children of the same family, the same blood, with the same first associations and habits, have some means of enjoyment in their power, which no subsequent connections can supply; and it must be by a long and unnatural estrangement, by a

divorce which no subsequent connection can justify, if such precious remains of the earliest attachments are ever entirely outlived. Too often, alas! it is so.—Fraternal love, sometimes almost every thing, is at others worse than nothing. But with William and Fanny Price, it was still a sentiment in all its prime and freshness, wounded by no opposition of interest, cooled by no separate attachment, and feeling the influence of time and absence only in its increase.[19]

Translation: biological siblings raised together—at least those who have not (yet) formed the "separate attachment" of marriage—share a primary and potentially enduring connection that can survive "time and absence." Such a tie exceeds "the conjugal" because longer established and consecrated by childhood "associations and habits." These "earliest attachments" will persist, even intensify, unless—and there's the rub—a new tie damages or destroys them. Should "fraternal love" become "worse than nothing," the blame resides, at least in part, with the differences that ensue from marriages that supplant allegiances to the first family, the very sort of marriages that initiate the action of this novel. If "the ties of blood" come to count for almost "nothing," as the narration describes the state of the case between Mrs. Price and Lady Bertram—"so long divided, and so differently situated"—then what was "an attachment [will] become a mere name," foreshadowing what will become the case between Maria and Julia Bertram (*MP* 290). "Too often, alas," a "separate attachment" destroys the ties to one's own family by creating new ones.[20] Far better, as in *Pride and Prejudice,* for sisters to marry best friends—or men with every chance of becoming so, as in *Sense and Sensibility*—than to divide themselves from one another.

On the face of it, then, the narrative takes the position that a relationship between siblings of "the same blood," being prior to "the conjugal," is also superior to it: while a preference for "single blessedness," which Mary Russell Mitford attributed to the unmarried Austen, is not directly invoked, there is more than a tinge of anti-marriage rhetoric here.[21] From this point of view, any marriage that disturbs the sibling bond would be a bad thing. Matrimony, however, cannot be construed as an entire evil to the family, for there can be no family—no socially sanctioned, legitimately constituted family—without it; as Mary Poovey comments on this passage, "If there were, finally, no family bonds, impervious to the effects of distance or time, there would be no basis for the society Austen wants to defend."[22] This narrator, then, would look with greater approbation on marriages that draw members of a family closer together. Children of "the same blood" who forge new unions might preserve their "earliest attachments" by choosing partners from families to which they are already connected, for such unions both generate new ties and sustain older ones.

As the historian Randolph Trumbach confirms, "The nature of English kinship made the sibling ties the strongest of bonds" and, at the same time, "brothers-in-law and sisters-in-law in the English kinship system were the closest of relatives."[23] Today the differences between a relation "in blood" and an in-law are taken as more or less obvious: much less so in the era of Austen's fiction, as exemplified in Mrs. Dashwood's remark that should Elinor marry Edward Ferrars, Marianne and Margaret "will gain a brother, a real, affectionate brother" or the favorable comments on "the attachment of the sisters" in referring to the afterlife of Elizabeth and Georgiana Darcy (SS 14; PP 249). Juxtaposing Emma Woodhouse's playful claim to Mr. Knightley that "we are not really so much brother and sister" with Lucy Steele's catty intelligence that Edward "looks upon [Elinor] and the other Miss Dashwoods, quite as his own sisters" demonstrates that sibling terminology is also available for characterizing ties among men and women connected by marriage (SS 112).[24]

To grasp this extra-metaphorical dimension of a sibling-in-law being understood as a brother or a sister, consider that while there was no impediment to a woman's marrying her half-brother's wife's brother (as in Sense and Sensibility) or her sister's husband's brother (as in Emma), such unions, while reinforcing existing ties, also brought new taboos into play. By the letter of church law, Margaret Dashwood could not legally marry Ferrars or Brandon in the event of Elinor or Marianne's untimely demise; nor would a widowed Emma be permitted to join hands in marriage with a bereaved John Knightley.[25] For according to the orthodox Anglican conception of sex, a married couple, "by their own oneness, incorporates each into the family of the other": as I explore in the next chapter, holy marriage makes a sister's husband or a brother's wife equivalent to a brother or sister of one's own.[26] Until more narrowly restricted by the emergent conjugal family formation, sister and brother could and did serve as umbrella terms for a range of female or male relatives, referring not only to the blood relationships of the birth family, as in the passage above from Mansfield Park, but also to affinal bonds. Through the workings of affinity, as I demonstrate in subsequent chapters, marriage creates something equivalent to consanguineal connection by asserting a likeness—or, for some commentators, an identity—among all women who occupy a sisterly position in relation to other women or men. Blood relation was not perceived as different in kind from affinity; both sorts of familial connection could, of course, equally become "a mere name"—and in some very basic sense are always just that.[27]

One might argue that it is the fiction of romantic love, to which *Pride and Prejudice* gives such stirring testimony, that partially enables the installation of a narrowly conjugal second family as the norm, weakening the force of sibling attachments by emphasizing the (still highly circumscribed) freedom to select mates without reference to the first family. But although the prospect of making a marriage so as to maintain or enhance "sibling solidarity" might strike us now as a highly unlikely ground for partner choice, many middle-class and elite people in the early nineteenth century would very likely have perceived marriages that deepen and extend extant family ties to hold pronounced advantages over bonds formed with "strangers."[28] Where those two groups diverged was on the degree and character of familial closeness such attachments should possess, for while the middle classes were still agitating to legalize a man's right to marry his dead wife's sister as late as the first years of the twentieth century, the aristocracy had secured the legitimacy of cousin-marriage three centuries earlier. Despite differing class attitudes—elites favored cousin-marriage as a strategy of incorporation and the middle classes preferred in-law marriage as a means of maintaining alliances—neither group perceived an existing membership in the family as a disqualification for marriage but rather as something of an incentive to it. Fanny's marrying Edmund would no more "[savor] of incest" from an aristocratic standpoint than would Elinor's marriage to Edward or Emma's union with Knightley from a middle-class perspective.

Idealizing first affections and critiquing their disruption, the narrative voice of *Mansfield Park* implies that marriage should support rather than nullify sibling ties; indeed, the ideological framework even for so-called companionate marriage encouraged the creation of new affinal bonds of comparable strength to consanguineal ones. Historically speaking, the affectionate nuclear model now constitutes the reproductive heterosexual norm, a vertical, intergenerational relation among father, mother, and offspring; meanwhile, the practice of making marriages with an eye to maintaining and reinforcing horizontal, intragenerational sibling bonds has almost (but not quite) fallen out of western cultural memory, as "cousins married cousins in the nineteenth century at a rate many times higher than would prevail in the twentieth."[29] Increasingly linked by late-nineteenth-century anthropologists to an earlier phase in the development of "the family," with its persistence among both the civilized and the savage a matter of some controversy, cousin-marriage no longer appears to be within the heterosexual marital norm, especially in the United States and increasingly in the United Kingdom as well.[30] It may well be the current unthinkability of such a marriage strategy that predisposes contemporary critics to read family unions in

Austen's fiction, particularly the marriage of Fanny to Edmund, as incestuous. Specifying the changing and particular historical provenance of incest, however, opens up other interpretive possibilities. Both Tuite's suggestion that "endogamous" marriage in *Mansfield Park* is "not a passion but 'a twist of the plot'" (*Romantic Austen* 100) and Daniel Cottom's designation of Fanny as "the intersection at a particular place and time of a great host of vagrant attachments" can inform a more historically responsive reading of what such a marriage means.[31] Following Eileen Cleere's lead, I hope to expand "discussions of incest [beyond] presumptions about affect" to take up issues of economics and status, thus problematizing the ahistorical conception of the nuclear family and the paradigms thought to govern it.[32]

The strand of Austen's fiction that represents marriage within the family as a good thing therefore requires an alternative stance on what we have taken to be the normative marriage plot. For the narrative commentary in *Mansfield Park,* like the novel as a whole, invites us to privilege "the family" over "the marriage," the latter construed not as an end in itself but as a means to an end: "The significance of marriage as a relationship between individuals in [Austen's] novels is always subordinate to its significance as a relationship between families."[33] (Indeed, this emphasis may itself be one reason why Austen's fiction is so susceptible to analyses that derive their theoretical grounding from anthropological studies of kinship.)[34] To proceed in this way means putting aside our critical preoccupation with the vicissitudes of the marriage plot and the fiction of romantic love between strangers to concentrate instead on the family plot, in which marriage figures as agent and instrument of breaking or making family bonds.

To grasp the priority of kin requires comparing familial forms and representations within Austen's fiction and analyzing in particular the class modalities of different family structures and their gendered implications. The opening chapters of *Sense and Sensibility,* for example, juxtapose a narrowly nuclear conjugal unit with another model that emphasizes, even exaggerates, the breadth of familial relationships.[35] John Dashwood's stance toward his dependent half-sisters and his stepmother (also referred to as his "mother-in-law") exemplifies "the lopping and diminishing of the extended family," observes Tuite, "the curtailing and cutting off of claims of kin": his definition of who counts as "family" displays both affective and economic stinginess (*SS* 3; *Romantic Austen* 103).[36] "Mr. John Dashwood had not the strong feelings of the rest of the family," an attitude nowhere more evident than in how he treats these relations—"with as much kindness as he could feel towards any body beyond himself, his wife, and their child" (*SS* 3, 5).

Restricting his sense of obligation to his conjugal family consolidates both feeling and wealth in a few intimates. "Related to him only by half blood," Elinor, Marianne, and Margaret are said to have no "possible claim" on their elder brother's "generosity"—are not even "*really* his sisters" to his wife's way of thinking—for "no affection was ever supposed to exist between the children of any man by different marriages" (*SS* 6, 7, 6, emphasis in original).[37] Understanding their tie "as no relationship at all" relieves the Norland heir of emotional or financial responsibility and "reinforces the legitimacy of a much narrower understanding of family" (*SS* 6).[38]

Such treatment also serves to indicate the particular class position to which John and Fanny Dashwood aspire at the moment of coming into his estate. As the only male offspring of a first marriage and the father of a son, John Dashwood could not be in a more favorable situation, with no competing claims to his patrilineal inheritance on either end of the generational chain so long as his son survives him. John's father's claim to the estate, by contrast, was a good deal less direct, resting solely on the childlessness of its previous possessor, who "had a constant companion and housekeeper in his sister" until her death led him "to supply her loss" by inviting John's father, his second wife, and their three daughters to live at Norland (*SS* 1). When John inherits, the new dispensation effaces another familial form: "Once the site of a family constructed by siblinghood," Perry concludes, Norland is now "transformed into the private castle of the conjugal family" (*Novel Relations* 141). While the historical privileges of primogeniture do not invariably outweigh the imperative of meeting obligations to kin, John and Fanny nonetheless readily set aside the latter in seeking to maximize their inherited capital. Rejecting John's proposal of an annuity for Mrs. Dashwood, Fanny offers an admonitory account of her mother's being "clogged with the payment of three to old superannuated servants by [Fanny's] father's will," which convinces John that "yearly drains on one's income" not only are "unpleasant" but also take "away one's independence" (*SS* 8). While servants once constituted part of the household, the nuclear conjugal ethic, pursued to an extreme, disallows their claims by restricting membership in "the family" to the smallest possible number. The problem with acknowledging a debt to those domestic dependents, John and Fanny agree, is that it makes "one's fortune... *not* one's own" (*SS* 8, emphasis in original). Extending this logic, so, too, may they dismiss the claims that even "half blood" should confer on the portionless daughters of a father's second marriage. One among several instances of its kind within Austen's fiction, the narrowing tactic that the Dashwood couple applies to reduce its obligations to John's father's second family-by-marriage complements a concerted strategy to amplify the status of Fanny's first family by means of marriage. Thus Fanny adamantly opposes any possible liaison between Elinor and her own brother Edward, taking "the first opportunity of affronting her mother-in-law on the occasion, talking to her so expressively of her brother's great expectations, of Mrs. Ferrars's resolution that both her sons should marry well, and of the danger attending any young woman who attempted to *draw him in*" (*SS* 19, emphasis in original).

What it means to "marry well" certainly differs across class fractions: for the Ferrars women, money is most important, whereas attitudes on cousin-unions among all members of the Elliot family in *Persuasion*—Anne excepted—share a common concern with rank. Operating from an inflated sense of their own status, Sir Walter and his eldest daughter pursue the heir to Kellynch, their paternal cousin William, as avidly as they seek the company of their Dalrymple relations. Cousin-marriage in this context possesses all the exclusive cachet of an exclusionary practice: Elizabeth "could see only in *him,* a proper match" that would satisfy her and her father's "strong family pride" (*Persuasion* 14, emphasis in original). Sharing her elders' perspective on the value of rank but having "merely connected herself with an old country family," Mary Musgrove is keenly alive to the impact that cousin-marriage with a lesser branch of her husband's family will have on her own diminished standing (*Persuasion* 12).[39] She opposes her sister(-in-law)'s alliance with a "less affluent" maternal first cousin, criticizing Charles Hayter's "pretensions" while betraying her own: "It would be quite a misfortune to have the existing connection between the families renewed—very sad for herself and her children," or so Mary laments (*Persuasion* 49, 75).

At the other end of the spectrum, Sir John Middleton's liberal construction of family ties in *Sense and Sensibility* offers more than just a comic counterpoint to the thrifty patrilineal family. Mrs. Dashwood's cousin behaves in a more traditionally benevolent way than does her stepson by making available "a small house, on very easy terms" to his distressed relations (*SS* 19). "In shewing kindness to his cousins therefore he had the real satisfaction of a good heart": Sir John fulfills the conventional duties of patriarch to kin through his generosity of both means and manners, indulging in the economic and affective largesse that lies beyond John and Fanny's ethical scope (*SS* 28). The miscellaneous connections to which Sir John lays claim, however, so broaden his circle, first at Barton and then again in London, that those who profit from his kindness—all of them women—must also submit to his extended sense of family, suffering company they would not elect for themselves. As her husband finds it "painful . . . even to keep a third cousin to himself," Lady Middleton must contemplate the prospect of the Steele sisters (consanguines to her, affines to him) not being sufficiently "fashionable" to suit her taste (*SS* 102). Even from Elinor's much less narcissistic perspective, so extended a connection has its drawbacks: "That kind of intimacy must be submitted to, which consists of sitting an hour or two together in the same room almost every day" in obedience to rules of politeness—or, as the narration baldly expresses Mrs. Jennings's point of view, "because they were all cousins and must put up with one another" (*SS* 107, 102). Sir John tells the Dashwood sisters that the Steeles "are your cousins, you know, after a fashion. *You* are my cousins, and they are my wife's, so you must be related" (*SS* 103, emphasis in original). Whereas what is owed to "half blood" matters little to John and Fanny, the web of relationship that Sir John weaves requires no blood ties at all and even extends affinal status beyond its already ample bounds. Sir John's characteristically aristocratic attitude to kin enables him to expand his conception of "his family" almost at will.

There is no danger in that to Sir John, but it courts potential risks as well as advantages for all those he claims as cousins. With "the idea of the extended family taken to such absurd lengths that it is almost meaningless," as Isobel Armstrong suggests, his somewhat fanciful assertion of relationship between his wife's relations and his own still has some currency, since family connections in Austen's age were not exclusively or even predominantly based on blood and biology.[40] And to be sure, his enlarged notion of family appears preferable within the moral framework of *Sense and Sensibility* to John and Fanny's bourgeois nuclear circle or to the narrowness that most of the Elliots display in *Persuasion*. Yet embracing so tenuous a connection as Sir John posits between the Steeles and the Dashwood women—a sense of relatedness which can make nearly anyone, "after a fashion," part of one's family—does generalize the terms of membership beyond any perceptible limits, though his sense of who constitutes his circle actually excludes many, many more people than it includes. Elinor's especial objection to Sir John's ways, we should note, rests in how it forces upon her a "kind of intimacy" with strangers, an unearned, unwarranted intimacy. Lucy Steele in particular will take full advantage of this familial familiarity by impressing Elinor with her longtime claim on Edward's affections (grounded in his prior residence in her uncle's household as a pupil) and by ingratiating herself with the members of his extended circle of friends and kin.

In proliferating linguistic acts through which "others" appropriate or perform familial standing, *Sense and Sensibility* thus registers a latent threat in the terminology that makes strangers into "cousins," "sisters," or "brothers": as Leila Silvana May argues in relation to mostly Victorian materials, "the overdetermined metaphorization of familial nomenclature" may potentially "prove destructive to the ideal of the family," or at least to "the family" in its emergent conjugal form.[41] More broadly still, *Sense and Sensibility* indicates that "a society based on the notion of extended family connections would be a nightmare of indefinite metonymic relationship"—even if, as we are only intermittently aware in reading Austen's fiction more generally, some people of varying class, ethnic, national, and racial positions would never qualify for inclusion in "the family."[42] Thinking about who can or cannot belong, who is or is not a stranger, and on what grounds Austen's fiction draws such conclusions, I suggest, enables us further to discriminate the instrumental role marriage plays in making and breaking family ties.

Would-be marriage-makers seek to secure their place by promoting the use of terms that will confer sibling status *avant la lettre,* and laying claim to sisterhood is an especially pronounced strategy for forwarding courtship in Austen's fiction. Isabella Thorpe's assertion that Catherine Morland would "be so infinitely dearer" to her than her own (birth) sisters at first strikes Catherine as an exaggeration, "a pitch of friendship beyond" any rational standard (*NA* 105, 106). But their jointly engineered "schemes of sisterly happiness" influence her to such an extent that she quickly comes to adopt the sibling language that Isabella deploys (*NA* 108). Having confided her lack of romantic interest in Isabella's brother John, Catherine aims to console her brother's fiancée with the thought that "we shall still be sisters" (*NA* 128). But knowing of Catherine's partiality to Henry Tilney and already plotting to drop Catherine's brother James in favor of Frederick Tilney, the mercenary Isabella's response both conceals an uneasy conscience and betrays a particular truth: " 'yes, yes,' (with a blush) 'there are more ways than one of our being sisters' " (*NA* 128).

Mary Crawford also grasps the value of claiming sisterhood in *Mansfield Park.* Arguing that Mary must come and live with them after he and Fanny marry, Henry disallows Mrs. Grant any right to her half-sister's company by emphasizing the double claim his household will possess: "Fanny will be so truly your sister!" (*MP* 201). While she does not willingly acknowledge it to her brother, Mary clearly believes that his courtship of Edmund's cousin will forward her own marriage plot, being "in a state of mind to rejoice in a connection with the Bertram family" that she hopes will gain her first a sister and then, in short order, a husband: "In Mary Crawford's world," Amy Wolf astutely remarks, "the links between women are always linking them to men" (*MP* 199).[43] Like Caroline Bingley—"more anxious to get Miss Darcy for her brother, from the notion that when there has been one intermarriage, she may have less trouble in achieving a second"—Mary believes "the marriage of one couple would assist that of the other," as Valerie Sanders puts it, "pairs of brother-sister marriages being especially delightful as a way of consolidating family and class alliances" (*PP* 80).[44] For both Isabella and Mary, claiming sisterhood should facilitate wifehood.

While the appropriation of kin terms to characterize friends who might or might not become relations may strike us as odd, the historian Naomi Tadmor has established through close linguistic analysis of primary documents that the "naming convention" of Austen's age enabled a person "to incorporate new members into his or her kinship group" regardless of the character of the relationship to those erstwhile strangers.[45] In a different key, the sisterhood to which Isabella and Mary self-interestedly aspire in pursuit of conjugal ends can also be interpreted as continuous with "the quest to forge, maintain, or recover a bond of sisterhood" that Susan Sniader Lanser identifies as "a quiet but persistent theme in virtually all of Austen's work, often paralleling and intertwining with the marital quest."[46] More pointedly than Lanser, Terry Castle remarks that "many of the final happy marriages" in Austen's fiction "seem designed not so much to bring about a union between hero and heroine as between the heroine and the hero's sister," in service of her larger claim that "sororal or pseudosororal attachments are arguably the most immediately gratifying human connections in Austen's imaginative universe."[47] And although she restricts her analysis to Victorian texts and does not always recognize the significant ways in which sisterhood and cousinship may overlap with "the plot of female amity," Marcus's extended discussion of women's friendships—"securely connected to domestic relationships, not simply by analogy but also through concrete interactions"—helps to illuminate the complex intertwining of courtship, friendship, and sisterhood in Austen's fiction, in which it is often though not always the case that "marriage makes female friends kin" (*Between Women* 82, 70, 83). Thus Henry Tilney and Catherine Morland are enabled to marry partially through the intervention of Eleanor, the friend who will become Catherine's sister; Darcy promotes Georgiana's maturation into discreet young ladyhood by taking Elizabeth as not only a wife for himself, but also a sister for his sister. Whether we agree with George E. Haggerty that "sisterly love . . . functions as an alternative to heteronormative desire" or, with Marcus, that all manner of ties between women were crucial to the institution of heterosexual marriage itself, "sisterhood" clearly provides a focal point for affective relations that cannot be limited strictly to the happy ending of the conjugal plot.[48]

In the two cases cited just above, new sororal relations promise authentically to fulfill the pledges of sisterhood that Isabella Thorpe or Mary Crawford only pretend to keep. But, following Lanser, we should also note that one of the heroine's birth sisters often joins the new kin circle that marriages forge, as is also true in the fictions of sisterhood covered in chapter 3: marriages create second-family sisters but do not necessarily require leaving first-family ones behind. The match between Jane and Bingley, on one hand, and her sister and his best friend, on the other, brings the two couples "within thirty miles of each other" (*PP* 278). Closer still, "Elinor's marriage divided her as little from her family as could well be contrived"; once Marianne marries Brandon, "between Barton and Delaford, there was that constant communication which strong family affection would naturally"—although not inevitably—"dictate" (*SS* 332, 335). Even without a double wedding, a sister's cohabitation may have a salutary effect: the presence of Susan Price at Mansfield partially permits Fanny's promotion from cousin and niece to wife and daughter, as "it was possible" for Lady Bertram "to part with her, because Susan remained to supply her place" and "became the stationary niece" (*MP* 320). Indeed, the breach between sisters created by the unequal alliances described at the opening of *Mansfield Park* is repaired in one branch of the next generation, as the felt need for proxy daughters ultimately enables two of the Price sisters to renew their attachment.

Whether the second family's configuration at novel's end includes a sister by birth or a sister-in-law or both, many sisters of either kind are also excluded from the final familial tableau (as with Maria and Julia Bertram) or treated as kin on a purely formal basis (as with Elizabeth Elliot and Lydia Wickham), granted the "mere name" of sister without the positive affective charge it carries in the other examples I have cited. That is to say, while some sisterly bonds are "immediately gratifying," many assuredly are not. Indeed, as May observes, Austen "peoples her novels with sisters, but of so many shades, hues, intensities, complexities and moral qualities that sisterhood often seems to become *mere* sisterhood."[49] In properly historical terms, neither attachment nor antagonism between kin can be inferred from the use of the sibling idiom, any more than we can necessarily infer greater social value in relationships between "children of the same blood" than among affinal relations. The point here is that Austen's family relations—even the closest ones—are made, not given. And anything that can be made through words can be unmade by other words at some later moment in the plot.

Accomplishing the movement from stranger to kin requires not only the persuasive rhetorical use of sibling terms but also a readiness on the part of the family to admit such strangers to it. Edmund Bertram first expresses his sense of the threat entailed by introducing outsiders on familial terms when protesting the advent of Charles Maddox at Mansfield, warning of "the mischief that *may*...the unpleasantness that *must,* arise from a young man being received in this manner—domesticated among us—authorized to come at all hours—and placed suddenly on a footing which must do away all restraints" (*MP* 108, emphasis in original). Intending to protect the interests and virtue of his sisters, Edmund is altogether less vigilant in guarding his own. Just a few chapters later, he regrets the exclusion of the Crawfords precipitated by his father's return and extends the perimeter so as to include them. Mary and Henry "have a claim," he tells Fanny: "They seem to belong to us—they seem to be part of ourselves," a sentiment that suggests how thoroughly he has incorporated them into the family (*MP* 135). Perhaps not coincidentally, Edmund's words precisely parallel how the narration later describes Sir Thomas's pained sense of his relationship to his sister(-in-law), Mrs. Norris: "She seemed a part of himself" (*MP* 316). The Crawfords' "presence at Mansfield Park creates a circumstance in which the boundaries between outside and inside, strangers and 'intimate friends,'" Pollak argues, "becomes difficult, if not impossible, to sustain," an observation that recalls the seemingly very different *Wuthering Heights* (*Incest* 182). Edmund's desire to marry Mary, which leads to his pressuring Fanny to say yes to Henry, increasingly shapes his perception of the relationship between the Bertrams and the Crawfords as an alliance of the families that will produce a single unit by means of a double wedding.

Very much later, when news of Henry and Maria's flight from Wimpole Street reaches Fanny at Portsmouth, her bodily response expresses moral disgust, suggesting that she, too—however unwillingly—has come to see the Crawfords as "part of ourselves":

> She passed only from feelings of sickness to shudderings of horror; and from hot fits of fever to cold. The event was so shocking, that there were moments even when her heart revolted from it as impossible— when she thought it could not be. A woman married only six months ago, a man professing himself devoted, even *engaged,* to another—that other her near relation—the whole family, both families connected as they were by tie upon tie, all friends, all intimate together!—it was too horrible a confusion of guilt, too gross a complication of evil, for human nature, not in a state of utter barbarism, to be capable of!—yet her judgment told her it was so. (*MP* 299, emphasis in original)

For the tremulous Fanny, the shock of Maria's adultery is very much compounded by Henry's partnership in it. For even if she does not want to think of either Mary or Henry as family, her response still betrays her internalization of the rhetorical constructions and institutionalized connections that have made these erstwhile strangers into something approaching kin. Maria and Henry's affair is a crime against "human nature," consistent only with "a state of utter barbarism."[50]

In this offense to "both families," Fanny potentially figures as its chief victim as she is both Maria's "near relation" and the object of Henry's professed devotion. D. A. Miller calls her moralizing response "extravagant," because it "retroactively masters the relationship she might have had with Henry Crawford by turning it into a torture" and "proleptically masters the relationship that is now possible with Edmund Bertram by turning the thought of it into a taboo" (but not, we should note, an incest taboo).[51] But we can differently account for it by noticing that Fanny is manifestly less concerned over any personal injury or benefit to her. Her immediate attention, rather, centers on the "taboo" already shattered, the impact of Maria and Henry's affair on "the whole family," which now includes Bertrams, Crawfords, and Rushworths. More than just another instance of Fanny's powers of displacement, her initial reaction explicitly emphasizes the "confusion" and "complication" that adultery introduces into the system of relationships that has taken hold among the three families, the interrelations among the previously unrelated of which (exogamous) marriage stands as the legitimate symbol and (quasi-incestuous) adultery its appalling counterpoint. Even in the face of her earlier exclamation, upon reading a letter from Edmund, that "the families would never be connected, if you did not connect them!" Fanny's response to the adulterous couple signifies that she, too, considers not just the Rushworths, but also the Crawfords as part of the family (*MP* 288).

As an unexpected, illegitimate outcome of forming "tie upon tie" with strangers, this event illustrates the risk that outsiders pose to the Mansfield family as well as Mansfield's internal susceptibility to that risk. But it also prevents any further injury from occurring by stopping the double marriage plot dead in its tracks, severing the ties between the Crawfords and the Bertrams, and promoting the eventual wedding of Fanny and Edmund. And therein lies one basis for the critical argument that cousin-marriage marks a means of conservative closure: "In marrying Edmund instead of Henry, Fanny indeed helps Sir Thomas to consolidate his empire and to protect his property from dispersion at the hands of outsiders."[52] According to the historical terms that Trumbach establishes, however, even as the denizens of Mansfield Park, in joining Edmund to Fanny, come to treat "marriage as an act of incorporation that preserved status rather than as an alliance that might advance it," the novel departs from the typical aristocratic paradigm for cousin-marriage that I cited above with reference to the first Eliza's story in *Sense and Sensibility:* this match is not finally effected to prevent "the loss of a family's name or land"; Fanny is no heiress and Edmund is no "father's brother's son."[53] As Perry further explains, "that Fanny and Edmund are maternal cousins means that no material advantage will accrue from the marriage—such as keeping a title or estate in the family" (*Novel Relations* 123). Even if we grant that marriage within the family may conservatively bar the door to difference, the significant permutation in the paradigm demands closer attention: Fanny's marriage within the family offers her a progressive trajectory upwards, in stark contrast to the downward spiral of the rich but relatively powerless Eliza.

As we shall see, the position Fanny occupies as the medium of conserving the Mansfield family, even before her marriage, enables her to make her own legitimate union within it, but she does not by this material fact escape the workings of the familial system that aims either to conserve the status quo or to extend family alliances. Instead, Fanny installs at the heart of the Bertram household—and the heart of the nineteenth-century novelistic tradition—a resistance to "exogamous" exchange that also functions to increase her own agency. The anomalies of her place at Mansfield permit her to give herself away without incurring the social death visited on either Eliza in *Sense and Sensibility* or, even more spectacularly, on her cousin Maria. For the familial "distinction" that has operated to separate Fanny from the Misses Bertram ultimately qualifies her to become a Mrs. Bertram.

Angling for a surrogate to ease her own domestic labors, Mrs. Norris counters Sir Thomas's initial objections to bringing a young, poor female relative into his house with the claim that an entanglement with her male cousins is "morally impossible": "Of all things upon earth, *that* is the least likely to happen, brought up as they would be, always together like brothers and sisters" (*MP* 7, emphasis in original). Regarding the niece as an adoptee, Tuite observes that "the acceptance of Fanny into the household becomes conditional... upon the institution of a fictive, or figurative" sibling-ship (*Romantic Austen* 108). And Mrs. Norris presents that as something of a prophylactic, "in fact, the only sure way of providing against the connection. Suppose her a pretty girl, and seen by Tom or Edmund for the first time seven years hence, and I dare say there would be mischief," since the blood tie of first cousinhood would form no moral or legal bar to so improvident a union (*MP* 7). "But breed her up with them from this time," she argues, "and suppose her even to have the beauty of an angel, and she will never be more to either than a sister" (*MP* 8). Making the poor relation's marriage to either brother "morally impossible" depends on Fanny's approximating an unmarriageable sister-in-blood rather than a marriageable first cousin.

In advocating that move, Aunt Norris invokes rules of attraction that pertain solely to (some) men's desires, assuming that a sister is not what a man is looking for in a wife: that this active, capable, and preeminently covetous character makes the argument also makes it doubly suspect. The scheme rests, however, on an unspoken assurance that Tom or Edmund will do all the choosing, that Fanny will have no desires of her own to prosecute—or at least no ability to prosecute them. Although Fanny's "complex interior life" is "inaccessible to [the] view" of every other character in the novel, it cannot be lost on us.[54] But if Fanny is less openly designing than her aunt, she turns out to be no less desirous—and even "repressed desire turns out, after all, to *be* desire."[55] Although Edmund does indeed, for much of the novel, see Fanny as a sister and fails to imagine her as a potential wife, Fanny's seeing Edmund as a brotherly cousin is the very basis for her choosing him as her only imaginable husband.

In Mrs. Norris's framework, bringing Fanny into the immediate family functions as the only sure way of keeping her out of it. At the very same time, however, Sir Thomas refuses to place Fanny on an equal footing with Tom and Edmund's sisters: his "adoption of the poor niece is a function of the master's charity," but not so much "a patriarchal duty" as it might appear to Sir John Middleton as "an individual action," which perhaps helps to explain why Sir Thomas apparently disadvantages Fanny even as he promotes her (*Romantic Austen* 104). "The distinction proper to be made between the girls as they grow up"—that "their rank, fortune, rights, and expectations, will always be different"—must delicately but forcefully drive home to this poor relation that her "admittance into the Bertram family is contingent upon a collective recognition of her inferior social status, and her own daily consciousness 'that she is not a *Miss Bertram*'": as Paula Marantz Cohen further suggests, "this difference of person and address is the starting point from which other, more subtle differences can be discerned and cultivated" (*MP* 10, emphasis in original).[56] Prescribing a "distinction" of class and gender, Sir Thomas here accentuates status differences between Fanny and her female cousins even as Mrs. Norris asserts the sister-brother link between her and her male cousins. The resulting configuration locates Miss Price in a virtual no-woman's-land when it comes to her marital prospects: like a sister to the boys, for Mrs. Norris, but not to their sisters, for Sir Thomas, Fanny is debarred by her aunt from marrying into the family but is not materially equipped by her uncle for marrying outside it. This asymmetry has a decided impact on both strands of Fanny's marriage plot.

Its propriety in Sir Thomas's eyes aside, the "distinction" between Fanny and her female cousins baffles Mary Crawford, who invokes a related but not identical distinction when she questions Tom and Edmund about Fanny's situation: "I begin now to understand you all, except Miss Price.... Pray, is she out, or is she not?—I am puzzled.—She dined at the parsonage, with the rest of you, which seemed like being *out;* and yet she says so little, that I can hardly suppose she *is*" (*MP* 36, emphasis in original).[57] As Fanny dines only with Mrs. Grant, and even then only in the company of Lady Bertram, while Maria and Julia visit in the neighborhood, Mary concludes, "the point is clear. Miss Price is *not* out" (*MP* 38, emphasis in original). That Mary has been somewhat "puzzled," however, somewhat puzzles her, for "in general, nothing can be more easily ascertained. The distinction is so broad. Manners as well as appearance are, generally speaking, so totally different" (*MP* 36). If Fanny's dining at the parsonage, as against her "manners" and "appearance," temporarily challenges Mary's sense-making capacities, it does not finally undermine the force of this other "distinction," established not only in Mary's mind but also "in general" and "generally speaking." According to the broader social world, where the making of good marriages is the most immediate priority—"every body should marry," Mary believes, "as soon as they can do it to advantage"— the terrain which unmarried young women of good family occupy is sharply divided in two: "out" or "not" (*MP* 32). The difference between them is only a matter of time. For those who are "not out" are always only *not yet* "out": the possibility of remaining "in" has no place at all on Mary's map. She does not so much perceive "a paradox in Fanny's position" as fail to recognize the possibility of an unmarried young woman *not* being on the market.[58]

But situated as Fanny is for most of the novel by Sir Thomas's stingy insistence on differentiating her from his own daughters, "in" would appear a far better term than "*not* out" for describing Fanny's position. She perplexes both Mary and Henry—"Is she solemn?—Is she queer?—Is she prudish?"— precisely because they have crossed into a world in which what they take to be the only relevant distinction among girls of a certain age and class doesn't apply (*MP* 158). One girl remains "in" at Mansfield so that the others may be "out" according to the initial discrimination of the labors of Fanny Price from those the Bertram sisters are supposed to perform: she runs the family's errands, cuts its roses, memorizes all its parts, so that Maria and Julia might work to "extend its respectable alliances" (*MP* 17). By posing the question of Fanny's status in slightly different terms, as a matter of "out" or "not out," Mary enables us to recognize that until Henry stakes his claim, no one at Mansfield besides Fanny has thought much about the possibility of her marrying anyone at all; even Fanny has concluded that the only man she wants "could be nothing under any circumstances—nothing dearer than a friend," here using that multivalent word in the sense we most often use it today (*MP* 181). It is absolutely the case that Fanny is "deliberately denied passage into the realm of exchange and prevented from becoming as interesting as her cousins": with the familial perception of her use-value to her aunts much exceeding her perceived exchange-value, and by analogy with the figure of the governess whose former quarters she haunts, she "does not circulate as an exogamous sexual commodity in the same way that [the Bertram] sisters do."[59] But it is also clear, however, that by being kept "in," Fanny does not finally lose out. On the contrary, it is by virtue of her liminal position, both in relation to the marriage market and to the family itself, that she finds room to maneuver.

For despite her failure to circulate, Fanny does get around—not so widely as Mary or the Bertram sisters, to be sure, but enough to attract Henry's attention well before the moment of her official début at the ball, which her uncle, who "could not avoid perceiving...that Mr. Crawford was somewhat distinguishing his niece," gives in her honor for what he takes to be their common advantage (*MP* 163). Once Sir Thomas grasps the price that Fanny could fetch in the marriage market, that is, he tries to erase the status difference he imposed on her when she first came to Mansfield, opening his argument in favor of Henry's suit by acknowledging "that there has been sometimes, in some points, a misplaced distinction" between Fanny and her female cousins—without admitting, of course, that he was the author of it (*MP* 212). Fanny herself has already understood this linguistic and material reversal very well, as her response to the honor of opening the ball suggests: "To be placed above so many elegant young women! The distinction was too great. It was treating her like her cousins!" (*MP* 189). Aiming to efface the "distinction" he had originally drawn between Julia and Mary and their cousin, Sir Thomas fails to recognize its permanent effects on Fanny's character.

Operating entirely within the purview of the "general," Henry has seen Fanny only as *not yet* "out," but what attracts him is precisely Fanny's distinction, shaped by the experience of being perpetually "in." He identifies her as potentially marriageable, but because she has not been "brought up to the trade of *coming out*," Fanny is pricier than most, not depreciated in Henry's jaded eyes by her participation in that arena (*MP* 183, emphasis in original). In this respect, Fanny's *not* being one of Sir Thomas's daughters is her greatest advantage. Once the so-very-out Maria and Julia have fled the scene for London, the privileged access the Crawfords have gained by their domestication at Mansfield—a level of access that arguably renders moot categories of "out" or "not"—affords Henry a remarkable opportunity to engage the affections of one whose charm lies in the fact that she is *not* on the market and never will be. Her exclusion from Maria and Julia's portion as the objects designated for "respectable alliances" paradoxically provides Fanny with all of the virtues Henry could ever wish for in a wife. In his seizing on Fanny's potential conjugal value—her "steadiness and regularity of conduct," her "high notion of honour, and such observance of decorum as might warrant any man in the fullest dependence on her faith and integrity"—we get a very clear sense of the particular advantage of her having remained "in," one that, to Henry's lasting "vexation and regret," Mansfield itself is not finally able to do without (*MP* 201, 318).

Even a girl not "brought up to the trade of *coming out*" may partially understand herself in its terms: albeit portionless, Fanny is capable in her own way of a silent and secret giving. Her "fond attachment" to Edmund undoubtedly originates in her feelings for her eldest brother, "whom she talked of most and wanted most to see" and to whom Edmund gives her the means of writing: her cousin's kindness in enabling her to correspond with William repairs that loss by also providing her with something on the order of a second attachment to Edmund himself (*MP* 57, 13). That the way to Fanny's heart lies through her brother is reaffirmed when Henry Crawford times his proposal so as to capitalize on the good will he has earned through his service to William. Yet the conditions of Fanny's second attachment differ dramatically in character from those of the first, contrary to Johnson's claim that "the difference between fraternal love and the 'other' is far from clear" (*Jane Austen* 117). In contrast to the presentation of her relation to William—"this unchecked, equal, fearless intercourse with the brother and friend" grounded in their shared experience of "the evil and good of their earliest years"—Fanny imagines her relationship to Edmund in the explicitly economic terms of value and debt: "In return for such services she loved him better than any body in the world except William," indeed "as an example of every thing good and great, as possessing worth, which no one but herself could ever appreciate, and as entitled to such gratitude from her, as no feelings could be strong enough to pay" (*MP* 161, 18, 28). Under obligation to Edmund without the means to compensate him for his "services," Fanny can attempt to pay their price only in the coin of her own "feelings," which, intense as they are, can never be "strong enough" to cover the debt.

Without sanction, then, Fanny bestows her heart and her allegiance on Edmund, with everyone from Mary and Henry to Sir Thomas and Edmund remaining unaware that she has already committed herself. And she makes this gift with almost no hope of return. Her presumption in giving herself away, rather than seeing herself as fully subject to being exchanged by others, certainly does occasion self-flagellation: the words she uses to describe her sense of being unworthy of Henry—"the higher his deserts, the more improper for me ever to have thought of him"—apply even more exactly to her feelings for Edmund (*MP* 240). But regardless of how "improper" it may be for her to form an attachment to someone she imagines to be so far above her, it is that very impropriety that safeguards "Fanny's heart" against both Henry Crawford's effort to engage it and Sir Thomas's belated effort to put her on the market by undoing the formative "distinction" he had himself installed (*MP* 158). Crucially, however, "that the love she silently bears is not exactly legitimate," in Johnson's words, has little to do with her biological relation to Edmund: if Fanny's love is illegitimate, it is because she bestows it without any sanction except her sense that her debt to Edmund is too great to cover by other means—a feeling born of class inferiority, to be sure, but also one that positions her as an active, responsible subject, a debtor, rather than as a pawn in someone else's game, or out of the game entirely (*Jane Austen* 117). The unequal terms of her membership in the family, which both place her on an uneven footing with the daughters of the house and temporarily make her Edmund's "only sister," enable her to remain within it on a permanent basis as his wife (*MP* 302).

In this respect, Fanny's plot does not so much break "the laws of exogamy and endogamy," which a generation of feminist theorists and critics of the nineteenth-century novel have understood as shaping both "the traffic in women" and the dominant narrative of heterosexual marriage, as it invites us to historicize those terms and their provenance in relation to the marriage plots of nineteenth-century English fiction (*Romantic Austen* 108).[60] The "law of exogamy," after all, has been understood to arise from a prior proscription of both incest and same-sex object choice, but since the definition of incest varies from one historical moment to another, the imperative to which this "law" purportedly gives rise is arguably something less than ironclad in the moment of *Mansfield Park*. In order for such a law to become hegemonic, alternative formulations of marriage had to be crowded out, a process that took place over the course of the entire nineteenth century. Like heterosexuality itself, exogamy and endogamy had to be invented and have to be understood as having a history, one that begins around Austen's moment. We forget too easily the force and scope the now-anomalous alternative plot of marriage within the family had for Austen's original audience. Its erasure from our histories of domestic fiction prematurely forecloses the possibility that there might have been something valuable for some female characters, and their authors, in that plot.

Mary Crawford most clearly articulates "the law" for women in this novel, but it seems not so much to prescribe whom one may or may not marry as to mandate that marry one must: as Pollak puts it, "What the incest taboo most decisively regulates...is not so much incest itself as the multiplicity of forms that, in the absence of that prohibition, it might be possible for sexuality to take" (*Incest* 10). Mary, Maria, and Julia all operate within the compulsory framework cast in the binary register of "out" or "not out," with marriage understood as their imminent destiny and final destination, while Fanny's remaining "in" or, alternately, debarred from "coming out" ultimately keeps her in the family by means of the marriage no character ever seriously thought she would make. Marriage within the family in *Mansfield Park,* then, represents less a critique of the infamous "traffic in women" or even an endorsement of the continuing power of "fraternal love" than a sustained investigation into how the reproduction of "the family," as a medium of inclusion and exclusion, both limits and enables the range of positions any female character might occupy in relation to compulsory wedlock, "exogamous" or not. At the same time, Austen's oeuvre also indicates that even within marriage, many female characters have opportunities to maintain and extend kinship ties, to other women and to men, through the creation of second families not exclusively centered on the heterosexual couple and its offspring. In this broader construction of "the family," which affords greater scope to a larger range of possible affective relations, we can see a fuller array of attachments that arguably rival heterosexual marriage itself in their intensity and duration.

Finally, in departing from the narrative she helped to pioneer, Austen significantly modifies the historical model of marriage within the family when she represents Fanny's originary circumstances in *Mansfield Park:* cousin and niece rather than sister and daughter; aligned on the mother's side rather than that of the father; a poor dependent rather than a rich heiress. These are critical factors in Fanny's fate because they disable her from participation in either "exogamous" or "endogamous" circuits of exchange—or, to put it in more historically appropriate terms, from being sought after by either strangers *or* kin in pursuit of rank, status, or cash. In this respect, Fanny Price and Elizabeth Bennet, despite their considerable differences, have more in common than appears at first blush, in that they make their marriages on the basis of character rather than connections, helping to advance the very fiction of individualism that, in other respects, Austen's novels challenge. Viewed in this context, Fanny becomes something other than a Maria Bertram or an Eliza Brandon, something different from the object of exchange subject to the patriarchal plots that designate marriage as a man's game and expel an errant object from the familial fold. Together with her ability to wait it out, Fanny's irregular position enables a degree of agency that makes her nobody's property but her own.[61]

✤ CHAPTER 3

Husband, Wife, and Sister: Making and Unmaking the Early Victorian Family

Had I not known were Love, at first a fear,
Grew after marriage to full height and form?
Yet after marriage, that mock-sister there—
Brother-in-law—the fiery nearness of it—
Unlawful and disloyal brotherhood—
What end but darkness could ensue from this
For all the three?

—Alfred, Lord Tennyson, "The Sisters," 1880

A husband is a thing very, very like a sister only he
doesn't interfere with one's sister at all.

—Minny Thackeray Stephen to Anny
    Thackeray, 1867

With ample selections from contemporary
family letters, the sixth chapter of E. M. Forster's *Marianne Thornton: A Domestic Biography* (1956), entitled "Deceased Wife's Sister," tells the story of
"a fantastic mishap" that his grandparents' generation "could only regard as
tragic."[1] After the death of his first wife, Harriet, in 1840, Henry Thornton decided to take another—no crime in that, except that his intended,
Emily Dealtry, was Harriet's younger sister. At once, "the situation became
very awkward" (*MT* 190). Having lived with Henry all her life, his sister
Marianne "behaved civilly" to Emily, who "had continued to frequent the
house" after Harriet's demise, helping "to look after her nephew and her
nieces," but another Thornton sister "refused to see her anywhere" (*MT* 190,
189). Spending "vast sums" without success "in trying to get the 1850 bill
passed" (*MT* 192), which would have repealed the 1835 statute invalidating
all such marriages contracted after the statute took effect, Henry took Emily,
her mother, and his own daughters abroad to solemnize the marriage in one
of the many European states where these unions were legal.

Appalled, the rest of his nine siblings, most of them married, worked to
maintain a united front. Upon Henry and Emily's return to England, the

susceptible Marianne was prevailed on to stay away from Battersea Rise; even "*a single visit*" from her, Forster's clerical grandfather insisted, "will be magnified into *countenance* and approval by a leading member of the family: and every artifice be employed to draw others in. . . . In the mind of society the family may become mixed with the offenders: and real injury be done without any resultant benefit" (*MT* 214, emphasis in original). By this act of "the Master, the Inheritor, who had betrayed his trust," Forster characterizes the other members of the family as "excluded for ever" from their ancestral home "unless they bent the knee to immorality, which was unthinkable" (*MT* 205). Enumerating Henry's alienation from his family as only one of the troubles that followed from his decision while simultaneously marking his own distance from Thornton family values, Forster comments that "to the moralist, so much discomfort will seem appropriate. To the amoralist it will offer yet another example of the cruelty and stupidity of the English law in matters of sex" (*MT* 210).

Forster knew a good deal at firsthand about that "cruelty and stupidity," of course, in all its multifarious forms. But reproving the manners and morals of a former age doesn't quite address the historical circumstances of his biographical subject, the loyal unmarried sister displaced not just by a new wife but also by one who cannot legally fill the place of the first. "Should the law be altered," Marianne Thornton writes, "probably the next [generation] will wonder at our scruples"; Forster confesses that "we do wonder at them," even as he purports to "remember the indignation of Orthodoxy" in 1907, when the prohibition was finally repealed (*MT* 190, 191, 217). Marianne, however, makes no reference to law and very little even to religion in characterizing her own attitude. "I have never thought alas as all my family do that it is very wrong," she tells a friend, "only that it is an *impossible* sort of idea—in short it seems not a sin—but a shame" (*MT* 190–91, emphasis in original). And the "shame" of it stems from "feelings that I fear nothing can eradicate—for they seem like an instinct planted in ones [*sic*] very nature"—albeit not in her brother's— "that in this generation cannot be worn out," though they were very much "worn out" by the time this Thornton family story found its way into print (*MT* 190). She subsequently gave those feelings a sharper profile in a letter to Henry: "My own brothers- and sisters-in-law have always appeared to me so exactly like real brothers and sisters that any other connection seems an impossibility. I cannot realise a different state of feeling" (*MT* 193).

Just thirty years before this Thornton family contretemps, Jane Austen's brother Charles married his sister(-in-law), another Harriet, who had taken her dead sister's place as "a careful and attentive mother" to her children: it had produced some "wonder and censure," in the words of Austen's mother but neither undue scandal nor much apparent familial discord.[2] Such remarks help clarify Marianne's claim about the feelings of "this generation," as opposed to those born slightly earlier and later. Lacking an historical grasp on Marianne's "state of feeling," we, too, might continue to interpret the long nineteenth-century debate about marriage with a dead wife's sister solely in the way that Forster does, as a species of Victorian foolishness in "matters of sex," rather than as, more neutrally, a sign of profound differences in the meanings of the family and incest. We are far removed from a time when some relations by marriage, commonly known as "affines," did figure by orthodox standards as "exactly like real brothers and sisters," those "consanguines" related to us by blood whom we cannot legally marry, So Marianne's "shame" may be difficult for us to fathom, as her assumptions about the family differ from those that underlie the now-naturalized nuclear model. As described in chapter 2, a sibling's marriage would not only create new ties between separate families, it would also expand and reshape one's very own family through its incorporation of new members. Regarded in this light, Marianne is herself, as Forster's chapter title attests, a "Deceased Wife's Sister" to the departed Harriet—with neither she nor Emily capable of forming "any other connection" to Henry than the one that already exists: neither sister, that is, can or should become his wife.

In the language she uses to express her feelings, Marianne observes a distinction between "real" siblings and those who are "exactly like" them that both forms a linchpin of the MDWS debate and reveals an ambiguity in the boundaries of the family. While "exactly like" suggests there is no difference between birth siblings and in-laws, the word "real" assigns priority to the former and dictates the rhetorical terms in which the latter were and still are represented: no one then or now ever says, for instance, "she's like a sister-in-law to me." Commonsensical as this distinction now appears, even the "real" of Marianne's statement is not entirely stable, though it most often designates those "children of the same family, the same blood, with the same first associations and habits" of whom Austen writes in *Mansfield Park*. Even if not always raised by the same parents, moreover, "real" siblings for Austen or Marianne Thornton must have shared more than "the same blood." For one thing, as Leonore Davidoff has argued, "the notion of a distinct 'blood relative'" may itself "be anachronistic when unproblematically projected on to the historical record": notions of family membership were not necessarily rooted in biological relation, as my study of Austen's fiction in chapter 2 indicates.[3] For another, having antecedents in common did not in and of itself form a barrier to marriage: the pervasiveness and legitimacy of cousin-marriage in nineteenth-century culture, so endemic as well in nineteenth-century fiction, suggests that a close degree of relatedness between marriage partners was something of an incentive rather than an impediment, at least among the upper classes. Even in a capacious sense of family, "real" siblings were nonetheless fully recognizable as different in kind from, say, cousins—and not only because one's cousin, unlike one's brother, could become one's spouse, as in *Mansfield Park*. That an in-law could become "exactly like" a "real" sister or a brother, however, helps especially to demonstrate the broader parameters of "the family" in the early nineteenth century. Proximity, association, and habits of language and thought produce not only first families, which may encompass birth, adoptive, and fostered siblings, but also second families, of which siblings by marriage form an integral part, in a far less narrowly nuclear sense of "family" than our contemporary usage denominates.[4]

As Leila Silvana May perceptively argues in *Disorderly Sisters,* her excellent study of sororal relations, "literal definitions of 'daughter' or 'sister'" constitute only a single dimension of their meaning; "extensions of those terms...produce metaphorical and metonymical parents and siblings."[5] To preview an example I discuss at length in chapter 6, Mrs. Hamley of Gaskell's *Wives and Daughters* can become "like" a mother to Molly Gibson, and her sons "like" Molly's brothers, by repeated use of familial analogy, in the absence of a "real" mother or "real" brothers of Molly's own and without any connection other than neighborly friendship between the Gibsons and the Hamleys. Whereas May emphasizes that the gap between the "real" and its likeness can be exploited for devious ends, as in the case of Austen's Isabella Thorpe or Mary Crawford, I follow Elizabeth Rose Gruner's lead in seeing the nineteenth-century family as both "born and made," as evident in Marianne Thornton's sense of relatedness to her siblings-in-law and Molly Gibson's family-by-analogy.[6] To privilege the "real" exclusively is to miss that kinship is and has always been a made thing, a human artifact, rather than (as some Victorian anthropologists would argue) a naturally occurring phenomenon based in blood. In a historical process that unfolded over a long period, the narrowing of the multivalent language of familial relationships to include only birth siblings (itself a vexed term in view of the widespread fact of adoptive relations) registers a slow but dramatic cultural shift away from the broader family that marriage had traditionally made, as the protracted span of the MDWS debate itself demonstrates.[7]

For much of the nineteenth century, sisterhood or brotherhood was conceived not only as a static relation fixed at and by birth but also as an achieved and achievable state of relationship to others. Siblingship was not just a legal or biological designation but also a more-than-metaphorical means of indicating proximity and connection that might both incite and prohibit romantic and sexual attachments. The installation of a norm emphasizing the exclusive (and exclusionary) bond of the conjugal, reproductive couple modified the older, larger "ideal of the family"; as Helena Michie suggests, "fusing two people with limited experience of the opposite sex, who often deeply identified with their families of origin and with communities of same-sex friends, into a conjugal unit that was to become their primary source of social and emotional identification" constitutes "difficult cultural work."[8] Drawing on Henry Maine's discussion in *Ancient Law* (1861) of the movement "from Status to Contract," Tony Tanner also notes that the genre of the novel itself not only traces the emergence of the individual from his or her obligations to the family but also dramatizes "ambivalent feelings" about that movement—ambivalence that attaches itself, I suggest, primarily to the figure of the unmarried or second sister.[9] This transformation of the meanings of marriage and the scope of the family generated extensive resistance and only qualified assent.

To illustrate the reshaping of "the family" among the early Victorians, I turn to pamphlets, speeches, and reports about MDWS published primarily between 1830 and 1860 that portray the second families formed by first marriages and the desire for second marriages they sometimes inspired. With few exceptions, the perspectives expressed in these male-authored representations support Margaret Morganroth Gullette's conclusion that "the MDWS controversy was mainly a battle between men" as well as Cynthia Fansler Behrman's comparable claim that it was "an issue that would concern men rather than women as a group."[10] Participants in the debate largely aimed either to broaden or to restrict middle-class male prerogative, to permit or to prohibit the fantasy that Karen Chase and Michael Levenson identify as central to both the quarrel and the culture: "that a husband will always have a second choice, a second sister, waiting nearby in domestic reserve."[11] Two contemporary novels by women—*Deerbrook,* by Harriet Martineau, and *The Inheritance of Evil, Or, the Consequences of Marrying a Deceased Wife's Sister,* by Felicia Skene—critique that prerogative and chastise that fantasy: the position of the second sister in the husband's affections reveals the contested role that marriage plays in constituting a second family. Yet these novels also reveal a corresponding female desire, which they likewise work to correct in the interest of solidifying the singular bond of the conjugal pair. Each stages the drama of the husband's illegitimate attraction to his sister(-in-law) against the backdrop of his wife's fierce attachment to the first-family sister whom she cannot or will not leave behind. The pervasive "jealousy" of the wife operates, I argue, as an ambivalent and ambiguous sign that conveys both desire and solidarity in a manner already familiar to us from Austen's fiction. Reading these novels against the fictions of relatedness constructed in the MDWS debate demonstrates a point that Forster somehow overlooked: that "matters of sex" are also family matters.

From almost-sister to second wife: an entirely unremarkable move to those Victorians who imagined "real" sisters as similar enough to make the substitution of the living for the dead an appropriate and desirable course for a widower to take. Although "the question of the relation between the sisters" could be posed in "a number of different ways," those who protested the MDWS ban most frequently cast the one as a living reminder of the other, naturalizing the second choice by emphasizing its inevitability.[12] "The heart, while yearning for a second love," in the words of a pamphlet that tells the widower's conventional story, "shrinks from all contact with that which wears not some impress, or cannot in some measure perpetuate the memory of the first":

> Consider how such a marriage is likely to originate. A man who marries the woman he loves, and loves the woman he has married, finds himself, after some years of conjugal happiness, a widower. He may or may not have children—if a father, there is before him the sight of those who vainly listen for a mother's voice; if childless, where is the face into which he can look for similitude of her that is gone?—in either case his bereavement is complete. If, then, in the hour of his desolation there come to him, with words of comfort and sympathy, one who in tone and feature—perhaps in heart and temper too—reminds him of his beloved departed, is it strange, though it may for a moment sadden him to
>
> > "view the dame
> > Resembling her, yet not the same,"
>
> that his heart should yearn towards her?... To whom but to *her* could he speak, as he would, of the lost one?—the one dear to, and lamented by, both—a bond of mutual sympathy and source of hallowed regret, alone sufficient to impart to such an union much more of a sacred than a sensual character.[13]

The likeness of the two is the widower's greatest comfort, for the sister "wears...some impress" of, bears a "similitude" to, the dead wife: in that familiar, familial comfort lies the origin of the new "union." The tenor of such a representation—and I could quote many, many more like it—leads the anthropologist Françoise Héritier to conclude that for grieving widowers and their apologists, "two sisters are essentially the same thing... replacing one sister with another amounts to the same."[14] But the use of the inset poetic quotation—taken from *The Giaour* (ll. 1093–94), of all things, by the infamously incestuous Byron—sharply qualifies Héritier's conclusion. "Resembling her, yet not the same," the second sister is not identical to the first, more aide-mémoire than exact replica. The point of difference—at a bare minimum, that dividing the living from the dead—enables the substitution, most effective when it makes the least difference. "It would be repugnant to my feeling to displace old associations, and to seek marriage elsewhere," one anonymous widower testified before the Royal Commission convened in 1847 to consider the state of the law. "My wife's sister disturbs nothing; she is already in the place of my wife" (*First Report* 66).

That a second sister might succeed a first wife, a move that casts them as both actual and "metaphoric replacements" for one another, does not then mean that they are "essentially the same thing."[15] Rather, each could occupy the same "place," namely that of wife, a position that could never be filled by a man's own first-family sister, rarely mentioned as a potential surrogate mother for the orphans who typically populate the standard tableau created by the advocates for repealing the ban. The latter as a rule subordinate the would-be wife's putative sisterhood to the widower to testimony that she has been a good sister to the departed. Indeed, the more a woman devoted herself to the memory of her dead sister and shared that unifying bond of grief with her brother(-in-law), the more likely that she would be an attentive mother to her nieces and nephews and a fit wife for their father. The widower thus quickly learns just how well or badly she would fill that empty "place," the latter being the case with Minny Stephen's sister, Anny Thackeray, who continued for a while to live with her brother(-in-law) Leslie and care for her niece Laura after Minny's death.[16]

Emphasizing that "sacred" rather than "sensual" feeling motivates such marriages, moreover, witnesses before the Royal Commission represented men as only heeding their dead wives' final wishes when they seek to take that momentous step: "it was the dying request of my first wife"; "she should die happy if I could marry her sister"; "my sister... on her death-bed expressed a wish, that if [her husband] married again, he should marry her sister" (*First Report* 69, 24, 76). The most assiduous wife might take a more active role: as one widower testified, "My former wife... expressed a very strong desire that, if I married again, I should marry her sister"; at the same time, "my former wife had also expressed to her sister her desire that if she married she should marry me, if such a marriage was legal; so that, in point of fact, we were both, it might be said, doubly tied up" (*First Report* 67). Matthew Arnold cleverly parodied the philistine lack of delicacy such arguments evince in *Friendship's Garland* (1871): "The place of poor Mrs. Bottles will be taken by her sister Hannah.... Nothing could be more proper; Mrs. Bottles wishes it, Miss Hannah wishes it, this reverend friend of the family [a Baptist minister], who has made a marriage of the same kind, wishes it, everybody wishes it."[17] For the grieving widower of the sentimental scenario, by contrast, honoring a wife's dying declaration, even when it means breaking the law, becomes another means of disavowing everything but the purest intentions and most enduring fidelity to the deceased. To reinforce "old associations" by forging "a second attachment [that] might seem like the continuance of the first"—resembling it, yet not the same—a widower needs a second wife who is like her dead sister and, presumably, whom her dead sister liked (*First Report* 88).[18]

But to make a wife from a sister(-in-law) is to deny that sisters-in-law are *really* a man's own sisters, and it was this point that advocates of the ban most fiercely contested. The Anglican divine Edward Pusey, a leading figure in the early years of the debate, consistently portrayed the effort to legitimate MDWS as an attack on the central principle of holy marriage, arguing that a married couple, "by their own oneness, incorporates each into the family of the other."[19] "Sexual union"—even outside marriage—"makes two people 'one flesh,'" with the doctrine of coverture proving to be the sticking point for the established church, as it was in the run-up to the Matrimonial Causes Act of 1857.[20] Such hard-line opponents of MDWS as Pusey did not distinguish between "consanguinity, a relation created by 'blood,'" and "affinity, a relation created by human law"; moreover, the two "were on precisely the same footing with regard...to incest" in the ecclesiastical courts.[21] And their polemics attempted to persuade others that they should not subscribe to it either: one contemporary essayist proposed, for example, that "in the actual state of public feeling and of the law, a man looks upon the sisters of his wife as upon his own sisters" and a woman regards them as "having such an interest in her husband's affection and attentions as his own sisters by blood. In life they are united as one family."[22] As the narration of *The Inheritance of Evil* states, even after the death of Elizabeth Maynard Clayton, whose body has created the bond between them, her sister Agnes is still the widower Richard's sister: "Death had dissolved the tie between Richard and Elizabeth in one sense only—it had not dissolved the relationship which that tie had produced—Agnes was still sister to her who mouldered in the dust—Richard was still one flesh with her—the fraternity between them remained unbroken as between children of the same parents."[23] "Those, then, who deny that the sister is akin to the husband must deny that the husband and wife are really one," and when Pusey says "really," he doesn't mean "exactly like."[24] "If of 'one flesh' with his wife, a man was related by blood to his wife's relations," as Nancy F. Anderson states: "If there were any meaning in those words at all," a clergyman tells Richard in *The Inheritance of Evil,* "the sister-in-law be in the sight of heaven counted as the sister in blood" (*IE* 44).[25] Concretely envisioning sisters as the same substance, opponents of MDWS posited identity rather than exact likeness between them: a man's sister-in-law is therefore *really,* as Marianne Thornton might agree, a sister of his own.

Although primarily religious in origin, some of these ideas also intersected with medical and legal constructions of the period. Citing a view that came under scrutiny later in the century, Anderson notes "the contention that sexual intercourse causes an actual physiological change in the marriage partners that makes them blood relations."[26] Chase and Levenson suggest that the lack of comparable discussion about a man marrying his dead brother's wife rested on a gendered asymmetry within contemporary thought about male and female physiology: "If the wife became the body in common between two men, then [the brothers'] blood would incestuously immorally mingle," because the body of the woman/wife, as Gullette further asserts, "is imagined as something like a permanent container of the first male flesh she experiences."[27] Even if the specter of homosexual incest was not routinely invoked, sex between in-laws was categorically differentiated in law from simple adultery because construed as incestuous, just as sex with a brother or sister "of the same blood" would be.

The effects of sex and marriage on first and second families were thus very much at issue in this aspect of the debate, and the varied interpretations of "one flesh" especially illustrated the contested claims about the impact of a man's first marriage on the parameters of the second family that every marriage created. In contrast with the view that would license such unions, the high church position asserted that when a man moves from his first family, where he is a son to his parents and (typically) a sibling among other siblings, to the one he originates as a husband and a father, the agency of holy marriage creates new, real siblings. Against the idea that the husband/father stands alone, accorded the right to take any second wife at his pleasure and convenience, Anglican orthodoxy enjoined that his second family reproduce elements of his first by establishing what William Hale Hale called "a real brotherhood and sisterhood" between in-laws.[28] As in most of Austen's fiction, marriage signified as an alliance not exclusively between individuals but between families, exemplified in Marianne Thornton's feelings of "real" kinship and in William Gladstone's parliamentary claim that by "the conjugal relation you bound families together."[29] A sister of one's wife thus becomes a sister to oneself: "The husband has not merely the opportunity, but the duty, of paying to his wife's sister those blameless and tender attentions which he pays to his own sister. He can pay them to no other woman except his own sister; he sees his wife's sister as he sees his own."[30]

This line of thought makes siblings-in-law available for intimacy within precisely the same legal and social limits that governed relationships between "children of the same parents." "In whatever degree the marriage law is relaxed," Pusey warned in his testimony before the Royal Commission, "in that degree are the domestic affections narrowed": if a more narrowly bounded idea of family and the contract model that deems marriage dissoluble (whether by death or divorce) work in tandem to loosen the ties of kinship by casting affinity as a merely metaphorical relationship, a sister-in-law will lose her privileged status as a sister (*First Report* 53). And a widowed brother(-in-law) will lose the benefit of her presence, since relaxing the law must drive her from his house according to the "rule of society that persons whom the law allows to marry cannot remain under the same roof unmarried" (*First Report* 53). (Note, by contrast, that in Forster's 1910 novel *Howards End,* when the Wilcox sisters' aunt, Mrs. Munt, offers "to go and keep house at Wickham Place" for her widowed brother-in-law, she could only do so "without impropriety," at least in her own mind, "before the passing of the Deceased Wife's Sister Bill" in 1907.)[31] "Change the sister of a wife into a young marriageable stranger," and "the union which is daily seen in families will, where it now exists, be broken": "The relation of brother-in-law and sister-in-law will cease" if not measured by the same standard that applies to "real" brothers and sisters.[32] One side emphasized likeness between first-family sisters as the basis for sanctioning second unions; the other cast the analogous relation between first and second families as grounds for prohibiting them.

With so much discord between the competing arguments, it is easy to lose track of where they overlap, but it is certainly the case that on both sides of the debate, "real brotherhood and sisterhood" between in-laws indicated an intimate non-sexual relationship that might generate a desire to marry. While some counseled that the very natural attraction to the second sister must be blocked—as the Queen's chaplain stated before the Royal Commission with some asperity, everyone has "desires to approximate, which they will naturally proceed to accomplish, except under powerful restraints"—an anonymous widower spoke for many others in testifying that "the intimate intercourse, which the present state of the law sanctions," itself "has been the cause of the attachment which subsists" (*First Report* 29, 80). A sister-in-law's presence in the household, as a sister to a brother, inspired the feelings the ban aimed to proscribe by allowing for the transfer and extension of "domestic affections" to a not-so-new, not-so-different object. The sides disagreed, then, on whether an attraction to the second sister was an appropriate outcome of family feeling or a hideous perversion of it, whether it was most "natural" or all too "natural." Differently valenced as that term was for each party, their joint appeal to nature demonstrated that neither commanded the full social assent to the premises each was attempting to legitimate.

Advocates of the ban feared that lifting it would contaminate all sibling bonds by admitting into the Victorian home the possibility of adulterous incest either before or after the first wife's demise; advocates of repeal—who posited likeness rather than identity between sisters, affinity rather than consanguinity between brother- and sister-in-law—denied the charge of incest and disputed the grounds on which it was based. "It is a curious idea of incest to call it incest to marry an alien in blood when it is not incest to marry a first cousin," a member of the House of Lords argued in the 1870s, invoking an increasingly frequent reference point for late-century opposition to the ban; "but are sisters-in-law sisters? This is just what they are not," he declared, enumerating legal distinctions of status between siblings and in-laws regarding the inheritance of property.[33] Cousin-marriage, to which no stigma was attached in Great Britain until about the 1860s, might have provided a model on which MDWS could have been made acceptable to the earlier Victorians, for "to many people at the time the idea that sex with such an in-law should be called incest," while marriage to a cousin was not, "seemed genuinely preposterous."[34] Undoubtedly it seemed so because to them, as to most of us, "one flesh" was only a metaphor, siblingship a relationship conferred only by the first family and, increasingly, marriage a potentially dissoluble contract between individuals rather than a union of families. If, metaphorically speaking, cousins were far away enough to marry, then wives' sisters stood at an even further remove from the family of origin.

Speaking for the forces of prohibition, the Royal Commissioners bluntly stated the rhetorical goal that they had so much trouble achieving— "to induce the husband to regard his wife's sister as his own," an end at which the repeated references to in-laws as relations "by blood" who are "united as one family" and the characterization of MDWS as "manifest incest" were clearly aimed (*First Report* x, 37). That such rhetoric alone kept the law in place seems unlikely, but it is just as improbable that the one-flesh metaphor, and the contest over the scope and membership of the second family that it generated, had no residual effect on how relationships between first and second families were conceived. "Preposterous" or not, the characterization

of in-law marriage as incestuous reminds us, moreover, that incest is a historically variable concept. Even as the Victorians progressively adopted a
more secular view of marriage, some remainder of the older dispensation
persisted: the figure of the wife's sister, at the apex of the triangle that forms
the second family, provided its focal point.

Responding to "the only objection" to repealing the law "worth
considering"—that it "would destroy the sanction under which the innocent familiarity allowed amongst brothers and sisters-in-law takes place"—
one pamphleteer argued that "this familiarity must be attributed to other
causes" than the law itself, going on to characterize those causes as something
other than familial feeling.[35] The author implied that a second sister would
continue to appear in the light of a potential marriage partner, even after a
first marriage, as a perennial "second choice":

> Up to the period when he makes his selection, the man necessarily
> regards all the sisters alike; it is absurd to suppose that, the moment
> he has married one, a complete revulsion in his moral being is to
> take place, and that he will be enabled to invest her near relations of
> his own age with the same ideal barrier, the same sin-repelling halo,
> which nature has cast around his own. If he did, he would never
> afterwards regard them as objects of sexual passion; for feelings of
> this kind are the product of habit, and cannot be put off and on with
> circumstances.[36]

"Men in general," he concluded, "undergo no such change" of perspective:
they do not come to see these new sisters as they see their own and as thus
immune to being regarded as "objects of sexual passion."[37] The very charms of
"familiarity" derived instead from those sisters having once auditioned for the
role of (first) wife, thus becoming sexualized to some extent simply by their
availability for male choice. For at the level of courtship ideology—think
of Mr. Collins confidently assessing all (but romancing only some) of the
Bennet sisters in *Pride and Prejudice*—women as a group were "not the choos-
ers but the chosen," a conclusion subsequently disputed in Darwin's theory
of sexual selection, "in which females were the ultimate decision makers and
males competed for female approval."[38] "A pretty, young, unmarried sister,"
in the view of a male character from Margaret Oliphant's *The Perpetual Curate*
(1864), "was perhaps the least objectionable encumbrance a woman could
have."[39] But if "a man changes his mind once," as Sarah Annes Brown remarks
of the hero of that quintessentially idealizing text, Coventry Patmore's *The
Angel in the House* (1856), "what is to stop him doing so again?"[40]

Based in the prerogative of unfettered selection, this point of view surely enabled the male fantasy of the "second choice" that Chase and Levenson analyze in the fiction of Dickens. Its scandalous appeal rests on the double charge of the second sister: both those who accept and discount the force of "one flesh" invariably construct her as at once an innocent familiar and a potential object of desire. This double charge involves double binds. On the one hand, the pamphleteer distinguished a man's attitude to his own sisters from what he might feel for his sisters-in-law, attributing the ban on the former to the quasi-religious feeling ("sin-repelling halo") that "nature" inspires in their brothers. On the other, he suggested that there is nothing natural about that "ideal barrier," pointing to the prohibition of sexual feeling as "the product of habit" rather than, say, instinctual taboo. If first-family sisters are not naturally off-limits, then second-family sisters are not even habitually so. Having "regard[ed] all the sisters alike," and all as unlike sisters of his own, generic man will see the woman he does not marry as a familiar domestic object that may be wife or sister, containing the latent capacity to occupy either place.

In *The Inheritance of Evil* as in *Deerbrook,* the woman who becomes the husband's sister is, from the very beginning of their acquaintance, an object of his desire. Narrated from the perspective of the suspicious and observant fiancée, the first meeting of Richard Clayton and Agnes Maynard causes Elizabeth "an indescribable pang": "Her future husband was standing with his eyes fixed on Agnes, gazing at her with a look of the most warm and unqualified admiration, a look such as had never been bestowed on herself" (*IE* 30). After the establishment of their joint household, Agnes fills a spot in Richard's daily life: "Annoyed and often irritated at" Elizabeth, he would "gladly turn from her to seek the society of Agnes," who forms "so pleasing a contrast to the anxious care-worn wife," "openly preferring" the one who is also "virtually his sister" (*IE* 36, 66, 102). Here what draws the husband to the sister(-in-law) is not her sameness but her difference: not being Richard's wife but still being close enough, as a virtual sister, to join him unchaperoned during "the long walks and rides which Elizabeth's enfeebled health prevented her from attempting," Agnes provides Richard with a source of female companionship that is both sisterly and sexualized (*IE* 37). In *Deerbrook,* by contrast, the husband's passion for the second sister does not arise from her domestication in the second family; it actually precedes it. Having learned that Hester Ibbotson loves him, Edward Hope, a Deerbrook doctor, proposes to the sister he has inadvertently attracted rather than to Margaret, the one he truly loves: "He decided at length how to act; and he decided wrong."[41] Although the narrative emphasizes his moral struggle, Hope finally chooses to act in a fashion convenient to his desires, knowing that marrying Hester will bring him Margaret as well: "He glanced forwards to his desolation when he should lose the society of both sisters—an event likely to happen almost immediately, unless he should so act as to retain them" (*Deerbrook* 140).[42] In both novels, then, the second family incorporates the sister on terms that make the husband's attraction to her an ongoing site of tension and conflict.

From the perspective of these male characters, "two sisters" are thus not "the same thing" at all; in both cases, neither wife nor sister is what she should be to the husband. With each novel asserting the shaping power of male choice, the fantasy of the second family turns out to be something of a nightmare for husbands, owing in part to the relationship between the sisters, whose first-family circumstances shape their entry into the second. Being orphans unites each pair very tightly: Elizabeth's dying mother had entreated her to "look upon [Agnes] henceforward as a sacred charge" and to promise "that no other tie or affection hereafter springing up in her life should interfere with this her earliest and most binding duty"; similarly, Hester and Margaret expect to be all in all to one another, "to be each other's only friend," when they arrive at the rural home of their distant relations after their father's death (*IE* 11; *Deerbrook* 21). Heeding her mother's request, on becoming engaged Elizabeth makes it "the sole condition of her marriage that Agnes should reside with" her and Richard "entirely, and that she should never be separated from her sister so long as [Agnes] remained unmarried" (*IE* 28). And in the prospect of Hester's marriage to Hope, "no one seemed to doubt for a moment that Margaret would live with her sister. There was no other home for her; she and Hester had never been parted; there seemed no reason for their parting now, and every inducement for their remaining together" (*Deerbrook* 162). Each new family formed by marriage, then, bears the imprint of a woman's first, with the sororal solidarity between orphans requiring that the husband embrace the sister as part of the new unit. Far from obeying "the imperative literally and figuratively to leave the birth family behind," which Michie represents as a defining feature of "conjugality," the second family dramatizes a variety of motives for resisting that imperative (*Victorian Honeymoons* 75).

Disaster threatens second-family life, however, not only because of the husband's fantasy and the sisters' bond but also because of the wife's temperament. Even before their marriages, both Elizabeth and Hester are represented as constitutionally jealous, possessed by a possessiveness that borders on mania. While still a child, Elizabeth's "affection for those she loved was of a nature so profound and exacting, that it had engendered that jealousy of disposition which makes such havoc of the soul that harbours it," and the advent of a potential husband focuses her "idolatrous love" on him (*IE* 8, 34). Explicating Elizabeth's jealous pang at Agnes and Richard's first meeting in the passage cited earlier, the narrative voice dwells on the "disposition" that gives rise to it: "Her affection for Richard Clayton was so absorbing that her whole heart and mind were bound up in it, and she had not a thought unconnected with him; she felt indeed that it had most utterly superseded all other sentiments and feelings, for at that moment she could have wished that the fairer and younger sister (her own dear Agnes!) had not been standing by her side, thus to rob her of a single look from one so passionately loved" (*IE* 30–31). Looking at Richard looking at Agnes, Elizabeth glimpses the possibility of a second choice in that gaze: coveting her fiancé's exclusive attention arouses her jealousy.[43]

Arguably, then, the problem at this point in *The Inheritance of Evil* is not so much the presence of the (sexualized) sister as the inconstancy of the husband and the insecurity of the wife; taken together, the flaws of the conjugal couple make for an imperfect union. The law aims to remedy their weaknesses: in Skene's scheme, the ban on the second sister not only prohibits the husband's desire for a familiar but also protects the wife from her own failings. Along these lines, Elizabeth initially rights herself by recalling the doctrine that will safeguard all parties from sin: "In another instant she repelled this unworthy feeling almost with horror, for she remembered how, in a very few days, Richard Clayton would hold for Agnes Maynard the sacred name of brother. They twain were about to be made by a most holy ordinance ONE FLESH, and from that hour her sister must be his sister also, in the sight of God and man" (*IE* 31). Had she been formed on a better model, the narrator implies, Elizabeth wouldn't have felt "jealous and suspicious" at all: adapted as it is to human frailty, the law ameliorates the lack of that better, purer self which it is the province of Christian doctrine to inculcate (*IE* 31). Knowing enough of religion to believe that Richard and Agnes can only ever be brother and sister to each other and in the eyes of God keeps Elizabeth's "unworthy feeling" in check—at least for a while.

Hester's possessiveness in *Deerbrook* also centers less on the perception of her sister as a rival and more on her desire for undivided affection, but it is her sister, rather than her husband, whose attention she craves. Hester covets Margaret's love as intensely as Elizabeth does Richard's in *The Inheritance of Evil,* claiming "there can never be the same friendship between three as between two" and attributing the operation of her "jealous temper" to the intensity of "the strongest affection I have in the world" (*Deerbrook* 21, 22). Contrary to May's assertion that "one source of the paranoid jealousy with which Hester torments herself" is that she intuits her husband's love for Margaret, Hester does not consistently see Hope as a rival for her sister's affections, nor as someone of whose affections she should be jealous: only once does Hester suspect, before the marriage, "that Margaret had been the more important of the two to him" (*Disorderly Sisters* 101; *Deerbrook* 117).[44] A more plausible "source" for Hester's insatiable need for her sister's undivided devotion emerges in a conversation early in the novel that gives her jealousy a first-family genealogy. Recalling the baby sibling they lost, Margaret wonders aloud "what difference it would have made between you and me, if we had had a brother" (*Deerbrook* 21). "He would now have been our companion,—growing into the stead of all other friends to us," Hester remarks, adding that "you and he would have been close friends,—always together, and I should have been left alone" (*Deerbrook* 21).[45] Fantasizing perpetual exclusion, she subsequently resents Margaret's intimacy with their new neighbor, Maria Young: "Hester found that Maria filled a large space in Margaret's mind, and that a new interest had risen up in which she had little share" (*Deerbrook* 70). And she turns that resentment against Margaret herself, from saying "a few pettish words" to loudly, even violently, lamenting the alienation of her sister's affections (*Deerbrook* 70). Such persistent suspicion provokes even the saintly Margaret to anger: "I have found a friend in Maria; and you poison my comfort in my friendship, and insult my friend. There is not an infant in a neighbour's house but you become jealous of it" (*Deerbrook* 288). But struggle as Hester may against her wickedness, Margaret's attention to her own nephew also disturbs her, leading Hester to accuse Margaret of having "not a thought to spare for any of us while she has baby in her arms. The little fellow has cut us all out" (*Deerbrook* 498). "The empty space that should be filled by the brother," May persuasively claims, "becomes the object of unfulfilled desire"; as the new baby replaces the dead one, Hester reproduces in her second family the feelings of loss and exclusion generated in the first (*Disorderly Sisters* 28).

While Martineau's Hester never learns the truth about her husband's feelings, Skene's Elizabeth undergoes the suffering induced by both her "idolatrous love" and the dying knowledge that her jealousy is not without foundation. Having managed to solace herself with help from the one-flesh doctrine, Elizabeth persuades herself that, after her death, "Richard would find some unknown stranger, fairer and dearer, to take her place in his love and in his home" (*IE* 38). Fixated as she is on her husband, "the one overpowering idea which was always present in [Elizabeth's] mind, was the conviction that his attachment for her fell far short of her own in depth and fervour" (*IE* 35). She experiences "the most complete consolation," when she lights upon an alternative scenario to the advent of that "unknown stranger": "Far from her place being filled by a rival," Agnes would stay on, after Elizabeth's demise, "and so long as she continued unmarried, she would prevent the possibility of another wife entering into the house of which she would be the beloved inmate," with Agnes remaining chief among the "memorials" to her sister and her enduring love (*IE* 39). Expressing her conviction that she would die in childbirth, but dissimulating her true motives, Elizabeth "repeatedly implored of them both to promise her that Agnes should always remain with her brother-in-law; urging as her reason for wishing it, that to her alone would she commit the care of her little daughter, and the new-born babe if it survived" (*IE* 40). The narrative thus casts the dying wife who pleads her sister's suitability as a second mother not as an angelic moral guardian aiming to superintend the family circle even from the grave, as proponents of MDWS would have it, but as someone so unprepared to give up worldly affections that "she longed, had it been possible, to have held [Richard] still within the stiff cold arms from which the warmth of life was fled" (*IE* 38).

The dénouement follows fast on Elizabeth's overhearing Richard, in a fortuitous conversation with a clerical friend about the prohibited degrees of affinity, speak "much of the advantage which might result from . . . procuring for the children of the deceased wife so kind and natural a protectress as their aunt": "There had been an energy and an anxiety in Richard's manner of expressing himself, which proved that, however unconsciously, it was yet for his own sake that he sought so earnestly to prove the truth of his assertions" (*IE* 43, 48). Albeit unredeemed by religious faith, Elizabeth nonetheless possesses "the instinctive delicacy of feeling with which a pure mind must revolt from a transaction so opposed to all that is just and holy," and the shock precipitates her final illness of both mind and body (*IE* 45). "Her gaze fell upon Agnes, and her heart revolted with unnatural horror against her dear and only sister," whom she throws against a wall before falling into a fit, delivering her child, and attempting to utter the words that will prevent the foul incestuous deed which, even just in the prospect, fills her with "unnatural horror" (*IE* 51). As Richard and Agnes sit by her bedside, reassuring her that they will honor her wish, Elizabeth can only listen to sentiments that once "would have been to her so inexpressibly soothing and consolatory" but instead "served only to madden and torture her" (*IE* 55). "In a few minutes more"—minutes that, as the text reminds us, she should be using to save her immortal soul— "she would be powerless to say the words with which she sought to separate them, to interdict their unhallowed union, that now came choking to the lips too palsied to articulate" (*IE* 58). When words do come, the ambiguous sentence they form is "Agnes . . . not . . . marry": as the misperceiving sister hastens to console Elizabeth with the pledge that "I will never leave this house," "an expression of utter hopelessness settled on [Elizabeth's] features—they had misunderstood her to the last!" (*IE* 59).[46] If the setup of the second household appears to fulfill the structural require- ments of the husband's fantasy, then it also closely corresponds to the shape of the wife's darker imaginings.

The truth of the matter notwithstanding—that both Elizabeth and Hes- ter *do* have reason to be jealous of their sisters, who *are* regarded as "objects of sexual passion" by their brothers(-in-law)—the desire for exclusive pos- session that motivates both wives, whether understood as excessive love or unmet need, intensifies with the addition of a third party (man, woman, or child) who threatens to cut them out of the picture. The male wish always to have a "second choice" close at hand joins, in very uneasy union, with the female fear of being excluded or replaced, not only by her sister but also in her sister's affections. The structural likeness of the fear to the wish suggests that they are actually two sides of the same marital coin, two desires that traverse the second family: Elizabeth's negatively coded "jealousy" comple- ments the male fantasy of plenitude.

While a wife's desire to retain her sister for herself even as she also gains a husband of her own may not look particularly scandalous, seeing it *as* desire helps us to recover a dimension of the husband–wife–sister triangle that both nineteenth-century analysts and contemporary critics have largely ignored.[47] In reading only for the wifely rivalry with the sister, we too readily accept the naturalness of the competitive structure between women implied by both sides in the MDWS debate: and whereas "nothing may seem more natural to us than female rivalry over men," as Sharon Marcus comments, "noth- ing seemed more odd to Victorian readers" (*Between Women* 106). As much recent queer criticism, including Marcus's own work, has usefully illumi- nated, we can consider sororal ties as promoting intimacy, for example, rather than enforcing competition. Eve Kosofsky Sedgwick notes parenthetically in "Jane Austen and the Masturbating Girl" that "there are important gen- eralizations yet to be made about the attachments of sisters, perhaps of any siblings, who live together as adults": one of those generalizations may be, as George E. Haggerty argues in relation to Austen's *Sense and Sensibility,* that "the most profoundly emotional and physical relations between women emerge from the family itself."[48] "Even for those [women] who deeply distrusted or disliked the nuclear family," Martha Vicinus concludes, "it remained an important source for imagining and constructing same-sex intimacy" into the early twentieth century.[49] Recognizing the wife's wish to possess sister *and* husband as comparable, indeed structurally parallel, to the husband's wish for "two sisters" enables us to inquire into the conjoined fate of male and female desire in these texts.

In ironic parody of pro-MDWS representations, Skene represents Elizabeth's death as joining brother and sister even more closely together, as it did Henry Thornton and Emily Dealtry. "He could not endure the society of any one excepting Agnes, with whom he could talk of his Elizabeth, and who in voice and manner so often reminded him of her"; "feeling that there was a bond between them in the love they had borne to the departed," Agnes "devoted herself to the task of soothing and consoling him" and of sustaining his sickly children (*IE* 62–63). Particularly chastised for being "weak and unstable in principle" and "following the inflexible law of his own inclination," Richard will acknowledge no limits on his freedom to choose (*IE* 27, 82). Thus ensues catastrophe, including social ostracism by almost every member of the community, the death of various offspring, and increasing alienation from the second sister who becomes his wife. Such punishment appears fit recompense for Richard's decision to defy God's ordinance in prosecuting his own selfish desires, with the achieved fantasy of a "second choice" exacting its price from one who would not conform to a higher law. Written in the service of Anglican orthodoxy, Skene's "novel with a purpose" predictably enacts its retribution in accord with divine will; that the work of a thoroughgoing Dissenter like Martineau pursues its narrative design in parallel fashion, however, is much more striking.

Although *Deerbrook* finally dispels all potentially evil consequences, its plot also overtly punishes the sins of a husband who has tried to mend his ways, with a decided emphasis on the need for the two made one by marriage to embody that unity in their conduct and feelings. In contrast with Richard Clayton, Edward Hope determines to squelch his inappropriate passion for Margaret, which persists and even intensifies after his marriage to Hester; he will not allow himself to treat his sister(-in-law) as a familiar or to regard her as a would-be wife. Lacking the explicit religious overtones of Skene's novel, *Deerbrook* trusts far more to norms of manly duty and self-denial even as it shows how difficult it is for Hope to live up to them: as May argues in the most thorough, interesting reading of the novel to date, "circumstances must conspire to bring the brother to his knees, to make him love the sister to whom he is married, to purify his feelings for his new 'sister,' and to get her out of the house" and into one of her own with the man she loves, Philip Enderby—who also happens to be secretly loved by Margaret's close friend, Maria Young (*Disorderly Sisters* 89).[50] By virtue of his marriage, Hope must labor to restrain the desire for the second sister that entering into that union enabled him only very imperfectly to fulfill; to make a sister of the woman he would have chosen for a wife, he must try to convert an "object of sexual passion" into a familiar sibling by cultivating those "feelings... [that] are the product of habit," a task he cannot accomplish without a major assist from Martineau's plot. For both Edward and Hester, renunciation of their shared desire for Margaret—love for that sister being the ground on which they are most united—is the critical element in making their marriage work, but it is no easy task. Taking up a more scandalous scenario than even Skene imagines, *Deerbrook* ultimately chastens both the husbandly and wifely fantasy of the second family, inciting a furor that publicly enacts a displaced punishment of domestic crime.

Although his attempt to "retain" both sisters by marrying the one and thus cohabiting with the other reveals a strand of selfishness in his character, Hope is not a light libertine on the order of Richard Clayton. Before he weds Hester and the trio sets up its joint household, he believes he can render the proper attitude to both women: "In his admiration of Hester, [Hope] thought as little as he could of Margaret," concluding "that he had deceived himself about his feelings" since "he could now receive from her the opening confidence of a sister; he could cordially agree to the arrangement of her living with them; he could co-operate with her in the preparation for the coming time, without any emotion which was inconsistent with his duty to Hester" (*Deerbrook* 165, 166). Upon returning from the honeymoon, however, he learns that he has not conquered his feelings after all: while "Margaret's eyes overflowed when Hester led her to Edward for his brotherly kiss," "Mr. Hope's mind was disturbed for one single moment that he had not given this kiss with all the heartiness and simplicity of a brother" (*Deerbrook* 199). Whereas May asserts that the kiss "exceeded the boundaries of brotherly propriety," I suggest that its lack of "heartiness and simplicity" shows that Hope actually falls short of appropriate brotherliness: he becomes momentarily conscious that it isn't the sort of kiss he'd like to give Margaret (*Disorderly Sisters* 97). The awkward physical contact with a desired object—the contact their new relationship permits, indeed by some lights requires—indicates that Margaret's proximity will severely test his self-restraint. Shortly thereafter, "a fearful suspicion... seized upon him. He was amazed at the return of his feelings about Margaret, and filled with horror"—like Skene, Martineau references the affect conventionally linked with incest— "when he thought of the days, and months, and years of close domestic companionship with her, from which there was no escape" (*Deerbrook* 205). With Hester remaining very much alive for the entire novel—and Margaret's own marriage plot imperiled by causes related to "the terrible secret of this household" which I discuss below—the second family affords Hope no opportunity for escape (*Deerbrook* 264). Even as he implicitly (and unfairly) holds his wife responsible for his dilemma, he tries to return her feelings—"he must devote himself wholly to her whose devotion to him had caused him his present struggles"—and to summon up considerable power of will, so that even "if Margaret did not, ere long, remove from the daily companionship which must be his sorest trial, he should grow perpetually stronger in his self-command" (*Deerbrook* 206). Unable to feel himself a brother or to fulfill his husbandly role, Hope occupies a false position toward both sisters.

And both sisters receive intimations of something amiss through Hope's various failures of brotherly and husbandly conduct. For her part, Margaret wonders at the lack of sibling intimacy that, "after all our longings for a brother," she had foreseen as a chief advantage of the marriage: "Her own gain was almost too great for gratitude: a home, a brother, and relief from the responsibility of her sister's peace" (*Deerbrook* 149, 164). Suffering under her own romantic troubles, Margaret's "great comfort was Edward . . . but even here she was compelled to own herself somewhat disappointed. This brotherly relation, for which she had longed all her life, did not bring the fulness [*sic*] of satisfaction which she had anticipated" (*Deerbrook* 232). Key to Margaret's distress is the quality of "the intercourse between themselves. That Edward was reserved,—that beneath his remarkable frankness there lay an uncommunicativeness of disposition,—no one could before his marriage have made her believe: yet it was certainly so"; "she felt that he did not win, and even did not desire, any intimate confidence" (*Deerbrook* 233). Margaret's experience shows that Hope cannot fulfill her expectation that a brother-in-law will be "exactly like" a "real" brother, yet it also demonstrates that he successfully avoids intimacy with this familiar.

One of Hester's comparably jarring moments occurs when Hope does not include her in the correspondence he conducts with his only brother, Frank, in India. When her husband receives Frank's response to a letter in which Hope had (unbeknownst to Hester) confessed his growing feelings for Margaret, Hester expects a sisterly pleasure: "She knew that the arrival of news from Frank was a great event in life to Edward. . . . She longed to share, for the first time, the confidence of a brother" (*Deerbrook* 338). Hope withholds the letter, which "re-awakened in his memory and imagination . . . the Margaret of last summer," so Hester complains that he denies her the familial access to which their marriage entitles her: "I believed that you would hold me your friend,—that no others were to come near my place in your confidence,—that all you cared for was to be equally mine,—that your brother himself was to be my brother" (*Deerbrook* 338, 340). Neither sister, then, gains the happy second family to which both aspired, owing to the consequences of Hope's fantasy-gone-wrong.

To be sure, Hope recognizes that keeping his secret prevents him from satisfying either Hester or Margaret, but he considers this his only means of protecting them from the ugly truth: "At my own table, by my own hearth, I cannot look up into the faces around me, nor say what I am thinking. In every act and every word I am in danger of disturbing the innocent—even of sullying the pure, and of breaking the bruised reed. Would to God I had never seen them!" (*Deerbrook* 246). With regard to Margaret, he laments that "I cannot even be to her what our relation warrants" (*Deerbrook* 247). Yet he cannot stand to lose her, so that when her engagement to Philip finally seems secure (although it is not), Hester gives voice to both her own and her husband's grief at losing Margaret:

> "We ought to rejoice with nothing but joy, Margaret," said she: "but I cannot see how we are to spare you. I do not believe I can live without you."
>
> Her husband started at this echo of the thoughts for which he was at the moment painfully rebuking himself. He had nothing to say; but gave his greeting in a brotherly kiss, like that which he had offered on his marriage with her sister, and on his entrance upon his home. (*Deerbrook* 327)

Reminding us of that earlier uneasy kiss, the text suggests that Margaret's impending marriage, which would be "another comfort" to Hope "if he could only feel it so," augments rather than alleviates his passion (*Deerbrook* 206). That his wife speaks aloud his secret thoughts also gives them another dimension, for if Margaret's presence poses a threat to their marriage, albeit one unknown to Hester, her absence would perhaps be no better. In their twin desire to keep the sister at their side, Hester and Hope draw closer together, but in a way that Hope alone understands.

Given that *Deerbrook* emphasizes her "jealous temper," Hester's blindness to Hope's true feelings for their sister seems unaccountable. But it makes a good deal more sense if we consider the plot of the novel as enacting the double fantasy the spouses harbor and the purifying chastisement each aspect of that fantasy demands, thus requiring them, as Ann Hobart suggests from a slightly different perspective, "to align their personal desires with the social roles they find themselves enacting."[51] For a long while, *Deerbrook* indirectly conspires to grant the Hopes their agonizing wish that Margaret will never leave them. The social circumstances of small-town life give their joint jealousy of

Margaret's affections broader scope, for the community compulsively polices its members—inventing crimes, pursuing petty grievances, disciplining its own for real and imagined improprieties—in both their public and domestic lives: in Deerbrook, "every man" and woman truly is, as Henry Tilney says in *Northanger Abbey,* "surrounded by a neighbourhood of voluntary spies" (*NA* 172). Thus even as Hope undergoes his private trials of domestication, he experiences a series of attacks on his professional reputation after committing "an act of public indiscretion."[52] His casting a vote that defies the wishes of the local gentry eventually leads the middling townspeople, in a plot twist that anticipates Lydgate's situation in *Middlemarch* (1871–72), "to give the benefit of their family practice to some one of better politics than Mr. Hope" (*Deerbrook* 230). "In another set of minds," among the laboring class, "a real fear of Mr. Hope, as a dangerous person, sprang up," which ultimately leads to the circulation "of stories about robbing churchyards, and of prejudices about dissection" and a complete boycott of Hope's practice (*Deerbrook* 230, 299).[53] And, as in *The Inheritance of Evil*—where "a laudable zeal for the well-being of society" induces a nasty neighborhood gossip (aptly named Mrs. Sharp) to cast the first stone "respecting the residence of Agnes Maynard with her brother-in-law" after Elizabeth's death—a local matron, Mrs. Rowland, purveys all manner of rumor about the Hope family in *Deerbrook* (*IE* 69).[54] Her particular grudge is the engagement between her brother Philip and Margaret, which, in another instance of sisterly jealousy of a brother's attention, she seeks to block by any means available. In all this there is much narratorial critique of the evil that men and women do—the town is ravaged by a fever so devastating that May refers to it as an "Old Testament–like curse"—as well as sympathy for the persecuted Hope ménage (*Disorderly Sisters* 93).

Yet even as the narrative both explicitly indicts the small-mindedness of small-town life and symbolically takes its revenge on it, the workings of the plot also convey another, still more censorious perspective on the Hope family. In Deerbrook's universal turn against the doctor for his purported crimes against the dead, we can read a displaced retribution for the sins of the living. The tyrannies of the village notwithstanding, the prolonged abuse of the Hope household helps to effect its breakup and reconstitution as a nuclear unit—without the second sister. The public ostracism all three undergo on account of the false charges functions to punish Hope for the secret offense he has committed: being "sent to Coventry," after all, was typically represented by both pro- and anti-MDWS forces as a potential outcome of an unmarried sister's residence in a widower's home, a source of "scandal," according to witnesses before the Royal Commission, especially in small towns where everybody's business might be known and judged (*Deerbrook* 240; *First Report* 10). Significantly, it is only after the boycott has reached its highest pitch that Mrs. Rowland makes a more accurate charge of private wrongdoing. Her "dreadful words," with their "mixture of truth," form the core of her brother Philip's allegation of Hope's malfeasance: that he married "the one sister out of compassion"; that Margaret returned his love, but sacrificed her happiness to her sister's; and that Hope is now giving Margaret to Philip for their "mutual security and consolation" and to avert the further opprobrium that the publication of such a report would incur (*Deerbrook* 452). This inaccurate tale never circulates fully—"no hint of it got abroad in Deerbrook"—and the novel, too, keeps Hope's actual secret from both the community and the sisters while ameliorating its effects (*Deerbrook* 482). Forcing Hester to conquer her demons by dedicating herself to her husband's interests, the penitential trial to which *Deerbrook* subjects both husband and wife ultimately consolidates the bond of two to which the sister's presence had been both so necessary and so disruptive.

If the novel never explicitly connects Hester's jealousy with Hope's secret passion, never represents the wife's desire to keep the sister in the family as perfectly aligned with the husband's parallel wish, it still reveals a core compatibility within the conjugal pair, united in its longing for a third. To fulfill the symbolic dictates of "one flesh," Hester and Hope indeed must "become a 'we,'" but the reduction of the family to the conjugal couple and its biological product occurs through the shared renunciation of the first-family sister who herself embodies the meaning of "one flesh" (*Disorderly Sisters* 91). Like *The Inheritance of Evil, Deerbrook* repudiates both iterations of the fantasy of possession, giving voice in the process to the ambivalent desire of the wife as well as the more obvious, expansive appetite of the husband. If, increasingly, as Michie states, "marriage required women and men to identify with their spouse and to carry out that identification in terms of the choices they made in their daily lives," then the plot of this novel, as with *The Inheritance of Evil,* forcibly punishes and corrects the bad choices of its characters even as it articulates just how onerous, how constricting, "that identification" could be (*Victorian Honeymoons* 21). In relation to the unruly desires of both wife and husband, the wife's sister figures, then, as symptom rather than cause: an index of the increasing pressure the marital couple faces in being nailed down to the nuclear form of the family and not, as she has been stereotypically represented, the source of division between husband and wife. In her persistence *as* a figure during seventy years of debate and discussion, I suggest, the wife's sister provides a fitting emblem of residual resistance to that narrowing, a screen on which the unmet needs of wives and husbands in nuclear family life might be projected.

In an important and exhaustive study, Ruth Perry argues that the triangular pattern of husband, wife, and sister that I have traced in this chapter is best viewed as a "cultural residual of consanguineal kin formations" (*Novel Relations* 9). In the trajectory that she outlines in literary and cultural history from Richardson to Austen, "the biologically given family into which one was born was gradually becoming secondary to the chosen family constructed by marriage" (*Novel Relations* 2). As a result, "it became less and less clear how much one owed to one's family of origin—to siblings and parents and even parents' siblings—and how much to the new family one made for oneself with a stranger" (*Novel Relations* 24–25). The comprehensive framework Perry develops is especially persuasive in elaborating the ways in which changing economic circumstances shaped and reshaped family formations, with a special emphasis on how women of all classes were massively disadvantaged: by changes in the rules of inheritance that made "women's hereditary rights in property... secondary to the imperative for accumulation"; by the modernizing practices of land enclosure; and by the diminution of female access to employment opportunities in the transition to wage labor, all of which added up to "a net loss of social power for women" (*Novel Relations* 49, 34). Perry carefully demonstrates that the push and pull toward conjugality as the central form of kinship edged out commitments to the first family, redefining the marriage plot in these terms as "the story of women scrambling to find new homes and to negotiate new families, their rights within the consanguineal family having been undercut by a shift in kinship priorities" (*Novel Relations* 7).

Although her overall thesis stresses the historical shift from first-family consanguinity to second-family conjugality, the main emphasis of Perry's discussion falls on the narrative patterns that derive from the "cultural residual" of consanguineal kinship. She examines a range of plots in which "paternal responsibility for daughters, fraternal responsibilities for sisters, the importance of maternal relatives"—all significantly less dominant in practice by the later eighteenth century because "law and custom increasingly defined women as wives rather than as daughters"—nonetheless constitute the major matter of domestic fiction (*Novel Relations* 9, 90). Retaining the sentimental force of an earlier dispensation, she argues, eighteenth-century novels relentlessly featured father-daughter reunion in "a nostalgic and compensatory recreation of a time when a father's word protected his daughter"; being "a family obligation from an earlier era, increasingly honored more in the breach than in the observance, brotherly love came to be a conventional ideal in fiction as it was eroded in life" (*Novel Relations* 90, 144). "In the wish-fulfillment of fiction," Perry concludes, "conjugal love creates new affinal sibling bonds that do not compete with earlier ties" (*Novel Relations* 145).

In reading both fictional and nonfictional early Victorian accounts of comparable circumstances, however, we can see not only the continued persistence of the "cultural residual" that Perry traces but also the basis it provides for a new resistance, especially on the part of men, to making a second marriage with "a stranger." "It is one of the many advantages of marriage with a sister in law," Henry Thornton wrote to his sister Marianne, "that all things connected with one's former life, instead of raising feelings of jealousy, acquire an increased interest and form a new bond of union" (*MT* 208). In undoing the difference that death has made, even adding a certain luster to what has been lost (and perhaps a necessary one in this case, if we credit Forster's claim that Henry "bore Harriet's decease phlegmatically"), Henry's second marriage continues, indeed renews, the first attachment (*MT* 156). Far from being lost, "the new family one made for oneself with a stranger" is enhanced by a second marriage to another member of that very same "new family"; the "jealousy" that a second wife from outside the second family might feel, in taking the place another had once filled, would not afflict Emily Dealtry. In mourning her sister's loss, she forms "a new bond of union" with the brother-widower, who is thereby spared the search for a new mate, a prospect so alarming for some men that it led one witness before the Royal Commission to claim that "to take a stranger into my house is in itself really a visitation" (*First Report* 64).

Indeed, the threat of the "stranger" to domestic security looms large in much of the pro-MDWS discourse, especially when the happiness of the children enters the equation: "The aunt, who already stand[s] in a suit of quasi-maternal relation to the children of the first wife, would, *cæteris paribus,* have a better chance than a stranger as a stepmother.... Such marriages have actually turned out happier marriages" (*First Report* 74). Another witness similarly prefers the known to the strange, with a special emphasis on his vulnerability to the latter: "With my habits of business, and want of comfort at home, I knew well that I should run great risks in marrying anybody that I might fancy, or that might be thrown in my way," making a fairly explicit reference to the sexual danger a man of some fortune might incur in being himself "thrown" onto (or venturing into) an open matrimonial market (*First Report* 82). "My present wife I had known as a child": if this remark has somewhat creepy overtones, the follow-up comment— "I knew her to be virtuous and good, and... that she would make me happy"—reemphasizes the importance of knowing the new wife's character from sustained familial association (*First Report* 82). In the male advocacy for what may be construed as an "endogamous" second union, the "exogamous" imperative that we typically associate with early Victorian marriage among the elite classes—and with the heterosexual courtship plot of nineteenth-century fiction—gives way to a preference for the security of the familiar and the familial. In seeking legal sanction for this "second attachment," arguments based on what men feel aim to legitimate "the desire never to have to leave home" and register "the longing of these widowed husbands to be allowed to stay within the domestic circle, not to be forced to look outside for a second wife but to find her here, already, the familiar sister."[55] One might say, then, that the increasing cultural emphasis on conjugality—the second family that a man makes with a first wife—plays a critical part in the formation of a widower's desire not to alter that second family any further than death has already done. We will see in subsequent chapters that the figure of "the stranger" that haunts MDWS discourse, embodying the anxiety over difference already glimpsed in the representation of the fascinating Crawfords of *Mansfield Park,* increasingly signifies in other contexts both the powerful inducement to remain within the familial fold and the class and racial exclusions performed in the service of producing a vision of familial autonomy.

For married women, no doubt, the situation differed from that of their male counterparts—but how, exactly? Perry's analysis affirms that "it was a mixed blessing for women to exchange whatever power and status they had in their families of origin for the power and status of women in conjugal families," that in "the movement from father patriarchy to husband patriarchy," daughters who became wives potentially lost sustaining connections to their first families (*Novel Relations* 2, 34). Becoming more isolated in marriage, albeit with the possibility of producing children of their own that might help to repair their losses, those women who could retain first-family ties to married or unmarried sisters—if they had the talent Michie identifies for "integrating sororal and conjugal love"—might meet a pressing emotional need (*Victorian Honeymoons* 66). Pitted against the ideological premium on conjugal loyalty, however, sisterly solidarity might run a poor second: for example, in an essay on the MDWS debate published more than two decades after *Deerbrook,* Martineau recommends to both wives and husbands that they exercise "that prudence which, in the conjugal case, should keep all friendships subordinate to the supreme bond,—all companionship secondary to the prime union,—all intercourses immeasurably below the open confidence and tenderness, and understood intimacy of the conjugal friendship."[56] Writing in full consciousness, to be sure, of the gender-differentiated consequences that might arise from any weakening of "the supreme bond," Martineau clearly subordinates first-family relationships to marital "confidence and tenderness," to "conjugal friendship." But her advice might be viewed as strategic rather than normative; it might, that is, spring from a recognition that a married woman's best chance at lasting security would lie with the husband who, for much of the century, controlled her person and her property almost as his own.

Finally, within a cultural framework that promoted matrimony as woman's destiny, to be the third where there should be only two, to be not a wife but a wife's sister with no living father or brother, as is the case in both *The Inheritance of Evil* and *Deerbrook,* would in the absence of economic independence make marriage a clear imperative for many, but a prospect that cohabitation with a sister and her husband might itself imperil. Reporting some secondhand family intelligence, Marianne Thornton proposes that Henry will choose to marry Emily in order to save her honor, so compromised by the scandal their situation has aroused that if he does not marry her, no one will: "He feels he has damaged her & owes it to her to make her retribution" (*MT* 198). Casting Emily as a fallen woman positions Henry as her seducer, who can make amends only by making an honest woman of her, even if doing so violates English law. One imagines that from his perspective, it is the *not* marrying her that would have constituted the real damage, in that whatever had (or had not) transpired between them had sullied her reputation and thus injured her marital chances. Moreover, in his position as scion of a large and influential Clapham Sect family, a father in his own right, an officer of an important local bank, and a leader in the community, Henry Thornton's personal reputation was also at stake, even if the stigma he might have incurred would have been broadly social rather than specifically sexual. His act of reparation, then, might constitute an effort to ward off the ruin of both parties, gender-differentiated though that ruin might be. So, too, could the differences between Henry's stance and Margaret's perspective arise from the gendered asymmetries at the intersection of sexuality and alliance in the family.

Discussing cousin-marriage and MDWS together as "two contested forms of marriage in eighteenth-century English culture" that "illustrate most clearly the cultural shift from consanguineal to conjugal loyalty," Perry suggests that the difference between the permissibility of the former and the prohibition on the latter in the eighteenth century depended "on whether or not marriage is understood to sever the consanguineal kin tie and replace it—whether or not marriage creates new families that retroactively suppress and replace the family of origin" (*Novel Relations* 119). She finds that cousin-marriage

is legitimate, because "the sibling tie" between the mothers or fathers of
the engaged couple was "dissolved by adulthood and marriage," while affinal marriage with an in-law was not, because a new "sibling tie" is created
by the very marriage that also creates the affinity (*Novel Relations* 121). My
research suggests, by contrast, that in nineteenth-century fictional and actual
cases of marriage within the family, the distinction that Perry draws between
consanguineal and conjugal (or affinal) families was not so clear-cut. That
distinction loses force under circumstances in which members of the first
family and those who populate the second are made analogous to birth siblings by the one-flesh doctrine. And it is decidedly blurred, as in my two
fictive examples, when married women retain their single sisters as members
of the new conjugal household. Both in-law and cousin unions remained, as
we shall see, "contested forms of marriage" through the nineteenth century,
with the terms that governed the debate about them shifting in relation to
developments in science and anthropology that took the determination of
"consanguinity" in particular as a central node of investigation.

Finally, the very plot points that, for Perry, exemplify the shift from consanguinity to conjugality— "daughters pressured to marry against their
wills, older brothers who gambled away the inheritance of younger children,
brothers who lived off the labors and savings of their sisters, mothers who
died leaving children ignorant of their paternity" as well as other "elements
of disrupted kinship"—so pervade nineteenth-century fiction as to suggest
a continuous cultural tension between the claims of the first family and
the dictates of the second (*Novel Relations* 30). Turning now to the fiction
of Charlotte Brontë, most of whose novels betray a decided kinship to the
eighteenth-century tradition that Perry traces, we will examine that tension through the lens of another nineteenth-century practice of making
families in which both consanguinity and affinity took on new and complex
meanings.

✌ CHAPTER 4

Orphan Stories: Adoption and Affinity in Charlotte Brontë

> My home is humble and unattractive to strangers, but to me it contains what I shall find nowhere else in the world—the profound, the intense affection which brothers and sisters feel for each other when their minds are cast in the same mould, their ideal drawn from the same source[,] when they have clung to each other from childhood, and when disputes have never sprung up to divide them.
>
> — Charlotte Brontë to Henry Nussey, 9 May 1841

Although the widowed Mrs. Pryor of *Shirley* (1849) cautions Caroline Helstone that "two people can never literally be as one," an exultant Jane Rochester, echoing Genesis, writes that "no woman was ever nearer to her mate than I am: ever more absolutely bone of his bone, and flesh of his flesh."[1] While advocates of marital reform would increasingly argue that women should retain separate legal personalities in marriage, Jane's biblically based assertion of physiological oneness between husband and wife was not an entirely dead metaphor: cultural conservatives who insisted on the unity of the conjugal couple, coming under siege at midcentury, even tried to ground it in biology. By positing an identity of substance between husband and wife, they appealed to the differences that the institution of marriage and the act of sexual intercourse make in the spiritual, social, and domestic lives of those individuals and families they join together. Those who regarded marriage as creating just a metaphorical affinity and disputed its equation with consanguinity, however, pointed to the lack of biblical or legal prohibition against another form of marriage involving a preexisting blood tie: "Why do you not absolutely interdict all marriages of first and second cousins," wrote Henry Rogers in 1853, who "are more nearly of kin than a wife's sister?"[2] "Cousins live habitually in much greater familiarity than brothers and sisters-in-law; they are not unfrequently brought up together, and their mutual feelings of affection have all the additional

strength that can be derived from actual blood-relationship, and from having been entertained from infancy," another MDWS advocate suggested in
1839.[3] "How society can forbid a man's marrying his wife's sister... and
yet allow him to marry his cousin—a proceeding generally unwise, and
sometimes absolutely wicked, I can not imagine," avers a character in Dinah
Mulock Craik's *Hannah* (1871), with the wisdom or wickedness of cousin-
marriage itself becoming a matter of scientific and cultural dispute even as it
remained socially viable and, in some instances, economically desirable.[4]

Among its other cultural functions and effects, the debate over affinal
marriage provides a forum for describing and determining the boundaries
of the family, a topic of increasing interest across a wide range of Victorian
discourses. Whatever the claims about blood and biology, this debate typically blurred the line between two of the central meanings of *affinity* itself,
a term that signifies not only a "relationship by marriage" but also a natural
(or naturalized) "inclination or attraction" (*OED*). Indeed, as we have seen,
pro-MDWS arguments often cast the former as the cause of the latter, with
shared domestic ties creating the conditions in which so-called natural affection might grow. As illustrated in chapter 3, opponents of the ban argued
that it enabled the very transgression it was ostensibly meant to prevent, by
sanctioning the sister(-in-law)'s presence in the widower's house; by permitting her to act in place of the dead wife and mother, the prohibition gave rise
to the very feelings it would proscribe. The affinity bred by a "relationship
by marriage," the familiarity that arises from familiality, thus may issue in an
"inclination or attraction" that cannot be readily assimilated to the fiction
of chaste sibling love. "Let people talk as they will about the ties of blood,"
argues another character from *Hannah,* "it is association which really produces the feeling which is termed 'natural affection.'"[5] On this model, the
family is united less by shared descent than by associative principles.

In this chapter, I look at adoption, another means of making or breaking
family ties, as it intersects with and diverges from the dispute over the scope
and meanings of affinity. Just as the debate over affinal marriage indicates
that the status of biological ties was still very much contested, the practice of
adoption typically demonstrates that such ties, however imagined, were not
the exclusive basis for family membership, that principles of association also
played a critical part. In that perception we can also identify fertile ground
for contemporary investigations into the emergence of "the family" as a crucial development in the history of humankind. Of the three "legal fictions"
that Henry Maine discusses in *Ancient Law,* for example, he assigns the greatest importance to "the Fiction of Adoption which permits the family tie to
be artificially created": without it, Maine claims, it would be "difficult to

understand how society would ever have escaped from its swaddling clothes, and taken its first steps towards civilization."[6] Although legal adoption as we know it did not come into being in England until 1926, "functional alternatives," such as taking kin or non-kin into the household as dependents, wards, or surrogates, "were readily available" throughout the nineteenth century.[7] Sheltering or rearing a child not "one's own" is as common in nineteenth-century fiction as bearing and tending biological offspring: indeed, "the predominant generic template of the nineteenth-century British novel blatantly undermines those ideologies of the family it is commonly thought to uphold," as Carolyn Dever argues, since "the Victorian novel conventionally opens with a scene of family rupture."[8] Orphans and wards—Pip and Estella, David Copperfield or Esther Summerson—have formal advantages, to be sure, for the favored plot of bildung. But one of the largely unremarked ideological functions of orphanhood is to throw into high relief the mechanisms of exclusion on which mid-Victorian fictions of family depend; as Laura Peters notes, "The ideal of the family . . . survives by continually producing and excluding that which endangers" it.[9]

Thinking about adoption—a practice that, like nineteenth-century marriage, could unite biological kin as well as "strangers" in a single unit—helps us to qualify the presumed preeminence of the "blood family" at mid-century. In particular, the racial politics of adoption in Charlotte Brontë's juvenilia combined with the focus on conflict and difference within the imperial family as she imagined it demonstrate that adoption may figure both exclusion and inclusion, hostility and affinity. Like ties of blood or marriage, adoptive ties also provoke and register intense feeling about who does and does not belong to "the family." An orphan story such as *Jane Eyre* largely supports a very narrow, nearly nuclear model, so much so that Nancy Armstrong has forcefully argued that the novel "universalizes a radically restricted notion of kinship based on the married couple and their biological offspring."[10] In my view, however, neither Jane nor her author articulates the shape of this unit on a solely biological basis: *Jane Eyre,* instead, attends to differences of class and power between maternal and paternal lines as a factor in adoptive relations, thus anticipating some emphases of early anthropology, and expands the scope of affinity to characterize feelings of relationship that may or may not coincide with actual kin connections. Jane's own quest, we should remember, moves her from one adoptive family to another, from a house in which, like Heathcliff, she had been degraded by her relatives almost to the status of a servant to a dwelling where she gains the power both to make a family of her own and to confer that privilege on others. When she tells St. John Rivers, "I never had a home, I never had brothers or sisters;

I must and will have them now," we are meant to recognize (not for the first time) that blood alone does not a family make, as both her exclusion from the Reed family circle and her reciprocal exclusion of them from her notion of "family" dramatically illustrate (*JE* 408).

By its juxtaposition of Reeds and Rivers, symmetrical families of first cousins differentiated from one another in almost every other respect, *Jane Eyre* exposes the limits of blood relation in the shape it gives to the orphan's plot. In the representation of such adoptive families, we see the fictions of biology as just one among other grounds for defining the family unit, including intersubjective experiences of connection and likeness—an increasingly dominant connotation of "affinity"—as well as hostility and difference. The practice of adoption establishes paradigms for family and marital relationships in which affinity, in the sense of the word as we typically use it today, takes precedence over consanguinity in determining kinship. Because the former is not sharply distinguished from the latter—or, to put it another way, because the dominant model of heterosexual union *as* affinity derives its force from the sanctifying aura of family love—the romantic drama of the female orphan unfolds within familial terms, in the language of brotherly/ sisterly connection. Sometimes one meaning of affinity trumps the other, as in the romantic relationships that Lucy Snowe and Jane Eyre forge with unrelated strangers on the basis of attraction and inclination. But it is worth noting at the outset that both orphans shape their romantic narratives by adhering to familial terms, by seeking from strangers the satisfactions of kin.

As we saw in chapter 1, in *Primitive Marriage* John McLennan locates the emergence of heterosexual monogamy as the transition point from primitive culture to civilized society, but Henry Maine, his rival, assigns a rather more central place to adoption in sketching his "view of the primeval condition of the human race" (*Ancient Law* 118). Best known today for the claim that "the movement of the progressive societies has hitherto been a movement *from Status to Contract,*" *Ancient Law* construes "the fiction of adoption" as a homosocial practice crucial to that very movement; moreover, as Sharon Marcus argues, it provides "a way to perpetuate and enlarge the family by means other than marriage and heterosexual reproduction" (*Ancient Law* 165, emphasis in original; *Between Women* 125). Focusing on ancient Rome and identifying the origins of the state in the family, Maine famously claims "the history of political ideas begins, in fact, with the assumption that kinship in blood is the sole possible ground of community in political functions," arguing that "all ancient societies regarded themselves as having proceeded from one original stock"; their first citizens understand themselves as "united by kinship in blood" (*Ancient Law* 124, 45, 46). But that "assumption," Maine also asserts, is itself a fiction: "Everywhere we discover traces of passages in their history when men of alien descent were admitted to, and amalgamated with, the original brotherhood" (*Ancient Law* 125).[11] Although "uniformly assumed to be natural"—that is, based on common "descent"—early Roman society "was nevertheless known to be in great measure artificial," as its citizens adopted "strangers" into their families who were obliged to *"feign themselves"* native-born (*Ancient Law* 125, 126, emphasis in original). "Men of alien descent," then, might join the community without either being born or marrying into it; moreover, "neither law nor opinion" would make "the slightest difference between a real and an adoptive connexion" (*Ancient Law* 128). So that the idea of the patriarchal family "remains what it always was," the fiction of adoption "affects to conceal" a prior authorizing fiction of blood relation (*Ancient Law* 25). Without it, Maine writes, "I do not see how any one of the primitive groups, . . . could have absorbed another, or on what terms any two of them could have combined, except those of absolute superiority on one side and absolute subjection on the other" (*Ancient Law* 126).

This way of conceiving the making of families—which aggregate over time as houses and tribes, ultimately leading to the commonwealth—does not and need not distinguish between blood and adoptive ties, one might speculate, because women have almost no part, not even a reproductive part, in Roman patriarchy as Maine envisions it. Indeed, adoption as both fiction and practice is especially crucial to this narrative because of the dominance of agnatic kinship, the reckoning of descent "exclusively through males," in Maine's account (*Ancient Law* 142). Agnation "excludes a number of persons whom we in our day should certainly consider of kin to ourselves"—for example, all of our mother's kin (unless related in their own right to our father)— "and it includes many more whom we should never reckon among our kindred" (*Ancient Law* 141–42). Maine's account of the patriarchal system, in which "men are first seen distributed in perfectly insulated groups held together by obedience to the [male] parent," denies women any share in the action even as, some feminists have argued, it seeks to open space for women's greater agency in England's progressive present (*Ancient Law* 121).[12] In Maine's view of patriarchy, marriage matters only insofar as it contributes to the making of agnates, and women matter only by reference to the men who father them; even though agnation includes the male and female descendants and any applicable adoptive kin of men, "none of the descendants of a female are included" (*Ancient Law* 143).[13] Through adoption, moreover, Roman men can make new children of either sex without female aid or intervention, bypassing the circuits of reproduction via a single (fictive) male progenitor who confers family membership.

McLennan would later take issue with Maine's representation as flawed at the root in that "it postulates that human history opens with perfect marriage, conjugal fidelity, and certainty of male parentage": for McLennan, all of these are accomplished only at the end of a long process (*Primitive Marriage* 107). Whereas Maine writes that "it is obvious that the organisation of primitive societies would have been confounded, if men had called themselves relatives of their mother's relatives," McLennan insists that that must have been the case because "the first kinship is the first possible—that through mothers, about whose parental relation to children there can be no mistake" (*Ancient Law* 144, *Primitive Marriage* 49n16). For McLennan, the cognatic system, which traces descent through both men and women, logically and temporally precedes the agnatic, since for him maternity is the one "physical fact" that early humans would have grasped: unlike Maine, moreover, McLennan strongly emphasizes the factual rather than the "factitious" status of the biological tie (*Primitive Marriage* 63; *Ancient Law* 127). That "adopted persons and their descendants through males were within the agnatic bond" McLennan grants, but a fiction of adoption could only flourish once descent "through males" could be more or less definitively determined (*Primitive Marriage* 94).

In McLennan's conjectural history, that "certainty" was a hard-won achievement a long time in the making. Before patriarchy, there is only matrilineage: the "men of alien descent" that Maine sees as necessarily imported into the family through adoption are, in McLennan's account, already present within the "stock-group." They are the sons of women captured from other tribes, identified at first as belonging to their foreign mothers, next as "a number of small brotherhoods," and only after a much longer period of time, as the male progeny of fathers who are brothers and, ultimately, of one father (*Primitive Marriage* 70). Kinship through a single male parent, that is, becomes imaginable only after primitive promiscuity has given way to a first form of polyandry (one woman, many men), then to a second (one wife, several brothers), and finally to marital monogamy. In McLennan's insistence on kinship as a physical reality, Anita Levy argues, "the signifier 'blood' comes to stand for a notion of *individuated, biological* similarity," with " 'blood-ties' [being] said to exist 'between certain of the individuals in the group,' " first between sons and mothers and only subsequently between sons and fathers.[14]

These two competing origin stories of "the family," then, make different claims about the "real" bases of kinship, as do the two sides in the MDWS debate. For Maine, it is the relatively peaceable adoption of "strangers"— "men of alien descent"—that creates progressive change and movement; their inclusion is founded not on the coercive ground of "absolute superiority . . . and absolute subjection" but rather through a common agreement not to distinguish or differentiate one man from another on the basis of his (always already fictive) blood relation to the rest of the group. For McLennan, whose "account of the rise of the idea of fatherhood" creates a violent conjectural prehistory for Maine's patriarchal family, the "reality" of blood ties, at first only recognizable in a child's relation to its mother, is indisputable and essential.[15] As Kathy Alexis Psomiades argues, Maine's narrative of the determining force of agnation, in which one is given status only via relation to the father, "imagines kinship . . . in patriarchal society not as based in a heterosexual union, and not even as exchanges between men."[16] By contrast, McLennan sees "heterosexual union" of a very particular kind—one man, one woman—as the crucial factor in producing a properly patriarchal society: "The first effect of kinship through males must have been to arrest the progress of heterogeneity" so that "the introduction of foreign women into a tribe no longer brought into it children accounted foreigners" but instead construed them as belonging to their father's tribe (*Primitive Marriage* 99). We might say that adoption, then, functions in Maine's text somewhat analogously to how monogamous marriage works in McLennan's: each becomes an instrument of incorporating those once understood as "strangers" or "foreigners" by fictively characterizing them in familial terms and, importantly, giving them a place in the father's line of descent, a place by which they may in time inherit the father's goods. Whatever their differences, that is, both would agree with their American contemporary Lewis Henry Morgan that "the family, as now constituted, and which grew out of the development of a knowledge of property, of its uses, and of its transmission by inheritance, lies at the foundation of the first civilization of mankind."[17]

While Brontë's juvenilia and her adult novels predate Maine and McLennan's conjectural fictions of blood and adoptive kinship, similar issues regarding gender, agnation, the adoptee's relation to its first (earthly) parents, and the question of "alien descent" trouble the origin stories that she writes for her adoptees. Almost from its very beginning, for example, *Jane Eyre* makes its orphan's progress a matter of finding her place in a patriarchal line. The "doleful" ballad that Bessie sings to Jane laments the exile of the friendless orphan even as it allegorizes every Christian soul's journey to an eternal end in the father's house (*JE* 22). "Though both of shelter and kindred despoiled" in this world, every "poor orphan child" has a dwelling in the next, for "Heaven is a home" and "God is a friend" (*JE* 23). By internalizing the

Christian message of this ballad, by learning to direct her thoughts upward, Jane gains—more accurately, regains—"shelter and kindred" in this world after leaving Gateshead, where she has felt herself "an uncongenial alien" to her mother's brother's wife and children and rebelled against their authority (*JE* 17). The ballad molds the orphan's path by giving her an immediate, particular paradigm of her experience and a figurative, universal emblem for each Christian's spiritual pilgrimage, initiating what Penny Boumelha terms "the providential theme" of the novel, "the story dispensed and directed by Our Father."[18] The allegory effaces both earthly and maternal origins in directing the soul's return to its true home: whatever Jane's status in this world, her father in heaven provides an authoritative parentage and a consoling vision. Ultimately, however, Jane's adherence to that heavenly father leads to her being placed within a happy home: while every orphan, like every Christian, has a father in heaven with a mansion of many rooms, only the fortunate few, Drew Lamonaca observes, find habitations here on earth.[19]

Maternal origins are not always erased from Charlotte Brontë's fiction, but they are usually vexed. As I argue below, there is no place for Jane and nothing to gain on the mother's side; as McLennan writes of "primitive" cultures, "a woman's children were held to be not of the kin of their mother but of their father," a claim with ironic resonance in light of the contemporary advocacy for greater gender equity in child custody matters (*Primitive Marriage* 94).[20] In "The African Queen's Lament" (1833), an earlier and equally "doleful" poem by Brontë, we do hear a mother's voice, but only as "a dying woman's moan" that sounds "like a requiem for the dead": she entrusts her orphaned son not to heavenly refuge with an eternal father but to worldly vengeance for an earthly father's sake.[21] The eponymous speaker of "The African Queen's Lament" interprets each natural sound—the "wild moan" of the palm trees, the "faint mingled cries" of the river—as "a sign, a warning token" of a future in which her child's loss of shelter and kindred will be avenged by his own hand rather than remediated by any god's love. Widow of the Great Sai Too Too Quamina, who led the Ashantee forces defeated by the Twelves at the Battle of Coomassie, the mother implores her sleeping son to hear the "sound of prophecy/Which speaks of bloody recompense" and enjoins him, when he reaches manhood, to "swift and bright as wand'ring star/Go piling heaps of dead" ("AQ" 6, 5). Adopted in "The Green Dwarf" (1833) by a fictive Duke of Wellington, "from whom he experienced as much care and tenderness as if he had been that monarch's son instead of his slave," Quashia Quamina aims nonetheless to live out the destiny his mother planned for him.[22] Far from being "amalgamated with" his new family by adoption and made part of their community, that is, and "notwithstanding the care with which he had been treated by his conquerors, he retained against them, as if by instinct, the most deeply rooted and inveterate hatred" ("GD" 179). Seeking to avenge the loss of familial and national autonomy, he raises an unsuccessful native rebellion against colonial authority and is executed by order of his foster-brother Zamorna, biological son of the Duke who had "nourished [Quashia Quamina] on his own hearth...with almost parental tenderness" ("GD" 180).

Reading these texts together, we can see how the status of the orphan and the adoption of the "alien," problematic in both cases, are differently inflected by gender, race, and national origin. Bessie's ballad, in its double instantiation of Jane's plot, achieves a generalizing tenor that enables Jane to enact this story because it belongs to no one in particular; she may successfully revise it through her own experiences, needs, and desires because it belongs to everyone, or at least to every English Christian, in common. In this context, the orphan figures a universal condition of earthly exile and homelessness: although Jane moves throughout the novel from one maternal substitute to another, she is never without a heavenly father. And by subduing (or sublimating) the anger and rage she feels as "an interloper" at Gateshead, the adult Jane makes earthly homes by finding congenial—that is, paternal—kin (*JE* 17). The voice of the avenging mother of "The African Queen's Lament," by contrast, speaks from and about a specific experience of violence and destruction that foreordains her child to carry out his dead father's mission, to fulfill her wish that he will his "father's mind [and] form,/His kingly soul inherit"; herself dying, her only real role is to reproduce him in her dead husband's image, an act that perpetuates Quashia Quamina's difference from those who would "amalgamate" him into their family/state ("AQ" 5). Perhaps anticipating Emily Brontë's Heathcliff, this son acts out a rage comparable to Jane's in an effort to destroy the adoptive imperial family that constitutes his oppression. His actions make clear that he regards his containment within the imperial family as requiring "absolute superiority on one side and absolute subjection on the other," terms to which he will submit no more than Jane does.

So the central motif of this black African adoptee's story and the keynote of his character, viewed from the perspective of his adoptive family, is treachery: "His mother's last advice will not, I imagine, be entirely lost upon him," the Duke of Wellington predicts, and "he may give our nation trouble yet" ("AQ" 3). "His disposition was bold, irritable, active, daring"; "at the age of seventeen," he had already "kindled in these wild savages a spirit of slumbering discontent and roused them to make an effort for regaining that independence as a nation which they had lost" ("GD" 179). Although "A Leaf from an Unopened Volume" (1834) portrays Quashia Quamina by the conventions of noble savagery—as "a man in whose person all the virtues of savage life were so nobly united"—the overwhelming tenor of his representation in the juvenilia is as "the young viper," "deeply treacherous," who, in the service of his mother's dream of revenge, foments rebellion against those who raised him ("GD" 179).[23] That Quashia Quamina is simultaneously inside and outside the imperial family, an African man domesticated among the creole colonizers, suggests a degree of fictive kinship with the girl orphan who both does and does not belong to the Reeds. But unlike Jane, who narrates only ill-treatment at the hands of her aunt and cousins, he stages rebellion against those who aim to allay his "inveterate hatred" by means of parental "care and tenderness." If Jane Eyre identifies and embraces an alternative script to the one that Gateshead writes for her, then Quashia Quamina remains wholly within his dead mother's patriarchal paradigm. Imagining a future rebellion by the Ashantees against the colonizers who seek, in Firdous Azim's words, to produce the adoptee through "education and the upbringing in an Angrian court...as *colonised* subject," the mother tells the story that becomes his, figuring adoption as itself a colonizing enterprise.[24]

In contrast with Maine's narrative of Romans adopting outsiders as a peaceable process, the adoptive relationship in nineteenth-century European fiction, as Patricia Howe observes, is "willed by one party and imposed on the other."[25] Orphans or adoptees get no say in where or with whom they are placed at the outset, and they are also much subject to the stories that others tell about them. What distinguishes Jane Eyre and Lucy Snowe from Brontë's comparable African characters, male and female alike, is that despite their initial position of relative powerlessness, these English heroines gain the power to tell their own stories, to rewrite the experience of being marginal to the (blood) family in ways that partially challenge its dominance—even if, in Jane Eyre's case, that rewriting can only be achieved once she has found her place within the father's house. By contrast, Quashia Quamina and other colonized adoptees have little or no access to narrative voice or agency: even if, as Susan Meyer argues, they both engage Brontë's imaginative sympathies and enact her recognition of the class and gender limits on her own racial privilege, they are, in some sense, also colonized by Brontë's ability to appropriate other worlds for her fictional empire.[26] That orphans and adoptees in the juvenilia are sometimes identified as (or with) characters of color means that they enter into white imperial families on even less advantaged terms than do Jane and Lucy. But their main function is not to figure the subordinated status of all orphans or to symbolize the oppressive force of race/class/gender inequities; they work, rather, primarily to indicate tensions within the internal dynamics of the adoptive imperial family, to illustrate that neither adoption nor blood ties nor marriage forms an unproblematic ground for family membership or family feeling.

Brontë and her erstwhile collaborator Branwell do not by any means attribute aggressive forces within the kingdom to Quashia Quamina alone, as Alexander Percy (later referred to as Northangerland) likewise figures throughout the juvenilia as an internal enemy to Wellington's son Zamorna (also known as the Emperor Adrian). Their political rivalry notwithstanding, Percy and Zamorna are inextricably intertwined through the marriages they arrange and contract for themselves or others, alliances undertaken for political ends in which both daughters and sons function as instruments for consolidating power. For example, in "an act of state by her father at a time when Percy and Zamorna were momentarily allied," Mary Percy is married off to Zamorna; subsequently, Zamorna's eldest legitimate son by a previous wife marries another of Percy's daughters, further extending the web of familial relationships between these two leading men and also intensifying their rivalry.[27] In "The Green Dwarf," Percy betrays imperial interests by warning Quashia Quamina of Zamorna's plan to attack the rebels under cover of darkness. And when Zamorna's army catches up with the African forces the next day, the rebel adoptee declares that "freedom would this night have received her death-stab from the hand of the White Tyrant [Zamorna] had not a traitor [Percy] arisen in the camp of oppression," even as Percy's intervention only delays the rebels' imminent defeat ("GD" 188). As Azim observes, the "fear of danger from outside (the unexplored and unsubdued natives) and from within (internal dissension, rivalries and corruption)...do not remain so schematically marked off from each other"; nor do treachery and loyalty break down neatly along racial lines (*Colonial Rise* 119). The betrayals of Zamorna that both his adoptive brother and his father-in-law perform in "The Green Dwarf" take shape in "the camp of oppression," where they seek to undermine the power of the Zamorna line from within. The charges of treachery that cling to Quashia Quamina are made in turn against the other major rival to Zamorna's power, who, like the adoptee— albeit for different reasons—cannot be said to be wholly inside or outside the parameters of the imperial family. Viewed in this light, both relations by marriage and relations by adoption mark the boundaries of membership in the colonial state—a state, not incidentally, constituted largely on the basis of kinship ties—and challenge its security.

As an orphan who turns on those who adopt him, Quashia Quamina foreshadows both Heathcliff, a more successful plotter, and the young Jane Eyre, who attributes her depiction of John Reed as "like a murderer...like a slave-driver...like the Roman emperors" to her reading of "Goldsmith's History of Rome" (*JE* 11). And like those other adoptees, Quashia comes to be an adoptive parent himself, bequeathing a legacy to his child that echoes his mother's wishes for him. Put to death by the Emperor Adrian at the very opening of "A Leaf" for his resistance to white rule, Quashia Quamina leaves behind a daughter named Zorayda who seeks to avenge him. While her narrative adheres to the conventions of foundling narrative more closely than his does, the racial and gendered differences between them are even more striking.[28] While he retains the memory of his mother's injunction to revenge, Zorayda does not even know the story of her own birth and identifies entirely with her adoptive context.[29] Her mother leaves her nothing but a ring, which subsequently proves her ancestry, while her allegiance to her African parent and her ultimate restoration to the care of her "true" father situate her exclusively as a counter within two competing patriarchal plots. If Quashia Quamina's fate is far more fatally fixed than his daughter's from the outset, then Zorayda's plot yet enacts a particularly feminine version of the adoption story, in which the politics of racial identification and membership also play a pivotal role.[30]

While Brontë obliquely casts the Ashantee leader as a sexual threat to white male prerogative in the "Roe Head Journal" (ca. 1836) and at the outset of the novella *Caroline Vernon* (1839), she depicts Zorayda as a sexual object who occasions a flare-up in the ongoing rivalry between the Emperor's twin sons, aptly named Alexander and Adrian after their grandfather and father, respectively.[31] As twins, Alexander declares, "our affection ought to be the stronger, but that circumstance, instead of generating an increase of love, has caused a greater degree of aversion": this unexplained "aversion" between very close kin affords the only motive for Alexander's plot to kidnap Zorayda from under Adrian's nose and make her his own ("Leaf" 342).[32] Zorayda initially appears to be unavailable to either brother. She resists assimilation into the court, at which she arrives with the secret intent of avenging her father's execution. But the primary site of her struggle lies in the boudoir, as she repudiates the possibility of marrying into the colonial elite. Adrian proposes a marriage "to which [she] will never consent," representing her birth as "an impossible barrier to our union" and evincing "an anxious sense of racial mixing as profane": "Never, never shall the blood of my race mingle with that of yours, Lord Adrian! It would *not* mingle! Dissensions and hatred of the deepest dye, the dissensions of near kindred, would be the result of such an unhallowed union" ("Leaf" 343–44, emphasis in original).[33] This passage metonymically links blood that "would *not* mingle"—literal and metaphorical sign of an impassable, "impossible" gulf between African girl and creole colonizer—with the "dissensions" among "near kindred" present in both the rivalry of the twins and the enmity between their father and grandfather. While Zorayda suggests that any effort to cross the racial gulf would create divisions within the family, the broader framework of the juvenilia makes it clear that rivalrous antagonisms already divide the extended family that constitutes the empire. With Zorayda's refusing a marriage she casts as potentially miscegenous and thus also a source of conflict, the narrative simultaneously foregrounds the existing differences that pit members of the royal family—putatively of one blood—against one another.

Representing the minoritized perspective of resistance to imperial oppression, Zorayda's plot ultimately restores her to a family she had lost. It does so by revealing that her "true" parentage lies not with the African nation but with the white tyrants and by establishing her place as a marriageable daughter within the agnatic chain of the white community. "Abducted by savages" along with her mother, daughter of an Angrian noble who "died shortly after her capture. . . . the infant was adopted by Quamina for his own daughter" ("Leaf" 365, 375). Following the generic conventions of the foundling plot, Zorayda turns out to be the noble Northangerland's granddaughter by a son he never acknowledged—owing to his expressed "aversion to male offspring"—and thus a cousin to the twins and related by blood to much of the rest of the imperial family ("Leaf" 377). Zorayda learns her own history only after she has tried and failed to emulate her (adoptive) father's example by becoming "the avenger of the unjustly slain," announcing herself as "Quamina's daughter" before the assembled court as she wields a knife at Zamorna ("Leaf" 371). Meeting the unharmed emperor's assertion that "Quamina was not your father" with "a glance of mingled surprise and indignation," she becomes "abashed and bewildered" at the revelation that "it is to a white man you owe existence; such a form was never the daughter of darkness": "Weeping and ashamed, she was led by her father and grandfather out of the imperial presence" ("Leaf" 372–73).

In one stroke, the assertion of Zorayda's "real" paternity, which confers on her a privileged majority status, blots out the racial identity she had been adopted into and which she had adopted for herself. With Zorayda stunned into silence and seemingly overcome by remorse, within three weeks' time, her marriage to "Prince Adrian was celebrated over all Adrianopolis in a style of regal magnificence suited to the rank of the high contracting parties": her adoptive identity is thus put at an even further remove once she is transferred from "real" father to royal husband ("Leaf" 377). In the resolution of her story, then, Zorayda's racialized identification with Africans is swept away by the discovery of her "true" biological identity, which makes her already a part of the white family whose internal ties her cousin-marriage will further consolidate. Within the tale, who she is, and how she functions within the framework of whiteness to which Brontë insistently calls attention, thus wholly depends on her birth father. Once Zorayda is restored to the agnatic chain, from which her adoptive father had excluded himself, even her attempt on the life of the emperor can be excused, undertaken as it was on the basis of a misconception as to where her loyalties actually should lie.

While the white tyrants reclaim Zorayda, the black rebels repudiate her. The architect of the revenge plot on the emperor's life, Shungaron, calls her his "last hope" for vengeance against Adrian the Magnificent but professes not to be surprised that Zorayda does not succeed in her effort: "The royal blood of Quamina did not really flow through her veins and how could constancy or courage be expected from the daughter of a white man?... In the hour of trial the pale alien has failed and been forgiven" ("Leaf" 375). Unlike Quashia Quamina, represented as always at some critical distance from his adoptive context, Zorayda's self-identification as "daughter of darkness" is so complete that she does not grasp her adoptive status as a "pale alien" until the emperor makes his announcement; once that racial reclassification is accomplished, we hear almost nothing more about her. On both sides of the struggle, then, Zorayda's "true" race and biological inheritance trump whatever sympathies and identifications her upbringing has created: from the perspective of both the ruling family and the insurgent Africans, as a character declares in the decidedly different context of George Eliot's *Silas Marner* (1860), "breed was stronger than pasture."[34] Restored to her "true" fathers, revealed to be "really" white, and married off as a Northangerland granddaughter to a Zamorna son, Zorayda functions to bridge the gulf between these two rivalrous lines within the white kingdom rather than to cross the "impossible barrier" between native African and creole colonizer.

"A Leaf" also juxtaposes the sudden erasure of Zorayda's adoptive identity, contrasted implicitly with Quashia Quamina's narrative of resistance to adoption-as-colonization, with another orphan story that entails both a divided racial legacy and an ambiguity about paternity. The tale of Finic seems to bear out Zorayda's claim that crossing the racialized lines between native and creole will issue in "dissensions," but it even more powerfully demonstrates the effort of the white tyrants to disown their miscegenous offspring, who blur the line between internal and external difference. Product of blood that ostensibly does "*not* mingle," the mute dwarf servant of

the Emperor Adrian who first appears in "The Foundling" (1833) resur-
faces in "A Leaf" to figure in his own person both racial difference and
kin-aversion within the royal household, representing in tangible form the
relation between elements metonymically joined but categorically separate in
the plotlines discussed above. "Misshapen and grotesque," in Azim's words,
Finic "stood about three feet high. His huge head was covered with a shock
of coal black hair," and "his horrible features received additional hideousness
from a pair of small bead-like eyes in which gleamed an expression of fiend-
ish malignity" (*Colonial Rise* 135).[35] Although the emperor has employed this
"miserable being" in his household, he remarks that Finic "was a thing of
which I had a particular and constant aversion, a disgust whose intensity was
unaccountable even to myself.... He stuck to me with a strange tenacity
for several years and as if we had been fated not to part" ("Leaf" 364). Only
moments before he sends Finic to the scaffold for his part in the plot against
his life does the emperor learn that the dwarf is actually his own son, born of
a long-ago liaison with an African woman named Sofala. Far from staying
the executioner's hand, this revelation seems to hasten it, as the narrative can
now account for the emperor's "aversion" and "disgust" by reference to a
blood tie of which he has heretofore been ignorant. No doubt intensified by
racial politics, his antipathy to his biological offspring once more strikes the
note of "aversion" and antagonism between blood relations, and especially
between closely related men, that characterizes so much of the juvenilia.

Although Azim asserts that Finic "stands as a warning against the sexual
transgression of racial boundaries," his uncle Shungaron offers another way
of interpreting Finic's monstrosity in "A Leaf" (*Colonial Rise* 135). He tells
a story in which, yet again, a mother's dream of revenge controls the fate
of her son: "When Sofala lay on her dying bed...she prayed that her child
might be a shame and a dishonour to its false father," who abandoned the
woman he subsequently calls "my lovely wife" even before Finic's birth
("Leaf" 376). Shungaron construes Finic's deformity as a result not of miscegenous intercourse but of the falsity of the "treacherous white man" to
Sofala, "who fell a victim to [the emperor's] perfidy twenty-five years since":
"when that deformed being was born it was as fair an infant as day ever
dawned upon, but soon after a hideous change came over it and ere long
it grew up to be what thou seest" ("Leaf" 376, 374, 376). The blighted
Finic—once "fair," now "hideous"—plots unsuccessfully against the father
who takes him into his household as a servant but not into his family as a
son. The tyrant Adrian—nostalgic for the memory of the "lovely wife" but
entirely unmoved by the presence of the child who literally embodies his
"shame" and "dishonour"—punishes the "treason and falsehood" of Sofala's

brother and son with death, while his own falsity, albeit emblematized in his
son's deformity, is hardly mentioned. Unlike the "pale alien" Zorayda, who
regains a lost racial and familial heritage by repatriation even as she loses the
established bearings of her identity, Finic knows his own origins. Yet that
knowledge leads not to a reunion with the father but to death at his hands.
The only words that, under coercion, this mute speaks—"Emperor, will you
torture your own son?"—are the very words that seal his doom ("Leaf" 375).
The effect of a specifically sexual treachery against a black woman is to make
"hideous" the "fair"; while Zorayda's crime is pardoned, Finic pays with his
life for his father's transgression.

In betraying his lover and then abandoning and disowning their child,
Adrian the Magnificent—once the putative hero of Charlotte Brontë's
juvenilia—is metaphorically "blackened" through his own treachery, including the crossing of racial lines that serves as one but by no means the sole
source of "dissensions" within the empire. The increasing ambivalence in
the representation of "the white tyrant" may exemplify the young Brontë's
own movement "from an unambiguous celebration of imperialist conquest
to a growing affirmation of various forms of rebellion against authoritarian
control."[36] Yet it is crucial to note that in these aversions and rivalries among
men related by blood, marriage, or adoption, such rebellion is put down or
cut off through the death of rebels against white colonial and patriarchal
power. Moreover, the African mothers who instigate their plots have limited efficacy as agents of resistance, typically expressed only in their efforts
to shape the course of their male offspring. Zorayda's strangely unhappy
happy ending, by sharp contrast, depends not at all on the recovery of an
inefficacious maternal legacy but on her being transferred from a black to
a white father. As Boumelha has observed of Jane Eyre, Zorayda, too, exists
largely within "the patriarchal determinations of kinship and inheritance"
as the foundling restored to her quintessentially feminine place as some man's
daughter, some man's wife, a place implicitly marked out for white women
alone (*Charlotte Brontë* 64). Only in the muting of her response to her new
access to status, fortune, and racial privilege do we hear the faintest critique
of the cost of the foundling's return.

To become somebody's daughter, somebody's wife, might thus appear the
ne plus ultra of the female orphan's plot, but this is not always so in Brontë's
adult fiction. "Just listen to the difference of our positions," Ginevra Fan-
shawe says to Lucy Snowe "in an expostulatory tone": with both accom-
plishments and admirers, "I am the daughter of a gentleman of family, and
though my father is not rich, I have expectations from an uncle"; lacking

either looks or lovers, "you are nobody's daughter...you have no relations."[37] "Lucy's orphanhood and exile are, of course, in one sense the basis of her dispossession and privation," as Boumelha glosses Ginevra's taunts, "but this very privation is also a kind of freedom, for it seems to place Lucy irretrievably outside the determining structures of class, family and patrilineage" (*Charlotte Brontë* 119).[38] The obscurity of Lucy's origins—more precisely, the origins she deliberately obscures—may deny her access to Ginevra's fantasy plot of female fulfillment, but being a nobody—*pace* Emily Dickinson— also keeps Lucy out of the patriarchal loop exemplified in the narrative of Paulina Home.

When Mrs. Bretton receives a disturbing letter in the first chapter of the novel, for example, Lucy "thought at first that it was from home, and trembled, expecting I knew not what disastrous communication" (*Villette* 6). As it turns out, the letter is indeed from Home, declaring the breakup of his household and announcing his daughter Paulina's impending arrival. "This little girl...had recently lost her mother; though indeed, Mrs. Bretton ere long subjoined, the loss was not so great as might at first appear": for to lose a no-good mother—"a giddy, careless woman, who had neglected her child, and disappointed and disheartened her husband"—is a fortunate fall, comparable to Rochester's "transplant[ing]" the orphaned Adèle Varens from "the slime and mud of Paris" to "the wholesome soil of an English country garden" (*Villette* 7; *JE* 151). All Paulina's "home sickness" concerns her separation from papa, mitigated in part by her precocious attachment to Graham (*Villette* 14). Her subsequently singleminded but doubly bestowed devotion to father and future husband—"a bond to both, an influence over each"—effaces any traces of her mother's unsettled past and its potential influence on her future (*Villette* 546). This motherless child is and always will be some man's daughter, some man's wife, in no small part because such a mother, within the patriarchal economy, can only be well lost.

Lucy Snowe's own plot circumvents Paulina's familial fate, so reminiscent of yet differently valenced from Zorayda's. In the final completed fiction of her career, Brontë conferred upon her heroine a radical homelessness that will not be ameliorated by a fairy-tale ending: "the well-loved dead, who had loved *me* well in life" will return only in dreams; they will only meet her "elsewhere, alienated" (*Villette* 197). Lucy is never at home, never happy at the adoptive home (of which we hear almost nothing) where she lives before she travels from England to Villette. She reports "the amiable conjecture" that upon leaving Bretton, "having been absent six months," she was "glad to return to the bosom of my kindred" in a tone as ironic as her reference to "my bereaved lot," in which she wears mourning for those she barely mentions, let alone mourns (*Villette* 42, 43). At least initially, Lucy approaches romantic attachment through a familial idiom of siblingship, as we shall see; but there's no effort in the novel to revivify "well-loved" kin and no dwelling on the shipwreck of the adoptive household. Borrowing a phrase from Elizabeth Barrett Browning's *Aurora Leigh,* we can say that "mother-want" afflicts all Brontë heroines, but *Jane Eyre,* closely allied in its framework to the archetypal foundling myth, pursues a very different tack in investigating the legacy of both of Jane's lost parents.[39]

While the fortuitous return in *Shirley* of the aptly named Mrs. Pryor recalls the fairy-tale foundling plot of familial reunion, Jane Eyre's mother and father, like those of Lucy Snowe, stay dead. What *Jane Eyre* relives instead are the inter- and intrafamilial conflicts and antagonisms earlier dramatized in the juvenilia, now stripped of their high-life trappings and transposed to a middling sphere in an ambiguously realist fiction, with many (though not all) of their racialized overtones displaced onto the bigamy plot. Every reader notices that the novel begins with one set of cousins and can only conclude once it finds another. But it is less often observed that cousinship in Jane's generation is overdetermined by in-law rivalries and jealousies in the earlier one— antagonisms among those who should, normatively, be affinal "friends" or "kin"—that are comparable to those within the Angrian court.[40] Dividing the heroine's mixed inheritance along maternal and paternal lines, the novel takes some pains to represent the conflict between first and second families as a critical factor in Jane's history that shapes her narrative possibilities. It fleshes out the universalizing orphan story of Bessie's ballad with quotidian detail, gradually peopling it with dead relatives whose living intentions make her seemingly singular plot a multifarious set of intersecting familial enmities and animosities. To cut off that conflict in her generation by her own hand, Jane must become not sister or daughter or even wife, but cousin to the long-lost relatives whose adoption of her as an adult undoes the injury of her childhood placement.

What the child Jane retains instead of her forgotten parents is another figure she cannot recall, whose former existence has secured for her only an uncertain place:

> I could not remember him; but I knew that he was my own uncle—my mother's brother—that he had taken me when a parentless infant to his house; and that in his last moments he had required a promise of Mrs. Reed that she would rear and maintain me as one of her own children. Mrs. Reed probably considered she had kept this promise; and so she had, I dare say, as well as her nature would permit her: but how could

she really like an interloper not of her race, and unconnected with her, after her husband's death, by any tie? It must have been most irksome to find herself bound by a hard-wrung pledge to stand in the stead of a parent to a strange child she could not love, and to see an uncongenial alien permanently intruded on her own family group. (*JE* 16–17)

Mr. Reed's death deprives Jane of the maternal uncle in whose goodness she continues to trust long after his demise: "I doubted not—had never doubted—that if Mr. Reed had been alive he would have treated me kindly," which is to say "as one of [his] own children" (*JE* 17). Like some latter-day Mrs. John Dashwood, who makes "no kin" of her husband's half-sisters on his father's side even in the face of her dying father-in-law's plea to provide for them, Mrs. Reed abjures the putative claims of kinship in relation to her sister(-in-law)'s child. Her husband's death, at least from Jane's narratorial perspective, cancels the bonds of obligation between the second family, which she now heads, and the first, from which her husband issued and to which he maintained fraternal ties; to put it in anthropological terms, Jane is not within the Reeds' agnatic line. Although she describes herself more than once as Jane's "friend" (*JE* 38, 42), while other characters refer to her as Jane's "benefactress," "patroness," and "natural guardian" (*JE* 12, 70, 93), to young Jane Mrs. Reed remains at best "my uncle's wife" and at worst "no relation of mine" (*JE* 74, 38). Indeed, Jane insists on differentiating herself from the Reeds: the "uncongenial alien," "an interloper not of her [aunt's] race," represents herself as a stranger within the "family group" and finds "an inexpressible relief, a soothing conviction of protection and security" in the presence of other strangers, in other words those "not belonging to Gateshead, and not related to Mrs. Reed" (*JE* 19).

As I have suggested, the trope of "the stranger" limns the difference between intimates and others. Here it is not only deployed to exclude someone who could readily be conceptualized as kin, according to cognatic reckoning, but also appropriated by Jane to represent her experience of exclusion. If Mrs. Reed limits the scope of her relations to her conjugal family only, then Jane also accepts that limit: even the way in which she phrases her complaint suggests that it is entirely reasonable for Mrs. Reed, "bound by a hard-wrung pledge" exacted by a dying man, not to "really like" her sister(-in-law)'s orphan child. Most importantly, when Jane adopts the terminology of "alien" and "interloper" to accentuate the difference between a relation by blood (her uncle) and one by marriage (her aunt), she posits that the absence of consanguinity, rather than the presence of affinity, is the root of both her lack of family feeling for Aunt Reed and Aunt Reed's reciprocal attitude toward her. Even though Jane might say just as truly of her Reed cousins what she later tells the Rivers siblings—that "half our blood on each side flows from the same source"—she significantly underplays her connection to John, Georgiana, and Eliza, representing herself instead as unrelated not just to her aunt-by-marriage but also to her maternal cousins (*JE* 405). Using an array of images and metaphors that "blacken" the Reeds, just as Brontë's juvenile narrators increasingly do to the Emperor Adrian, Jane further distances herself from her maternal relations, representing the "impossible barrier" between them in terms that clearly echo the racialized discourses of the juvenilia by dramatizing her lack of affinity with and for them.

The "insuperable and rooted aversion" between aunt and niece, related only by law, thus is (or becomes) mutual (*JE* 27). Chastising her aunt for her cruelty, Jane demands to know "what would Uncle Reed say to you if he were alive?" (*JE* 28). Here, as Boumelha observes, "the archetypal 'bad mother' figure is rebuked by means of the authority of the father figure," who, along with Jane's dead parents, "can see all you do and think" (*Charlotte Brontë* 66; *JE* 28). Jane seeks to raise a spark of familial conscience in her aunt, which only comes to fruition much later in the novel as Aunt Reed lies on her deathbed, by summoning the dead uncle back to life: though a living uncle might make all the difference at this point in her history, the ghostly one she conjures in the red room inspires only horror. But Aunt Reed blocks access to Jane's living uncle for reasons other than or in addition to those Jane assigns to her. While Jane represents her circumstances at Gateshead as a matter of being excluded from the "family group" as "an interloper" to whom her uncle's wife has no blood tie, Mrs. Reed sees Jane as her mother's living avatar, standing between her and her husband.

When, for example, the niece asks her dying aunt why she wishes Jane Eyre dead, Mrs. Reed situates her aversion to Jane within a longer familial history: "I had a dislike to her mother always; for she was my husband's only sister, and a great favourite with him. . . . When news came of her death, he wept like a simpleton" and had his dead sister's child brought to his house. The wife's envy of her sister-in-law's status as "favourite" is not slaked by her death but rather finds a new object in Jane. The orphan also freshly occasions Mrs. Reed's jealousy in relation to her own children: she "hated [the baby] the first time I set my eyes on it," but "Reed pitied it; and he used to nurse it and notice it as if it had been his own: more, indeed, than he ever noticed his own at that age" (*JE* 243). Perceived by Mrs. Reed to usurp her children's rightful primacy in their father's affections, Jane bears the brunt of her aunt's own displaced feelings of exclusion: Mrs. Reed cuts Jane out of the "family group," we may speculate, because she has experienced what it is to be cut out by the first-family tie between brother and sister that her husband did not or would not relinquish upon marriage. By withholding John Eyre's offer of adoption, Aunt Reed may be able to exact her "revenge"—"for you to be adopted by your uncle and placed in a state of ease and comfort was what I could not endure" because "I disliked you too fixedly and thoroughly ever to lend a hand in lifting you to prosperity"—but neither her aversion to Jane nor Jane's conduct to her is its sole source or cause (*JE* 251, 250).

In the final analysis, Aunt Reed's "revenge" only defers access to the "ease and comfort" she aims to deny Jane outright: though she never enters his presence, Jane will come to inherit an uncle's estate by a circuitous route. Significantly, the absent uncle is a rich relation on the father's side who has gotten on in the world at the expense of others: as Azim argues, it is the disposition of the "colonial possession and wealth" accumulated by a childless man that will "restore her to the family of origin (her Uncle Eyre/her *father's* brother)" (*Colonial Rise* 177, emphasis in original). There is no such possibility of fortune through the mother, as the daughter's status follows from her father's: already disowned by her parents for marrying a poor clergyman, Jane's mother leaves "nothing to bequeath" her daughter except the protection of her only brother's care (*JE* 250). When Aunt Reed claims that she "would as soon have been charged with a pauper brat out of a work-house," she expresses in the starkest terms the extent of Jane's maternal disinheritance (*JE* 243).

In taking the first step toward claiming her legacy, Jane unknowingly and altogether fortuitously sets in motion the chain of events that will endow her with both a fortune and a family on the father's side. As she confronts the "annoyance and degradation" she feels in being showered with expensive gifts and "dressed like a doll" by her master-turned-lover, Jane imagines that "if I had but a prospect of one day bringing to Mr. Rochester an accession of fortune, I could better endure to be kept by him now" (*JE* 281–82). Writing to Madeira to announce her continuing existence and impending marriage, Jane forges the first of "a formless lump of links" that will be "drawn out straight" by St. John Rivers, who "reconstructs Jane's relationship to her uncle, procures her fortune for her, and provides her with three cousins in himself and his two sisters," in a sibling configuration that precisely matches yet radically revises Jane's first adoptive family of maternal cousins (*JE* 404).[41] That letter leads not only to the revelation of Rochester's bigamous plot and her exile from Thornfield but also to her eventual discovery of paternal kin.[42]

Azim's point—that Jane inherits wealth and kin on the *father's* side—has been subordinated even in those interpretations of the novel that recognize the importance to Jane's plot of finding a family to which she is tied by both blood and affinity. Maurianne Adams argues that in moving from Gateshead to Lowood to Thornfield, Jane Eyre "supplants bad foster-families with good," emphasizing the narrative fact that "prior to establishing a family by marriage" with Rochester at Ferndean, "she regains and reunites a family of origin" at Marsh End.[43] In contrast with John Kucich's claim that Jane's "rediscovery of her female cousins remains only a minor event, firmly relegated to the background of the novel," Adams suggests that it "prepares for the marital resolution with Rochester, in which affinity, monetary inheritance, social status and mutual interdependence are of a piece"; more recently, James Buzard has also pointed out that "Jane's marriage is supplemented by her other intimacy, both chosen *and* discovered, with her new found blood relations, her Rivers cousins."[44] But why does Brontë identify Jane's true or good "family of origin" with her paternal relatives? Why must she inherit kin and fortune from an Eyre rather than a Reed? The short answer, already suggested, is that mothers are dispossessed or disowned by patriarchal marriage, so that to be a girl child without parents or portion in the home of "rich, maternal relations"—like Fanny Price at Mansfield—is quite literally to be "nobody's daughter" (*JE* 399).[45] But a closer look at the circumstances of the Rivers of Moor House, who also suffer through a failure of maternal kin, complicates this picture.

Like Jane's lack of loving family ties, the Rivers siblings' loss of fortune originates in the unresolved conflicts of the generation that preceded them. Before they discover their cousinhood, Diana tells the story of how their maternal uncle (Jane's father's brother) led his brother-in-law (Diana's father) to ruin:

> We have never seen him or known him. He was my mother's brother. My father and he quarreled long ago. It was by his advice that my father risked most of his property in the speculation that ruined him. Mutual recriminations passed between them.... [I]t appears he realised a fortune of twenty thousand pounds. He was never married, and had no near kindred but ourselves, and one other person, not more closely related than we. My father always cherished the idea that he would atone for his error, by leaving his possessions to us: that letter informs us that he has bequeathed every penny to the other relation. (*JE* 376–77)

Although he is the figure within the Rivers family who stands in a parallel place to Uncle Reed, this mother's brother does not take a protective role toward either his sister or her children; he can be more readily assimilated in historical terms to the entrepreneurial and enterprising men whose circumstances

Leonore Davidoff and Catherine Hall studied in *Family Fortunes,* drawing on the in-law network that marriage creates for (colonial) investment capital.[46] In this fictional case, financial ruin precipitates a familial falling out; while the father of the Rivers children believed that recompense was due them for what he had lost by "speculation," those "mutual recriminations" over a deal gone bad would presumably have played a part in Uncle John's decision to make his brother's child his sole heir. Here again, although in a different key, affinal relations—specifically those on the mother's side—both fail to live up to a normative conception of family feeling and expose the asymmetries in gendered privilege, leaving a sister's children with nothing while endowing a brother's child with ample means. Although Diana casts the as-yet-unknown cousin as "not more closely related" to their uncle than she and her siblings are, Jane's status as the child of a brother rather than of a sister may also factor into their uncle's decision: a brother's child may indeed be understood as "more closely related" from the point of view of agnation, so Jane has a stronger claim to be her uncle's sole heir.

Ultimately placed in a position where she can compensate the disregarded mother's children by making the amends her uncle John would not, Jane undoes the fate of disinheritance that her own mother had endured, symbolically repairing the broken link between brother and sister. To be sure, her generosity follows in part from her friendship with Diana and Mary, established in advance of knowing they are kin. With each alive to "the pleasure arising from perfect congeniality of tastes, sentiments, and principles," "our natures dovetailed: mutual affection—of the strongest kind—was the result" (*JE* 368, 369). Here what Jane certainly casts as natural "inclination or attraction," an affinity arising from familiarity and compatibility, precedes the discovery of biological relationship, so that Jane may later remark, "When I knew them but as mere strangers, they had inspired me with genuine affection and admiration" (*JE* 405). Such "congeniality" lends credence to Jane's earlier assertion that "sympathies" exist "between far-distant, long-absent, wholly estranged relatives," but the force of that claim itself rests on the fact of biological likeness, in that what is said to promote "sympathies" between the otherwise "estranged" is "the unity of the source to which each traces his origin" (*JE* 231). The discovery, then, that "half our blood on each side flows from the same source" retroactively goes to show why these three cousins get on so well from the outset, even as shared blood leads only to aversion on the other side of Jane's family. If the initial affinity of the Eyre cousins is in some sense predicated on their common biological inheritance, then it also makes the sharing of the material inheritance a critical element of the "integration of blood and kinship ties" that paves the way for Jane's marriage.[47]

That marriage, however, does not further consolidate the extended family in quite the way that it might. Consider for a moment where Jane's newly discovered position as heiress and cousin, in a novel by another, perhaps an earlier, author might lead: not to a division of the estate in four equal parts but to its being concentrated, through a cross-cousin marriage, in St. John's hands. And consider, too, Zorayda's fate, once her "true" identity is discovered and she is rapidly assumed into a patriarchal structure. Repudiating his claim that she is "formed for labour, not for love," Jane famously rejects St. John's business-like proposal, implicitly linking cousin-marriage to coercion, as in *Pride and Prejudice* or *Sense and Sensibility* (although not in *Mansfield Park*), but without any reference to the economic advantage such a marriage would bring to him (*JE* 424). In the aristocratic paradigm for cousin-marriage we encountered in chapter 2, an heiress such as Colonel Brandon's Eliza could be obliged to marry her cousin to keep the fortune on the male side, while the maternal relation Fanny Price makes an unlikely, unconventional marriage within the Mansfield family in that it does not advance the economic fortunes of the Bertrams. Jane Eyre marrying St. John Rivers would unite the daughter and son of a brother and a sister, respectively, repairing the material difference between the two Eyre offspring that a third (childless) sibling had opened up between them. In stopping short of marrying her father's sister's son, however, Jane breaks with the economic logic that underpins the dominant form of cousin-marriage so that Brontë may spread the narrative wealth more widely, having chosen not to concentrate the family fortune in one man's hands, but rather to make possible the separate settlements that enable Diana and Mary also to marry the men of their choice.

By choosing Rochester over St. John, moreover, Jane prefers the claims of spiritual to biological kinship, turning away from the brotherly cousin whose nature (unlike those of his sisters) is partially alien to her own and toward the lover who is defined and experienced as kin. In so doing, she prefers the affinity that she identifies in her connection to Rochester—"I felt at times, as if he were my relation, rather than my master.... So gratified did I become with this new interest added to life that I ceased to pine after kindred"—which has some of the satisfactions she associates with the experience of family life that she has never had (*JE* 153). As Catherine might say of Heathcliff, so Jane says of Rochester: "I feel akin to him,—I understand the language of his countenance and movements: though rank and wealth sever us widely, I have something in my brain and heart, in my blood and nerves, that assimilates me to him" (*JE* 184). If it is possible to say that "theirs is a bond of kinship," as Deborah Epstein Nord remarks, and "not only of [romantic] love," then it is also critically important to recognize the extent to which Brontë's fiction challenges any firm distinction between the two.[48] Or, to put it another way, romantic love and marriage function analogously to adoption, making kin—as marriage was still widely held to do—of those who once were strangers.

In marrying the man who is *like* a relation, rather than the man who actually *is* one, Jane creates both a surrogate first family and a second family in marriage, keeping them literally and metaphorically separate, bringing into being two families where once she had only a single, radically insufficient one. By constantly referring to her Rivers cousins as her brother and sisters, moreover, she installs a rhetorical impediment to marital union with St. John where no actual impediment exists: although cousin-marriage came under increasing scrutiny after 1860, roughly coinciding with the early stirrings of eugenics, it remained perfectly legal in England (though not in the United States), and fairly common, especially among elites. At the same time, Jane and Rochester's affinity for one another is repeatedly referred to on a quasi-familial basis, as romantic love and family attachment coincide in the safe space of a nonbiological relationship, in "an affinity based on moral and spiritual qualities."[49] Although Jane refuses marriage within the family on the one hand, she embraces a version of it on the other. But does Brontë effect this division between (brotherly) cousin and (unrelated) lover in an effort to shore up the distinction between the two or to collapse it? In Foucauldian terms, we might ask if the shape of Jane's choice signifies the wavering import of alliance in the face of sexuality or the persistence of alliance at sexuality's core. The task of the orphan-heroine in Brontë's fiction, I submit, is to navigate and negotiate the overlapping discourses of kinship and romance that intersect in the doubled term *affinity,* sometimes to collapse distinctions between the two, as in *Jane Eyre,* and sometimes to demarcate their differences to her narrative advantage.

Aptly citing *Villette* as their key example, Boone and Nord argue that "the rhetoric of sibling identification and/or affection can also serve as a mode of wooing, precisely by clearing a linguistic space for erotic sparring between otherwise undeclared lovers."[50] M. Paul frames his assertion of sameness, however, by first identifying differences:

> You are patient, and I am choleric; you are quiet and pale, and I am tanned and fiery; you are a strict Protestant, and I am a sort of lay Jesuit: but we are alike—there is affinity. Do you see it, mademoiselle, when you look in the glass? Do you observe that your forehead is shaped like mine—that your eyes are cut like mine? Do you hear that you have some of my tones

of voice? Do you know that you have many of my looks? I perceive all this, and believe that you were born under my star. (*Villette* 460)

The likeness Paul remarks—in appearance, tone, and expression—approaches the biological, casting Lucy as his physical twin or double and minimizing their disparities of belief, background, and temperament. Brontë's use of the term *affinity* here draws on yet another meaning of this multivalent word, one that would become increasingly useful in all the human sciences. For linguists and natural historians, *affinity* denoted a "structural resemblance" between objects of study (languages, animals, plants) that indicated "their origin from a common stock" (*OED*), so that when Paul tells Lucy that she was "born under [his] star," he is asserting a family likeness that links them as closely as fruit from the same tree or blossoms from the same flower.[51] Yet if their likeness lays the ground for establishing a brother-sister bond, at least rhetorically, so, too, does their difference contribute to it, in that elements of both connection and disjuncture, identity and otherness, mark *all* relationships between the sexes in Brontë's fiction; as Valerie Sanders observes, "Brontë heroines search for an 'affinity' with a man . . . but this may be achieved only after many bouts of sibling-like squabbling."[52] While a sister can always figure a second self, Brontë's vision of gender (also supported, in *Villette,* by religious and national distinctions) predominantly casts sexual difference as antagonism or opposition—as in the "erotic sparring" identified by Boone and Nord, the "squabbling" discussed by Sanders, the representation of "sexual union as a battleground" that Kucich finds in *Shirley.*[53] Cross-sex siblings and heterosexual lovers, distinguished from one another in some important ways, do at least have difference in common.

Paul begins to deploy the language of siblingship in defining his relationship to Lucy in order to differentiate it from romance. For Lucy, this rhetoric is closely allied with friendship:

"Knowing me thoroughly now—all my antecedents, all my responsibilities—having long known my faults, can you and I still be friends?"

"If monsieur wants a friend in me, I shall be glad to have a friend in him."

"But a close friend I mean—intimate and real—kindred in all but blood?"

"Is monsieur quite serious? Does he really think he needs me, and can take an interest in me as a sister?"

"Surely, surely," said he; "a lonely man like me, who has no sister, must be but too glad to find in some woman's heart a sister's pure affection." (*Villette* 509–10)

Paul refines Lucy's offer of friendship by redesignating what he seeks as "kin-dred"—"intimate and real," nearly connected "in all but blood." Closer than friendship, just short of siblingship, approximated to affinity, this relationship, as Paul imagines it, is difficult for Lucy to assimilate to her existing models for cross-gender bonding, yet it is clear to her that the "pure affection" for which he asks is not sexual. Never having been a sister to anyone, as far as we know, Lucy nevertheless has a tacit conception of how a brother might behave: "My wish was to get a more thorough comprehension of this frater-nal alliance: to note with how much of the brother he would demean himself when we met again," so that she may judge his assertion of "fraternal" desire by both deeds and words (*Villette* 513). Yet Lucy also sets herself an emotional task—"to prove how much of the sister was in my own feelings"—that she is more readily able to fulfill (*Villette* 513–14). Her final take on Paul's offer demonstrates her wariness of using sisterhood as the frame for her relation to him: "I was willing to be his sister on condition that he did not invite me to fill that relation to some future wife of his" (*Villette* 513).[54] Having accepted his self-representation as "a sort of lay Jesuit," Lucy calculates that "tacitly vowed as he was to celibacy, of this dilemma there seemed little danger," but the very fact of making the calculation suggests that Lucy's "own feelings" are not asexually "pure," that is, sisterly in Paul's sense (*Villette* 513).

Reimagining herself as a potentially jealous sister(-in-law), Lucy gestures toward the conflictual relations between first and second families epitomized by Mrs. Reed and avoided, through her choice of Rochester over St. John, by Jane Eyre. Here, I think, we can glimpse the positive aspects of being nobody's sister or daughter or cousin or niece, the freedom from the family ties that bind, which Lucy Snowe surely if ambivalently possesses. Yet even as orphanhood opens a space for feminine self-fashioning in Brontë's fiction, the discourse of the familial exerts a familiar sway, especially in the sphere of romance. Facilitating the intimacy that springs from spiritual affinity and effecting a sense of kinship between those who are technically not kin, the pervasive emphasis on making and remaking family in the orphan's romance also prepares the ground for conflict by peopling the world with family figures.

Fully embraced by neither party, the language of siblingship thus serves only as a way station in *Villette,* a transitional point on the road to romance at which Paul, already encumbered by "antecedents" and "responsibilities" of a familial kind, takes temporary refuge. "I call myself your brother," he tells Lucy, but "I hardly know what I am—brother—friend—I cannot tell" (*Vil-lette* 523). Paul's doubts appear genuine, whereas Lucy's provisional accep-tance of sisterhood, on the terms noted above, has a strategic quality. "Could it be that he was becoming more than friend or brother? Did his look speak a kindness beyond fraternity or amity?": these questions are not the products of an overheated and discursive imagination but ones to which Lucy surely already knows the answers (*Villette* 553). While it might at first appear to be wholly an impediment, especially to Lucy herself, Paul's use of the sibling idiom in *Villette* enables the movement into a full-blown romance plot in that it permits a deepening intimacy that springs from spiritual affinity, a sense of kinship between those who are not kin that is comparable to Jane's feeling for Rochester. Use of sibling terms "allows an easy slippage into a discreetly sexual relationship": calling Lucy a sister might then be imagined as an erotic apéritif, an inducement rather than an obstacle to heterosexual love.[55] His plea for "pure affection" notwithstanding, sibling language for Paul is itself erotically charged: for in his sending her down the path from friend to sister to fiancée, roles that are supposed to be distinct from one another, we may also read an inevitable progression and intensification of affect that tends to blur the distinctions among them.

No family of nineteenth-century writers has garnered more attention than the Brontës, and much of that attention concerns their status as a family. Under the eyes of loyal servants, a patriarchal papa, and their maiden aunt—a wife's sister who fills the dead mother's place but not, in this instance, that of the dead wife—the surviving children created worlds of their own from the raw materials of their father's library, contemporary magazines and journals, and their own imaginative resources. In "the participatory creations that claimed all the Brontës," as Bette London argues against the grain of interpretations that read the juvenilia in terms of a developmental, individualist plot of literary apprenticeship, "collaboration was the necessary mode for generating and sustaining, as well as recording, ongoing collective fantasies."[56] Within the walls of the parsonage or out on the surrounding moors, together they created a home that alternately satisfied and stifled them; away from Haworth, they pined for the shared world that they identified not only with the romance and adventure that adult workaday life sadly lacks but also with the family affection that sustained and supported them.

The epigraph to this chapter, with its remarks on the common affection and family likeness among brothers and sisters, in many ways anticipates the forms of heterosexual romance to which Brontë's fiction gives voice, as in Jane's assertion of kinship with Rochester or Lucy and Paul's joint if uneasy negotiation of sibling terms. Giving this statement its most bland (or most stereotypically "Victorian") interpretation, we might read its embrace of sameness and refusal of division as evidence of an idealization so "profound" and "intense" that it makes sibling solidarity the sole source of a true, sustaining intersubjectivity: as in *Shirley*, "family jarring vulgarizes—family union elevates" (*Shirley* 113). "Some of Brontë's energy," Buzard writes, "always harks back to this ideal, lost condition of sibling togetherness."[57] Such a vision of "the family" is, of course, almost nowhere present in the mature fiction of Charlotte, Emily, or Anne, for what Kucich terms "a militant and anarchic competition between individual selves" takes place both "in the world" that their heroines and heroes encounter and in most of the homes they inhabit as well.[58] But within the representation of those homes, the petty "disputes" and vulgar "jarring" that we see between the Linton children, the Reed sisters' alienation from one another's interests, and the "elevated" sisterly community at Moor House all serve as foils within the broader charting of the central Brontëan protagonists' unsettled relationship to home, family, and personal identity. Only if we identify Charlotte Brontë's representation of siblings whose "minds are cast in the same mould" with a shared "ideal" of intersubjective engagement can we begin to grasp the ways in which experiences of siblingship frame familial and romantic fictions in her work. The familiarity bred by the languages of familiality in these orphan stories shapes the romance narrative, in which both Lucy Snowe and Jane Eyre choose men (with "minds cast in the same mould") who appeal to them in a familial and familiar way.

✺ CHAPTER 5

Intercrossing, Interbreeding, and *The Mill on the Floss*

> The nature of European men has its roots intertwined with the past, and can only be developed by allowing those roots to remain undisturbed while the process of development is going on, until that perfect ripeness of the seed which carries with it a life independent of the root.
>
> —Marian Evans, "The Natural History of German Life," 1856

Stronger than the death that does not divide them, matched in affective intensity only by Heathcliff's quite literal ambition to come between Edgar and Catherine Linton in the grave, the tie between Maggie and Tom Tulliver in *The Mill on the Floss* provides supreme testimony to the persistence of the first-family bond in the nineteenth-century English tradition. Having renounced her cousin Lucy's fiancé on the ground that there can be no conception of duty, no moral compass by which to steer, "if the past is not to bind us," Maggie returns to the fold of the sibling dyad.[1] Recalling the force of the claim in *Mansfield Park* that "children of the same family, the same blood, with the same first associations and habits" have an attachment to one another that "no subsequent connections can supply" and evoking "the intense affection" of the Brontë siblings, Tom and Maggie sink together into a final embrace foreshadowed in the novel's very first sentence, an embrace that is almost inevitably read as transgressive. Referring specifically to *The Mill on the Floss,* Tony Tanner writes that "there are cases when the bourgeois novel avoids adultery only by permitting and even pursuing something that is very close to incest"; more boldly, William A. Cohen comments that *The Mill on the Floss* is "as fully perverse a work as one could desire," offering "a range of alternatives to the marriage plot" that includes not only incest and adultery, but also homoeroticism.[2] As for the latter, the epigraph that doubles as Tom and Maggie's epitaph invokes both the brother-sister bond and, more explicitly, the loving tie of Jonathan and David—friends, soldiers, and brothers(-in-law).[3] Although Cohen reads the allusion as "[eliding] the distinctively female character of Maggie's misfortunes," we might understand it instead as reinforcing the conception of a love that refuses both gendered and sexual difference in its preference for sameness, "the identification of brother and sister" that Gillian Beer links to the *Antigone*—as significant a text for George Eliot as it was for Virginia Woolf—in which "love, duty, kinship, passion and death" all commingle.[4]

As I have been arguing, such bonds, such intensities, far from being some marked deviation from a nineteenth-century English "exogamous" norm, themselves constituted a significant norm in their own right. When we use the imprecise yet ideologically loaded term *incestuous* to characterize them, we fail to register the difference of the past; the aura of the unnatural that incest evokes is so strong that any casual use of the term tends to block rather than promote further analysis. Moreover, for middle-class Victorians, it is certainly arguable that the rejection of family likeness—broadly construed in Brontëan terms as affinity—in favor of the different, the other, or the strange is the truly aberrant or unnatural. Even when nineteenth-century intellectuals began to question the wisdom of preferences for the familiar under the influence of the nascent sciences of heredity, they did so suspiciously, weighing the risks of sheltering difference at home, in the broader society, and in the empire.

It is in pursuit of understanding the emergent discourse around the promise and perils of mixture that this chapter focuses not on first-family sibling erotics but on the biological making of second-family ties that came to preoccupy some very eminent Victorians after midcentury. Like her contemporary Charles Darwin and her partner George Henry Lewes, Eliot, too, pursued the meanings of family likeness, of inheritance, and of the historical/cultural/biological production of difference. These intellectuals all sought answers to questions of origin, influence, and descent. In Eliot's case, as in Darwin's, such questions no doubt had biographical determinants: Mary Ann Evans effected her flight from the family, famously aborted by Maggie Tulliver, only after the demise of her father and at the cost of the familial death inflicted by her brother's long, disapproving silence at her liaison with the married Lewes. Along with so many of George Eliot's protagonists—Maggie Tulliver, Esther Lyon, Dorothea Brooke, and Daniel Deronda among them—Marian Evans must have wondered how it was that she came to be so much at odds with the milieu in which she was born and raised, why her interests and values varied so dramatically from those of her first family.[5] Most painfully, she was troubled by the persistence of "the profound, the intense affection"

that she, like Charlotte Brontë, felt for her siblings—especially her brother—
even though she knew all too well that their minds had not been "cast in the
same mould." Some years after the break with Isaac Evans, she continued to
mourn his loss: "I cling strongly to kith and kin," she wrote to Barbara Bodichon with a bitter pathos in late December 1869, "even though they reject
me."[6] Such feelings animate not only *The Mill on the Floss* but also a range of
other contemporary investigations into the dynamics of variation.

Discourses of breeding significantly shaped norms of biological reproduction among humans, and how to produce or prevent "variation" was a key
issue. "Linnaeus' sexual system of classification"—a central taxonomy for
nineteenth-century professional and lay botanizing—"was not only imbued
with social-sexual language," remarks Amy M. King, "but also constructed
by an explicit social-sexual system of analogy between humans and plants."[7]
The traffic between the human and the animal was just as busy, so that "worries about the concupiscence of human females structured the theory and
practice of animal breeding," according to Harriet Ritvo, "and the emergence
of racially based nationalism conditioned discussions of species, variety, and
breed in animals."[8] In imagining relationships within families, biological or
adoptive, Eliot and her contemporaries—especially the venerable Darwin—
returned again and again to analogy, the rhetorical figure "between metaphor and substantiality" that enables the representation of human relations
in vegetable or animal terms; the increasing scientific authority granted to
those analogical relations was underwritten by techniques of close observation associated with natural history, domestic breeding, and literary realism
itself.[9] Yet for all Victorians, such analogies could be highly problematic, and
the use of analogy in argument—as Beer brilliantly analyzes—was anything
but a stable ground for truth claims, although it licensed imaginative leaps,
a point to which we shall return.[10] So, too, was breeding a mystery beyond
human comprehension: with no knowledge of genetics, it was as much the
limits as the scope of human control over biological reproduction that per-
plexed contemporary makers of family fictions.

Eliot thus launched her career as a novelist with a sensibility very much
informed by the convergence of these ways of seeing the construction of
human families through imperfect but creative lenses ground by the analogical habit. Locating some of her early work in relation to these ways of seeing,
I aim to illuminate the connections across discourses that increasingly problematize the production and reproduction of humans and their families, with
specific reference to contemporaneous debates about cousin-marriage and the
findings of lay breeders and professional scientists. In contrast with the long
MDWS controversy, the dispute over cousin-marriage focused intensively on

its impact on marital offspring. Scientific debates—close kin to those within early anthropology—rhetorically constructed analogies among human, plant, and animal reproduction that illustrated the shifting dynamics of this instance of marriage within the family, with "interbreeding" and "intercrossing" each understood in terms of class and race and inflected by gender asymmetry. Increasingly, sex and marriage with those construed either as "too near" or "too far" were characterized in comparable fashion. Situating *The Mill on the Floss* in relation to writings by Darwin and Lewes in which the risks and rewards of both interbreeding and intercrossing are fully canvassed, I argue that the new racialized fictions of heredity shaped Eliot's early historicism, particularly her conception of character as historically constructed.

In Eliot's metaphorical garden, from the vantage point of an "invisible spectator whose eye rested on her like morning on the flowers," we see Hetty Sorrel seeing herself in the mirror of her vanity.[11] "In those exquisite lines of cheek and lip and chin, in those eyelids delicate as petals, in those long lashes curled like the stamen of a flower," Adam Bede reads the features that "nature has written out" for him as emblems of "his bride's character" and peoples their projected future with children who will "hang about [Hetty] like florets around the central flower" (*AB* 144). The narration gives the face-as-flower still closer scrutiny, dissecting the blossom's constituent parts; it is those long, curling lashes that particularly arrest attention as it hastens to correct Adam's "hasty reading," which misinterprets nature's language and extracts "the very opposite of her real meaning" (*AB* 145). For while it is "impossible" even for the discerning narrative voice "not to expect some depth of soul behind a deep grey eye with a long dark eyelash," that expectation is fatally misguided (*AB* 145). Hetty is one of those "plants that have hardly any roots; you may tear them from their native nook of rock or wall, and just lay them over your ornamental flower-pot, and they blossom none the worse" (*AB* 146). Unlike her opposite number, Dinah Morris, who is "not free to leave Snowfield, where I was first planted, and have grown deep into it, like the small grass on the hill-top," the depthless, rootless Hetty, all pollen-y stamen and no seed-bearing pistil, can go anywhere, with no "loving thought of her second parents—of the children she had helped to tend—of any youthful companion, any pet animal, any relic of her own childhood even" to keep her fixed in one dear perpetual place (*AB* 83, 145–46).

What made her this way lies mainly beyond the ken of the narrative.[12] Having voiced the suspicion "that there is no direct correlation between eyelashes and morals," the text hazards that the former may "express the disposition of the fair one's grandmother"—or not (*AB* 145). There is no real accounting for "family likeness" in *Adam Bede,* nor any consistent schema for doing so (*AB* 38). Notwithstanding Mrs. Poyser's observation to Dinah that she is "th' image o' [her] poor Aunt Judith," the sort of talk that would imply a causal relation between Hetty's emptiness and the character of her Poyser kin or the conditions of her environment is almost entirely absent from the text (*AB* 72). Although relentlessly anthropomorphized, neither plants nor animals have much of a history, and some characters just *are* flowers, or kittens, or suckling pigs. The "organic metaphors for change" that Rosemarie Bodenheimer identifies in the early letters of Mary Ann Evans, "in which the life of plants figures the human potential for social evolution," make no appearance here.[13] The animal and plant analogies of *Adam Bede* trace resemblances only.

Consider by contrast the very early conversation in *The Mill on the Floss* between the miller and his wife, in which the two attempt to account for the unaccountable characteristics of their children by reference to family origins:

> "Tom hasn't got the right sort o' brains for a smart fellow. I doubt he's a bit slowish. He takes after your family, Bessy."
>
> "Yes, that he does," said Mrs. Tulliver, accepting the last proposition entirely on its own merits; "he's wonderful for liking a deal o' salt in his broth. That was my brother's way, and my father's before him."
>
> "It seems a bit of a pity, though," said Mr. Tulliver, "as the lad should take after the mother's side istead o' the little wench. That's the worst on't wi' the crossing o' breeds: you can never justly calkilate what'll come on't." (*MF* 11–12)

Leaving aside for the moment what the Tullivers say, let us note first the mere fact of their saying it. As against the silence of *Adam Bede* on this point, *The Mill on the Floss* inquires into the origins of character from the beginning: it introduces the lay language of family resemblances ("taking after") and the discourse of breeding in an effort to identify how these children come to be who they are—or appear to be. Alternately aided or ironized by the text, Dodsons and Tullivers chart likenesses and discover unexpected differences, gauge the success or failure of human efforts to select for outcomes, and generally grapple with this aspect of nature in all its puzzling complexity. This element of *The Mill on the Floss* not only marks a difference in how Eliot imagines the task, style, and generic valence of her second novel, it also functions as a crucial element of her historicism. That *Adam Bede,* published just a year earlier, poses few questions about the genesis of character indicates Eliot's conception of that historical moment as Keatsian cold pastoral; the emphasis of *The Mill on the Floss,* set about thirty years later and deeply concerned with generational and gendered sameness and difference, falls much more heavily on the mechanisms of change, deploying animal and plant analogies that are all about process.

The language of the cross generates that emphasis almost from the outset. Whether a deliberate strategy for inducing change or an accidental result of sexual contact between closely allied varieties, *intercrossing* functions as an agent of modification that operates over time to the benefit of the organism. "With animals and plants a cross between different varieties, or between individuals of the same variety but of another strain, gives vigour and fertility to the offspring," Darwin argued in *The Origin of Species* (1859), with that additional power bestowing an advantage on the crossed individuals within "the economy of nature": "If any one species does not become modified and improved in a corresponding degree with its competitors, it will soon be exterminated."[14] By contrast, the whole point of *interbreeding* is to select desirable traits and reproduce them in successive generations, as in the efforts of breeders to shape perfect progeny. From a Darwinian point of view, crosses are a crucial motor of change, but the attempt to establish particular traits as the direct outcome of (natural) inheritance or, in Mr. Tulliver's case, to control character by exercising (artificial) selection is faulty and limited. The narration of *The Mill on the Floss* thus remarks that nature, with "the deep cunning which hides itself under the appearance of openness," will refute the "confident prophecies" of "simple people": as Darwin writes in *The Origin of Species,* "the laws of inheritance are quite unknown: no one can say why the same peculiarity in different individuals of the same species, and in individuals of different species, is sometimes inherited, and sometimes not so" (*MF* 29; *OS* 76). The unpredictability in "the crossing o' breeds," which I examine in this section especially in relation to gender, poses decided obstacles to Tulliver's plans, as neither Maggie nor Tom breeds to specification.

In the tracing of family resemblances that dominates the early books of *The Mill on the Floss,* Tom appears more Dodson than Tulliver, Maggie more Tulliver than Dodson, with their mother and father perceiving them each according to her or his own needs and criteria. For example, Mrs. Tulliver considers her son's taste for salty broth as something on the order of an acquired characteristic, passed down to Tom from her male relatives. Notable as one of very few references in the entire book to Dodson men—among them the invocation of the dead brother whose unseen sons, Mrs. Glegg fervently hopes, "supported the Dodson name on the family land, far away in the Wolds"—it is also a relatively idiosyncratic attribution of Dodsonness, most often identified with the feminine possession of "particular ways" in "household management and social demeanour," an observation made by the sister who is "the merest epitome of the family habits and traditions" (*MF* 170, 38). Unable to identify her own daughter as visibly descended from her first family, Bessy is all the more eager to trace a relationship between her son and the Dodson men, "to have one child who took after her own family, at least in his features and complexion, in liking salt and in eating beans, which a Tulliver never did" (*MF* 38). With Tom initially appearing in the novel as "one of those lads that grow everywhere in England, and, at twelve or thirteen years of age, look as much alike as goslings," independent testimony from the good people of St. Ogg's subsequently supports the claim that he "takes after his mother's family" at sixteen (*MF* 29, 186). Yet in its immediate context, the attribution of resemblance says more about Mrs. Tulliver than it does about her son: Tom's display of characteristically male Dodson tastes becomes a convenient peg on which she hangs her "self-serving and self-revealing" desire for a child who confirms her place in her first family, as one of the sisters committed to the patronymic of which their marriages have legally, but not socially, deprived them.[15]

A pity, then, "as the lad should take after the mother's side istead o' the little wench": Mr. Tulliver concurs in his wife's ascription of Dodsonness to Tom, although he locates it in his paucity of "brains" rather than his partiality to broth or beans. Preoccupied with her daughter's difference from herself and gratified by finding a way to link Tom to her male kin, Bessy does not even notice the snub in her husband's words, which deplore the migration of his intelligence to a child of the opposite (and wrong) sex. But as in his wife's case, Mr. Tulliver's relationship to his first family certainly shapes his view of second-family likeness. With her daughter "inferior enough to Maggie in fire and strength of expression, to make the resemblance between the two entirely flattering to Mr. Tulliver's fatherly love," sister Gritty sees Lizzy Moss as her older cousin's double, with her brother remarking that "both take after our mother" (*MF* 69). Qualifying Jules Law's claim that all such talk is "pure postulation," others confirm the visible resemblances among Tulliver women ("Water" 57). Obviously implying that Maggie is heading for the same fate, the Dodson sisters decidedly make the connection: "It was agreed" that Maggie "was the picture of her aunt Moss, Mr. Tulliver's sister,—a large-boned woman, who had married as poorly as could be; had no china, and had a husband who had much ado to pay his rent" (*MF* 52).

As Tom follows in the Dodson male line, then, Maggie appears to follow the Tulliver females. Her likeness to his mother, sister, and niece does not so much gratify her father's vanity as revivify his fraternal piety: moved to contemplate his children's future by Gritty's reminder that "there's but two of 'em, like you and me, brother," Mr. Tulliver "was not long in seeing his relation to his own sister side by side with Tom's relation to Maggie. Would the little wench ever be poorly off," he wonders, "and Tom rather hard upon her?" (*MF* 69). Provoked by the structural parallel to consider the possibility that Tom could take after him in another sense, he consciously if inefficaciously aims to shape that future by patterning his current (in)action—not calling in the Mosses' debt—on how he would have his son act toward his daughter. Although Tulliver's connection to his first family is differently configured from his wife's, having a child who takes after "his people," specifically his closest female kin, similarly enables him to understand himself as linked to that past. As is the case for Eliot's contemporary creation Silas Marner, in whose imagination the "sleeping child" on his hearth recalls the "little sister whom he had carried about in his arms for a year before she died" and conveys "a message come to him from that far-off life," Tulliver's past returns to him embodied in female form.[16]

A child perceived as taking after you and yours, whether in looks, manners, or acts, confirms your connection to your first family and, perhaps, earns a special place in your heart: each Tulliver parent has a particular fondness for the opposite-sex child identified as belonging to their respective first families. And the implicit expectation among Tullivers and Dodsons is that a child should take after one family or the other, never both. Among the very few points on which Mr. Tulliver and Mrs. Glegg agree, for example, is that Maggie resembles the Tullivers in all respects: echoing an earlier claim to the same effect by Mr. Tulliver, Aunt Glegg says "there isn't a bit of our family in her" (*MF* 68, 178). To be sure, "there were some Dodsons less like the family than others—that was admitted"; even if Philip Wakem "takes after his mother in the face," "he's got his father's blood in him too" (*MF* 38, 133, 154). But for the most part, the older generation tends to regard the younger members of the family in dichotomous terms, as if each were only a Dodson or a Tulliver, rather than a blend of two lines; even when they do see mixture, as we shall see, they represent the meeting of the two "breeds" as a union of antitheses.

As should already be apparent, the other key expectation and desire that underlies such talk in the novel is that children ought to take after their same-sex parents. But if the resemblances they identify across gender difference please the Tullivers, then the differences that arise within gender sameness puzzle them. The "assumption that character is normatively inherited along lines of gender," as Law writes, is first ironized in the narrative's reference to Maggie as "this small mistake of nature" ("Water" 57; *MF* 12). More tellingly, the assumption of same-sex transmission has an important corollary: that the father's contribution to the makeup of his offspring of either sex should out-weigh that of the mother. Eliot may here be parodying the androcentric bias of "the consensus of breeders" at the time of the novel, that "the male par-ent dominated in shaping offspring": although Ritvo notes that "an absolute assertion of male dominance needed modification in view of the obvious tendency of young animals to resemble both their parents," animal husbandry experts "still reserved the more vigorous genetic role for the stud."[17]

George Henry Lewes, for one, contested the assumption of male pre-dominance in determining the character of offspring by reference to Buffon, where he found "the most decisive example we could quote of the twofold influence of parents." A she-wolf and a setter dog give birth to a male and female cub. The son looks like its dog-father; the daughter is like her wolf-mother: so far, so good. But "the cubs manifested a striking difference in disposition, in each case *resembling in character* the parent it did not *resemble in appearance* and in sex; thus the male cub, which had all the appearance of a dog, was fierce and untameable as the wolf; the female cub, which had all the appearance of a wolf, was familiar, gentle, and caressing even to impor-tunity." Regarding "these hybrids," Lewes concluded, "the wide differences in the aspect and nature of the parents enables us to separate, as it were, the influence of each."[18] In a similar key, Darwin's doctrine of "pangenesis," expounded in *The Descent of Man, and Selection in Relation to Sex* (1871), pos-ited that secondary sex characteristics "are present in both sexes," which only becomes apparent when two species intercross, "for each transmits the char-acters proper to its own male and female sex to the hybrid offspring of either sex."[19] Extrapolating from this to an admittedly different human context, the potential consequences for the "hybrid offspring" of the cross would be a sort of latent gender hybridity within all individuals, each bearing a doubly gendered potential.

Generally speaking, Darwin believed that "equal transmission of characters to both sexes is the commonest form of inheritance," although he added the qualifier that "characters are somewhat commonly transferred exclusively to that sex, in which they first appear" (*DM* 266). Mr. Tulliver has trusted largely to the latter, to a natural asymmetry of reproductive power, recount-ing to Mr. Riley the calculations that led him to choose Bessy as a mate:

> "It's the wonderful'st thing"—here he lowered his voice—"as I picked the mother because she wasn't o'er 'cute—bein' a good-looking woman too, an' come of a rare family for managing; but I picked her from her sisters o' purpose, 'cause she was a bit weak, like; for I wasn't agoin' to be told the rights o' things by my own fireside. But you see when a

man's got brains himself, there's no knowing where they'll run to; an'
a pleasant sort o' soft woman may go on breeding you stupid lads and
'cute wenches, till it's like as if the world was turned topsy-turvy. It's
an uncommon puzzlin' thing." (*MF* 18)

Having expected his traits to descend to sons and his wife's to daughters,
Mr. Tulliver retrospectively claims to have based his selection of Bessy from
the pool of available Dodson women on her good looks, her family's reputation "for managing," and her "soft" temperament and moderate intelligence, qualities that contrast strongly, he believes, with his own. Compare this
principle of complementarity with the alternative ground of likeness on
which Mr. Glegg picks "the eldest Miss Dodson as a handsome embodiment
of female prudence and thrift," since he was "himself of a money-getting,
money-keeping turn" (*MF* 102). In his effort to control outcomes—the
course of his marriage, the character of his children—through a deliberate
process of selection, Tulliver thus has assumed not only that sons would take
after fathers but also that his strength would surmount feminine weakness
in all aspects of the marriage; Bessy's "pleasant," stereotypically female soft-
ness inspired him with a confidence he could not have felt in marrying the
dictatorial Jane. If nature did indeed behave in human ways, then his genetic
contribution would always trump that of his wife.

In representing his selection of a mate who would produce offspring with
gender-appropriate qualities, the miller anticipates the spirit of Darwin's
views on sexual selection among humans. In a passage very near the end of
The Descent of Man, Darwin wondered at the disparity between the deliberation men exercise in mating their animals and the relative lack of concern
with which they decide on the women who would bear their children: "Man
scans with scrupulous care the character and pedigree of his horses, cattle, and
dogs before he matches them: but when he comes to his own marriage he
rarely, or never, takes any such care. He is impelled by nearly the same motives
as the lower animals, when they are left to their own free choice....Yet he
might by selection do something not only for the bodily constitution and
frame of his offspring, but for their intellectual and moral qualities" (*DM* 688).
That more men did not choose wives "with scrupulous care" had social and
political implications for all humankind, as he indicated earlier in *The Descent
of Man:* "A want of care, or care wrongly directed, leads to the degeneration
of a domestic race"; indeed, "no one who has attended to the breeding of
domestic animals will doubt that this must be highly injurious to the race of
man" (*DM* 159). In consciously, deliberately choosing a human mate (whom
he construes as) very different from himself, Tulliver thus partially adopts a

breeder's logic to forward his aims in a fashion that Darwin might condone, even if Tulliver does not select for the particular qualities that would enhance "the race of man" according to quasi-eugenicist values, even if scientist and miller alike are "profoundly ignorant of both the causes of variation and the precise means by which favorable variations were preserved and accumulated."[20] One may yet wonder, however, if Darwin's advocacy of more careful selection would mandate a man choosing a mate very much different from or very much like himself—or if, in spite of his monogenist stance, he would nonetheless have seen biological differences between strangers and near kin as meaningful. For in Darwin's model, most humans, whose "breeding has never long been controlled, either by methodical or unconscious selection," were already "hybrid offspring" of generation upon generation of crosses; their uniformity of character—itself a product of "natural selection preserving the favourable variations"—was what gave rise to the classification of humans as a breed or type (*DM* 46; *OS* 149).

Not coincidentally, the narrative, too, casts its human children as the hybrid progeny of a cross between stable types known as Tulliver and Dodson, at least in part. From the vantage point of Eliot's characters, each child is conceived as the product of a union between two distinctly marked varieties, while ostensibly sex-linked traits are unaccountably scrambled. And the language of categorical difference strikingly expresses the lay perception of this unpredictable mixture when Maggie's failure to take after her mother so perplexes Mrs. Tulliver that she voices her discomfiture at Maggie's departure from Dodsonness, in both looks and manners, by a racialized term. With the shining example of the well-behaved Lucy ever before her—a girl who "takes more after me nor my own child does" and is "more like *my* child than sister Deane's"—Bessy wonders how Maggie came to vary so much from the Dodson female norm while "the thinnest and sallowest of all the Miss Dodsons" had borne a fair, plump girl (*MF* 12, 37, 52). To put it in Darwinian terms, having placed her faith in the stability of the type and imagined herself a more strongly marked representative of it than Lucy's mother, Bessy simply cannot account for her daughter's difference from the Dodson norm: Maggie's dreamy ways make her appear "half an idiot i' some things," and "that niver run i' my family, thank God, no more nor a brown skin as makes her look like a mulatter" (*MF* 12).[21] It's unclear what, aside from the shade of Maggie's complexion, this might mean—perhaps nothing at all.[22] But in marking this difference between herself and her daughter, which follows from the distinction between Dodson mother and Tulliver father, Bessy's word helps to initiate another crucial strand of the discourse on animal and human reproduction, in which the messy metaphorics of mixture associated with intercrossing unsettle the self-regarding attributions of "taking after."

Early in the novel, we encounter something like a folk perspective on the dubious wisdom of breeding animals to select for a specific trait that serves no practical purpose. As Maggie belatedly inquires into the health of Tom's "lop-eared rabbits" starved to death by neglect, the head miller Luke "soothingly" claims that these artificially engineered creatures "happen ha' died, if they'd been fed," for "things out o' natur niver thrive: God A'mighty doesn't like 'em. He made the rabbits' ears to lie back, an' it's nothin' but contrairiness to make 'em hing down like a mastiff dog's" (*MF* 28). Invoking divine opposition to human interference, Luke targets an especially useless variation, one that might indeed disadvantage a rabbit, whose permanently perked-up ears presumably serve a protective function. Moreover, there's no place for such "nash things," either in the mill or "in that far tool-house, an' it was nobody's business to see to 'em," because they don't fit the working model of the enterprise (*MF* 28, 27). When next we hear of Tom (having resisted the doubtful attraction of ferrets) procuring an animal, we know that the "little black spaniel" that Bob Jakin secures as a gift for Lucy Deane (ten years and hundreds of pages later) will fare much better than those unnatural, unnourished bunnies (*MF* 316). Being not only "a rare bit o' breed" but also a true pet, committed to the care of a mistress who "was fond of feeding dependent creatures, and knew the private tastes of all the animals about the house," Lucy's purebred puppy has its designated place in the Deane household economy (*MF* 316, 299). That Tom has chosen such a pet for such a cousin—whom it would be most advantageous for him to marry and for whom the novel obliquely indicates he has a serious liking—shows how well he has come to understand the symbolic function of breeding.[23]

Although he is happy to oblige Tom, for his own part Bob prefers a mutt: "Mumps is as fine a cross as you'll see anywhere along the Floss," and he defends its mixed birth against all comers, advancing its superior claim to intelligence as against its lack of ornamental charms (*MF* 232). Arriving at the mill "followed closely by [this] bull-terrier of brindled coat and defiant aspect" (*MF* 230), Bob offers Maggie a puppy for company—"better friends nor any Christian"—adducing the virtues of the cross and also reversing the typical direction of analogical comparisons:

> There's a pup—if you didn't mind about it not being thoroughbred: its
> mother acts in the Punch show—an uncommon sensable bitch—she
> means more sense wi' her bark nor half the chaps can put into their

talk from breakfast to sundown. There's one chap carries pots,—a poor low trade as any on the road,—he says, "Why, Toby's nought but a mongrel—there's nought to look at in her." But I says to him, "Why, what are you yoursen but a mongrel? There wasn't much pickin' o' *your* feyther an' mother, to look at you." (*MF* 231, emphasis in original)[24]

Although Toby provides nothing much "to look at," she has more to say, "means more sense," than do most humans. Redeeming Toby from the potman's snobbish aspersions, Bob turns the tables to link dog to chap, identifying both as mixed-breed "mongrels" and, at least in the dog's case, none the worse for it. For the potman, with his "poor low trade," to prefer something "to look at" over something to listen to in a dog strikes Bob as a mistake. A decorative dog purely bred for the Deane drawing room is all well and good in its place, but a working dog that performs "in the Punch show" or travels with a packman or a potman is an altogether different thing. As against the pride of parentage and commitment to bloodline that privileges the pure over the mixed, Bob vindicates the cross and casts it as the implicit norm for ordinary human breeding as well. As a heterogeneous thing that Eliot's contemporaries were increasingly coming to understand as a figure for the English themselves—a people of hybrid stock, mixed in blood and character—a mongrel is an eminently useful creature whose very "vigour and fertility" ensures its ability not just to survive but also to propagate its mixed kind.[25]

The perspectives that Luke and Bob take on the animal world are partially compatible with Mr. Tulliver's attitude in that he, too, clearly aims to breed children for use—although a daughter's value is also partially measured, of course, by her being something "to look at." Persistently assessing Tom and Maggie's traits, or "points," according to the markets for professional labor and marriage, the son's dullness and the daughter's acuity don't measure up: Tom's father fears, for example, that Dodson "brains" alone will not make "a smart fellow." Projecting a future in which his son would attain professional status rather than take up a (Dodson) managerial position or a (Tulliver) small proprietorship, that Tom shows no aptitude for schooling (while Maggie does) threatens to frustrate Mr. Tulliver's best-laid plans. But having exerted control to the best of his ability, he only puzzles over the results, offering what remedies occur to him as practicable—a haircut for Maggie, a gentleman's education for Tom. Although he does not voice precisely the same sentiments as Luke, there is a comparable degree of resignation to the power of unknown forces and no further effort on his part to analyze what goes awry. It is the Dodson sisters, rather, who explicate these exasperating children by more direct reference to blood, reifying the perceived differences between Tulliver and Dodson, as in Bessy's representation of Maggie as a "mulatter." With Bob Jakin's preference for the mongrel very much a minority view, these characters introduce the racialized note in an largely negative mode: "Poor Bessy's children were Tullivers," "Tom, notwithstanding he had the Dodson complexion, was likely to be as 'contrary' as his father," and so on. In telling contrast with the favorable Deane-Dodson product, Bessy's children prove that "the Tulliver blood did not mix well with the Dodson blood" (*MF* 52).

Such comments clearly contribute to the aura of inevitability that many critics have taken as the fundamental meaning of heredity in the novel, solicited and supported by the representation of Tulliver and Dodson as opposed types, which provides a heuristic key for what George Levine has called "the inevitable development of [Maggie and Tom's] characters according to the pressures of heredity."[26] Expanding the Dodson analysis, Sally Shuttleworth attributes the careers of Maggie and Tom to a biological determinism as powerful as any flood in the claim that "the mixing of Tulliver and Dodson blood rendered Maggie"—but, seemingly, not Tom—"unfit for survival in her environment"; this recalls U. C. Knoepflmacher's assertion that "the outside forces affecting Maggie," "irrevocably determined" by her father's genes, "are withstood by her brother by virtue of his Dodson tenacity."[27] As Josephine McDonagh argues in more general terms, Eliot creates "a world in which natural forces are always determining, . . . exerting their ineluctable control over the form of human life"; "natural features are seen to behave like people, and people, by extension, like nature."[28] But we may wonder if we should so confidently identify this perspective with Eliot's own: Is the Dodson sisters' view really shared by the narrative voice? Is "nature" a highly reliable arbiter of human character in the novel, as irrevocable or ineluctable as the onward flow of the Floss? That the river is itself diverted for human ends implies just the opposite.

As Law argues, by reading a symbolic element of the novel like the river as a virtual "allegory of inexorability," we underestimate Eliot's interest in "circumstances which are genuinely, objectively uncertain" ("Water" 53, 60). Those who contend that it is the mixture of antagonistic qualities in the offspring of Tulliver-Dodson sex that constitutes the problem of the "nature" of Tom and especially Maggie accord a kind of certainty to scientific and lay perceptions about reproduction that the novel—conceived and written at a moment when those perceptions were very much in flux—does not. *The Mill on the Floss* is not "a story about the power of biological inheritance to overcome the individual will," as Deborah Epstein Nord has characterized

The Spanish Gypsy (1868), and Maggie's character and destiny cannot be solely the outcome or result of what Eliot called, in describing the origins of that text, "an inherited organization."[29] Although Law's central example for illustrating "the unexpectedness of endings and the unpredictability of consequences" centers on Mr. Tulliver's lawsuit against Pivart over water rights, we have already seen that the emphasis on the unexpected and unforeseeable is very much present, too, in the discourses of breeding and crossing ("Water" 64). These prove to be, as Susan Meyer recognizes, "an endless preoccupation in this novel," perhaps because they are so closely allied to the discourses of racial/national/ethnic character formation, which constitute a critical element in both Eliot's and Lewes's thinking on heredity.[30] The notion of failed mixture—not only the default Dodson position but also a mainstay of contemporary racial science—undergoes a good bit of transformation in the narrative's accounting for these hybrid children.

In the context in which Eliot wrote, Mrs. Tulliver's use of the term "mulatter" implies hybridity and sterility, with which racial mixture is frequently associated in contemporary discourses of reproduction.[31] One dominant view of the times is that blood that does not "mix well"—or that achieves what Alfred Henry Huth called "a mixture without a blending"—indicates a failure of "fusion" among incompatible elements.[32] And though Darwin did not consider "the races of men... sufficiently distinct to inhabit the same country without fusion," the failure to mix or blend "affords the usual and best test of specific distinctness" among animals (*DM* 202). Under the emergent term *miscegenation,* however, which did posit that polygenist "distinctness" between (or even among) Europeans and others, the crossing of widely separated "breeds" or "races" was purported to "produce mediocrity and reversion to a primitive and unimproved type," resulting in decreased fertility and degenerate offspring.[33] While "the accumulation of well-attested examples of fertile interspecific hybrids undermined the essentialist position," since it provided proof of fertility across putative borders, Robert J. C. Young proposes that "the claim of degeneration," which could only be judged true or false over time by close observation of offspring, constituted "the final, and undoubtedly the most powerful, retort to any apparent demonstration of the fertility of mixed unions."[34]

From another perspective, a miscegenous union could have outcomes that might be understood in Eurocentric terms as positive: in advancing the lesser group, Darwin surmised, "a cross with civilised races at once gives to an aboriginal race an immunity from the evil consequences of changed conditions," conditions no doubt forcibly "changed" through the impact of

European colonial and imperial expansion (*DM* 221). But considering only the impact on the dominant culture, the price exacted for mixing would be degeneration: the very virtues of vigor and fertility that Darwin attributes to the cross in plants and animals are those reproductive qualities that it allegedly most imperiled among "civilised" humans who mixed with "an aboriginal race."[35] So "a lively debate was generated by the question of whether racial mixing brings down civilization"—in what Werner Sollors terms "the familiar racialist position"—"or stimulates and invigorates cultural activity."[36] What is not under dispute in this debate is that crossing leads to change, whether perceived as degeneration or development, and thus functions as a motor of history—even if, in the very long run of reproductive history, the crossing of closely related varieties leads to the production of a stable type.

Relying on both Auguste Comte and Herbert Spencer for his analysis, Lewes's review of contemporary books on human and animal breeding—which appeared in the very same number of the *Westminster Review* as "The Natural History of German Life" (1856), Marian Lewes's important article on the sociological writing of W. H. Riehl—attributes to intercrossing among humans the power of making change but focuses especially on the power of interbreeding to arrest it. He argues that "a whole dynasty of blockheads would never produce a man of genius by intermarriage with blockheads"; a union with a member of another group "must introduce 'new blood' " in order for "the man of genius" to issue from it, because "the variation must have its cause."[37] Along with other theorists of heredity, Lewes categorizes "blockheads" as a "fixed type," unalterable after a long history of interbreeding: an outcome of too little intercourse with others over too a long period of time, blockheadedness—or "hereditary genius," as Darwin's cousin Francis Galton would argue in the book of that name, published in 1869—becomes a trait passed down from parent to child. In positing both that variation requires the introduction of a new strain and that "we inherit the acquired experience of our forefathers—their tendencies, their aptitudes, their habits," Lewes fixed the boundaries of the type.[38]

All this leads to a theory of national/ethnic/racial character as "the acquired experience of our forefathers" writ large, produced at the rhetorical expense of those people civilized races should avoid. Lewes's discussion of the "Moral Sense" provides a partial key to his thinking here. Following Comte, he asserted that in the "slow subjection of the egotistic to the sympathetic impulses" lies the path of "the development of the Human Family," as of the individual, for "what is organically acquired becomes organically transmitted." Thus among "lesser" people—"Australians," "Hindoos," and "Papuans"—"the *sympathetic* emotions are quite rudimentary," because such savages "have not acquired" them from earlier generations.[39] Lewes characterizes the "Moral Sense" as "the aptitude to be affected by actions in their moral bearings," and asserts that "this aptitude to be so affected is a part and parcel of the heritage transmitted from forefathers." If we assume constant interbreeding within a given population, then those whose progenitors lack the "Moral Sense" cannot possibly inherit (or perhaps even develop) it; conversely, "just as the puppy pointer has inherited an aptitude to 'point'... so also has the European boy inherited an aptitude for a certain moral life, which to the Papuan would be impossible." Announcing that "heritage, for the first time, is made the basis of a psychological system," Lewes quotes approvingly to that effect from Spencer's *Principles of Psychology* (1855): "A modified form of constitution, produced by new habits of life, is bequeathed to future generations"; "the modified nervous tendencies produced by such new habits of life are also bequeathed; and if the new habits of life become permanent, the tendencies become permanent." In other words, once "the transmitted organization" of a people has been fixed as national, racial, or ethnic character, Lewes asserts, no individual representative of that people "altogether merges his original peculiarities in that of the people among whom he dwells."[40] Turning from savages elsewhere to aliens and animals at home, he concludes that it "is little more remarkable" that "the Jew should preserve his Judaic character while living among Austrians or English... than that the Englishman should preserve his Anglo-Saxon type while living among oxen and sheep": for so long as there is no intercourse between separate types, "no important change in the race can take place."[41]

At the very end of her career, George Eliot argued in the essay entitled "The Modern Hep! Hep! Hep!" (1879) that a distinctively English national identity could be endangered by "a premature fusion with immigrants of alien blood," for "the tendency of things is towards the quicker or slower fusion of races."[42] Although that analysis differed from Lewes's much earlier one, she, too, sounded the Comtean note regarding the "Moral Sense," asserting that "all we can do is to moderate [the tendency] so as to hinder it from degrading the moral status of societies by a too rapid effacement of those national traditions and customs which are the language of the national genius."[43] She suggested, in other words, that Lewes's confident positing of the fixed type might be undermined by "the tendency" to fusion, attributing to "immigrants of alien blood" the power to alter and degrade the character of their host by eroding its "traditions and customs."[44] Crossing with "others" might lead to cultural degeneration of "the national genius." And yet before her literary career had even begun, Mary Ann Evans had advanced the claim that a *lack* of intercrossing among humans would pose the same threat: "The law by which privileged classes degenerate from continued intermarriage must act on a larger scale in deteriorating whole races."[45] Other writers echoed this perception. In a passage from the unpublished essay "Cassandra," Florence Nightingale both considered cousin-marriage "the only natural thing" and pronounced it "in direct contravention of the laws of nature for the well-being of the race," citing the examples of "the Quakers, the Spanish grandees, the royal races, the secluded valleys of mountainous countries" as reproductive sites at which "madness, degeneration of race, defective organization and cretinism flourish and multiply."[46] Her tone and tenor recalls what Tom Paine had to say on the subject a good fifty years earlier: "Aristocracy has a tendency to degenerate the human species. By the universal economy of nature it is known, and by the instance of the Jews it is proved, that the human species has a tendency to degenerate, in any small number of persons, when separated from the general stock of society, and intermarrying constantly with each other."[47] Breeding out or breeding in may well lead to the same end.

When they published these essays in the *Westminster,* the Leweses were less concerned with the possibilities of cross-racial fusion—a central trope of *Daniel Deronda* (1876)—than with the historical production through "continued intermarriage" of the *type,* a term that "came into widespread use in the 1850s" and "brought together the implications of both species and race."[48] In her account of the persistence of the type in "The Natural History of German Life," which closely parallels his essay in its emphasis on the agency of interbreeding, we can grasp the emergent racial basis for George Eliot's historical vision. Drawing on her observations of such objects as artworks and peasants during her travels in Germany two years earlier, Marian Lewes related a story in which the fixed type that results from "continued intermarriage" is everywhere apparent:

> In one part of the country we find a longer-legged, in another a broader-shouldered race, which has inherited these peculiarities for centuries. For example, in certain districts of Hesse are seen long faces, with high foreheads, long, straight noses, and small eyes with arched eyebrows and large eyelids. On comparing these physiognomies with the sculptures in the church of St. Elizabeth, at Marburg, executed in the thirteenth century, it will be found that the same old Hessian type of face has subsisted unchanged, with this distinction only, that the sculptures represent princes and nobles, whose features then bore the stamp of their race, while that stamp is now to be found only among the peasants. A painter who wants to draw medieval characters with historic truth,

must seek his models among the peasantry. This explains why the old German painters gave the heads of their subjects a greater uniformity of type than the painters of our day: the race had not attained to a high degree of individualization in features and expression. It indicates, too, that the cultured man acts more as an individual; the peasant, more as one of a group. . . . [M]any thousands of men are as like each other in thoughts and habits as so many sheep or oysters.[49]

To identify physical "peculiarities" among members of a group as "inherited" traits is clearly to assume that no modifying influence—or "new blood"—has intervened to shorten Bavarian legs or narrow Prussian shoulders: reproductive sexual relations within a single, separate cohort (like Lewes's blockheads or Galton's geniuses) rather than between different ones has been the historical norm. So, too, does "the same old Hessian face," at least six hundred years in the making, persist "unchanged": echoing Disraeli's *Coningsby* (1844) as well as anticipating Hardy's *Tess of the d'Urbervilles* (1891), Marian Lewes reported that it was peasants rather than princes who now possessed it.[50] Whether this physiognomic survival derives from the degeneration of a once-privileged class through "continued intermarriage" or from an incomplete conquest that did not "amalgamate" the blood of conquerors and conquered, she did not (and probably knew she could not) say. But the outcome is clear: peasants were providing for artists a visible, physical record of a "historic truth" that could only have been preserved in the absence of intercrossing or in the Hessian failure to fuse with different ethnic/racial groups.

Those thirteenth-century artworks also present another ideological truth, aesthetically expressed. As their makers represent "a greater uniformity of type than the painters of our day," they demonstrate that "a high degree of individualization" is the product of a process, an outcome rather than a cause of historical change. "The race had not attained" that "high degree" because of its lack of traffic with others, because it had remained stable and stationary; even what Spencer called "nervous tendencies," and not simply physical traits like broad shoulders, can only become the permanent heritable property of a more highly organized race that in its intercourse with others has increased the capacities of its stock. The essay thus demonstrates, as Catherine Gallagher argues in a slightly different vein, "a consequentialist materialism in delineating consciousness, which tended to exclude the appearance of high levels of moral sensibility among people at low levels of social progress."[51] Here, too, then, can we see "heritage" becoming "the basis of a psychological system" in which intercrossing results in complex offspring. Individuality thus marks "the cultured man" rather than members of a group who are as alike "as so many sheep or oysters" and as distinct from the members of other groups as "oxen" are from "sheep"—and, by implication, as Jews from Anglo-Saxons. Where "uniformity of type" prevails, there "individualization" is not: to make the individual, as Darwin will agree, requires something on the order of a cross. And in this context, Mrs. Tulliver's reference to her daughter as a "mulatter" suggests that Maggie's individuality—her high level of moral sensibility compared to the "emmet-like Dodsons and Tullivers" from whom she springs—derives from her own diversified lineage (*MF* 222).

In marginally annotating a series of essays by Walter Bagehot that appeared in the *Fortnightly Review* in 1868 and were later published under the title *Physics and Politics,* Darwin crystallized a view implicit in much of his own work, linking increasing heterogeneity to mobility and migration: "nations which *wander* & cross would be most likely to vary."[52] Whether one group dominates and the other capitulates, or the two meet on more friendly terms, contact with others creates the possibility for reproductive sex, and reproductive sex is a key agent of variation. By this logic, an already mixed parent crossed with another mixed parent will produce progeny ever more mixed: unlike the Hessians that Marian Lewes analyzed, whose failure to roam insures they will remain a stable racial type, those who travel (and presumably conquer, in an imperial framework) alter the stock of potentially inheritable traits for their progeny. As we have already seen, particular groups are typically singled out for *not* mixing with others: for sundry reasons, savages and peasants, Jews and aristocrats—like oxen, oysters, and sheep—are all alleged to keep to themselves and so are routinely alleged either to commit incest or to be committed to class/race endogamy. And we have seen as well that different shades of opinion on the desirability of mixing imply comparably different attitudes about what would advance or injure the health and progress of any race, species, or breed. That Darwin's stand on these issues underwent some variation of its own during the period between the publication of *The Origin of Species* and *The Descent of Man* helps to elucidate the broader cultural tensions evoked by either promoting or prohibiting mixture, even as it also sheds light on Eliot's similarly complex, changing views.

In 1862, the erstwhile botanist concluded a long treatise with a long title, *On the Various Contrivances by which British and Foreign Orchids are Fertilised by Insects, and on the Good Effects of Intercrossing,* that proved the preeminence of cross-fertilization among certain orchids by inviting his readers to join him in an imaginative leap. Given the ease with which an orchid possessed of both stamen and pistil might always have fertilized itself, Darwin yet observed that it does not and extrapolated a speculative inference from that "astonishing fact" in his very last sentences:

> That self-fertilisation should not have been an habitual occurrence. . . . apparently demonstrates to us that there must be something injurious in the process. Nature thus tells us, in the most emphatic manner, that she abhors perpetual self-fertilisation. This conclusion seems to be of high importance. . . . For may we not further infer as probable, in accordance with the belief of the vast majority of the breeders of our domestic productions, that marriage between near relations is likewise in some way injurious,—that some unknown great good is derived from the union of individuals which have been kept distinct for many generations?[53]

Having inferred the value of the cross from his own observations and the reports of others, he reiterated a few years later, in *The Variation of Animals and Plants under Domestication* (1868), that "the existence of a great law of nature is almost proved; namely, that the crossing of animals and plants which are not closely related to each other is highly beneficial or even necessary, and that interbreeding prolonged during many generations is highly injurious."[54] Within the next decade, however, Darwin had backed away from his own conclusions: he removed the final sentence quoted above from the 1877 edition of the orchid treatise, hence abandoning the prospect of the "unknown great good" to be attributed to intercrossing, and deleted the "highly" that modified "injurious" from the *Variation*'s second edition in 1875.[55] Without disowning his position on intercrossing, Darwin thereby partially retracted the conclusion that interbreeding—or, by his own analogy, "marriage between near relations"—was dangerous.

If the analogical leap from orchids to humans is itself somewhat "astonishing," then the revisionism is perhaps only slightly less so. Both Nancy F. Anderson and Martin Ottenheimer surmise that Darwin was influenced in the early 1870s by the researches of his son George, who undertook a study of first-cousin marriage using the statistical tools developed by Galton.[56] Published in the *Journal of the Statistical Society* in 1875, the younger Darwin's study concludes that "the practice might be quite all right for the rich but bad for the poor," a finding that may have given his father some comfort even if, as I argued in chapter 1, it inspired anxiety in those who surveilled the urban poor, whose sexual habits increasingly preoccupied social reformers.[57] George Darwin began his essay by referring to the efforts of Sir John Lubbock—anthropologist, animal breeder, and Member of Parliament, whose writings are frequently cited throughout *The Descent of Man*—to insert a question about first-cousin marriage in the Census Act of 1871, which was rejected by a 2–1 margin "amidst the scornful laughter of the House."[58] What Darwin *fils* did not say is that it was Darwin *père,* eager to locate and assemble empirical evidence on which he could reconsider his own findings, who had asked his neighbor Lubbock to advocate the question's inclusion.[59] The census would give Darwin information on the scale, of the kind, and in the format he wanted so that he could give human breeding the close scrutiny that his own numerous observations of and worldwide correspondence concerning the reproductive history of ducks, vines, pigeons, and other domesticated fauna and flora enabled. Just after that motion was defeated, he wrote somewhat bitterly in *The Descent of Man* that "when the principles of breeding and inheritance are better understood, we shall not hear ignorant members of our legislature rejecting with scorn a plan for ascertaining whether or not consanguineous marriages are injurious to man" (*DM* 688).[60]

However much Darwin later qualified his views on the perils of interbreeding, his pointed and no doubt strategically placed remarks in *Orchids* had an immediate impact. Jonathan Smith has established that as early as 1862, "Darwin's botany...entered an ongoing debate, primarily involving agriculturalists but increasingly concerned with humans, about the effects of in-breeding"; the widely read and cited *Orchids,* little known today, "was almost immediately absorbed into discussions about whether or not cousin marriages...should be outlawed on the grounds that the children of such unions were disproportionately inferior both physically and mentally."[61] As I have suggested in earlier chapters, numerous critics of the MDWS ban had long pointed to "the incongruity of forbidding marriages of affinity while allowing unions between close blood relatives."[62] The emergent concern about cousin-marriage focused not on the degree of relationship between partners to the union, however, but on the risk to its potential offspring. It is the quality and character, the mental and physical health, of the children who populate the second family that commanded attention, with the increasing biologization of all families providing the specific impetus for concern. Disputing their purported evils, one contemporary writer listed the "effects in the human subject which consanguineous marriages are alleged to produce": they include "deaf-mutism, idiocy, albinism, defective vision, scrofula, consumption, epilepsy, and spasmodic disease."[63] Darwin's own union with Emma Wedgwood, who bore ten children, eight of whom lived to adulthood, was one of four first-cousin marriages in their generation of Darwins and Wedgwoods. Recent biographers suggest that he attributed the early deaths of some, and general ill-health of most of the rest, to hereditary factors: "His own constitutional weakness had been passed on, accentuated by Emma's Wedgwood blood."[64] If Darwin indeed came to feel that inherited disorders would haunt the offspring of closely related mates, then crossing distinct breeds or stocks would introduce a necessary, salutary difference. While his anxieties were not purely personal, in the immediate circumstances of his own reproductive practices, he found some strong reasons to wonder about the value of the cross.

That interbreeding would lead directly to degeneration of the species over time was the conclusion that critics of Darwin's original position sought to counter. Published in the *Westminster Review* in 1863, an article by G. W. Child, a doctor, entitled "Marriages of Consanguinity" locates Darwin's *Orchids* in the context of works by French medical researchers who claimed to have identified the evil effects of cousin-marriages on their progeny, with the inclusion of Darwin's botanical volume in a review otherwise concerned with human reproduction indicating that the analogy of plant to human had struck a chord—or, perhaps, hit a nerve. Child took issue with the reduction of a complex process to a single chain of cause and effect: "as the antecedents upon which the condition of any offspring depends are...extremely complicated,...nothing less than a very large and very unequivocal experience can justify us in asserting that, in a particular case, this, that, or the other phenomenon in the offspring is the result of this, that, or the other individual antecedent in the parents."[65] He stringently limited the scope of such claims: that "the marriages of blood relations are more likely, *cæteris paribus,* to produce unhealthy offspring than others where no hereditary taint exists," this he granted; that the offspring of two people "related in blood, even at so distant a degree as that of second cousins...will, as a rule, be degenerate" was another matter entirely ("Marriages" 42). Moreover, Child rejected the argument from analogy that what is true among animals bred in-and-in will also be true for humans. Here he uses the celebrated example of a closely interbred bull: "Even if it were established that such breeding as that from which 'Comet' was descended had invariably led to degeneracy and disease, we should not be thereby warranted in arguing from it that an occasional marriage of cousins among mankind have [*sic*] even the slightest tendency to produce similar results" ("Marriages" 44). Darwin's own "inference," he argued, "is drawn not from the rule but from the exception": "The difference of degree between the cases is so great as to destroy all analogy between them, and render the reasoning which might be sound in the one case totally inapplicable to the other" ("Marriages" 47, 48).

Darwin, of course, had made his inferences based not solely on his study of orchids but on a whole host of experiments and practical demonstrations—which led to predictably mixed conclusions. On the one hand, observations of plant and animal life indicated that interbreeding led to "loss of constitutional vigour, size, and fertility" (*VAP* II, 143); on the other, he considered it "a fact of some importance" that "certain domestic races seem to prefer breeding with their own kind" (*VAP* II, 102). A range of other commentators argued that the effects of interbreeding among humans, by analogy with other species, would be largely positive. Since the eighteenth century, animal breeders had learned that the surest way to guarantee the desired results was by "persistent inbreeding," which Ritvo further describes as "the quickest method of fixing desirable characteristics and getting them to breed true"; "so satisfactory were the results," she reports, "that they were repeatedly urged as justification for similarly hygienic practices among people—at least marriages between first cousins, if not between members of the same nuclear family—so long as 'the parties' were not 'both predisposed to the same disease.'"[66] For decades, "in-and-in breeding lacked either a political or a religious charge" in animal and vegetable contexts, and so drew no fire; "crossing within a restricted lineage of animals selected for desirable characteristics was simply an effective technique for increasing control over the quality of the next generation."[67] The "close interbreeding" of animals and plants conducted by fanciers and gardeners was far closer than anything one would find among humans; moreover, such practices were, from one perspective, radically distinct from what were taken to be the operations of nature itself. "In-and-in breeding is perfectly well known to have a tendency to fix the type so that it never changes," a desirable end for breeders and fanciers, but precisely the problem for Darwin, in that unchanging, fixed types would ultimately be doomed to extinction.[68]

Thus the question of whether animals "naturally" inclined toward mating with close relatives or were somehow impelled to look further afield for their sexual partners took on specific importance. Lacking reliable human evidence, observations of "the higher anthropomorphous apes" might do, for Darwin claims—against the contrary argument of McLennan—"whatever conclusion we arrive at in regard to the higher animals may be safely extended to man" (*VAP* I, 124).[69] Citing the anthropologist E. B. Tylor's *Early History of Man* (1865) on "the almost universal prohibition of closely-related marriages" in the first edition of the *Variation,* Darwin went looking for a comparable taboo among apes and gorillas. He wondered if, among primates, "any inherited instinctive feeling, from being beneficial, has been generated, leading the young males and females of the same family to prefer pairing with distinct families, and to dislike pairing with each other"—if, in other words, nature works to encourage intercrossing by instilling an instinct for "exogamous" relations because such unions have evolutionary advantages for their offspring (*VAP* I, 123). If such a feeling were discernible, there would then be "no need to suppose that the incest taboo had been deliberately enacted," for "natural selection would have done its work" by inspiring animals—including human ones—to breed out for evolutionary ends.[70]

Darwin posited, then, that sex between those "not of the same family" would require some additional inducement; even a "slight feeling, arising from the sexual excitement of novelty" and impelling apes to look elsewhere for partners, "would be augmented through natural selection, and thus might become instinctive" (*VAP* I, 123). That is, while he declared that "the almost universal practice of all races at all times of avoiding closely-related marriages is an argument of considerable weight" even as he explicitly rejects "the belief... that the abhorrence of incest is due to our possessing a special God-implanted conscience," Darwin imagined that, in the general course of things, interbreeding had to be forcibly supplanted by intercrossing—not because it was wrong or bad or dangerous or violated human and divine law but because it did not advance the strength and vigor of individuals or the race (*VAP* I, 124; *DM* 139). That preference among "certain domestic races" for "breeding with their own kind" notwithstanding, apes—and, by implication, humans—would in selecting mates have to be motivated to choose outside their families, impelled not just by "the sexual excitement of novelty" but by the invisible hand of natural selection, which implants an instinct for mixing with others where once there was, perhaps, only desire for those closer to home.

Aiming to identify a mechanism that would promote intercrossing even as he articulated a rationale and observed discrete preferences for interbreeding, Darwin consistently held to the position Beer describes: that whereas "man breeds plants and animals to serve *man's* ends"—a redder rose, a faster thoroughbred—"natural processes breed always for the good of the individuals of the race concerned."[71] If interbreeding among apes or humans were indeed deleterious to species survival, the real proof of that danger would evince itself negatively, in the gradual disappearance of the practice rather than in documented cases of the sort that a census would provide. Its persistence, by contrast, would indicate either that interbreeding was not so counter to nature's ways after all or that the interbred—among whom, perhaps, the desire for one's own kind was stronger than the thrill of "novelty"—would eventually die out. Since from the point of view of the health and survival of the species, the cross was advantageous, natural selection had to be as active a shaper as any cattle-breeder, even if nature worked to encourage "exogamous" mixture rather than to promote "endogamous" purity. So, too, could humans exercise a like discretion and discrimination in making reproductive choices, even lacking a thorough knowledge of the laws of inheritance. If the biological advantages of marrying out were in Darwin's view indisputable, then any preference for marrying in—a preference that he, like many of his contemporaries, had indulged—would have to be justified on alternative grounds.

While Dodsons and Tullivers sharply distinguish themselves from one another, they by no means qualify in the nineteenth century's racialist terms as widely separated types whose crossing issues in degenerate offspring. In the narrative's overarching framework, they are much more alike than not. Even to cast the one family as "the forces of convention uncomprehended and rigidified" and the other as "the forces of blind spontaneity of feeling" overly polarizes them, since both subscribe to many of the same fundamental notions, attitudes, and practices.[72] In the famous opening chapter of the fourth book, "The Valley of Humiliation," the narrative does attribute some particular "family traditions" to Dodsons alone after summing up what they have in common with Tullivers, who share the "conventional worldly notions and habits without instruction and without polish" that the critic E. S. Dallas termed "a purely bestial life of vulgar respectability" (MF 222).[73] Only Dodsons are specifically identified, that is, with "the thorough scouring of wooden and copper utensils, the hoarding of coins likely to disappear from the currency, the production of first-rate commodities for the market, and the general preference for whatever was home-made," habits of "faithfulness to kindred, industry, rigid honesty, thrift" that have been passed on from one generation to the next (MF 223). Here, however, and by analogical sleight of hand, the narrative introduces a biogenetic note, assimilating the handing down of customs to the mysteries of hereditary transmission: "The same sort of traditional belief ran in the Tulliver veins, but it was carried in richer blood, having elements of generous imprudence, warm affection, and hot-tempered rashness" (MF 224).[74] As if by means of heredity, Dodsons and Tullivers, too, pass on "the same sort of traditional belief," with the "richer blood" of the latter providing a more intense medium than that of the former.

"Blood" here and elsewhere in the novel's discourse functions as metaphorical shorthand that conflates, perhaps deliberately, biological and social transmission. Such a formulation might indeed reflect what George W. Stocking Jr. characterizes as the "implicit biological rationale in the Lamarckian (and Spencerian) assumption of the inheritance of acquired characteristics, which...provided a mechanism by which habitual behavior became instinctive, and cultural inheritance became part of biological heredity."[75] We might also say, however, that like Darwin, Eliot sought to show how it was that "habitual behavior" did *not* become "instinctive," why some stray from the fold and diverge from their parents: in considering natural selection as a mechanism for deterring anthropomorphous apes from their preference for interbreeding and positing mixture as prerequisite for the development of the species and the individual, Darwin aimed, in a sense, to answer the very question that Eliot, too, pursued.

The frequent invocation of the power of "blood" in *The Mill on the Floss* never features, either within the narratorial commentary or among the younger set, as a means of explicating what come instead to be called Tom and Maggie's "natures." If the narration represents Dodson and Tulliver "blood" as differing in degree rather than kind, then it also takes great pains to establish that their children differ from the older generation (and also from each other) in other ways, not according to the criteria that parents and aunts employ to measure resemblance but by virtue of something that it casts as historical necessity. Telling Emily Davies some years after the publication of *The Mill on the Floss* that her "sole purpose in writing it was to show the conflict which is going on everywhere when the younger generation with its higher culture comes into collision with the older," Eliot made the ideological move that Daniel Cottom has identified as pervading all her fiction: via "the characterization of representation of any sort as a symbolic entrance into the universal," Tom and Maggie are made to stand in for "the younger generation."[76]

The passage from the novel that most closely articulates this stance also appears in the opening chapter of the fourth book. Here the narrative juxtaposes the "ruined villages" on the Rhone, which figure collectively as "the sign of a sordid life," with "those ruins on the castled Rhine" that "belong to the grand historic life of humanity" and convey "a sense of poetry" (*MF* 221–22). The "narrow, ugly, grovelling existence" on the Rhone, as on the Floss, lacks even "the poetry of peasant life"; "the mental condition of these emmet-like Dodsons and Tullivers" weighs upon both the text and its imagined audience as an "oppressive narrowness" (*MF* 222). We must be made to feel it, too, "if we care to understand how it acted on the lives of Tom and Maggie—how it has acted on young natures in many generations, that in the onward tendency of human things have risen above the mental level of the generation before them" (*MF* 222). From Tom and Maggie to you and me, the narrator suggests to her contemporaries, is not so great a leap, perhaps less than the distance between them and their parents, as this conflict between parents and children also repeats itself "in many generations" and is "going on everywhere." This is perhaps the paradigmatic instance of the rhetorical pattern that Bodenheimer identifies in Eliot's novels, in which we overhear the narrative voice "telling the imaginary reader that he

is thinking something that an actual reader has most likely had little inclination to think"; the "assumption of shared experience," in Cottom's phrase,
underlies the universalizing appeal to readers "everywhere."[77]

In another ideological precept masquerading as a general truth, the narrative attributes Tom and Maggie's rise "above the mental level of the generation before them" to "the onward tendency of human things." Echoing
as it does the single most important metaphor of the novel, the phrase constructs an analogical relationship between a force of nature, like the river, and
the progressive course of "human things." Here we may again be inclined
to interpret the river as an "allegory of inexorability": the Floss rolls on,
bearing Tom and Maggie along with it, lifting them above the insect intelligence of their birth family only to consign them to the watery deeps. That
"onward tendency" may be identified as an instance of Eliot's commitment
to the philosophical schema of historical development that underpins her
representation of St. Ogg's as "a society which has not yet moved beyond the
egoism of man's animal beginnings to the sympathy and benevolence which
Feuerbach and Comte believed would grow out of egoism."[78] But we might
also say that it makes itself most dramatically felt, as in the essay on Riehl, as
a movement from the "uniformity of type" demonstrated by Dodsons and
Tullivers to the "high degree of individualization" exhibited by their offspring. For where their parents see and speak about conflicts of blood, these
new "young natures," with their "higher culture," experience inter- and
intragenerational conflict in terms provided by the emergent psychological
discourse that both George Henry and Marian Lewes located in Spencer, as
when Maggie tells Tom, "our natures are very different. You don't know how
differently things affect me from what they do you" (*MF* 318). These terms
also echo in the comments of an anonymous contemporary reviewer who
asserted that the novel reveals "not alone the inner workings of two very different natures, but the effect the two natures have upon one another."[79] The
conflict between Dodson and Tulliver "blood," I suggest, is transferred to an
interior psychological terrain, the higher "mental level," on which both Tom
and Maggie live, struggle, and die.

As distinct as these generationally marked discourses may appear, then, the
novel and its narrative voice mystify a fundamental continuity between them.
The experiments in breeding and crossing in which the older generation
indulge may not establish the precise new variations they aim to bring
about, but they are effectively transmuted into another, "higher" idiom. The
increasing individuation of the younger generation produces, in Tom's case,
"a nature in which family feeling had lost the character of clanship by taking
on a doubly deep dye of personal pride" and, in Maggie's, the internal conflict

that keeps her perpetually at war "against formidable, never permanently conquerable 'savages'" within her own psyche (*MF* 404).[80] That both Maggie and Tom ultimately function as types of the modern individual—the divided feminine self, the man of maxims—suggests the continuing if muted power of the racialized discourses of reproduction that *The Mill on the Floss* deploys in its effort to distinguish nature's role in making individual natures.

❧ CHAPTER 6

Fictive Kinship and Natural Affinities in *Wives and Daughters*

> The Cinderella story warns little girls that it is
> dangerous to be left alone with a widowed father, for
> a widowed father must remarry, and the daughter's
> fate depends upon his choice of a wife. In some
> variants of the tale, the daughter suffers because the
> father replaces her mother with a cruel stepmother. In
> others, the daughter suffers because the father wishes
> to marry her himself.
>
> —Judith Lewis Herman, with Lisa Hirschman,
>   *Father-Daughter Incest,* 1981

Of the three families in the foreground of Elizabeth Gaskell's *Wives and Daughters,* only one is constructed through the discourse of breeding and heredity that pervades the early books of *The Mill on the Floss,* set at the same historical moment but within a distinctly different provincial milieu. In representing the Hamleys, Gaskell devotes specific attention to intergenerational family resemblances and divergences in a way that recalls, but does not exactly repeat, Eliot's text. Parents of different socio-economic backgrounds—the daughter of a London merchant and the only son of "a very old family, if not aborigines"—produce two boys.[1] "Osborne, the eldest—so called after his mother's maiden name"—is to be the sole heir to the estate; he "was full of tastes, and had some talent. His appearance had all the grace and refinement of his mother's"; as a boy, he was "almost as demonstrative as a girl" (*WD* 43). "He takes after madam's side," his father asserts, "who . . . can't tell who was their grandfather" (*WD* 74). Roger, the younger, who will have to make his own way, is "clumsy and heavily built, like his father," and appeared as a child "little likely to distinguish himself in intellectual pursuits" (*WD* 43). "Roger is like me," says the squire, "a Hamley of Hamley, and no one who sees him in the street will ever think that red-brown, big-boned, clumsy chap is of gentle blood" (*WD* 74). On the face of it, then, the elder son follows the mother; the younger "takes after" the father. If Osborne's association with poetry and sentiment further feminizes him, then the rugged Roger's manliness is also written on the body: the elder dies, the younger thrives.

Frederick Greenwood, the *Cornhill* editor who provided the postscript to Gaskell's unfinished novel, took the "likeness in unlikeness" of the two offspring as both biologically and aesthetically appropriate: "When Squire Hamley took a wife, it was then provided that his two boys should be as naturally one and diverse as the fruit and the bloom on the bramble. . . . These differences are precisely what might have been expected from the union of Squire Hamley with the town-bred, refined, delicate-minded woman whom he married" (*WD* 652). More recent efforts to stabilize the meanings of heredity in *Wives and Daughters* also read the death of one brother and the survival of the other as bioculturally determined. For Mary Debrabant, "the Hamley plot comprises distinct criticism of social customs," such as primogeniture and class endogamy, "superseded by the implications of Darwinian evolution"; the novel thus instantiates an "essential evolutionary law, the necessity to adapt, failing which certain groups are exterminated."[2] For Louise Henson, who has illustrated the ways in which Gaskell's fiction is not so much specifically Darwinian as informed by the scientific thinking that paved the way for *The Origin of Species*, "the children of this 'mixed' marriage, Osborne a sickly aesthete, and the robust and dynamic Roger, are associated with clear cultural developments, which the survival of one and the eradication of the other confirms"; the overdetermined fates of the two underline that "the narrative impetus of the novel is towards social and political change," so the unfit heir must give way to the better-endowed second son.[3]

To read the novel in this way, however, requires repressing both the messiness of contemporary scientific theory, which we explored in chapter 5, and the greater complexity of biological inheritance as Gaskell represents it: in the words of an earlier fictional representation that takes up related questions, "we've allas summut uh orther side in us" (*WH* 192). With each boy given the same educational opportunities, Osborne squanders his fellowship chance, while Roger throws off his dullness to become Senior Wrangler. The elder turns out to be no more inventive or "adventurous" than his father's people, whom he does not otherwise resemble and who "never traded, or speculated, or tried agricultural improvements of any kind," while the younger entrepreneurially adopts the mercantilism associated with his mother's side, albeit in a professional vein, by selling his talents "to the highest bidder" (*WD* 41, 350).[4] But even though Osborne follows his invalid mother to the grave, he leaves behind a son by his marriage to Aimée, in a sign of reproductive vigor that belies the text's insistence on his enervation.[5]

Neither son, then, completely follows the parent that he is said to favor, and their parents' "mixed" marriage is hardly a recipe for degeneration. Much like Eliot's novel, this family plot invokes what Karen Boiko calls "the random variability of heredity," such that "physical characteristics can be misleading in the social realm just as they are in the animal kingdom": "The fate of the two sons," Deirdre D'Albertis remarks, "reinforces Gaskell's insistence on the erratic patterning of descent," which Pam Morris classes among the novel's "comically ironic reversals."[6] As in *The Mill on the Floss,* paternal plans are fixed, but outcomes are uncertain; like falling in love, human sexual reproduction is less a matter of rational calculation than imaginative speculation.[7] The Hamleys, like the contemporary Tullivers, derive the fictions they create about their sons and their sons' futures—underpinned as they are not only by observable resemblances to each parent but also by those parents' own desires—not so much from outworn cultural practices doomed to extinction as from the available fictive means of generating the continuity that constitutes family history. And, to be sure, the Hamleys' fictions mark only one instance of family-making within an increasingly crowded cultural field that situates the family's development, from its primitive state to its civilized form, as an important component of the progressive plot of "social and political change" to which Gaskell indeed subscribes.

Naturalizing the family resemblances of the Hamleys so that the divergence of each son from his "proper" parent goes relatively unremarked, *Wives and Daughters* instead highlights a different basis for understanding and representing family in the representation of its central unit, a "blended" family, to use today's terminology, in which blood ties form only one ground for asserting kinship. Two second families, disrupted by death rather than divorce, merge to create a third, with husband, wife, and respective daughters joined as one unit by two second marriages. Through this union, old parent-child ties are renegotiated, and new bonds, including siblingship, are formed, but in no very smooth way. When Molly Gibson's stepsister Cynthia Kirkpatrick says on her arrival in Hollingford, "we're all in a very awkward position together, aren't we?" she uses the adjective that best characterizes the uncharted territory into which all the novel's major figures wander (*WD* 216). *Awkward* captures the prevailing sense of unease that marks both the effort to forge new familial relationships among unrelated strangers and the concomitant need to adjust extant relationships to new conditions; as Jennifer Uglow notes, Gaskell "almost never writes about 'normal' families."[8] In displaying the making of the blended family in this novel, which also centrally concerns the making of marriages, she offers us a highly self-conscious representation of family as a made thing, constructed from not only the prior relationships and attitudes that pertain among its members but also the family fictions that precede it.

The novel itself is something of an intertextual hybrid: in the words of Ruth Bernard Yeazell, *Wives and Daughters* is "a virtual compendium of the strategies by which the English novel has traditionally managed to represent the young woman's courtship."[9] So, too, does it deploy the familial frameworks developed by Austen, the Brontës, Eliot, and other women writers and shaped by the cultural debates about affinity, adoption, and consanguinity. For example, Gaskell revises the use of sibling terminology to characterize the affinal tie between men and women connected by or contemplating marriage that we explored in chapters 2 and 3: there is almost no talk of marriage making husband, wife, and their kin "one flesh" but quite a lot of family language that characterizes unrelated strangers as "friends," in the older, broader sense of that word.[10] Gaskell also revisits the theme of adoption, as we shall see, emphasizing its fictive quality in a way that resonates with Austen and Eliot and with the anthropological thinking of her time, deploying analogy as a rhetorical figure that enables the construction of family likeness. Pursuing these and other resemblances, my aim is decidedly not to contest the novel's claims to originality, nor to undermine Gaskell's current, hard-won reputation as one of the nineteenth century's most innovative and versatile novelists; rather, I demonstrate that by working within and thus modifying particular aspects of her own literary inheritance, she produced a critique of the family fictions that underpin the novel form. My method in this chapter, then, is to explore a series of plots and plot structures in *Wives and Daughters* by reading them through their modification of some of the central paradigms that I have already identified while also branching out to situate the text in relation to discourses of family thinking in the late nineteenth century.

Current anthropological thinking about kinship, which has engaged its nineteenth-century origins in its effort to reconfigure kinship norms as responsive to changing and dynamic forms of "family," partially informs my approach. Borrowing from the work of the anthropologist David Schneider and expanding Sarah Franklin and Susan McKinnon's claim that contemporary practices of affiliation are "no longer conceptualized as grounded in a singular and fixed idea of 'natural' relation, but... [are] seen to be self-consciously assembled from a multiplicity of possible bits and pieces," Judith Butler comments "that kinship itself is a kind of doing," "a practice that enacts that assemblage of significations as it takes place" (*Undoing* 126). Whether enforcing or contesting the norms, we shape and reshape kinship's "bits and pieces" from the range of discourses that constitute it, recontextualizing and thus modifying those fragments. Understanding kinship as enacted practice—in Franklin and McKinnon's words, as "a medium through which relations are naturalized and naturalized relations are transformed into cultural form"—enables us to see that Gaskell conceives relations of family not as fixed or given, predetermined by biology or blood (although those "bits and pieces" of an emergent norm still pertain).[11] They are instead malleable, situational, and fungible, a matter of doing more than being, action more than essence. "Rather than instating biological determinism," as Linda K. Hughes and Michael Lund observe of the novel's title, *Wives and Daughters* works "to loosen the connection between biology and motherhood."[12] Like contemporary reinventions of kinship, it "self-consciously assemble[s]" its family plots "from a multiplicity of possible bits and pieces" and, in the process, fashions something truly distinctive.

If, near the point at which the novel breaks off, Mr. Gibson admits in conversation with Roger Hamley that "losing one's daughter is a necessary evil," then his unwillingness to make that concession at any earlier point suggests just how much of an "evil" he has felt it to be (*WD* 643). For in an earlier round in the contest of "Lover *versus* father!"—which, over the long run, "lover wins"—Mr. Gibson had put up a much stronger fight, battling young Mr. Coxe with all the weapons at his disposal (*WD* 644, emphasis in original). As Yeazell points out, that he concedes victory to Roger without firing a shot simply appears to confirm that his prospective son-in-law has already assumed "the father's place" by virtue of having first taken on a brother's role (*Fictions* 200). For in fortuitously discovering her at the very moment she begins to grieve her father's impending remarriage and to lament her own displacement, Roger treats Molly with a fraternal kindness, which is reiterated for the remainder of her first stay at Hamley, just as Edmund Bertram salves Fanny Price's grief at missing her brother William in *Mansfield Park*. And in the effort to rationalize a father's action, Roger explicitly assigns a fatherly motive to Mr. Gibson's act: "It must be almost a duty," he surmises, "to find some one to be a substitute for the mother" (*WD* 116). Gibson's deferral of the performance of this duty for well over ten years, however, suggests that it is not Molly alone who believes that "Two is company/Three is trumpery" (*WD* 133). Although both Miss Phoebe and Mrs. Hamley invoke an ideal of constancy to "the memory of his wife" to explain how "a young widower, with a little girl" should not have secured a second partner, Gibson's failure to provide "a substitute for the mother" until Molly is almost seventeen disrupts the normative construction of the widower's duty on multiple fronts (*WD* 68, 72).

Contemplating the possibility of her own demise in a letter written in 1841, Gaskell expresses a "mother's fears" in asking her sister-in-law to promise that she would, "as much as circumstances would permit," keep watch over her children "in case of my death," as "we all know the probability of widowers marrying again."[13] Herself a motherless daughter whose own father remarried rather quickly and started a new family, Gaskell implies both the likelihood of and the social sanction for a man's second marriage, a move that the community in *Wives and Daughters* fully supports. The wealthy widower Lord Hollingford, who has "only boys," advises Mr. Gibson to find a woman "to manage your home" so as to "be free from any thought of household cares" (*WD* 101). The never-married Miss Browning, like Roger Hamley, also refers to second marriage as based in "a sense of duty of one kind or another" so that men may acquire "a housekeeper" or "a mother for their children" (*WD* 144–45). Although as Squire Hamley acknowledges, "a step-mother to a girl is a different thing to a second wife to a man," even Mr. Gibson reluctantly comes to believe that "a second marriage was the very best way of cutting the Gordian knot of domestic difficulties" (*WD* 74, 89). As in the MDWS debate, the normative ideal says that a widower with a child or children must be in want of a wife; the advocates of second marriage in this novel, however, make no claim that second unions need be inspired by affection but simply construct it a matter of practical convenience. Why, then, does the eminently practical Gibson put off remarriage until his domestic situation requires immediate redress?

The novel offers a series of possibilities, about which we, like its characters, can only speculate. Unusually isolated in his circumstances, Gibson has no visible relations and is rumored to be illegitimate. We know nothing about the first family of his wife—perhaps an only child, since Molly has no visible cousins—except that Gibson's medical predecessor in Hollingford was her great-uncle. Father and daughter thus have no extended kin network on which to rely. Moreover, although other characters idealize the memory of the dead mother, the narrative tells us that from Mr. Gibson's perspective, Mary Pearson was "good, pretty, sensible, and beloved" but "not his second; no, nor his third love" (*WD* 143). Undermining the ideal of fidelity to Mary's memory by giving us access to Gibson's inner thoughts and, more generally, sketching his commitment to reason as "lord of all," the narrative obliquely suggests that his first marriage to the boss's great-niece, if not solely made for convenience, may have served primarily to consolidate his professional position (*WD* 32). From that point of view, there would be nothing to gain from a second alliance: "There was no one equal to himself among the men"—or women—"with whom he associated" (*WD* 39).

Seemingly "settled for life" after his wife's death, Gibson first confronts his family situation years before Mr. Coxe arrives on the scene (*WD* 32).

The issue explicitly arises in relation to the professional interest of taking on apprentices: "As Molly grew to be a little girl instead of a child, when she was about eight years old, her father perceived the awkwardness of having her breakfasts and dinners so often alone with the pupils" (*WD* 33). This would seem to be a proper juncture for settling on a second wife and substitute mother; instead, he chooses "a respectable woman" from "a destitute family" as Molly's governess (*WD* 33). But as neither Gibson nor Gaskell pursues the governess romance, the ironically named Miss Eyre—hired more to make conversation with the apprentices than to educate Molly—makes no second wife.[14] Even when he first renews his acquaintance with Mrs. Kirkpatrick, who uses her "most winning manner" on him at the end of the novel's second chapter, Gibson does not take the bait (*WD* 29). Though he will not wear the chain on his leg that Molly proposes as a means of permanently fastening them together, his inaction early in the novel rests on the strong feeling that "he did not want to lose the companionship of his child," supporting Hilary M. Schor's observation that "the most important fact of their relationship is its exclusivity, and the shared joy in what seems its repetition of marriage" (*WD* 45).[15]

Most critics agree that what keeps Mr. Gibson from remarrying until Molly reaches the age of seventeen is his desire to keep his daughter to himself, "but," as the narrative voice remarks in a related context, "he put it to himself in quite a different way" (*WD* 45). In his lament "that he could not guard her as he would have wished" and in his "idea that all young men," even the very gentlemanly Roger and Osborne Hamley, "were wolves in chase of his one ewe-lamb," Gibson constructs a vision of predatory male sexuality that mandates Molly's protection from men both inside and outside his home—even from the apprentice Coxe, whom he begins to address as "a member of my family" only after he discovers the apprentice's designs on his daughter (*WD* 52, 54–55, 56). Although the doctor thinks of and treats her as a child, Coxe's letter leads him to see, as he tells Molly, "people consider you as a young woman now" (*WD* 59).

In his muted recollections of his romantic life before marriage, we can read Mr. Gibson's new identification of Molly with the first, second, and third loves he pursued as a much younger man: as Emily Blair observes, the remembrance of "'poor Jeanie' provides the detail that introduces Mr. Gibson's own sexual experience as the motivation for his response to Mr. Coxe's letter."[16] Arguing that "it is not Molly but her father's view of her that has changed," Margaret Homans provocatively suggests that "the transformation this letter effects in Molly, sexualizing her, causes her father to send her away as much from himself as from Mr. Coxe" (*Bearing* 253). Gibson's resistance to inserting Molly into the marriage market, and thus losing her "companionship,"

ironically backfires: "The very gestures by which Dr. [*sic*] Gibson attempts
to stave off the future effectively serve to bring it on," Yeazell points out,
"as when he tries to keep his daughter out of contact with the lovestruck
apprentice only to send her off to the home of her future husband" (*Fictions*
198). Moreover, when he does select a wife, as Elizabeth Langland has amply
demonstrated, the second Mrs. Gibson makes it her business to groom Molly
for marriage, conceiving it as the better part of her maternal "duty."[17] In
triangulating Gibson's relation to his daughter by introducing a third who
disrupts the father-daughter dyad, Gaskell acts to "protect" her heroine
from the knowledge of men's desires—but in a way that emphasizes Molly's
father's pursuit of his own. If the new wife's job will be to control male
access to his daughter, thereby deferring Molly's marriageability, one effect
of Mrs. Kirkpatrick's incorporation by marriage is that she regulates her
husband's access to Molly. A daughter, then, unlike a wife's sister, cannot (or
should not) be (or even approximate) a wife: the text at once acknowledges
and defuses the potentially erotic charge between father and daughter in
representing the delayed fulfillment of the widower's "duty."[18]

It is important to acknowledge that the father's wish to keep his daughter to himself, as Gaskell imagines it, structures the novel and poses a central problem for the heroine's plot. When Coral Lansbury asserts that "no
girl can become a woman and eventually a wife until she has ceased to be a
daughter" or when Langland criticizes "the dangers in Molly's unhealthy
idealization of her father," each gestures toward the fiction of development
that requires the daughter to renounce a desire for the father as a prerequisite
for achieving adult (heterosexual) womanhood, a plot that the novel enacts
from its fairy-tale opening onward.[19] Yet the father, too, must redirect his
desire away from the daughter if she is to "become a woman and eventually a wife." Schor grasps the asymmetry between the father's plot and the
daughter's, noting that from Mr. Gibson's point of view, "keeping Molly
sexually untouched is more essential to their intimacy than keeping himself
single."[20] That insight enables us to articulate more clearly the ambivalence
that the text evinces in relation to the father, who deprives his daughter of
the opportunity to reach out for what he ultimately takes for himself, even as
he aims to represent his remarriage as undertaken in Molly's interests.

For despite all the talk of second marriage as "desirable and expedi-
ent" (*WD* 109), the novel stages the doctor's proposal to Mrs. Kirkpatrick as
induced by something more than mere convenience:

Her voice was so soft, her accent so pleasant, that it struck him as particularly agreeable after the broad country accent he was perpetually

hearing. Then the harmonious colours of her dress, and her slow and graceful movements, had something of the same soothing effect upon his nerves that a cat's purring has upon some people's. He began to think that he should be fortunate if he could win her, for his own sake. Yesterday he had looked upon her more as a possible stepmother for Molly; to-day he thought more of her as a wife for himself. (*WD* 105)

If "his domestic affections [had been] centred on little Molly" since his first wife's death, they will be so no longer; in taking a second plunge into matrimony, Gibson is much aided by his perception of Mrs. Kirkpatrick's womanly charms, altogether sophisticated and distinctly different from the tomboy ways of his daughter (*WD* 32). The second wife no doubt disrupts the idyll of father-daughter communion, but Gibson's sensitivity to her attractions, that is, her ability to perform the class-coded gestures of femininity, suggests the compensations he identifies in taking "a wife for himself." The narrative voice's knowingness about what (or whom) Mr. Gibson wants makes it difficult not to read the consequences of his choice as punitive. But it is difficult to say, I think, for which of his sins he is being punished—keeping his daughter too close, or pushing her away.

With the rapid progress of her father's courtship of another woman screened from her view, Molly herself will only begin to understand how her father "had come to like Mrs. Kirkpatrick enough to wish to marry her" when she watches Roger fall under Cynthia's spell (*WD* 127). The events leading up to her father's second marriage initiate the "displacements and delaying actions" or "substitute representations" that, as Yeazell argues, constitute Molly's education in both family and romance (*Fictions* 199). While it is "very disagreeable," as Lady Cumnor says, "to have a stepmother coming in between her father and herself," Molly's displacement from the center of her father's world is naturalized as a necessary thing (*WD* 131). But in sending her to Hamley, Mr. Gibson belatedly gives his daughter the chance to replace him.

About midway through the novel, as Molly tortures herself with the thought that Cynthia does not return Roger's affection, she vows to do what she can to support his suit:

Cynthia's love was the moon Roger yearned for; and Molly saw that it was far away and out of reach, else would she have strained her heart-chords to give it to Roger.

"I am his sister," she would say to herself. "That old bond is not done away with, though he is too much absorbed by Cynthia to speak about it just now. His mother called me 'Fanny'; it was almost like an adoption. I must wait and watch, and see if I can do anything for my brother." (*WD* 354)

Even though "Molly did not know her own feelings," she does know Roger's as well as Cynthia's: with "keen insight into her 'sister's' heart," Molly can read Cynthia's character even before she knows her secrets (*WD* 354). In all this and more, Molly is a second Fanny: a surrogate for the Hamleys' dead daughter and sister of that name and the literary descendant of Fanny Price, who moves from cousin to sister to wife over the course of *Mansfield Park* and who similarly watches and worries as her brother entertains another potential bride, a stranger who is also, ambiguously, a sister.[21]

In describing her connection to Roger's mother as "almost like an adoption," Molly follows the lead of the Hamleys (and the narrative voice) by defining her position among them in familial terms. But whereas Fanny Price actually *is* family at Mansfield Park, Molly Gibson *becomes* family at Hamley Hall, and not only by virtue of her projected marriage at novel's end. The extralegal status of adoption itself enables this way of thinking, which pervades *Wives and Daughters*. Taken into the Hamley household at the moment at which her own is undergoing significant disruption, Molly juxtaposes the informal but meaningful ties that she builds over time with the socially sanctioned stepfamily that her father's remarriage imposes on her. So when the second Mrs. Gibson admonishes her for grieving for the dying Mrs. Hamley by telling Molly that "you're no relation, so you need not feel it so much," the stepmother both asserts her own status as kin-by-marriage and discounts the strength and depth of Molly's feelings for those who are not (*WD* 199). Here and elsewhere, by casting the non-related Hamleys as familiars and the related-by-marriage Kirkpatricks as strangers, Gaskell revises Austen's binary structure by adding a third term. Whereas Fanny Price essentially exchanges Portsmouth for Mansfield, losing her place in her first family and finding it in her second one, Molly Gibson has at least three distinct experiences of family in *Wives and Daughters,* with the relationship to the Hamleys mediating between the two forms that the Gibson household takes.

Gaskell's treatment of the patriarchal bar that governs Molly's relation to the men who will become her brothers obviously recalls Austen's plot even as it alters it. Yeazell concisely demonstrates that "the central triangle of Austen's novel anticipated Gaskell's": "Its courtship plot begins when the modest young woman arrives in the home of her future husband, and . . . the resident patriarch immediately fears lest one of his sons fall in love" with her (*Fictions*

211–12).[22] To be sure, Molly arrives at Hamley not as a girl cousin whose surplus status impels her removal from her parents' house but as a young woman whose only family, aside from the servants and the governess who have raised her, is the man who has been "her mother as well as her father" (*WD* 55). On the Gibson side, the decision to send Molly away from the home to which she will return, under its changed conditions, has less to do with economics than erotics. But on the Hamley side, Molly's visit, as a favor granted to Mr. Gibson that his daughter repays by the services to the squire and his wife that earn her daughterly status, at first evokes Mansfield-like concerns about potential danger to the host family.

The prohibition that Squire Hamley installs cites Molly's lack of rank (and, secondarily, money) in the case of Osborne, and Roger's need to "make his own way, and earn his own bread" (*WD* 57). When Miss Eyre's absence prolongs Molly's stay and threatens to bring her into close contact with his sons, despite his wife's confident (and correct) assurance that "she's not at all the sort of girl young men of their age would take to," the squire worries "that it's a very dangerous thing to shut two young men of one and three and twenty up in a country-house like this, with a girl of seventeen" (*WD* 79). This perception simply reverses her father's view of her circumstances at home: "It was very awkward, [Mr. Gibson] considered, to have a motherless girl grow- ing up into womanhood in the same house with two young men" (*WD* 50). Only Mrs. Hamley's presence as a second or surrogate mother sanctions Molly's continuing if intermittent residence at Hamley; before her death, she takes up the mother's position in a way that makes Molly and Hamley safe for one another. It is, in other words, by making Molly like family rather than keeping her a stranger that the Hamleys effectively enact the prohibition on marriage; it is also through that active making of a stranger into kin, however, that the prohibition is gradually eroded.

The adoption plot of *Wives and Daughters* thus creates fictive kinship between Molly and the Hamleys well before the projected ending of the (unfinished) novel. If Gibson needs a mother to supervise his daughter, then the Hamleys need a daughter, whom they receive on very favorable terms. As Homans writes, because Molly is not actually a relative and thus "of no immediate consequence to the family," they are under no obligation to make sure that she is "adequately provided for," as Sir Thomas Bertram imagines his duty to Fanny Price, or to prepare her for marriage and "a creditable establishment" of her own (*Bearing* 255; *MP* 7). She will not be a means to "extend" their "respectable alliances" in the way that the Hamleys' own dead daughter, requiring a portion to enter the marriage market, assuredly would have been (*MP* 17). This lack of economic interest in Molly's potential as a wife, dovetailing as it does with her father's wish to keep her to himself, enables a deeper investment in her as a surrogate "daughter of the house" (*WD* 81). She fulfills "all the pretty offices of a daughter" for Squire Hamley and occupies "the place of a daughter in [Mrs. Hamley's] heart"; the squire is "only too willing to appropriate Molly when he or his wife feels the need for some daughterly affection" (*WD* 147, 148).[23] As at Mansfield Park, albeit more rapidly, the new arrival fills a gap, as the Hamleys replace the girl they could not afford with one who costs them nothing; something like a dead wife's sister, Molly suitably fills an empty place. Moreover, after Mrs. Hamley's death, husband and sons cast Molly in the part of the lost wife and mother: "As receiver of secrets, and as selfless mediator and 'third person' who erases her own presence," Homans notes, "Molly has inherited Mrs. Hamley's own role" (*Bearing* 256). Like quite a few other Gaskell heroines but also like Fanny Price, Molly undertakes the emotional labor of meeting people's needs—in thinking "more of others than of oneself," as Roger puts it—by taking a daughterly position that further expands with Mrs. Hamley's death (*WD* 117).[24]

While Molly's first visit to Hamley severs the exclusive bond between her and her father, it also provides her with an alternative to it through the birth of her intimacy with Squire and Mrs. Hamley, and with Roger, who comes to occupy the place of the father she feels she has lost by becoming the brother she has never had. In this context, we can reread the events that lead to Molly's achieving surrogate status at Hamley not simply as the effect of her father's actions, in which Molly remains passive, but also as part of the novel's interrogation of Molly's limited experience of the structures of family and romance. Perceiving first her exile and then her father's remarriage as exclusion, Molly finds the family that enables her to repair her losses as a daughter while also introducing her to the role of sister, a role that both promises and polices cross-gender intimacy. While sending Molly away affords her a surrogate family that mediates her acquisition of a new, legitimate one, her status at Hamley is contingent on her ability to play all the vacant feminine parts. That from this position Molly ultimately enters into Fanny Price's place suggests the agency that yet inheres in this apparently inauspicious situation. Molly is not just a substitute in an endless chain of signifiers, as Homans argues, but an agent who seeks to find substitutes to fill vacant roles in a drama of her own.[25]

Identifying her relation to the Hamleys, especially to Mrs. Hamley, as almost-adoptive certainly provides Molly with a prior defense against the claims of the stepfamily, but it also provides Gaskell with an alternative discourse for characterizing relationships among those who are, technically speaking, not related. The claim to adoptive status asserts a kinship that is not governed by birth or even by marriage. The use of kin terms between Molly and the Hamleys marks even as it makes affinity among them: as in *Deerbrook* or *Jane Eyre,* a natural (or naturalized) "inclination or attraction" among individuals incites the use of family language, and that language in turn shapes each one's sense of the connection. Explicitly fictitious in this instance, family language domesticates Molly at Hamley as an almost-daughter and virtual sister. Like Austen's Fanny, this quasi-adoptee will be made to appear non-marriageable—or, as Mrs. Norris says in *Mansfield Park,* not capable of being "more to either" Osborne or Roger "than a sister"—which will, in the long run, make her all the more so (*MP* 8). By including her in the family on terms that seem explicitly to exclude her from permanent membership in it, the fiction of adoption also provides the language through which Molly can begin to articulate the sexual feelings that, much more even than Fanny Price, she cloaks in sibling language, an idiom that both denies and acknowledges her desire for her brother.

More broadly, then, Molly's adoption by the Hamleys promotes the narrative of courtship that it was ostensibly designed to avert. It produces the tie between Molly and all members of the family that ultimately facilitates Roger's turn from Cynthia to her, like Edmund Bertram's from Mary Crawford to Fanny Price, as a second choice. If Mr. Gibson's marriage aims to create new relations for Molly by giving her a mother who should normatively provide the "tender supervision which . . . all girls of that age require," then her appropriation by the Hamleys enables her marriage by analogical means: Molly becomes a wife to Roger by passing through a chain of family likenesses, which assimilates her to a vacant "place" (*WD* 101). From being "a stranger in the household," she becomes more and more "like a child of the house almost"—conflated by the dying Mrs. Hamley with the dead Fanny, "liker [*sic*] a child of mine than a stranger" to the widowed squire, and "like a sister" to both of the Hamley brothers (*WD* 85, 201–2, 581, 245). By virtue of becoming "like one of us," as Osborne puts it, Molly actually makes it so: more and more like a sister and a daughter than a stranger, she ultimately becomes a wife (*WD* 494). By the repeated use of analogy—in being *like* a sister or a daughter without being one in either legal or biological terms—Molly takes her place in their family long before the (unwritten) conclusion of the novel, when such a marriage would appear to be the most natural thing in the world.

Molly's figuration as a "stranger" differs significantly from the paradigms we encounter in other, earlier adoption plots in that she is not really all that strange, hardly "foreign" or "other" to the Hamleys. By contrast with *Jane Eyre* and some of its antecedents within the juvenilia, in which adoptees represent themselves (or are represented) as aliens to, and alienated from, their new families, Molly's joining the Hamleys in *Wives and Daughters* constitutes a turn toward rather than an exile from "true" kin. As against both Brontë and Gaskell, Eliot had imagined the adoptee in her early fiction as a work of nature that would either transform or be transformed by those who give her a new home: non- or even anti-biological fictions of adoption issue in forms of family that blend or hybridize distinctly different forms. The aristocratic Cheverels in "Mr. Gilfil's Love Story" (1858), who take Caterina Sarti from her Milanese home, approach the labor of adoption from a botanical perspective. Like Henry Maine just a few years later, who refers to the adoptive family as "the people on whom [men of alien descent] were engrafted," the narrative voice indicates that the Cheverels' intention is to "graft as much English fruit as possible on the Italian stem," to hybridize a plant not native to English soil (*Ancient Law* 126).[26] Seeking to naturalize a wild, non-native growth in a new environment and to adjust it to "new soil," these adoptive parents neutralize the force of Squire Lammeter's old-school claim in *Silas Marner*—that "breed was stronger than pasture"—by undercutting the distinction between the two and, as Marianne Novy argues, so challenging "the opposition between adoption and nature."[27] In different ways and via different discourses, Brontë and Eliot emphasize the adoptee's otherness: whether or not the adoptee can be domesticated within the adoptive unit is the central question.

But for all the talk about Molly as an outsider, there is very little in *Wives and Daughters* to separate her from the increasingly impoverished Hamleys; even the squire's reverence for rank looks like an empty signifier, as the markers of his family's distinction decay and other forces of change take center stage. Not differentiated from the Hamleys by race or nation or upbringing—as are the French Aimée, the Frenchified Cynthia, and "the black folk" whose "peculiarity of complexion," Mr. Gibson predicts, "will only make [Roger] appreciate white skins the more"—Molly's adoption into the Hamley family need not be figured as grafting or hybridization (*WD* 391). She can become a member of the family over the course of the novel largely because she is already a member of "the family" in a broader sense: what qualifies and permits her to join the Hamleys is her thoroughgoing likeness to them, a similarity further underlined by and through her acquisition of a stepfamily.

Where once Molly had just a sole parent, Gaskell endows her heroine with two additional families. But the new family formations to which Molly belongs are by no means equivalent, partly in that they are constructed by different discourses. As we have seen, the language of "like" governs Molly's interactions with the Hamleys, an idiom others first deploy that she comes to accept and use. She becomes "like a child of the house almost" by visibly enacting or performing the conventional gestures associated with sisterhood and daughterhood, "reinforcing the notion," as Boiko remarks of the novel in another context, "that it is what you do...that counts" in establishing this fictive form of kinship.[28] Following Darwin, one might say that Molly comes to look "like" a family member by adaptation to the Hamley environment; the particular qualities she has developed as a father's only daughter fit her to play a comparable part. The ground for Molly's use of analogy, however, rests not just on the resemblance between her position at home, before the advent of a second Mrs. Gibson, and the one she takes up at Hamley but also on how the Hamleys come to approximate the familial relations she lacks, the mother and brothers she does not have. (It's worth noting that no matter how much she sympathizes with him, Molly never uses family language to describe the squire.)

Analogy, then, clearly functions to establish fictive kinship. Although it "enables a way of thinking," as George Levine writes of its use in the contemporary scientific context, analogy "has no empirical authority."[29] As the new Mrs. Gibson often reminds her, Molly is not "really" the Hamleys' daughter any more than Hareton Earnshaw and Catherine Linton are Ellen Dean's children (*WH* 246). By contrast with the assertions of natural(ized) affinity that MDWS opponents installed at the heart of that debate or even with the attributions of spiritual affinity (or being "like kin") that punctuate Brontë's fiction, Gaskell's deployment of affinity is patently and quite openly fictitious, much closer in spirit to the "feigning" associated with Maine's fiction of adoption that we encountered in chapter 4. But even Maine seeks to naturalize the adoptive relationship by deploying the idiom of plant and animal breeding, as noted above, understanding hybridity as the product of deliberate human cultivation. Naturalizing the relation of adoptee to host aims to eliminate any trace of a difference between them over time: "The incoming population should *feign themselves* to be descended from the same stock" so that the perceived difference between the graft and the stock will become no difference at all (*Ancient Law* 126, emphasis in original). Gaskell deploys no such metaphors.

The precise value of analogy for the novel's rethinking of family relations, as Gillian Beer describes the workings of this figure, is that it may "claim more than it proves."[30] It announces its own fictive status while aspiring to persuade with its imaginative truth; it gives us critical purchase on other

domains, like the biological or the legal, perceived to possess greater "empirical authority." However often the novel reminds us that Molly is not kin to
the Hamleys—which it arguably does every time it uses the word *like*—it also
invites us to consider the basis on which family membership is determined
by highlighting its performative dimension. As Maine helps to establish, the
ability to feign family ties and to experience that feigning as authentic is
to problematize the understanding of "the family" as naturally or biologically given. What are the differences between actually being a daughter or
a mother or a sister and being "like" a daughter or a mother or a sister? On
what grounds does the novel (and the culture) construct these differences,
and how much do they matter?

These questions become especially pressing when we consider Molly's
new stepmother, whose claims have the sanction of law and custom, backed
by Mr. Gibson's authority. On returning from his honeymoon, he prescribes
the course he expects his daughter to take in giving "the name long appropriated in her mind to some one else—to her own dead mother"—to his
second wife: "Why shouldn't you call her 'mamma'? I'm sure she means to
do the duty of a mother to you.... At any rate let us start with a family bond
between us" (*WD* 172, 174). The "family bond," in Mr. Gibson's framework,
follows from the establishment of the new legal relation of marriage; using
the normative terms and enacting the naturalized roles they connote—as in
the evocation of "duty"—should be a simple matter of observing the forms.
(Interestingly, Mr. Gibson always remains "Mr. Gibson," never "papa," to
Cynthia.) Yet *Wives and Daughters* also undermines this position: the legal
relation created by the father's second marriage gives a certain force, but not
much content, to the positions that these virtual strangers occupy in relation
to one another. "Mother" and "daughter" name formal obligations and roles,
but without establishing affinity, in either the legal or spiritual sense, between
those who are obliged to feign them; with respect to the blended unit that
two second marriages make, a "family bond" is not where you begin, and
only perhaps where you might end.

At one level, Gaskell's representation of the stepmother reinforces the priority of what Austen calls "first associations and habits" in forming Molly's
sense of a "mother": that Mrs. Hamley much more closely approximates
than does the second Mrs. Gibson Molly's sense of what a mother should be,
and of what her own mother was, partially shapes her resistance to the "new
mamma." And that Mrs. Gibson does not behave "like a mother" even in
relation to her own daughter also foregrounds how the ideological construction of motherhood exceeds any individual's performance of it. In profess-
ing to love Molly "better than any one" on ten days' acquaintance, Cynthia

quite sincerely confides, "I don't think love for one's mother quite comes by nature": her remark underlines Hyacinth's failure to enact the affective aspect of the maternal ideal after Mr. Kirkpatrick's demise as one reason for the absence of "a family bond between" them (*WD* 219, 220). Here Gaskell represents mother-daughter affection as an effect of practice, rather than an essential, natural given.

Indeed, *Wives and Daughters* effectively splits off the affective function of the mother from maternal "duty," normatively construed, by opposing Mrs. Hamley to Mrs. Gibson, who, significantly, never meet. Langland's reading of the novel recuperates the productive force of the latter, who by inserting Molly into class- and gender-coded scripts enables her finally to fit the part of an eminently marriageable woman; she thus carries out to the letter this aspect of the mother's duty, in Homans's words, "the transformation of daughters into wives" (*Bearing* 251).[31] Without diminishing the importance of this necessary and functional role, the step-relation can yet be subtly distinguished from the analogical relation in that Mrs. Gibson performs "as" a mother—occupying that place and carrying out its nominal duties as a result—while Mrs. Hamley, "like" a mother in affective terms, but without the formal burdens of maternal "duty," is freer to approximate for Molly the less coercive aspects of the maternal ideal. The difference between being "like" a mother and acting "as" one is not simply that one "is" while the other "does": both are performances, albeit explicitly and self-consciously constructed in different discursive registers. Where they differ lies in Molly's experience of them and our readerly perception of them: although Molly may call Mrs. Gibson "mamma," she always thinks of her as "papa's wife," less like a mother than a rival for Mr. Gibson's attention (*WD* 437). And in this, Mrs. Gibson's place as a wife—the place Molly once felt herself to hold as a daughter—does provide the ground for a further instance of analogical thinking. For in coming to see the making of her father's marriage through the lens provided by Roger's courtship of Cynthia, Molly puzzles through the complexities of her own displacement and exclusion, first from her father's confidence and then from her brother's attention, by her "new mamma" and her stepsister.

Preparing for her wedding, the soon-to-be stepmother certainly thinks of herself largely as a future wife, once again free to lounge about "in the drawing-room like a lady," as she did "when poor Kirkpatrick was alive" (*WD* 98). Inciting her to remember "the reason why it does not do to have Molly at home just at present," Gibson also reminds himself of "one of the good reasons for the step he had taken" (*WD* 133, 134). More attentive than

Hyacinth to what directly concerns her, Molly is conscious only that the concealed "reason" pertains to some mystery about herself:

> She had been sent from home for some reason, kept a secret from her, but told to this strange woman. Was there to be perfect confidence between these two, and she to be for ever shut out? Was she, and what concerned her—though how, she did not know—to be discussed between them for the future, and she to be kept in the dark? A bitter pang of jealousy made her heart-sick. (*WD* 134)

Realizing that "a secret" has been and is being kept from her, Molly is mystified by her father's deliberate withholding of it: not knowing that the secret involves Coxe's letter, she has no way of accounting for her father's action. Of course, by the time Molly learns the truth about the secret, she is far "too tired to be amused, or even interested" by it, burdened as she has been with keeping secrets not her own and with concealing (from herself, though not from us) the nature of her feelings for Roger (*WD* 561).[32] But in denying her full access to his "reasons" for marrying Mrs. Kirkpatrick, Mr. Gibson enables Molly's sense that he is substituting another woman for her—not a stepmother who takes the dead mother's place but a wife who fills the place Molly once occupied.

In *Miss Marjoribanks* (1865–66) by Margaret Oliphant, the imperious Lucilla responds to a visit from the local curate, who tells her that she stands "so much in need of a mother's care" that "we must try to find some one to fill her place," with "a scream of genuine alarm and dismay."[33] Not every Victorian heroine—or antiheroine, in the case of *Miss Marjoribanks*—turns inward to suppress her shock at the prospect of a stepmother, and even Molly herself breaks out on occasion to protest her lot. That the introduction of this third mother produces more than one "bitter pang of jealousy," however, is parodically mirrored by the responses of Mrs. Kirkpatrick, whose capacity for affecting sentiment far outlasts her ability to produce a blush. When she says even before the wedding that she's "almost jealous sometimes" of Gibson's love for his daughter, she mimics the second wife's conventional reaction to a stepdaughter, the sort of reaction MDWS advocates represented as a powerful disincentive to taking a "stranger" into the family (*WD* 126). But as Molly comes to recognize her father's unhappiness, "papa's wife" features less in her eyes as a rival for his affection and more as an impediment between them. Mrs. Gibson erects "perpetual obstacles" between her husband and stepdaughter, depriving Molly of things that she "did not value, yet which she, like the dog in the manger, prevented Molly enjoying," and putting "stumbling-blocks in the way of their unrestrained intercourse, which was the one thing they desired to have, free and open, and without the constant dread of her jealousy" (*WD* 371, 424). When the new mamma goes off to London with Cynthia (which leads a neighbor to tell Mr. Gibson that "it will be like being a widower over again!"), father and daughter are invited to tea everywhere, "quite like bride and bridegroom" (*WD* 439, 440). When Hyacinth returns to Hollingford without Cynthia, Molly learns "that perpetual *tête-à-têtes* with Mrs. Gibson" are almost more "tiresome" than she or, by implication, her father can bear (*WD* 446).

Mrs. Gibson does not, however, simply affect being jealous: like the first wives I analyzed in chapter 3, she is represented as constitutionally so. Although her jealousy is not given a first-family genealogy, as in the case of Skene's Elizabeth or Martineau's Hester, the text does obliquely indicate the ongoing influence of a second-family plot that shapes her actions. On the face of it, Hyacinth's desire for exclusive possession—of good things to eat and valuable information, of "intimacy with great people" like the Cumnors—leads her to "place quiet obstacles in the way of a too frequent intercourse" between Molly and Lady Harriet, just as, in a different key, she blocks Molly's access to Mr. Gibson (*WD* 294, 355). But of no one does she appear to be more authentically jealous than of her own daughter. As her rival for Preston—a secret kept offstage for much of the novel, mainly alluded to via gossip, and never fully confided to Molly— Cynthia has stood in the way of another second marriage that Mrs. Kirkpatrick was aspiring to make. Gaskell keeps this plot in the background of the novel as a subtextual presence, comparable in form though not in substance to the intermittent allusions to Mr. Gibson's romantic past. Yet it continually functions, as one of the novel's suppressed stories, to indicate how much more there is to tell than we ever hear.

Mrs. Gibson's references to her first husband are always prefaced by either "poor" or "dear" or both (*WD* 21, 199, 225, 385, 489, 522). While the narrative voice tells us that "if Mrs. Gibson had ever felt anything acutely it was the death of Mr. Kirkpatrick," her appeals to his memory aim to establish her primacy with him, "who did so dislike the notion of second marriages" (*WD* 393, 109). "Whenever anything went wrong, poor Mr. Kirkpatrick was regretted and mourned over, nay, almost blamed, as if, had he only given himself the trouble of living, he could have helped it": nostalgically recalling his "walking five miles into Stratford to buy me a muffin," Mrs. Gibson remarks that "it really was selfish of him" to die without considering "the forlorn state in which I should be left" (*WD* 447).[34] Although she tells Molly that "one always does call" fatherless daughters "poor dears," her daughter's loss of a father, which also partially deprived her of her mother, carried hardly any weight with the new widow (*WD* 214). Cynthia's memory of what transpired on the father's death is that her mother discounted her feelings: "I heard mamma say to a caller, not a fortnight after his funeral,—'Oh, no, Cynthia is too young; she has quite forgotten him'—and I bit my lips, to keep from crying out" (*WD* 220). Given a variant on her mother's name purportedly at her dead father's request, Cynthia "has a way of attracting men," her mother says, which "she must have inherited from me" (*WD* 540; cf. 491). On the basis of these cues, we can conclude that the mother was "almost jealous sometimes" of a husband's love for their daughter, whom she constructs as her double and who later becomes her rival.

In light of all this, it is all the more interesting that in sketching the plot of the novel in a letter of 1864, Gaskell emphasizes not (step)mother-(step)daughter rivalries but a conflict in which the stepsisters—whom she describes as "not sisters but living *as* sisters in the same house"—become "unconscious rivals" for the same man.[35] Gaskell's summary underplays the conscious intergenerational rivalries among the women who constitute the new blended family: the competition for Mr. Gibson between Molly and the new wife, which Molly (necessarily) loses; the earlier, offstage struggle between Cynthia and her mother for the attentions of Mr. Preston, which Cynthia (unfortunately) wins. Gaskell clearly subordinates these antagonisms and the bad feelings they breed in highlighting the happier if still conflicted tie between sisters: Molly and Cynthia, whom the author described in the same letter as "contrasting characters," are pitted against one another as "rivals" for Roger's hand.[36] But this sketch offers an important way of reading the story of the "two sisters" in their relation to Roger as it repeats and condenses the other triangles that compose this complex family romance. In the homosocial triangle that Gaskell creates, which displaces the intergenerational stories of competition between (step)mother and (step)daughter, Cynthia's entry into the family as mediator and rival initiates Molly into the adult plot of desire from which her father had excluded her; in being something like, if not quite like, a sister to Molly, Cynthia demonstrates the scope and limits of that role within the romance plot.

Whereas Molly resists the replacement "mamma," she initially embraces the idea of the new sister wholeheartedly: "Oh, what a pleasure it would be to have a companion, a girl, a sister of her own age!" (*WD* 213). Her enthusiasm for a new relation is in part conditioned by the fact that Cynthia takes no one's place; until this point in the novel, Molly has not had even one same-sex peer relationship, so that if she has been like a sister to Roger and Osborne, no one has approximated that relation to her. Cynthia and Molly become each other's "sister" by filling an empty position, much as Cynthia's mother takes

on the maternal role to Molly and Molly's father embodies paternal authority for Cynthia. But unlike the stepparent positions, which evoke norms of
"duty" and obligation, the exact form that Molly and Cynthia's siblingship
will take is much more ambiguous, as the narration parenthetically registers:
"Ever since she had heard of the probability of her having a sister—(she
called her a sister, but whether it was a Scotch sister, or a sister *à la mode de
Brétagne,* would have puzzled most people)—Molly had allowed her fancy to
dwell much on the idea of Cynthia's coming" (*WD* 216–17).[37] Using locu-
tions that invoke differing conventions of kinship in Scotland (her father's
putative native country) and France (where Cynthia has been at school)
and thereby relativizing the meaning of kinship itself, Gaskell also avoids the
much less puzzling term *stepsister.* What it will mean to live "*as* sisters" is
negotiated over the course of the novel, rather than given in advance; Molly's
initial stance toward her new friend is unfixed.

A similar provisionality attends the narration's description of Molly's
response to Cynthia on their first meeting: transfixed by "the contemplation
of Cynthia's beauty," "Molly fell in love with her, so to speak, on the instant"
(*WD* 215, 216). "In love" attests to the intensity of both Molly's attraction
and Cynthia's attractiveness, with the latter represented as a "most exquisite
power of adaptation," "something that can neither be described nor reasoned
upon": "A woman will have this charm, not only over men but over her own
sex," and Cynthia possesses this "unconscious power of fascination" over
"the susceptible" in spades (*WD* 217). Molly's feeling for Cynthia is her first
truly passionate attachment to someone other than a parent or parent figure. "Her little wavering maiden fancy" for "the unseen Osborne"—"now
a troubadour, and now a knight" but never anything other than a literary
fiction—is routed even before she learns, just ahead of Cynthia's arrival, that
he is already married (*WD* 147).[38] Nor has Roger yet become more than "a
Pope" to Molly, with each of them "imagining some one very different for the
future owner of their [*sic*] whole heart" (*WD* 147). The narrative's use of the
qualifying "so to speak" suggests that "in love," as a way of characterizing
one girl's feeling for another, much more closely approximates the real thing
than anything Molly has felt thus far. Having already acknowledged the
ambiguity of "living as sisters," the novel effectively says that Molly both is
and is not "in love" with the girl who both is and is not her sister.

Cynthia figures a sort of undecidability in being neither completely sisterly
nor fully eroticized in Molly's eyes. Sarah Annes Brown argues that "Molly's
fascinated interest in Cynthia represents her awakening (hetero)sexuality
even though it manifests itself as a covert lesbian attraction," while Amy K.
Levin calls Cynthia's effect on Molly "akin to a seduction."[39] Each of these

characterizations, like Gaskell's own, implicitly acknowledges that Cynthia's main narrative function is to instigate desire in Molly: in Sharon Marcus's terms, the relationship becomes "a vehicle for depicting a heroine's erotic excitability while skirting, so to speak, the strictures on female heterosexual assertion" (*Between Women* 83).[40] This desire precedes and also precipitates the rivalry that Gaskell subsequently constructs between the two; it is legitimated, indeed produced, by the remarriage plot, which scripts positions for stepparents toward stepdaughters but not for stepsiblings in their relations to one another. Making Cynthia serve as both same-sex object of desire and sister-surrogate, Gaskell constructs the blended (rather than the biological or surrogate) family as the site at which Molly's multivalent desire is generated through the introduction of a stranger whose "power of adaptation" has been shaped by first-family circumstances very different from Molly's own.

If Molly learns what it is to desire in this sisterly relation, then Cynthia also teaches her, in the mediating presence of another familial third, what it is to be desired as something other than a sister. This opens up a gap between familial and romantic love by differentiating them in a way that is new to Molly. Given her own experience, it is no surprise that she is "the first to discover the nature of Roger's attraction" to Cynthia, perhaps even before Cynthia does: "Of all the victims to Cynthia's charms"—including Molly herself—"he fell most prone and abject. Molly saw it all" (*WD* 310, 239). And although "Roger's attraction" to Cynthia does not change his attitude toward Molly—"his manner had had just the brotherly kindness of old times"—she sees the difference in "the manner he had to Cynthia; and Molly half thought she would have preferred the latter" (*WD* 242). Molly's observation of how Roger looks at Cynthia—in a way that she identifies as not-brotherly by reference to his treatment of her—leads her to desire to be looked at by Roger in the way that both she and Roger look at Cynthia, or to put it differently, to be herself no longer regarded only as Roger's or Cynthia's safely un-sexual sister. While Molly's passion for Cynthia has been commensurate with their relatively undefined and unpoliced relationship "*as* sisters living in the same house," observing how Cynthia's powerful charm attracts Roger inserts the thin wedge of rivalry between the stepsisters, which, at times, leads Molly to renounce the sisterhood she had previously claimed. Cynthia mediates Molly's desire for Roger, along the lines established by René Girard: as Leila Silvana May writes of a comparable episode in *Deerbrook,* Molly "desires to *be*" Cynthia and thus also "to become...her rival" (*Disorderly Sisters* 92, emphasis in original).[41]

To be sure, at no point does Cynthia deliberately or intentionally compete with Molly for Roger's attention. In a brief, early conversation between them, Roger tells Cynthia that "I look upon [Molly] almost as a sister," which Cynthia clearly takes as a sign that he is not sexually interested in her (*WD* 269). While Molly would interpret that statement as an avowal of strong affection, her more worldly and experienced sister—almost a second Mary Crawford—posits a difference between what Roger would feel for a sister and what he is starting to feel for her. Although she becomes engaged to him, Cynthia herself has no passion for Roger, only liking, appreciation, and respect; he fulfills her wish, at this point in the novel, to be desired by someone who is more worthy (and less possessive) than Preston, someone in whose eyes she is as nearly perfect as she can be (*WD* 353–54). It is, rather, Molly who comes to see Cynthia as standing between her and her brother, diverting his attention away from her: "Molly suddenly felt as if she could scarcely keep from crying—a minute ago he had been so near to her, and talking so pleasantly and confidentially; and now he almost seemed as if he had forgotten her existence" (*WD* 270).

The advent of Roger's desire for Cynthia restages events that Molly has not herself previously seen, events that she experiences as the disruption of a bond that she has felt to be exclusive and unique. Having turned to Roger in part because her father has turned away from her, Molly once more undergoes a gendered trauma of sexual exclusion, witnessing what she constructs as "perfect confidence between these two" with herself "for ever shut out." This time around, however, the exclusion is redoubled: her own complex attraction to Cynthia is displaced, even diminished, in the interests of the heterosexual plot, as desire for the brother trumps that for the sister. That what develops between Roger and Cynthia is quite different from Mr. Gibson and Mrs. Kirkpatrick's hasty courtship is less relevant here, I think, than that Molly registers it as a repetition both of that earlier series of incidents and, as Levin notes, of the loss of familial connection to Roger and Cynthia alike.[42] Being able to observe the genesis of Roger's feelings for Cynthia teaches her something about what motivated Mr. Gibson's second marriage, and it "elicits in Molly a response similar to that produced formerly when a stranger laid claim to her father."[43] But it also leads her to resist Cynthia's sisterly claims, as is most specifically registered in the description in the text that "Molly's love for Cynthia was fast and unwavering, but if anything tried it, it was the habit Roger had fallen into of always calling Cynthia Molly's sister in speaking to the latter" (*WD* 312). Roger's naming of Cynthia as part of Molly's family evokes an affect comparable to that induced by Mr. Gibson's insistence that Molly call the new Mrs. Gibson "mamma." Molly thus comes to equate Roger's romance with Cynthia with that between her father and Mrs. Kirkpatrick and, at some level, to repudiate the Kirkpatrick women, whom she views as having twice replaced her.

The chapter in which Roger proposes to Cynthia, entitled "A Lover's Mistake," nicely illustrates these repetitions even as it also suggests a difference between them. It opens with Molly speculating "as to whether her father was quite aware of her stepmother's perpetual lapses from truth; and whether his blindness was willful or not," language that recalls her earlier wonder at "Roger's blindness in coming so willingly to be entrapped" by the snares of that "plotter," Mrs. Gibson (WD 371, 346). Its central incident is Roger's proposal, which takes place out of Molly's view (and out of the reader's view as well). She responds to the news with shock and horror, as she did in hearing about that earlier engagement, although here she understands and feels "nothing. . . . as if she were dead," in contrast with the "cries and screams" with which she once longed to counter her father's words (WD 372, 111). It concludes, however, with a conversation in which Cynthia, accused by Molly of telling "lies," in effect speaks the truth of Molly's feelings—"One might think you cared for him yourself"—while Molly "spoke the truth as she believed it, though not the real actual truth": "I am proud to remember that he has been to me as a brother, and I love him as a sister, and I love you doubly because he has honoured you with his love" (WD 377). By her own account, Molly should now love Cynthia "doubly" because her sister is going to marry the man who has been "as"—rather than "like"—a brother to her: within the framework of affinity-by-marriage, a brother's wife will also become a "real" sister of one's own. Yet the doubleness of Molly's putative sisterhood to Cynthia, made by law and language, conceals "the real actual truth." The narrative intervention here surely functions to point out the duplicity of Molly's own words, how she takes cover under the fiction of pure sibling affection that has come to serve as her own particular form of "blindness," a form of not-knowing that strikingly links her situation both to her father's and to Roger's.[44]

The structured repetition that Gaskell creates in "the two sisters" plot thus makes Molly privy to "the wrong side of the tapestry," concealed from her when she first went to Hamley, even as it leads her *not* to see her implication in the romance plot, to which her use of family language blinds her (WD 346, 451). In being replaced again by a second Kirkpatrick, she loses the brother she substituted for the father, and this, too, it would seem, is a necessary loss, effected in part by her sister's mediation. Linking herself and her mother as "interlopers," Cynthia demonstrates the limits of analogical relationship by showing Molly that a sister will never come first if there is a wife in the cards (WD 437). In order to regain Roger, this time as a lover, Molly must cease to be his sister and become, if only temporarily, something more like a stranger.

In identifying Roger's courtship of Cynthia with her father's remarriage, Molly rearticulates emotions associated with loss of the one in relation to loss of the other, as when Cynthia inquires into the nature of Molly's feelings for "mamma":

> "She is papa's wife," said Molly, quietly. "I don't mean to say that I am not often very sorry to feel I am no longer first with him; but it was"—the violent colour flushed into her face till even her eyes burnt, and she suddenly found herself on the point of crying; the weeping ash-tree, the misery, the slow dropping comfort; and the comforters [sic] came all so vividly before her;—"it was Roger!"—she went on looking up at Cynthia, as she overcame her slight hesitation at mentioning his name—"Roger, who told me how I ought to take papa's marriage, when I was first startled and grieved at the news. Oh, Cynthia, what a great thing it is to be loved by him!" (WD 437–38)

Now "no longer first" with anyone, Molly's recollection of losing her father's undivided attention focuses not so much on him as on the memory of the brother's "comfort": "very sorry" though she still is about "papa," she only begins to falter on the verge of saying Roger's name. Although Cynthia has taken Molly's place with Roger, demonstrating that a fiancée has superior claims to a sister (as a wife does to a daughter), Molly does not entirely yield her own claim any more than she has with her father, with her "great power of loving" forming its basis: "She did not believe that Cynthia cared enough for him; at any rate, not with the sort of love that she herself would have bestowed, if she had been so happy—no, that was not—if she had been in Cynthia's place" (WD 345, 411). Her covert resistance to both her stepmother and her stepsister issues in a refusal to engage in plotting, which she comes to see as a common behavior of both Kirkpatrick women. Cynthia's underhanded dealings with Preston may have a different valence than her mother's more overt designs, but Molly rejects their practices even though compelled by her loyalty to both Cynthia and Roger to participate in and resolve that intrigue.

Until *Wives and Daughters* nears its end, Gaskell's own plotting consists of these structured repetitions—"everything in the story is duplicated, triplicated," Felicia Bonaparte notes—whereby Molly keeps losing her place in the plot.[45] If she comes to read her father's remarriage through the lens provided by Roger's pursuit of Cynthia, then she also imagines Roger and Cynthia's projected marriage as a union of two who are as unsuited to one another as her father and stepmother have proven to be. Moreover, in identifying courtship with conscious design and deliberation on the part of women, based on what she sees after her father's marriage, Molly also rejects any possibility of positioning herself either as a manager of events or as "conscious if passive bait" (*WD* 346). So when Cynthia, having broken her engagement to Roger by letter, "started up stung with a new idea"— "Roger will marry you! See if it is not so!"— "Molly pushed her away with a sudden violence of repulsion," going "crimson with shame and indignation" (*WD* 549). Regarding this passage, Homans argues that "Cynthia's understanding of Roger's ability to seek out substitutes . . . allows for Molly's inclusion as the next in that series" (*Bearing* 269). Viewed in this light, only Molly's "maidenly modesty" forcibly intervenes to differentiate her, in her own eyes and perhaps also in ours, from the stepsister whose perception that Roger will be both "changeable" and "consolable" proves correct (*WD* 549).[46] But only partially correct, I think, in that Molly and Roger's romance repeats, yet rather more emphatically revises, the second-chance narratives we have already considered.

If we recall the infamous final chapter of *Mansfield Park,* for example, in which dramatic action yields to narratorial exposition, we might see Roger's position as analogous to Edmund Bertram's. Neither had long "to wait and wish with vacant affections for an object worthy to succeed" his first faulty choice: "Scarcely had [Edmund] done regretting Mary Crawford, and observing to Fanny how impossible it was that he should ever meet with such another woman, before it began to strike him whether a very different kind of woman might not do just as well—or a great deal better" (*MP* 318, 319). Edmund's second attachment is upright, inevitable, and based on long familial association; with Fanny's "mind in so great a degree formed by his care, and her comfort depending on his kindness," the narrative voice asks in that familiar ironic tone, "What could be more natural than the change," which takes place "exactly at the time when it was quite natural that it should be so, and not a week earlier" (*MP* 319). Whatever "change," if any, may take place in Edmund's feelings is for all intents and purposes non-narratable: describing his undertaking "to persuade her that her warm and sisterly regard for him would be foundation enough for wedded love," the narration simply identifies the very "foundation" of Edmund's own fraternal "regard" for her (*MP* 319). Everything that has made Fanny an endearing cousin and "only sister" will also make her a fitting wife. All that has really changed is Edmund's estimation of what a wife should be: not "very different" from oneself but very much the same.

Roger's stance is certainly comparable to Edmund's. Although Cynthia is not quite "the false Duessa" Roger makes her out to be, in order "to express [his] sense of the difference between her and Molly as strongly as [he] could," he, too, takes "a very different kind of woman" as his second object (*WD* 643). But this narrative dramatizes both the change in Roger's feelings for Molly and his self-conscious plan to avoid even the appearance of repetition. When they both stay at the Towers, Roger feels "a sort of desire to obtain her good opinion in a manner very different to his old familiar friendliness"; he becomes jealous and possessive when her attention is "pre-occupied" by other men and "annoyed at her so constantly conjecturing what he must be feeling on the subject of Cynthia's marriage" (*WD* 616, 618). Subsequently kept at a distance by Molly, Roger misreads the "air of constraint" that governs their interactions as a sign of her disdain: he feels no longer "at liberty to speak to her in the old straight-forward brotherly way" (*WD* 629, 633). If Austen permits Fanny to fall into her cousin's arms with no compunction at all, then Gaskell makes Roger work at winning Molly, thus effacing rather than building on the "foundation" of his "old familiar friendliness."

Roger's perception of Molly's "changed treatment of him" (*WD* 635) also precipitates his deliberate effort to depart from the culturally sanctioned plot in which a second sister replaces a first. Suspecting that Molly "had come to view all the symptoms of his growing love for her... as disgusting inconstancy to the inconstant Cynthia; that she had felt that an attachment which could be so soon transferred to another was not worth having" (*WD* 635), Roger resolves not to repeat what has gone before so as to mark the distinction between the first and second "attachment":

> He was very jealous on her behalf. Was that love worthy of her which had once been given to Cynthia? Was not this affair too much a mocking mimicry of the last? Again just on the point of leaving England for a considerable time! If he followed her now to her own home,—in the very drawing-room where he had once offered to Cynthia!... Until his return he would not even attempt to win more of her love than he already had. But once safe home again, no weak fancies as to what might or might not be her answer should prevent his running all chances to gain the woman who was to him the one who excelled all. (*WD* 636)

As he subsequently confides to Mr. Gibson, "I determined not to repeat the former scene in the former place": conscious of the structural symmetry, Roger effectively cancels it out in refusing the available, tempting trajectory (*WD* 643). He marks the distinction between Cynthia and Molly, "the one who excelled all," by treating her as not interchangeable with her stepsister, "a person so inferior to herself" (*WD* 643). "Jealous" *for* her rather than *of* her, Roger aims to make it clear that he values Molly in her difference from Cynthia by according her different treatment.

Although Molly is not Cynthia, she also cannot be the sister he has known if Roger is to fall in love with her. During his two years away, she is "not changed," as Mr. Gibson describes Roger himself after his return from Africa, "and yet not the same"—words that recall the lines from Byron's *Giaour,* quoted in chapter 3, used to describe the dead wife's sister (*WD* 589). To be sure, the changes in Molly are effected in part by her step-relations; their designs have shaped her growth into young womanhood in more ways than one. Her changed attitude to Roger, however, has everything to do with her unwillingness to be herself designing or part of another's design. Spurred into consciousness by overhearing Mrs. Goodenough's speculation that Mrs. Gibson has laid a new plan for engaging Roger's affections by sending her stepdaughter on a visit to Hamley (to which Roger has returned from Africa upon his brother's death), Molly tries to avoid even the appearance of "impropriety" (*WD* 626). She modifies her manner, with the effect on him noted above. Molly's dilemma thus bears some further comparison with that of the dead wife's sister, whose "natural" desire to comfort her brother (-in-law) and his bereaved family could give rise to similar speculation as to her motives. Even if genuinely and exclusively inspired by familial love, as one witness before the Royal Commission had testified, "Such an [*sic*] one would shrink from exposing herself to the suspicion of others, or even of her own conscience, that selfishness was mingling itself with her benevolence; and that, in devoting herself to the consolation of her sister's husband,... she might, at the same time, be perhaps influenced by the secret desire of engaging his affections, and of ultimately becoming his wife" (*First Report* 112). Although Roger is not tabooed to Molly, either by her stepsisterhood to Cynthia or the squire's earlier objection—indeed, the squire seeks to promote their marriage during this visit—she suffers the same anxiety regarding her conduct to Roger as would one to whom any relation other than sisterhood is prohibited (*WD* 632–33).

That Molly's own "secret desire," which also recalls that of Fanny Price, is at this point in the novel potentially realizable and perfectly legitimate suggests that the impediment to revealing it lies only in her apprehension of sexual "impropriety." The question for Molly, then, on her visit to Hamley becomes how to act:

All that Molly could do was to resolve on a single eye to the dear old squire, and his mental and bodily comforts; to try and heal up any breaches which might have occurred between him and Aimée; and to ignore Roger as much as possible.... It would be very hard to avoid him as much as was consistent with common politeness; but it would be right to do it; and when she was with him she must be as natural as possible, or he might observe some difference; but what was natural? How much ought she avoid being with him? Would he even notice if she was more chary of her company, more calculating of her words? (*WD* 627)

If what once felt "natural"—her "almost brotherly intimacy" with Roger—was actually a product of Molly's informal, analogical adoption by the Hamleys, then the newly obvious potential for marriage makes Molly uncomfortable and self-conscious, "chary" and "calculating" against her will in ways that she implicitly identifies with the Kirkpatricks (*WD* 619). The narrative underlines how Molly's effort to avoid designing yet issues in something quite the opposite: "She made laws for herself . . . but her perfect freedom was gone; and with it half her chance"; in any other context, being "stiff and"—yet again—"awkward," the very opposite of "natural," would have spoiled the impression she might make (*WD* 627). But because Molly is staying not with "strangers who had not known her before" but with familiars, her being "so different from her usual self"—putting distance between herself and Roger, trying to act like the stranger she is not rather than the sister she has been—generates the very uncertainty and anxiety in him that has effected the change in his behavior to her (*WD* 627). In this sense, Molly is indeed "influenced by the secret desire of engaging his affections" and manages to do so without seeming to know how she did it.

The deliberateness with which Gaskell represents Molly's non-deliberate success at capturing Roger's attention, precipitated both by his will not to repeat and her movement from acting "naturally" to behaving "awkwardly," rings one last change on the theme of unintended consequences that *Wives and Daughters* develops over its course. As when Mr. Gibson sent her away in order to keep her to himself, only to lose her through his own actions, Molly's effort not to be designing furthers Gaskell's own design, which has been implicit in the novel from its fairy-tale beginning. "The old rigmarole of childhood" presents us with a sleeping princess, who awakens not once, but twice, to find her future stepmother at her side with her father nowhere in sight (*WD* 5). The Cinderella story Gaskell shapes, however, subtly reveals the connection between the two "variants of the tale" identified in this chapter's epigraph. Molly surely does suffer because "the father replaces her mother with a cruel stepmother," but this is a move that Mr. Gibson makes, as Homans and Schor imply, "because the father wishes to marry her himself." Represented in this novel as the "natural" outcome of their mutual and exclusive tie, father-daughter love has the potential to transgress both nature and culture. In choosing Mrs. Kirkpatrick, Mr. Gibson protects his daughter from himself, albeit not from suffering; through his story, Gaskell also makes plain the concealed imperative for Molly to move out from underneath her father's eye. Being replaced brings Molly pain and loss, and yet her second experience of this, at Roger's hands, not only repeats but also alters the circumstances of the first event. In the willed nonrepetition that she structures into the novel's presumed yet unwritten conclusion, Gaskell creatively revises the family fictions of her novelistic predecessors. Moreover, *Wives and Daughters* further demonstrates, in a highly particular and historically responsive way, that family affections—biologically or analogically based; inter- or intragenerational; same-sex as well as cross-gender—have a very prominent place in generating narratives of desire.

✒ CHAPTER 7

Virginia Woolf and
Victorian "Incests"

> Many narratives by survivors of incest and sexual
> abuse indicate that the trauma resides as much in
> secrecy as in sexual abuse—the burden not to tell
> creates its own network of psychic wounds that far
> exceed the event itself.
>
> —Ann Cvetkovich, *An Archive of Feelings,* 2003

> Would it not have been better (if there is any sense
> in saying good and better when there is no possible
> judge, no standard) to go on feeling, as at St. Ives,
> the rush and tumble of family life? To be family
> surrounded; to go on exploring and adventuring
> privately while all the while the family as a whole
> continued its prosaic, rumbling progress; would this
> not have been better than to have had that protection
> removed; to have been tumbled out of the family
> shelter; to have had it cracked and gashed; to have
> become critical and skeptical of the family—?
>
> —Virginia Woolf, "A Sketch of the Past," 1939–40

> It is so hard to talk even to ones [*sic*] own brothers
> and sisters.
>
> —Virginia Stephen to Violet Dickinson, 1904

In "A Sketch of the Past," Virginia Woolf
sought once more to come to terms with "the past" in writing—but flinched
at the task. "I do not want to go into my room at Hyde Park Gate. I shrink
from the years 1897–1904, the seven unhappy years" when the Stephen sisters
"were fully exposed without protection to the full blast of that strange character," "the alternately loved and hated father" ("SP" 136, 107, 116). Orches-
trated by George Duckworth, the "Greek slave years" of "coming out" were
filled with "drudgery and tyranny," as the sisters suffered under the "accepted
standards" of "upper middle class Victorian society" that he embodied and
enforced ("SP" 106, 151, 150). These were the years of which Woolf wrote,

"the division in our lives was curious. Downstairs there was pure convention; upstairs pure intellect," and, further, that "there was no connection.
There were deep divisions" ("SP" 157, 158). But the "divisions" were not so
sharp as she insisted. For the room she did not "want to go into"—"'done
up' at George's cost" after Stella's death, complete with a "long Chippendale
(imitation) looking glass, given me by George in the hope that I should look
into it"—not only sheltered "pure intellect" but also enabled bodily violation
("SP" 122). As she wrote in an earlier memoir, "There would be a tap at the
door; the light would be turned out and George would fling himself on my
bed, cuddling and kissing and otherwise embracing me in order, as he told
Dr. Savage later, to comfort me for the fatal illness of my father."[1] These were
the years, then, when sexual attention from an older sibling compounded the
serious difficulties of being Virginia Stephen and becoming Virginia Woolf.

"The impact of childhood sexual abuse" on Woolf's "life and work"
has been a topic of scholarly debate at least since the publication of Louise
DeSalvo's important, if tendentious, 1989 study.[2] Woolf's multiple accounts of
George Duckworth's "cuddling and kissing," combined with her single report
of Gerald Duckworth's "hand going under [her] clothes" when she was a very
young child, "going firmly and steadily lower and lower," have inspired an
array of critical responses too varied for quick synthesis here ("SP" 69). Most
of this scholarship locates Woolf's experiences within our contemporary
paradigm for understanding and representing incest as sexual trauma. Not
published until late in the twentieth century, a moment when the prevalence of incest was being rediscovered under new, but not entirely different,
historical and discursive conditions, Woolf's autobiographical writings offer
testimony from someone we might now characterize as a "survivor." But as the
previous chapters of this book should suggest, I will read "childhood sexual
abuse" in the life and work of Virginia Woolf within the historical parameters of nineteenth-century discourses on sex and marriage within the family,
which differ in some substantive ways from those that currently constitute
(incestuous) sexual abuse.[3] Although recent theoretical work on trauma aims
to conceptualize its political and historical dimensions, I highlight Victorian
discursive legacies in my analysis in an effort to isolate the terms through
which Woolf fictionalized and analyzed her experiences, born as she was at
a moment when, as I argue in chapter 1, incest and its cultural meanings were
being renegotiated.[4] For all its emphasis on the development of a uniquely
sensitive and strikingly idiosyncratic creative sensibility, "A Sketch of the
Past" also explicates incestuous sexual abuse and a child's response to it in
historical and anthropological terms, situating it within the affective intensities of the Victorian family system.

The gendered asymmetries of power and privilege that shape familial bonds and marital ties form the object of Woolf's critique. On this point, the theoretical and critical insights of trauma studies do play a part in my thinking, in that the polarity between what is and is not said subtends her writing almost from start to finish: "How deep they drove themselves into me," she writes of "all that I never said" to Leslie Stephen, "the things it was impossible to say aloud" ("SP" 108). *The Years* famously enacts multiple censorships, being in many ways that "novel about Silence" that Terence Hewet imagines in *The Voyage Out,* a novel about "the things people don't say."[5] As Christine Froula has definitively established, "Woolf's negotiations with internal and external censorship" are nowhere more apparent than in her writings of the 1930s, when she struggled to write a book that would open the door on "the sexual life of women" and shatter the "silence inspired by fear," a task that she could achieve only by trying to "break every mould & find a fresh form of being, that is of expression, for everything I feel & think."[6] I contend that for all Woolf's difficulties with "the family" and with the writing of *The Years* itself, it is as a *critique* of family life—with that word connoting an exploration of both its scope *and* its limits—that her writing illuminates the historical configuration of its emotional ties.

Woolf's autobiographical writing reveals the force of patriarchal power in the domestic sphere, embodied by "the alternately loved and hated father" old enough to be her grandfather, dependent on wives, daughters, and other female kin for all his comforts. It charts the shifting relations between two sisters who not only forge a "close conspiracy," a "private nucleus" "in that world of many men, coming and going, in that big house of innumerable rooms," but also, like the fictional sisters of Martineau, Skene, or Gaskell, contend with one another in an ongoing bid for exclusive attention ("SP" 143). "Woolf built her political analysis of her culture on her experience of her childhood," writes Hermione Lee, further noting that "Stella [Duckworth]'s relationship with Leslie [Stephen] became the basis for…Woolf's analysis of the tyranny and hypocrisy of the Victorian fathers."[7] While I share this assessment, I focus on the rhetorical, historical, and discursive dimensions of her autobiographical representations of the Stephen-Duckworth ménage—a particularly complex "blended" or third family that included a widower and his daughter, a widow and her three children, the four children born to this second marriage, and myriad other first- and second-family kin on both sides. Experience is Woolf's starting point, but the analysis of the Victorian fathers who did not support their daughters' efforts to make independent lives that she undertook in *Three Guineas* (1938) also depends on her reading of the biographies of "the daughters of educated men," which enabled her to historicize her position within a broader context (*TG* 4). To put this in today's terms, Woolf came to interpret her own first-family situation as symptomatic of a dysfunction within her culture, and she used all of the tools at her disposal to diagnose it.

This chapter proceeds, then, from an analysis of the key themes and discourses in Woolf's autobiographical writing about "the Victorian family" to a brief reading of *The Years,* which I undertake in the context of her abandoned attempt to combine fact and fiction in *The Pargiters.* This latter work contains her most sustained effort to articulate the impact of childhood sexual experience on both girls and boys. I largely set aside her well-known portraits of her parents in favor of attending more closely to the relationships among their various real and fictive children, relationships that proved not only painful but also powerfully formative for their daughter. It is especially striking in view of Woolf's conflicts with her four brothers that her late works of fiction imagine and reimagine a sister-brother bond that, as Diana L. Swanson argues, "becomes the female-male relationship of importance . . . for developing new egalitarian male-female relationships," especially in *The Years.*[8] Like a number of the other women writers considered here, Woolf's sibling connections were intense and lasting: the "bond . . . was from my earliest childhood so close with both Nessa and Thoby that if I describe myself I must describe them" ("SP" 125). Ultimately, I hope to suggest, in the words Woolf gave to Ralph Denham in *Night and Day,* "all that brotherhood and sisterhood, and a common childhood in a common past mean, all the stability, the unambitious comradeship, and tacit understanding of family life at its best," is as central to her vision as the "horror of family life" at its worst.[9] We cannot fully appreciate its "horror" unless we also understand the value Woolf locates in "family life."

In chapter 1, we encountered the strange coincidence of Virginia Stephen's writing of "Reminiscences" with the passage of the laws legalizing MDWS in 1907 and criminalizing sexual intercourse between (some) blood relations in 1908. Although the memoir does not directly refer to either form of "incest," veiling its discussion of the "scandalous" relationship between Jack Hills and Vanessa Stephen and only hinting at the sexual charge in George Duckworth's opposition to the liaison, it subtly reveals the circumstances that incite both. "Reminiscences" mythologizes the structuring gender relations of the Stephen-Duckworth household, in which women occupy the space of sacrificial victims and resisting rebels, complying with male demands and looking to escape from them, while men seek in their closest relations the satisfactions and solace that ostensibly only these women can provide. Such demands emanate not only from the father, but also from elder brothers, who resist the loss of sisters to marriage and prefer instead to keep those women to and for themselves. This family, then, looks like a closed unit: its women do not circulate and are not exchanged with others; it operates by replacing from within the women who depart from the family only by death.

Thus the fourth chapter narrates the competing claims on Vanessa Stephen's attention in the wake of the death of Stella Hills. Having lost a first wife (temporarily replaced by that wife's sister, Anny Thackeray), then a second, and then a stepdaughter, Leslie Stephen "was quite prepared to take Vanessa for his next victim" ("Reminiscences" 56). So was George Duckworth, who, "on the full tide of emotion, insisted upon a closer and more mature friendship with us" ("Reminiscences" 44). The new widower also turned to his sister(-in-law) for comfort, as almost six decades of debate had suggested that he inevitably—if illicitly—would. Of these three men, only Jack Hills held out to Vanessa Stephen the possibility of partial noncompliance with her inherited role, just as he had "offered" to Stella Duckworth "a very refreshing revolt" against "the compact which she had made with her stepfather" by promising her "the prospect of an independent life, a life at least which depended upon one person only" ("Reminiscences" 48). If the turn to a surviving sister was "natural" for Jack Hills—enacting as it did a cultural script that put the dead wife's sister in the widower's immediate path—then it may have been partially strategic for Vanessa Stephen to turn to him, as a way of resisting the sharper demands of her father and her eldest brother ("Reminiscences" 56).[10]

Narrating a late Victorian version of the MDWS plot, "Reminiscences" rehearses the critical perspective that the sisters came to share on their use and abuse by the men of their family. To be sure, when Virginia Stephen wrote of what her dead mother and sister might have felt, she undoubtedly invented, constructing a point of view on their situation in which they figure as representative "victims" of the Stephen-Duckworth family's tendency simultaneously to idealize and cannibalize its women. As Woolf came to fictionalize her in *To the Lighthouse* (1927), Julia Stephen was sometimes complicit in this tendency, having "the whole of the other sex under her protection," "presiding with immutable calm over destinies which she completely failed to understand," while her daughters "sport with infidel ideas which they had brewed for themselves of a life different from hers" (*TtL* 6, 50, 6–7). Their mother, Woolf later wrote, "was too willing, as I think now, to sacrifice us" to her husband ("SP" 133). Most plaintively, however, "Reminiscences" exposes "the damage that [Julia's and Stella's] deaths inflicted" on the family structure as a whole, and on the sisters in particular, in having that idealized "protection removed": "Had there been a mother or sister to intervene, much pain and anger and loneliness might have been spared" ("SP" 136, 137; "Reminiscences" 56).

Representing her sister's effort to manage the competing demands of father, brother, and brother(-in-law), Virginia Stephen also implicitly protested her own particular loss of her sister's "protection." In the patriarchal family's privileging of men's needs as primary—a key element of MDWS rhetoric—she occupied a secondary place as the motherless girl-child whose own needs went unmet, a detail that resonates with Woolf's representation of Cam in *To the Lighthouse* and Rose in *The Years,* both of whom suffer gendered wounds at the hands of boys and men. Putatively a portrait of Vanessa, the memoir subtextually speaks from and about the Brontëan position, described in chapter 4, of the orphaned and abandoned child, deprived of a mother or maternal surrogates by death, marriage, or both. Explicitly focusing on the three men who had laid claim to the surviving sister, "Reminiscences" yet indicates that its author was another, less powerful supplicant for Vanessa Stephen's attention after Stella Hills died; Virginia's unresolved feelings at "losing" Stella to marriage and motherhood in 1897 may have been rekindled by Jack's courtship of a second sister who also served as a maternal proxy.[11] The shared "sorrow" of three, "sharpened" by animosity toward Leslie Stephen, gave way to a bond of two, as Jack and Vanessa gradually came together: Vanessa "began to have more of Jack's confidence and favour than I did; and directly any such favour is shown it becomes more marked and endures" ("Reminiscences" 56). As in the women's fictions we encountered in chapter 3, "Reminiscences" configures jealousy as both *of* the sister and *for* the sister: Virginia expresses resentment "that Jack did not see all our efforts," that he did not sufficiently appreciate Vanessa, and that Vanessa herself "met [Virginia's] plaints" with "silence" ("Reminiscences" 59).

Tacitly marked by Virginia Stephen's responses to the exclusivity of heterosexual romance, the text also conceals a significant parallel between the moment of writing and the moment written about: the situation of Vanessa and Clive Bell in 1907, newly married and expecting a baby, structurally repeated that of Stella and Jack Hills, who ten years earlier conceived a child that died along with its mother. Conscious of the parallel or not, Virginia Stephen wrote her living sister's present into her construction of the past, perhaps willing her to break with their dead sister's example, even as her account is also shaped by other exigencies of the current moment.[12] For when Vanessa married Clive, as when she threw in with Jack, Virginia—anxious about the implications of the marriage for her own life—"was sometimes jealous" ("Reminiscences" 59). The intimacy she later forged with Clive—a living sister's husband—not only recalled her ambivalent responses first to Stella's marrying Jack and then to Jack's subsequent relationship with Vanessa but also restaged elements of an earlier, even more persistent competition between the Stephen sisters for the attention of their brother Thoby, who died in 1906.[13] It is thus significant in a number of ways, not least of which is "the difficulty of describing Vanessa's affair with Jack," that jealousy—one way of naming Virginia's desire exclusively to possess her sister in both 1897 and 1907—is the emotional note on which the memoir breaks off.[14]

On balance, then, Virginia Stephen's first sustained representation of the messy psychodynamics of the Stephen-Duckworth family shows them to be continuous with, rather than some monstrous transgression of, the cultural paradigm for upper-middle-class Victorian family life, characterized in particular by intense intragenerational bonds. By 1907–08 she had formulated a critique of the sexism that subordinated the interests of women and children to those of men. She had limned but not fully elaborated the psychic structures that propelled Leslie, Jack, and George toward Vanessa as surrogate and substitute for the women they had lost and that also, perhaps, impelled Vanessa toward first Jack, then Clive, to repair her own losses. She had begun to explore the triangular configurations that her childhood installed and that shaped her relationships with her parents and siblings; she had also reproduced them—or, we might say, acted them out—in her writing and behavior. Woolf would subsequently construe rivalry, competition, and jealousy among family members as writ large in the public sphere. These emotions, concretely situated in the conditions of her own early life, would become material that she would persistently work through in her fiction, ultimately historicizing them as the cultural and psychic residual of the Victorian family system.

Returning to the dead wife's sister plot thirty years later in "A Sketch of the Past," Virginia Woolf expanded on an image Virginia Stephen had introduced in the earlier memoir to emblematize the desolation that followed from Stella's death: "I remember the shape of a small tree which stood in a little hollow in front of us, and how, as I sat holding Jack's hand, I came to conceive this tree as the symbol of sorrow, for it was silent, enduring and without fruit" ("Reminiscences" 56). In the earlier memoir, Jack "talked, when he talked, of Stella and the past" ("Reminiscences" 56). In the later one, as Woolf recalled this "leafless bush," she interpreted his broken sentences as expressions of his grief and longing: "Subconsciously, I knew that he meant his sexual desires tore him asunder; I knew that he felt that at the same time as his agony at Stella's death.... And the tree outside in the August summer half light was giving me, as he groaned, a symbol of his agony; of our sterile agony; was summing it all up" ("SP" 140–41). Far more explicit than "Reminiscences" about Jack's sexual frustration and her "subconscious" recognition of it, so, too, does "A Sketch" more directly link Jack's desires to George's antagonism. For when that tree started once more to flower, "to grow little red chill buds," the whole family's "sterile agony" burst into bitter bloom: "The misery, the quarrels, the irritations, . . . the insinuations, which as soon as family life started again began to prove that Stella's death had not left us more united; as father said; but had left us all ill adjusted; growing painfully into relations that her death had distorted" ("SP" 141). As Froula argues, "this tree and the incestuous desire it summed up" persistently figures in Woolf's writing, "a symbol at once of blight and of potential rebirth."[15]

In "another garden scene" in "A Sketch" that follows directly on that one, George implores Virginia to set things right, and she puts her willingness to please on display:

> George singled me out, and walked me off round the lawn. I cannot remember any phrase exactly. A sound of mumbling comes back; his pressure on my hand; and then I gathered that very emotionally and ambiguously, with many such words as "Darling old Goat," "old party," and so on he was telling me that people were saying that Vanessa was in love with Jack; it was illegal; their marriage he meant; could I not speak to her; persuade her—It was a blurred night talk; with the usual resonance of emotional chords; and I was flattered; perhaps felt important; and must have promised I would say whatever it was he wanted me to say. ("SP" 141–42)

Using Virginia as a tool to coerce Vanessa, George "flattered" her, makes her "feel important," trades on her affection for him so that she will take his side. But once she "realised that [Vanessa] had her side," too, Virginia took her sister's part, in an instance of her overriding loyalty to her closest ally ("SP" 142). Vulnerable to George's pressure, she also implied the continuity between this form of sexual coercion and another. For in that "blurred night talk," as Woolf recalled it, "usual" rather than exceptional in George's pathetic striking of "emotional chords," we can hear echoes of the "emotionally and ambiguously" charged incident that Woolf reported at the end of "22 Hyde Park Gate," when, "creaking stealthily, the door opened; treading gingerly, someone entered" her room, and George "flung himself on my bed, and took me in his arms."[16]

Regarding her "knuckl[ing] under to [George's] authority," Woolf wrote, "I must obey because he had force—age, wealth, tradition—behind him"

("SP" 152, 154). Trying to explicate "his desire to make us share his views," she "cannot find the true reason" but asserted that "his motives were—as indeed they always were—mixed": "Some crude wish to dominate there was; some jealousy, of Jack no doubt; some desire to carry off the prize; and, as became obvious later, some sexual urge" ("SP" 154). Paramount among the "relations that Stella's death had distorted" were George's "relations" with his two younger half-sisters. But in the moment of writing, armed with the analysis she had been developing over several decades, Woolf contextualized his "crude wish to dominate" within a feminist critique of the Stephen-Duckworth family, indicting "that great patriarchal machine" which "stamped and moulded" fathers and brothers and tortured young women: "The machine into which our rebellious bodies were inserted in 1900 not only held us tight in its framework, but bit into us with innumerable sharp teeth"; "a girl had no chance against its fangs" ("SP" 153, 152, 157).

The machine thus provides one of the chief metaphors by which Woolf critiqued upper-middle-class Victorian society as a system for producing and reproducing class and gender relations of power, which both men and women live at the level of the body. "The intellectual machine" makes the career, from which all else follows, by subjecting boys to the pattern for making professional men ("SP" 153). Excluded for good and ill from that aspect of the system, the Stephen women yet have their part to play, as George's successful entrance into "the social machine" requires his sisters' assistance ("SP" 153). A second metaphor illustrates "the pressure" it exerts: "Though we could and indeed must, sit passive and applaud the Victorian males when they went through the intellectual hoops, George's hoops—his social triumphs—needed our help" ("SP" 150, 154). Identifying a source for "the outsider's feeling" that she elaborated as the basis for resistance to patriarchy in *Three Guineas,* Woolf remarked that she "felt as a gipsy or child feels who stands at the flap of the tent"—perhaps lacking the price of admission—"and sees the circus going on inside.... I saw George as an acrobat jumping through hoops" ("SP" 152–53). Along with the machine, then, the circus and the game become interchangeable images, contributing to the overall impression of "the social" and "the intellectual" as constituted by performance and display and as constitutive of human types. Only the presence of that "good friend who is with me still, upheld me; that sense of the spectacle; the dispassionate separate sense" enables the critical detachment from and resistance to being "stamped and moulded" in the conventional, rule-bound way ("SP" 155).

In her analysis of upper-middle-class conventions in "A Sketch of the Past," Woolf participated in the "broad reversal of assumptions" about the continuum between savagery and civility that Christopher Herbert identifies as emerging in the late nineteenth century.[17] "As discipline increasingly took on negative connotations in late-Victorian discourse," intellectuals began to valorize their own freedoms by recasting primitives as rule-bound, governed by what Herbert Spencer called "a considerable amount of ceremonial regulations."[18] A generation or two later, in order to primitivize the society in which she was raised, Woolf portrayed the Victorians—especially Victorian men—as mechanically conforming to ritual: she represented the "savagery" within civilization as the "spectacle of controls exerted systematically upon the smallest details of daily life," focusing (as did Victorian anthropologists) on gender and sexual relations as a key site at which such controls were naturalized and enforced.[19] Woolf's own "sense of the spectacle," however, is neither fully "separate" nor entirely "dispassionate": "the outsider's feeling" is itself generated and shaped by the events observed and subsequently narrated. In "the show ring," for example, Woolf glossed her recollected perception of George "jumping through hoops" as tinged "perhaps with fear, perhaps with admiration"—not as neutral and objective but as colored by conflicting emotions ("SP" 153).

This ambivalent stance on past events can be connected to another rhetorical position that Woolf takes up in "A Sketch" when she conducts her reading of a not-entirely-vanished past, situating herself and Vanessa at a temporal and spatial distance from the men of her family:

> While we looked into the future, we were completely under the power of the past. Explorers and revolutionists, as we both were by nature, we lived under the sway of a society that was about fifty years too old for us. It was this curious fact that made our struggle so bitter and so violent. For the society in which we lived was still the Victorian society. Father himself was a typical Victorian. George and Gerald were consenting and approving Victorians. So that we had two quarrels to wage; two fights to fight; one with them individually; and one with them socially. We were living say in 1910; they were living in 1860. ("SP" 147)

Although she had indeed lived at the same time as her father (fifty years her senior) and her half-brothers (fourteen and twelve years older, respectively), Woolf both denied the generational difference between father and stepsons by freezing them all in a high Victorian past and minimized the intragenerational sibling links between George and Gerald, on the one hand, and the Stephen sisters, on the other.[20] To be sure, the three Duckworths and the mysteriously disabled Laura Stephen had always been set apart from their younger siblings. With their distinction from the Duckworth brothers further "symbolized by our separate rooms" after Stella's marriage, "'us four' as we called ourselves had become separate," yet "not so separate," she adds, "as boys and girls, brothers and sisters, often become when the boys go to public schools and the sisters stay at home," for grief had "united us" ("SP" 125). With Gerald and George's rooms placed "on the floor below" her own, the spatial divisions of the upper-middle-class house, so carefully enumerated in "A Sketch," further enabled the fiction of temporal distance that underpinned her "denial of coevalness," a rhetorical strategy that Johannes Fabian has identified in colonial and imperial western discourse by which contemporary nonwestern peoples are represented as stuck in an earlier developmental moment ("SP" 123).[21] If Leslie, George, and Gerald are not hereby explicitly made primitive, then Woolf's rhetorical move of placing them in a high Victorian past marks them as survivals, in the anthropological sense, whose continuing presence creates a disturbance in the field of futurity (or "modernity") in which she represented Vanessa and herself as adventuring and exploring.

To be "under the power" and "the sway" of a still-living "Victorian" past, when one is "by nature" a child of "the future," resulted in a "struggle so bitter and so violent" that Woolf repeatedly invoked these distancing fictions, tinged with emotion recollected in something other than tranquility, in order to clarify and classify that past as the medium for cruelty.[22] If her representation of "this past is much affected by the present moment"—note that Woolf wrote "A Sketch" under the shadow of the coming war, which seemed to portend the atavistic triumph of barbarity over civilization—then it also constituted "the present moment" as formed by and continuous with 1860, 1882, 1897, or 1904 ("SP" 75). Within this framework, George becomes "a fossil" who "had taken every crease and wrinkle of the conventions of upper middle class society between 1870 and 1900" ("SP" 151). Recalling Eliot's representation of "emmet-like Dodsons and Tullivers," analyzed in chapter 5, Woolf wrote that a day in the life of the Stephen-Duckworth household "as we lived it about 1900" could provide "a complete model of Victorian society," "like one of those sections with glass covers in which ants and bees are shown going about their tasks" ("SP" 147). In a startling variant on the circus metaphor, the home itself became a "cage," she "a nervous, gibbering, little monkey" and her father "a lion who was sulky and angry and injured; and suddenly ferocious, and then very humble, and then majestic" ("SP" 116).[23] His "violent displays of rage" had "something blind, animal, savage in them": repeating the words of Roger Fry, Woolf concluded that if "civilization means awareness," then her father "was uncivilized in his extreme unawareness" ("SP" 146). As Julia Briggs observes, Woolf invoked Conrad's foundational metaphor of the dark heart of "civilization" both early in her career and in her very last novels.[24] It provided a critical image for conveying the survival of "savagery" in "upper middle class Victorian society," which had disavowed "savage" practices, like incest itself, through discursive means and projected them onto class and race others.

Two final instances from "A Sketch" show the variable uses to which Woolf put this reverse-discourse. In an early scene of *The Years,* Milly and Delia Pargiter sit "at the round table in the front drawing-room of the house in Abercorn Terrace," waiting for the kettle to boil and the rest of the family to come home, looking out the window to relieve their culturally enforced boredom; in "A Sketch," describing the front drawing room at 22 Hyde Park Gate "facing the street," Woolf once again recalled "the round table in the middle" of the room, "the very hearth and centre of family life" ("SP" 117, 118).[25] Like the Pargiter men, "in the evening back they would all come; Adrian from Westminster; Jack from Lincoln's Inn Fields; Gerald from Dents; George from the Post office or the Treasury, back to the focus, the tea table, where Nessa and I presided" ("SP" 143). Only boys and men voyage out, while their sisters remain at home, trying to light the flame—or, perhaps, "guarding the door of Darkness."[26] Woolf revised that emblem of Victorian civility and the meaning of that ritual in an ethnographic vein:

> The tea table rather than the dinner table was the centre of Victorian family life—in our family at least. Savages I suppose have some tree, or fire place, round which they congregate; the round table marked that focal, that sacred spot in our house. It was the centre, the heart of the family. It was the centre to which the sons returned from their work in the evening; the hearth whose fire was tended by the mother, pouring out tea. (118)[27]

Continuous with rather than differentiated from the "primitive" customs of "savages," tea-table gatherings, like "tea-table training," reflect the habitual, rule-bound, "sacred" order that constitutes and is constituted by the gendered division between domestic and professional labor, the very order that the Stephen sisters would both inherit and contest. Like the furniture and knickknacks of Abercorn Terrace, which turn up scattered about other houses and flats throughout *The Years,* some portion of the tea table survived in its new context, remainder and reminder of the bright and dark heart(h) of family life.[28]

An earlier set of references in "A Sketch" reaches even further back in time to analyze young Virginia Stephen's responses to two of Virginia

Woolf's memories: first, her shame at the "habit of looking at my face" in the "small looking-glass in the hall at Talland House," a "habit" to which "a strong feeling of guilt seemed naturally attached" ("SP" 68, 67, 68); and second, her "resenting" and "disliking" Gerald Duckworth touching her "private parts" ("SP" 69). Along with their close textual proximity and their shared focus on the affective dimension of bodily experience, a discourse of inheritance links these two passages. Trying to understand the first emotion, Woolf theorized that enjoying her own image—a legacy from her mother and Stella, whose beauty "gave me as early as I can remember, pride and pleasure"—must have been thwarted by "some opposite instinct," "checked by some ancestral dread" ("SP" 68). Borrowing from Darwinian discourse in being "almost inclined to think that I inherited a streak of the puritan" from the "spartan, ascetic" ("SP" 68) father and grandfather, Woolf looked to her immediate ancestors and her mixed lineage for the source of her sensations.

When it comes to describing her response to Gerald's molestation, however, she constructed a much longer timeline and an exclusively matrilineal inheritance to account for her feelings:

> I remember how I hoped that he would stop; how I stiffened and wriggled as his hand approached my private parts. But it did not stop. His hand explored my private parts too. I remember resenting, disliking it—what is the word for so dumb and mixed a feeling?... This seems to show that a feeling about certain parts of the body; how they must not be touched; how it is wrong to allow them to be touched; must be instinctive. It proves that Virginia Stephen was not born on the 25th January 1882, but was born many thousands of years ago; and had from the very first to encounter instincts already acquired by thousands of ancestresses in the past. ("SP" 69)

Here, too, the adult Woolf attributed the feelings of her younger self to "instincts," defining them in the idiom of the Victorian discourse of inheritance as the product of experiences "acquired" by many "ancestresses" throughout the ages. These "instincts" installed a two-part taboo. Within the immediate context of the experience she was describing, the statement "they must not be touched" implies rather than states a grammatical subject: it only implies, that is, a taboo on (incestuous) sexual abuse rather than naming it outright, so that a prohibition on touching could conceivably extend to masturbation, another Victorian taboo endlessly pronounced and transgressed. That "it is wrong to allow them to be touched," within the broader context of a Victorian girlhood, suggests the patriarchal premium on female chastity that Woolf redeployed to feminist ends in *Three Guineas,* even as it also lodges some responsibility for that "wrong" with the child, who cannot help but "allow" the imposition that produces "so dumb and mixed a feeling." However we interpret Woolf's analysis, in representing herself as born "many thousands of years ago," she located her responses to her brother's violation of her bodily boundaries as continuous with those of an imaginary but imaginable line of "ancestresses." In doing so, she also primitivized the practice of (incestuous) sexual abuse as the inheritance of a "savage" past that was continuous with and survives into the "civilized" present.

Fictionalizing sexual abuse in *The Pargiters,* the "novel-essay" or "essay-novel" that she began late in 1932 only to abandon early in 1933, Woolf made a deliberate attempt not only to analyze but also to historicize the "dumb and mixed...feeling" she experienced. Part of the difficulty in doing so lay in the absence of nineteenth-century accounts of sexual abuse that would flesh out her "novel of fact" (*Pargiters* 9).[29] It should have been simple to demonstrate that nothing "influenced the lives of the Pargiters in March 1880 more powerfully and more completely than the principle of that love which—to distinguish it from the different loves of the drawing room—may be called street love, common love, love in general," which mandated that "Eleanor and Milly and Delia could not possibly go for a walk alone" (*Pargiters* 36, 37).[30] But neither the particular event that traumatizes their younger sister Rose nor Rose's response to it has any precedent in literary sources:

> This instinct to turn away and hide the true nature of the experience, either because it is too complex to explain or because of the sense of guilt that seems to adhere to it and to make concealment necessary, has, of course, prevented...the novelist from dealing with it in fiction—it would be impossible to find any mention of such feelings in the novels that were being written by Trollope, Mrs. Gaskell, Mrs. Oliphant, George Meredith, during the eighties; and if the novelists ignore it, this is largely because the biographers and autobiographers also ignore it, and thus reduce the material which the novelist has to work upon to a minimum. (*Pargiters* 51)

While "ignore" is probably the wrong word here to explain the silence of fiction, biography, and autobiography alike about the (incestuous) sexual abuse of children, there was at least one fictional representation of incest published in the 1880s, which Woolf might have known, that subscribes entirely to the discursive conventions examined in chapter 1. Relocating the scene of the crime from overcrowded urban rooms to "cabins no better than sties" in a "foul little fen village," Vernon Lee's *Miss Brown* (1884) describes "the pools of sin" in which "miserable creatures have gradually come to live worse than animals," and "the condition of brutish sin" in which "they grow, and let their children in turn grow up."[31] With the novel published in the immediate wake of *The Bitter Cry of Outcast London*, Lee's images and assertions closely resemble those of the social investigators and parliamentary commissioners who painted "incest" as the preferred vice and habitual practice of working-class "savages": "It's been going on for generations," exclaims one of the novel's characters (*MB* 160).

That the children of incest are discursively aggregated as "the starving, unwashed, and unlettered million" who mechanically go on to perpetrate incest with children of their own helps account for why "such feelings" as Rose Pargiter's have no history, or at least no recorded history, on which Woolf could draw (*MB* 197). For the only feelings that matter in such a context belong to middle-class observers, who luxuriate in the expression of the "outrage" that characterizes such representations.[32] In the context of Woolf's project, *Miss Brown* and the contemporary texts it echoes—not at all concerned with the experiences of actual abuse that Woolf sought to analyze—still help to illuminate a series of broader disconnects that also shape her representations. In characterizing the context of her own incestuous sexual abuse, Woolf deployed the discourse of incest as a "savage" practice to primitivize the ways of "consenting and approving Victorians"; but in her fictionalized accounts, she reproduced some of the conventional associations that sustained that discourse by objectifying and stigmatizing victims.

The failure of fiction and memoir to document, or even to imagine, an experience like Rose's demonstrates the operation of "a convention" that Woolf critically and self-consciously uses in representing the man who exposes his genitals to Rose at the pillar-box.[33] In *The Pargiters*, though not in *The Years*, the sentence in question reads, "As she ran past him, he gibbered some nonsense at her, sucking his lips in & out; & began to undo his clothes" (*Pargiters* 43). The sentence trails off into an ellipsis, "a convention, supported by law, which forbids, *whether rightly or wrongly*, any plain description of the sight that Rose, in common with many other little girls, saw under the lamp post by the pillar box in the dusk of that March evening" (*Pargiters* 51, emphasis added). Woolf implied that its legally adjudged "indecency" would have prohibited a "plain description" of sexual abuse from being circulated in the 1880s (or even in the 1930s, for that matter, in the aftermath of obscenity prosecutions against the works of D. H. Lawrence, James Joyce, and Radclyffe Hall).[34] As the journalist George Sims wrote in *Horrible London* (1889), "Were I . . . to go into the details of ordinary life in a London slum, the story would be one which no journal enjoying a general circulation could possibly print."[35]

But the equivocal "rightly or wrongly" also invokes another convention. Woolf's words here gloss the practice of euphemism—which "seeks to conceal what it renames while simultaneously conveying the information it hides"—in the public discussion of (incestuous) sexual abuse.[36] The use of such "pargeting" phrases as "nameless outrages," "cruel immoralities," "grave evils," or "brutish sin" both does and does not reveal the sexual nature of the crime.[37] To be sure, the use of euphemism was not restricted to cases of sexual abuse: as William A. Cohen observes, "Sexuality in the nineteenth century became the subject routinely and paradoxically signaled by its ineffability— a subject that consequently produces volatile effects... when it approaches explicit articulation."[38] Whether the subject is sexual contact between men, the major focus of Cohen's work, or between adults and children, the use of particular phrases no doubt conjured up precisely the images they ostensibly sought to obscure; as the historian Carol Smart remarks, "there was common knowledge about adult-child sexual contact.... It was not simply silenced or invisible."[39] However, even had Woolf consulted the archive of sources authorized to describe and discuss (incestuous) sexual abuse—for example, the annual reports of the child-protection organizations that came into being around 1885 with the passage of the Criminal Law Amendment, which raised the age of consent from 13 to 16—she would have found little about the feelings of those who experienced it, and not much in the way of "plain description."[40]

As Louise A. Jackson argues in her analysis of child protection rhetoric, such organizations as the National Society for the Prevention of Cruelty to Children deployed euphemism to maintain "the silence which must... of necessity surround [sexual abuse] because the details of cases were too delicate to report."[41] According to Jackson and other historians, the delicacy of the cases, which might in our time mandate anonymity to protect sexual-assault survivors, instead resided in their potential effects on others: both the representation of "nameless outrages" and the children upon whom these "grave evils" were visited were "a dangerously polluting presence" in the print media and the (working-class) home (*Child* 58).[42] To be the object of (incestuous) sexual abuse was not only to be contaminated but also to become a source of potential contamination; to write plainly about (incestuous) sexual abuse would diffuse and extend its contaminating force to "innocent" readers.[43] Until the 1920s, working-class girls who had been sexually abused—whether in the family, on the job, or in the street—were routinely removed from their homes and placed in institutional settings where they could be "reformed" and their influence contained; moreover, "child victims of incest were more likely to be sent to an institution than those who had been assaulted by strangers" (*Child* 66). So Woolf's equivocation signals a deeper uncertainty, which she partially shared, about the social impact of representing "nameless outrages." At the same time, both the absence of accounts in the print sources on which Woolf relied to reconstruct the Victorian past and the presence of euphemism in the "official" materials that she did not (apparently) consult challenge the naturalness of the acquired "instinct" she attributed to Rose, "the sense of guilt that seems to adhere to" the victim of (incestuous) sexual abuse "and to make concealment necessary."

Woolf was no doubt correct in her perception of "the actual fact—that children of Rose's age are frequently assaulted, and sometimes far more brutally than she was," which would be "familiar to any one who reads the Police Court news" (*Pargiters* 50). Yet in stating that "fact," Woolf was participating in another discursive convention, also marked by class, race, and gender, that "rightly or wrongly" assigns sexual assault as an aspect of "street love" to places entirely off-limits to the Pargiter sisters (with the exception of Eleanor, whom I will discuss below), places where they could scarcely be imagined venturing in 1880—even if "they had a maid or a brother with them" (*Pargiters* 50). Perhaps relying in part on accounts from "the Police Court news," Woolf wrote that "even today, a mother in the poorer parts of London will make an effort that her small daughter shall not run round to the grocer's shop after dark without a little brother or sister to go with her" (*Pargiters* 50). Purportedly a sign of how little had changed between 1880 and 1932, Woolf's association of (known and reported) instances of sexual assault with "the poorer parts of London" more dramatically papers over—or pargets—what she knew from her own experience, even if she had no way of judging how typical or anomalous her circumstances had been.[44]

Woolf's representation of Rose's assault by a stranger on a public street, which recasts the conditions of her own abuse, can be verified by recent historical research. Jackson's study of 1,146 cases of sexual assault tried on indictment in Yorkshire and Middlesex between 1830 and 1910 notes that "where details of specific circumstances are available, a large proportion of court cases involved allegations of abuse in public places by total strangers"; moreover, "when cases involving men known to their victims were reported, they tended to implicate male lodgers, neighbours and employers rather than blood relatives" (*Child* 43). Of the 250 cases in which "details of the relationship between the victim and the alleged abuser were traced," incidents of familial sexual abuse accounted for only 12 percent of the total (*Child* 167n88).[45] As for the class profile of those involved in the cases, Jackson finds "the majority of abuse cases," unsurprisingly, "concerned complainants and defendants of similar social rank: working class and petite bourgeoisie"

(*Child* 29). For reasons we encountered in chapter 1, "the middle-class male and, indeed, the middle-class home, was less likely to be the subject of surveillance or scrutiny," so very few incidents of sexual assault, incestuous or not, involving middle-class people were ever prosecuted (*Child* 8). As Roger Davidson argues in a Scottish context, when "child abuse was removed from the home and placed on the street, in the park, in the cinema," it was represented as "something that happened to girls"—presumably of any class, race, or ethnicity—"when they wandered to a dangerous place and encountered a strange man," not as something that also "happened to girls" at home.[46]

Construed in this light, then, Woolf's representation of Rose's fictive experience and of the typical site and scene of sexual assault, as reported to the police and recounted in the media, coincides with the historical record, such as it is. That record indicates the stringent limits to what we can know about the prevalence of (incestuous) sexual abuse during this era, and it also reminds us that, "even today," it is impossible to be certain about the incidence of private-sphere malfeasance, whatever the social stratum. But Woolf's choices also indicate the pargeting of her own incestuous abuse, the papering over of experiences to which she could have testified with the culturally acceptable fiction that sexual abuse was confined to "the poorer streets of London": Margot Gayle Backus is surely right to claim that when an aspect of the "cycle of incestuous appropriation" characterizing the Stephen-Duckworth family was represented in a text intended for publication, "the feelings pertaining to it can only be experienced and encrypted" by being "attributed to a sexual assault stemming from outside the family."[47] My point, however, is not that Woolf should have "come out" in *The Pargiters* or *The Years* as a victim of (incestuous) sexual abuse but rather that the fictive Rose's experience relies on even as it contests aspects of the cover story that relegated such abuse to the margins of representability, a choice on Woolf's part that tended to confirm rather than undermine the association of sexual crimes against female children exclusively with the poorer classes. Creating a middle-class victim of abuse in *The Pargiters* opened a possibility for intervening in that association, but Woolf limited her public critique of the structures and systems that she more explicitly indicted in her private writings, like "A Sketch of the Past" and even the two memoirs she read to her intimates in the Memoir Club. Only in Rose's bedtime hallucination that "the man was actually in the room with her" can we locate a potentially different and far more difficult story to tell (*Years* 40).

There is some evidence that Woolf had planned to provide a detailed view of "the poorer parts of London" and those who lived there than the published

version of *The Years* contains.[48] Much of that view would have been presented through Eleanor, whose doubled position—as a surrogate mother to
Rose and the only Pargiter daughter in the first section of *The Years* to have
anything like a life outside the home—marks a crucial intersection between
widely separated knowledges and experiences. For Eleanor represents, among
other things, a familiar figure of the 1880s and 1890s, the middle-class female
philanthropist who visits the East End poor: she is "sized... up" by an anonymous man on a bus as "a well-known type" (*Years* 102).[49] In the "1891" section, Woolf represented through Eleanor's consciousness a series of cross-class
encounters that indicate an expanding knowledge of "the poor" and how
they live. Even in light of the muting and silencing that Woolf performed in
the movement from *The Pargiters* to *The Years,* she constituted this character,
more than any other, as a witness of public and private life in different class
contexts.

One such encounter takes place in the committee room, when an "ex-
mill hand," "scenting condescension," and a "retired shopkeeper" argue with
Eleanor and Major Porter, who are "both of the same social standing" (*Years*
95, 96). Another occurs when, after adopting the "upper middle-class tone
she detested," Eleanor threatens to fire the man who built her houses in Peter
Street, only "five years" old "and yet everything wanted repairing" (*Years*
100, 99). Here she also notices, almost in passing, that "Mrs. Toms, the downstairs lodger," has "another baby coming, after all I told her" (*Years* 97). It is
not until Eleanor goes to look for her sister Delia, who has left her father's
house and now "lodges in a St. Pancras' slum," that the more ominous rhetoric of working-class urban life infiltrates her vision.[50] "Here was the vice, the
obscenity, the reality of London," signified not by those she meets—for she
encounters no people—but by the "dingy and decrepit" streets and squares
and buildings "that seemed to have been degraded from their past dignity,"
the warrens of the poor that the late Victorians, although not Eleanor, would
designate as the sites of overcrowding that produced incestuous abuse (*Years*
114). "The whole neighbourhood seemed to her foreign and sinister": thinking of Delia's personal safety, Eleanor reflects, "she must often come back
this way at night alone" (*Years* 114, 115). In such passages, the adult Eleanor
(about thirty-five years old in the "1891" section) is fully aware of the difficulty of lives other than her own, lived in far less privileged circumstances,
and understands things about sexuality and sexual danger. However much
shaped by the rhetoric of working-class "vice," her point of view contains
elements of actual perception about threats to the security of all women.

That such understanding is partly a function of Eleanor's cross-class travels
becomes clearer when we return to earlier moments in both *The Pargiters* and

The Years. In a passage from the first chapter of *The Pargiters,* Milly asks her sister what she would do with her life had she the freedom to choose, and Eleanor projects a very different existence from the one she currently is leading: "I should take a room, somewhere [...] but in a poor neighborhood: & [...] pull down all these awful slums &—well, start things fresh,—if I had the money" (*Pargiters* 23).[51] "Eleanor's relations with 'the poor,'" "discussed by the Pargiters [...] as if they were in a book," "amused her family": what strikes Eleanor about "the poor" is that "everything's discussed" openly (*Pargiters* 21, 22). She (silently) compares this to the "reticence" that "existed between the sisters" of Abercorn Terrace even as she also reproduces that "reticence": her dealings with "the Levys & the Gages & the Zwarts" of "Lisson Grove" in St. John's Wood "had taught Eleanor a great deal about marriage," but she did not "discuss it with her family" (*Pargiters* 23, 21, 24). Reflecting Woolf's thorough excision of explicit content about "the sexual life of women" over the course of the novel, it is instead Eleanor's "dreams, her plans," her wish to live among the poor, that "she did not want to discuss" with her sister or her brother Morris in *The Years:* "She never told him about the Levys either, except by way of a joke" (*Years* 31, 34). Thinking about her sisters' confinement to "the cage" of Abercorn Terrace, what she says is that "the poor enjoy themselves more than we do"; what she seems to mean is that they express thoughts and feelings on a range of topics, including sexuality, more openly than do members of her own family (*Years* 30; *Pargiters* 21).

To be sure, from a Foucauldian perspective, we could dismiss Eleanor's perception, steeped in class and race constructs, as an image of the other—less bound by propriety, more frank and free about sexuality—created by the dominant discourse, which Woolf then deploys against the respectable "reticent" class, whose members are presented as insuring their own "inhibition" by internalizing and enforcing speech prohibitions. While this is a plausible reading of Eleanor's speech and thoughts in both *The Pargiters* and *The Years,* it doesn't do full justice to this character, the only member of the first Pargiter generation who makes a sustained and genuine, if imperfect, effort at what her niece Peggy calls "living differently" (*Years* 391). Indeed, there may be a significant, though submerged, link between Eleanor's role as a visitor to "the poorer streets of London" and her position as the eldest daughter whose situation at home, in relation to her father and her siblings, locates her at the center of the family's intensities and antagonisms; who stands in the place of a mother to her youngest sister and, ultimately, of a wife/sister/daughter to her widowed father; and who suffers exclusion from the world of boys and men. It is Eleanor, after all, to whom Rose tries and fails to relate her frightening experience with the man at the pillar-box; who "knew that Rose's fright had nothing to do with the cats" in Miss Pym's garden; who tells her that her father and brother "would never let a robber come into your room"; and who recognizes that "something was being hidden from her...something horrible" (*Years* 41, 42).[52]

We might conclude that the Eleanor of *The Years* lacks the knowledge of the analytical narrative voice of *The Pargiters* and thus does not have the ability to hear what, "absent an audience within the text, Rose herself hardly knows" and does not have the words to say.[53] Having learned "a great deal about marriage" from "the poor" in *The Pargiters,* Eleanor is less specifically knowledgeable about sexuality in *The Years;* she is, however, quite attuned to the tenor of her little sister's experience, thoroughly aware of her fear and fright. Although Eleanor may not know exactly what has happened to Rose on the street, she does share the experience of another gendered wound that derives from the division of their world into masculine and feminine prerogatives and rituals: Woolf associates Rose's traumatic experience at the pillar-box with the entry of her brother Bobby (renamed Martin in *The Years*) into the world of boys and men.[54] Through this link, Woolf marks Rose as female by giving her new knowledge of sexual difference and by invoking a gendered binary that defuses the sense of power, underwritten by imperial discourses, that Rose had derived from her identification with her father and her brother, an identification rerouted in her adult role as a militant suffragette.[55]

In a different key, Eleanor and Morris, too, were also once "conspirators," "in league together"; "they had been such friends when they were children" (*Pargiters* 25, 26). But as adult brother and sister, "Morris was giving up telling her about his cases; & she kept back a good deal about the Levys" (*Pargiters* 26). "That was the worst of growing up," Eleanor thinks in *The Years:* "They couldn't share things as they used to share them," a somewhat sentimental perception that belies the deeper silence between siblings (*Years* 34). For part of what is "kept back" is the knowledge of sexuality each sibling has independently obtained, knowledge that, if shared between brothers and sisters, could potentially unite and protect rather than divide and injure them. The prohibition on articulating and communicating what Eleanor and her siblings know, enforced by gender and class constraints, symptomatizes a broader problem surrounding sexuality within the late Victorian family and late Victorian culture that leaves all children vulnerable to sexual abuse.

In *The Pargiters,* both Rose's identification with her military father, who "had lost his fingers 'fighting savages,'" and her childhood alliance with Bobby, who has become "a proper schoolboy" no longer interested in playing "the Red Indian game," are challenged (*Pargiters* 14, 40, 41).[56] Walking alone to the corner store after Bobby refuses to go with her, Rose's "raid into the enemy's country," carrying a "secret message which she had to deliver to the English who were besieged in a fortress," ends in her encounter with the gibbering man on her way back from the corner store (*Pargiters* 41, 42). *The Pargiters* focuses on how that experience produces not just a new knowledge of sexual difference—"Rose, next day, of course, began to observe Bobby more closely"—but also a new idea of her brother as thereafter "in the enemy's camp": she is excluded from his "rights and privileges" as part of "the fellowship of men together" and partially recognizes the grounds on which her exclusion is enforced (*Pargiters* 51, 55, 54). This is but one in "a series of abuses" that "Woolf identified as girls' experience of the transit from infancy to womanhood."[57]

The analytical voice of *The Pargiters,* however, indicates that what is hidden from Rose in Bobby's experience is the functional analogue to the girl-child's troubling introduction to a predatory male sexuality:

> But though Bobby Pargiter lived a far freer life than Rose,...there sprang, partly from this freedom which was so oddly combined with secrecy...a mass of feelings, of reserves, of licenses, and of controls which made his life at school so difficult, strange, and so unnatural that Rose had no just cause for her bitter anger, for her floods of tears in the bathroom. Had she known what her brother was going through at school, she would very likely have decided,...that instead of being henceforth members of opposite camps, they ought, on the contrary, to combine together in blood brotherhood. Before Bobby went to school, this was symbolized by tying red thread around their wrists. (*Pargiters* 55–56)

Even more vaguely described than the pillar-box incident, Bobby's school experience is "difficult," "strange," even "unnatural," comprising "a knowledge of sex which at twelve surpassed not only Rose's but Milly's and Delia's"—though not, importantly, Eleanor's (*Pargiters* 55). We may speculate that in addition to an understanding of prostitution acquired from other boys, it includes knowledge of sexual assault by older boys against younger ones, a matter of widespread concern at the end of the nineteenth century in the public school context (*Pargiters* 53–54).[58] Although she constructs Bobby as "the enemy," linking him directly with the gibbering man on the basis of his sex and her exclusion from his perquisites, had Rose known the ways in which Bobby, too, was actually or potentially exposed to sexual violence, the analytical voice suggests, she might have seen her brother as less free and powerful: that is, as also subjected, in gender- and class-specific ways, to experiences of bodily vulnerability.

Juxtaposing this material in *The Pargiters* to the representation of Edward Pargiter at Oxford reading the *Antigone* and thinking of Kitty Malone, Woolf also invoked the contemporary discourse on masturbation in late Victorian culture. Having "taken no exercise for some weeks"—"exercise was one way," he reminds himself, "to conquer" a "degrading" and "bestial" feeling—Edward tries to resist his impulse to masturbate, recalling his own public school experience as a prefect who, on the instruction of the masters, "had always broken up those sinister little groups of boys lounging about at the edge of the playing fields" (*Pargiters* 66, 67). "Like Bobby," Woolf wrote in the essay that glosses this episode, Edward "had been free from a very early age to walk about London alone; and the knowledge that he acquired from the streets was soon supplemented by the boys at school." He learned "the dangers of love; and the best method of exorcising love" and "considered it to be one of his duties to exterminate the forms of love that were considered objectionable"—in himself, it would appear, as well as in others (*Pargiters* 81). Imbued with the "outlawed emotions" that Regenia Gagnier has analyzed in public school memoirs of the late Victorian and Edwardian periods, "boyhood erotic activity"—marked in many cases by expressions of shame and secrecy, recalling "the sense of guilt that . . . make[s] concealment necessary"—implies both complicity with and resistance to the cruel hierarchies of a homosocial institution.[59] In the parallel episode from the "1880" section of *The Years,* Woolf gives Edward's somewhat sadistic determination "to exterminate the . . . objectionable" an even sharper edge, "tortur[ing]" his lover Ashley by entertaining the sporting Gibbs (who will later become Edward's brother-in-law): "Edward began to relish the situation; he played up to it maliciously" (*Years* 55). Woolf's representations of the sexual life of men constitute a counterpart both to Rose's childhood experience and, we might speculate, to her adult lesbian sexuality, to which *The Years* in its final form only alludes.[60]

Rather than "being henceforth members of opposite camps," nursing "an enmity which lasted until a very queer scene . . . fifteen years later," Rose and her brother might have worn that "red thread" on their wrists for the rest of their lives; instead, each is scarred in and by her or his isolation (*Pargiters* 56). Separated by gendered norms and by differently gendered experiences of sexuality that they cannot communicate to one another as children, all Rose and Martin can finally agree on as adults—in that "queer scene" in the "1908" chapter of *The Years* at the house on Abercorn Terrace, in which each remembers events from the night of Rose's assault—is that they have both been damaged: " 'What awful lives children live!' he said. . . . 'Don't they, Rose?' 'Yes,' said Rose. 'And they can't tell anybody' " (*Years* 159).

In this chapter Rose relates her memories of "that row when the micro-scope was broken," a mishap for which she feels she was unjustly blamed, claiming that Martin's friend Erridge (whom she has just run into during a suffrage speaking tour in the north of England) was the culprit (*Years* 157). Even as Martin and Rose agree in remembering "that row" as "one of the worst," a further "memory seemed to have come back to her" of Martin ask-ing her afterwards "to go beetling... in the Round Pond" (*Years* 157–58):

> "And you said, 'I'll ask you three times; and if you don't answer the third time, I'll go alone.' And I swore, 'I'll let him go alone.'" Her blue eyes blazed.
>
> "I can see you," said Martin. "Wearing a pink frock, with a knife in your hand."
>
> "And you went," Rose said; she spoke with suppressed vehemence. "And I dashed into the bathroom and cut this gash"—she held out her wrist.... There was a thin white scar just above the wrist joint. (*Years* 158)

We know from internal evidence that this incident, which precisely reverses the circumstances of Rose's solo trip to the corner store, happens on the very same day that Rose meets the man at the pillar-box in the "1880" section. Martin here recollects Rose "wearing a pink frock," as she is on the evening that she encounters the gibbering man; even more concretely, in the "1880" section, Rose does "not want to go in" to the nursery to ask Martin to go with her, for "they had quarrelled first about Erridge and the microscope and then about shooting Miss Pym's cats next door" (*Years* 10, 17). The consequences of these solitary excursions are not the same, of course—in emulating her brother's journey, Rose comes to a different end—but it is significant that Rose cuts herself after her brother has not only accused her and defended his friend but also demonstrated that he can "go alone" in ways that her gendered embodiment as a girl does not permit. Rose's "thin white scar" attests to the significant link Woolf made between Martin's (potentially dangerous) freedom to "go alone" and the limits on Rose's mobil-ity, which are not caused by but actually precede the pillar-box incident. Precipitated by gender, this self-inflicted wound stands in for that other, specifically sexual injury, to which Rose wrongly supposes Martin to be immune.

In this context, it would seem that only Rose still wears the "red thread" of sibling connection around her wrist, though now it has become a "white scar," never to disappear. But Martin does indeed also make a link, albeit a tenuous one, to that past, which provides a different narrative means of registering the asymmetrical sexual danger to boys and girls. As is the case for his sister in this episode, "some memory from his childhood came over him as he saw Rose sitting there at the tea table with her fist still clenched. He saw her standing with her back to the schoolroom door; very red in the face, with her lips tight shut as they were now. She had wanted him to do something. And he had crumpled a ball of paper in his hand and shied it at her" (*Years* 159; cf. 17). Two faces precipitate Martin's ability to recollect that moment so precisely: Rose's face before him at the tea table, again with "lips shut tight," and "the placid, smiling picture of their mother" that "had ceased to be his mother" and "become a work of art" which "wants cleaning," so dirty that he can no longer see the "little blue flower" that he remembers from childhood (*Years* 150, 149, 158, 159). In these two survivals of the past into the present—the living sister, wearing the same look she once wore; the dead mother, killed into art and then defaced by time—we find two emblems for memory that call up the past without enabling Martin to recall it fully and certainly not to change (or "clean") it. Had Rose gone with Martin to the Round Pool, perhaps he would have gone with her to the corner store; had Martin gone with Rose to the corner store, perhaps the adventure would have taken another, less frightening form. But that Martin recalls that memory at all, in the context of these two female faces, suggests a buried recognition of the differential harm to him and to Rose on which the narrative hinges.

Entering the room where her sister and brother are still squabbling after thirty years, Eleanor enters as well into the fragmented recollections that Rose, in this section as in the next ("1910"), and Martin bring to the surface. Her reflections on Renan's *Life of Jesus* gloss her unknowingness about both of her siblings' lives: "What vast gaps there were, what blank spaces, she thought, leaning back in her chair, in her knowledge! How little she knew about anything" (*Years* 155). Yet Eleanor also begins to listen for the silences that separate them all. As Martin tries but fails to discuss their dead aunt Eugénie's affairs—his cousin Maggie will laughingly ask, in the "1914" section, "Are we brother and sister?" in response to Martin's speculation that his father was in love with his brother's wife—Eleanor muses on Martin's similarly unmentionable sexual life (*Years* 247). "It came over her that he must have a great many love affairs" about which he does not tell her (*Years* 155). Similarly, Eleanor either does not know or does not remember that Rose had cut herself, but that "there was something queer about the memory, Eleanor could see. [Rose] spoke with a curious intensity" (*Years* 158). Her consciousness in this episode mediates the joint and separate memories of Rose and Martin, revealing the "vast gaps" and "blank spaces" in her own knowledge of a past that they lived together but never fully shared; what she, like other characters, knows is articulated through patterns of silence and speech. Even in light of the muting and silencing of "the sexual life of women" that Woolf performed in the movement from *The Pargiters* to *The Years,* however, this character, more than any other, is constituted as the witness to loss—the "real and consequential loss" that Judith Butler identifies in the *Antigone,* a play that resonates throughout Woolf's writings from the 1930s—generated from within the family that *The Years* ultimately seeks to grieve.[61]

Eleanor's position in this scene brings together those memorial family images cited above. In "1908," she is still "fumbling with the wick" of the tea-kettle, as Milly does in the "1880" section; still counting out "one, two, three, four" teaspoons for the pot like those "virgins and spinsters with hands that had staunched the sores of Bermondsey and Hoxton," working-class districts mentioned in the prelude to the "1880" section (*Years* 151, 10–12, 4). She is also still living with her father, with whom, according to "1891," she "got on extremely well . . . almost like brother and sister," so much so that she even once mistakenly refers to her cousin Maggie as her niece, while her father considers confiding in her about his longtime mistress (*Years* 92, 103–4). In being at once the dead mother and the living sister in relation to both father and siblings, Eleanor may seem to exist in the "borderland between life and death," as the narration describes the condition of Delia and her dying mother, also named Rose, in "1880" (*Years* 25). Or perhaps, as Mitchell Leaska claims, she has "been dealt a fate worse than Sara's," another Pargiter cousin whose reflections on the *Antigone* constitute an important node in the "1907" section: Woolf "has left Eleanor alone with a possessive and indul-gent father," Leaska argues, "and by casting her in that role the author has in effect buried Eleanor—like Antigone—alive" (*Years* 132–37).[62] That Oedi-pus and Antigone were both father and daughter *and* (half-) brother and sister, however, suggests that Eleanor is not simply a living figure for a dead past; that she has taken the place of a mother to her siblings, and of a sister or even a wife to her father, points to the complexity inherent in "living the equivocations that unravel the purity and universality of those structuralist rules," as Butler has written, that would keep each familial function in its proper, fixed place: rules that so many families break as well as maintain, for good as well as for ill (*Antigone's Claim* 18).

Like the wounded children of Oedipus, Eleanor does not marry and bears no children, and in *The Years* more generally, the conventional marriage plot of nineteenth-century fiction is almost entirely erased: "In Kitty's case, as in Delia's, Maggie's, and Milly's, Woolf simply refuses to portray courtship and marriage as the major events in a woman's life."[63] "No marriage-bed" for

Eleanor, Rose, or Sara; "no marriage-song" for Martin or Edward; perhaps "no child to rear" for their niece Peggy either.[64] Vexed as they are, fraught with the difficulties of intimacy bred by the silences of the family system, the primary commitments of the Pargiter siblings are to one another: in the family tableau of sisters and brothers that forms at the very end of the novel, at the dawn of a new day, we may sense sadness or hope, loss or potential, but we can also grasp a figure for and of survival.

With this point in mind, I have framed my reading of *The Years* against Jane Marcus's guiding assumption that "all of Virginia Woolf's work is an attack on the patriarchal family."[65] To be sure, the novel itself persistently critiques the patriarchal, but more surprising in Woolf's oeuvre is the impulse to reconstitute, recuperate, refigure, and reimagine familial life in affectively gratifying egalitarian forms, such that individuals will have the opportunity to reconceive their relations in new ways on new models. As Marcus notes about *The Years,* its "last scene is a 'family reunion'": she characterizes "the family whose life is celebrated" as "the *political* family of antifascists, the left's ideal replacement of the moribund patriarchal family."[66] But the family that gathers in the "Present Day" section includes all of the Pargiter children (some married and identifiably heterosexual, others not) and their descendants; cousins of their own generation; unrelated but affiliated friends whose political loyalties in the present, like their memories of the past, collide and conflict. While not all may be "celebrated," all are included—and by that inclusion, I suggest, Woolf was aiming at something other than making an image of "the left's ideal": she was aiming, that is, at reconfiguring kinship for new uses in new times, without pargeting.[67] And in her repeated returns to her own Victorian family past, she also works to refigure and refashion the discourses of incest in ways that may, even now, prove both limiting and productive.

Conclusion

> The many and varied activities of the educated man's
> daughter in the nineteenth century were clearly not
> simply or even mainly directed towards breaking
> the laws. They were, on the contrary, endeavours
> of an experimental kind to discover what are the
> unwritten laws; that is the private laws that should
> regulate certain instincts, passions, mental and physical
> desires.... [S]uch laws... have to be discovered afresh
> by successive generations, largely by their own efforts
> of reason and imagination.
>
> —Virginia Woolf, *Three Guineas,* 1938

"Can the family be redeemed?" Eve Kosofsky
Sedgwick poses this question in an illuminating discussion of "queer tutelage" published in the early 1990s. It is this question I have also sought to
address by feminist historicist means in the wake of queer theory. Suggesting that knowledge of more expansive practices in the past, comparable to
the ones I have analyzed here, might provide precedent for projecting "into
the future a vision of 'family' elastic enough to do justice to the depth and
sometimes durability" of intimate "bonds," Sedgwick holds out an alluring
prospect: that "the family of the *present* can show this heterosexist structure always already awash with homosexual energies and potentials, whose
making-visible might then require only an adjustment of the interrogatory
optic, the bringing *to* the family structure of the pressure of our different
claims, our different needs."[1] The cultural work that Sedgwick herself performs in her essay, however, doesn't so much "redeem" the family as question
its future as a site of resistance to, rather than a key apparatus of, the normative. Having entertained the possibility of refocusing the past so as to bring
a different version of it into view, she rejects that move as insufficient to the
contemporary situation: "The word, the name, the *signifier* 'family' is already
installed unbudgeably at the center of a cultural value system—so much
so that a rearrangement or reassignment of its *signifieds* need have no effect
whatever" (*Tendencies* 72, emphases in original).[2]

Nearly two decades after these words were written, they are that much harder to argue with. Pervasively, indeed oppressively, deployed in U.S. culture against those of us who do not do our best to approximate the norm, the discourse of "family values" may have its most pernicious impact on those who actively seek the recognition and legitimation that the state withholds, those who desire access to the institutions of marriage or family. Their continued exclusion maintains, even as it troubles, the boundaries between who's in and who's out, who does or does not qualify for access to the full social, economic, and civil privileges that being married and adhering to the hegemonic family form can convey. As I have argued throughout this book, nineteenth-century conceptions of "the family" were also premised on exclusions—based in concepts of blood and biology, shaped by racialized and class limits that forged distinctions, institutionalized by civil law and religious precept. Yet like comparable contests in our own time, the continuous resistance to emergent forms also helped to keep alternative practices, extra-legal arrangements, and other models for intimate relation in play. Whereas Sedgwick concludes that redeploying "family," even in new contexts with new players, "can only add to the numinous prestige of a term whose origins, histories, and uses may have little in common with our own recognizable needs," I must conclude otherwise: that in the effort to make institutional forms responsive to our heterogeneous needs, an effort for which there is a good deal of historical precedent, we have an opportunity to reshape the forms themselves (*Tendencies* 72).

To be sure, that task is fraught with risks of its own. In a moving and incisive essay entitled "Is Kinship Always Already Heterosexual?" Judith Butler emphasizes the danger entailed by the quest for legitimacy that she identifies in the movement for gay marriage. If, "on the one hand, living without norms of recognition results in significant suffering and forms of disenfranchisement," including economic and social disabilities, then advocacy for inclusion potentially produces further exclusions with no less painful material effects:

> The demand to be recognized . . . can lead to new and invidious forms of social hierarchy, to a precipitous foreclosure of the sexual field, and to new ways of supporting and extending state power, if it does not institute a critical challenge to the very norms of recognition supplied and required by state legitimation. . . . What would it mean to exclude from the field of potential legitimation those who are outside of marriage, those who live nonmonogamously, those who live alone, those who are in whatever arrangements they are in that are not the marriage form? (*Undoing* 115–16)

Keeping the political demand for legitimation in play while maintaining a critical stance toward it, Butler makes us mindful of the losses that even a "successful" demand for recognition could entail. While Sedgwick concludes that "redeeming the family isn't, finally, an option but a compulsion; the question would be how to *stop* redeeming the family," Butler's work most broadly suggests that just stopping is no answer at all (*Tendencies* 72, emphasis in original). Opting out simply cedes all power to the state for determining who counts and who doesn't, or on what basis the rights we accord to persons are distributed. If we cannot and should not just "stop," even as we aim to make change in how social goods are allocated, perhaps it is still possible if not to "redeem" then at least to reinvent and reappropriate "the family," on the basis of both its past histories and current articulations in the interests of a more open future.

A site of actual and potential good as well as harm, care as well as injury, recognition as well as violation, the family is a thing of our own making that also always precedes and exceeds us. For some who will read these words, as for me who writes them, it is no haven in a heartless world, no respite from the rigors of the competitive marketplace, and decidedly not the homey place where we are truly known, best understood, or most fully valued for who we are or have become. For some but by no means all of us, first families give shelter to gendered, sexual, racial, and class violence and exploitation; some of us have worked hard not to reproduce, have indeed had to unlearn, these formative experiences in our intimate adult relations to others and in our broader relations to children and elders, strangers and friends. But one thing I have learned, in part as a consequence of researching and writing this book, is to take almost as a given the persistence of family formations that have differed—and are differing—from the heterosexist, biologically bounded, procreative, self-contained, other-excluding, white middle-class norm at the center of Anglo-American public discourse. After 9/11, in the context of transnational migration and the ever-increasing feminization of poverty within and beyond the United States, for example, the state-sponsored norm appears all the more a figment of the national imaginary, "a fantasy of normativity that projects and delineates an ideological account of kinship, at the moment when it is undergoing social challenge and dissemination"; calling it "a fantasy" especially underlines its tenacious hold and power (*Undoing* 116). In studying the nineteenth century—thought to be, and even celebrated by some conservatives as being, the moment at which the hegemonic family/marriage norm unproblematically emerged—I have become increasingly aware of the fictiveness of the norm itself, then and now. Don't we (perhaps inadvertently) perpetuate exclusions by continuing to insist on its unchanging hegemony? Couldn't we gain some purchase on the present by realizing that "the family" of the past was also a site of cultural contestation and conflict? For me, one crucial aspect of doing the historical work that Sedgwick rejects lies in the opportunity of discovering, not for the first time, the heterogeneity and mutability that now-normative fictions both conceal and contest.

Queering "the family" or marriage, in the present and for the future, would also enable, perhaps even require, queering the past so as to demonstrate a degree of historical flexibility in forms of intimacy that could become a resource for making change, and that historicist effort is already well underway. To take an example of a parallel project that I have referenced throughout this book, Sharon Marcus's provocative reconstruction of Victorian "female marriage" in *Between Women* rereads a range of materials through the adjusted "optic" Sedgwick invokes, explicitly challenging the immutability of marriage as an institution that has always been and should always be reserved for one man and one woman only.[3] From another angle, Helena Michie's work on that most canonical of conjugal institutions—the honeymoon—partially explores its "heterosexualizing imperative" in the writing of John Addington Symonds, whose "self-situation with respect to normative modes of Victorian sexuality can help us both to defamiliarize that norm and to feel anew its familiar" (and sometimes familial) "pressures" (*Victorian Honeymoons* 79). Among its other purposes, such scholarship lets us historicize the heterosexual and, in so doing, grasp the variable modes of connection that nineteenth-century women and men lived and valued.

Like marriage plots and other related fantasies, fictions of family are culturally shaped and culturally shaping: not lies, but not truths either; enmeshed in power relations, but also sites of resistance and, yes, potential and actual change. Whether or not holy marriage makes "one flesh," for example, was a central question with a decided, definite answer for many Victorians: "yes" for some, who defended it on the basis of a highly literalist reading of scripture; "no" for others, who dissented from the institutional Anglican norm with the support of what we would today call a constructionist framework for interpreting and historicizing Leviticus and Deuteronomy. More important and more interesting than the clash of belief systems and interpretive frames, however, are the particular forms of relationship that adherence to or dissent from "one flesh" clearly licensed or sharply prohibited; the narratives of familial inclusion and exclusion that adoption, affinity, and consanguinity generated and underwrote; and the means by which first and second marriage might make strangers into friends and family or keep them at a distance. So, too, does the current contest over norms in the ongoing, sometimes virulent debates about access to marriage or adoption rights—the hegemonic constraints of "familialism," "the trouble with normal" that many of us experience, the attacks from cultural conservatives that stigmatize queer life—suggest the scope and limits of what we can make of these institutionalized forms of belonging, which have been shaped and reshaped in the past, lived and challenged in the present, and may be renovated or perhaps discarded by posterity (*Tendencies* 72).[4] A justifiable skepticism notwithstanding, I do take, have taken, and will probably continue to take family fictions as a resource for making change in the ways we live now and for generating a fuller future, because those fictions, viewed in historical perspective, themselves instantiate the very possibility of change. Whether or not change entails greater liveability, as Butler might say, is partially up to us.

At the same time, I have been concerned throughout this project not simply to indicate the potential richness of the past as a resource for the present, a richness that Sedgwick clearly recognizes and yet rejects as inadequate to her politics. I have aimed also to complicate and challenge the static versions of the past that circulate in our time, even among academics, by emphasizing aspects of its strangeness and difference; its messiness and complexity, especially around questions of otherness; its failure to stand still and be one thing, much as we might like it to be. I have found that variety, moreover, through exploring some of the nineteenth century's most canonical fiction: by emphasizing the diversity within Austen's representations of family, marriage, and the relation between the two; by construing both adoption and biological reproduction as key sites at which the Brontës, Eliot, and Gaskell differently articulate the shifting relations among affinity, consanguinity, and the politics of familial, national, or imperial belonging; by identifying the differences within marital, sexual, and familial practices that we have too readily relegated to the convenient but misleading shorthand of "incestuous," "exogamous," or "heterosexual." As other literary scholars and historians have begun and will continue to demonstrate, the frameworks for analysis that feminist critics and theorists developed to critique marriage and family in the wake of structuralism, in the 1970s, and identity politics, in the 1980s, deployed an "interrogatory optic" that made some things brilliantly clear, while others went entirely out of focus. Shifting the point from which we observe as well as grinding some new lenses can give us a transformed and transformative perspective on even the most familiar texts and the conceptual schemes we have used to read them.

In this regard, Butler's rereading of Hegel, Lévi-Strauss, and Lacan is exemplary in that it revisits and revises foundational texts from the perspective of a transformed present, looking to construct new conceptual frameworks "that might well accommodate change within kinship relations" (*Antigone's Claim* 18). She seeks to "put into question the assumption that the incest taboo legitimates and normalizes kinship based in biological reproduction and the heterosexualization of the family"; the prohibition on (parent-child, and particularly mother-son) incest "makes sense only in terms of kinship relations in which various 'positions' are established within the family according to an exogamic mandate" (*Antigone's Claim* 66, 18). Critiquing the structuralist indifference to the rigidity of these symbolic "positions," their resistance to change, Butler invokes in the place of Oedipus the figure of Antigone: sister to her father; aunt to her brothers; never married to the mother's brother's son for whom her uncle (aiming to shore up his own claim to political power) "endogamously" intends her. Antigone thus occupies and is occupied by more than one of the "positions"; in that multiplicity she can be represented, as I have represented Woolf's Eleanor Pargiter in chapter 7, as "living the equivocations that unravel the purity and universality of those structuralist rules" (*Antigone's Claim* 18).

More hopeful than Sedgwick, Butler rethinks structuralist frameworks in light of new social and familial formations—including but not limited to gay, single, and adoptive parenting, and non-nuclear, nonbiological kinships—that are reconfiguring how we "do" family. And that project, in my view, can partially take its bearings from new perspectives on the past, in that before such rules begin to be adduced as the founding precepts of civilization and formulated as "the law" by anthropologists and early psychoanalysts in the latter half of the nineteenth century, such sisters as Marianne Thornton and Emily Dealtry, Emily and Charlotte Brontë, and many other women writers and female characters I have considered here also lived the equivocations of being multiply positioned within families and among friends. If Antigone can be an emblem of and for our present, in which rigid "positions" do not hold, that both she and her often-forgotten sister Ismene may also figure the "positions" created by and imposed on women writers of the past suggests that the rules are themselves subject to change. Moreover, the criticality that Butler posits as necessary in pursuing the demand for recognition now can also be identified, especially though not exclusively, in writings by and about women. Without positing a time before "the law," I believe that it is still important to suspend our belief in its "universality" in approaching historical materials created under the aegis of different rules.

As illuminated by both Butler and Woolf, the situation of Antigone (and Ismene too) provides a means of thinking back through our sisters as we reread the nineteenth-century tradition of women's domestic fiction for evidence of its difference from the normatively exogamous heterosexual plot that has come to dominate our understanding. Each text I have considered here may be understood as intertextually revising the others, as indicated especially in chapter 6, but all register the multiplicity of the "positions" women occupy within residual and emergent familial fictions of the times, a multiplicity that the *Antigone* has continued to exemplify. Woolf herself first read the play as early as "1902, when she had taken Greek lessons with Janet Case," and then again in 1932, 1934, and 1937; it "seemed to accumulate meaning for her as she grew older," and *The Years* contains a number of significant references to it.[5] Yet in one particular episode, an early version of the scene that Woolf originally imagined as "the turn of the book," a character's reading of the *Antigone* is interrupted by the mention of another text that foregrounds its female characters' resistance to *and* compliance with the "positions" assigned to them.[6] "Buried alive" in her bedroom within the patriarchal household as she reads her cousin Edward's translation of the play while her sister Maggie, who will marry and raise children, attends a society party with their parents, Sara "spills milk over [the] books" on her bedside table (*Years* 136).[7] The *Antigone* is spared, but her copy of *Wives and Daughters* is soaked.

As Gaskell repeated and departed from Austen, Martineau, and Eliot, rewriting their plots to accommodate a shifting conception of kinship-as-fiction, so Woolf here consciously invoked Gaskell, choosing not only the most maternal of metaphors but also one of the prescribed elements in her regimen for maintaining health with which to signify the intertextual relation. A dead metaphor brought back to life, spilled milk conveys Woolf's ambivalence toward the narrative Molly Gibson makes and is made by, a narrative in which multiple forms of familial relation—forged through biology, affinity, and analogy—both incite and prohibit desire, with a heroine who is as much an Ismene as an Antigone, if not more so.[8] It is not hard to imagine Woolf reading *Wives and Daughters* as comic elegy, permeated by the first Mrs. Gibson's absence—the loss that sets the whole plot in motion—but giving us nothing much to cry over in the end. Yet in the fact that Woolf considered both "Sons & Daughters" and "Daughters & Sons" as possible titles for her own novel, we can glimpse the imperative she felt to revise that narrative of maternal loss—which was also, at some level, a variant of her own story—once more.[9] Preferring the latter title, because it "would give a rhythm more unlike Sons & Lovers, or Wives & Daughters," Woolf clearly wanted *not* to echo either of those specifically, distinctively gendered versions of the parent-centered family romance.[10] Yet her fiction places itself in relation to Gaskell's (and also to D. H. Lawrence's), invoking and disowning the plot that structures it, repeating but reshaping the fictive forms of family.

As Woolf did especially in *Three Guineas,* Eliot also emphasized the irrec-
oncilable demands to which the *Antigone* gives voice, taking them as a point
of departure for the sister's plot in *The Mill on the Floss.* On the front flyleaf
of her commonplace notebook, Eliot inscribed the line from the play that
Woolf would later deem "worth all the sermons of all the archbishops,"
words Woolf knew in translation as " 'tis not my nature to join in hating, but
in loving" (*TG* 82).[11] Eliot's essay on the play, "The *Antigone* and its Moral"
(1856), locates its conflict in a "dramatic collision": "The impulse of sisterly
piety, which allies itself with reverence for the Gods, clashes with the duties
of citizenship," or giving allegiance to Creon, who brooks no challenge to
his authority.[12] Eliot aimed to separate family from polity in a way that was
consistent with the nineteenth-century liberal tradition, representing the two
as distinct and even opposed to one another, with each the locus of different
values. Yet in its action, *The Mill on the Floss* partially collapses that distinction,
anticipating Woolf's claim in *Three Guineas* that "the public and the private
worlds are inseparably connected; that the tyrannies and servilities of the one
are the tyrannies and servilities of the other" (*TG* 142).

As Madelyn Detloff points out, the ambiguity of Antigone's multiple
positions "confounds any clear separation between forms of kinship and the
state"; moreover, Woolf's analysis of the rage expressed by actual Victorian
fathers, including those of Charlotte Brontë and Elizabeth Barrett, at their
daughters' bids for independent lives suggests that a pervasively patriarchal
power over both spheres similarly "confounds" the distinction and separation of the two (*TG* 130–38).[13] In Maggie Tulliver's case, where the tyrant is
also close kin—not father or uncle but brother—the oppressive force within
the family mirrors and is mirrored by an unyielding social structure that
would sacrifice the daughter, striving to realize the individuality with which
Eliot anomalously and precipitously endowed her, to its demand for confor-
mity. Unlike either Antigone, who responds to Creon's fiat by invoking the
community's unspoken support for her action ("All these would say that they
approved my act/Did fear not mute them") or Theresa of Avila, deterred
from the childhood pursuit of martyrdom among the Moors when "domestic reality ... in the shape of uncles" bring her and her brother home, Maggie Tulliver lacks a "coherent social faith and order" on which to rely.[14] In
the absence of that communal backing, tragically at odds with "the world's
wife," Maggie is an unwilling outlaw from her first and only family, whose
norms she has honored even in the breach; biographically speaking, of course,
the same could be said of Mary Ann Evans (*MF* 397).

Like Woolf, who distinguished in *Three Guineas* between "the private
brother, whom many of us have reason to respect," and the "monstrous male"

who, in "the society relationship of brother and sister," bars the door to women's participation in (and potential transformation of) public life, Eliot sometimes minimized the cruelties of the private house and adopted a more forgiving posture (*TG* 105). Many have read this as a sign of Eliot's complicity with patriarchal ends: "sisterly piety" alone, in the absence of any broader framework, may make Ismenes of all those who, in honoring the norms and fearing the consequences of their transgression, fail to support the making of a "coherent" stance in relation to others that would affirm not just "the duties of citizenship" but access to its rights and privileges as well.

Finally, however, it is Maggie Tulliver's mother, her wronged cousin Lucy, and even her typically censorious Aunt Glegg, in "an unexpected line of conduct," who forgive and support her: as the narration asks from the latter's point of view, "If you were not to stand by your 'kin'..., pray what were you to stand by?" (*MF* 403). "People as don't belong to you," however sad their fall may be, aren't worth the tears you shed for them; people as do, no matter how compromised—or incomprehensible—their actions, command your loyalty (*MF* 50). That Ismene never repudiates any of her kin, however un-brave that may seem when set beside her sister's actions, also suggests that we shouldn't repudiate her. Today "the relations of kinship arrive at boundaries that call into question the distinguishability of kinship from community," permitting "the durable tie to be thought outside of the conjugal frame and thus open[ing] kinship to a set of community ties that are irreducible to family"; in the past, those boundaries were arguably just as permeable (*Undoing* 127). If not for Mrs. Glegg—for whom, "in the matter of wills, personal qualities were subordinate to the great fundamental fact of blood"—then certainly for a range of other fictional and actual nineteenth-century women and men, who does or does not "belong to you" is, finally, the real question (*MF* 109). Only by sustained, collective "efforts of reason and imagination" and many ongoing "endeavours of an experimental kind" will we be able to answer it, for our own ends, in our own time.

✄ Notes

Preface

1. Helena Michie, *Victorian Honeymoons: Journeys to the Conjugal* (Cambridge, 2006).

2. Ruth Perry, *Novel Relations: The Transformation of Kinship in English Literature and Culture, 1748–1818* (Cambridge, 2004).

Chapter 1. Making and Breaking the Rules: An Introduction

1. Virginia Woolf, "Reminiscences," in *Moments of Being: A Collection of Autobiographical Writing,* ed. Jeanne Schulkind (San Diego, 1985), 55, 57; hereafter cited in the text.

2. Most commentators on this episode strike the note of "scandal" without attending to context. Noel Annan, however, suggests that George's opposition to the relationship was based on his concern for "the scandal—his career—Virginia's marital prospects—*his own* marital prospects." See *Leslie Stephen: The Godless Victorian* (London, 1984), 122. Claudia Nelson provides a useful introduction to the issues I analyze here. Nelson, *Family Ties in Victorian England* (Westport, CT, 2007), 119–23.

3. *Hansard* 3 (Lords), vol. 214, col. 1902, 13 March 1873.

4. See Hermione Lee, *Virginia Woolf* (New York, 1997), 139. In "A Sketch of the Past," Woolf referred to Vanessa's "detesting... in particular Aunt Mary [Fisher, née Jackson], who had viciously interfered" in the affair with Jack. *Moments of Being,* 143; hereafter cited in the text. For the fictional scene between Katharine and her aunt, see Virginia Woolf, *Night and Day* (San Diego, 1973), 404–10.

5. Virginia Woolf, *Mrs. Dalloway* (San Diego, 1981), 75.

6. Virginia Woolf, "22 Hyde Park Gate," in *Moments of Being,* 177.

7. Sybil Wolfram, *In-Laws and Outlaws: Kinship and Marriage in England* (London, 1987), 43.

8. Ibid., 42.

9. Ibid., 43.

10. Judith Butler, *Undoing Gender* (London, 2004), 157; hereafter cited in the text.

11. Ellen Pollak, *Incest and the English Novel, 1684–1814* (Baltimore, 2003), 187; hereafter cited in the text.

12. Michel Foucault, *The History of Sexuality, Volume I: An Introduction,* trans. Robert Hurley (New York, 1978), 127; hereafter cited in the text.

13. Elizabeth Wilson, "'Not in This House': Incest, Denial, and Doubt in the White Middle Class Family," *Yale Journal of Criticism* 8 (1995): 38, 41.

14. Rosemary Jann, "Darwin and the Anthropologists: Sexual Selection and its Discontents," *Victorian Studies* 37 (1994): 287.

15. Andrew Mearns, *The Bitter Cry of Outcast London,* ed. Anthony S. Wohl (Leicester, 1970), 61.

16. Daniel Bivona and Roger B. Henkle, *The Imagination of Class: Masculinity and the Victorian Urban Poor* (Columbus, 2006), 1, emphasis in original.

17. George R. Sims, *"How the Poor Live" and "Horrible London"* (New York, 1984), 45.

18. Anthony S. Wohl, *The Eternal Slum: Housing and Social Policy in Victorian London* (Montreal, 1977), 217; *First Report of the Commissioners on the Housing of the Working Classes [England and Wales]* (Shannon, 1970), vol. 2, 100; hereafter cited as *CHWC.*

19. Quoted in John Hollingshead, *Ragged London in 1861* (New York, 1985), 233.

20. Edwin Chadwick, *Report on the Sanitary Condition of the Labouring Population of Great Britain,* ed. M. W. Flinn (Edinburgh, 1965), 88, 192, 190.

21. Ibid., 191, 193, 423.

22. Benjamin Disraeli, *Sybil; or, The Two Nations,* ed. Sheila M. Smith (Oxford, 1986), 172.

23. Judith R. Walkowitz, *City of Dreadful Delight: Narratives of Sexual Danger in Late-Victorian London* (Chicago, 1992), 18.

24. Polly Morris, "Incest or Survival Strategy? Plebeian Marriage within the Prohibited Degrees in Somerset, 1730–1835," in *Forbidden History: The State, Society, and the Regulation of Sexuality in Modern Europe,* ed. John C. Fout (Chicago, 1992), 139.

25. William Acton, *Prostitution, Considered in its Moral, Social, & Sanitary Aspects, in London and Other Large Cities: with Proposals for the Mitigation and Prevention of its Attendant Evils* (1870), 3d ed., ed. Peter Fryer (New York, 1968), 130.

26. *Hansard* 4 (Lords), vol. 42, col. 1199, 10 July 1896.

27. Seth Koven, *Slumming: Sexual and Social Politics in Victorian London* (Princeton, 2004), 61.

28. Henry Mayhew, *London Labour and the London Poor,* vol. 4, ed. John D. Rosenberg (New York, 1968), 259.

29. *First Report of the Commissioners Appointed to Inquire into the State and Operation of the Law of Marriage as Relating to the Prohibited Degrees of Affinity, and to Marriages Solemnised Abroad or in the British Colonies* (Shannon, 1969), 77, ix; hereafter cited in the text.

30. Alexander James Beresford-Hope, *The Report of Her Majesty's Commission on the Laws of Marriage, Relative to Marriage with a Deceased Wife's Sister* (London, 1849), 149.

31. Incestuous adultery was and remained, even after the passage of the MDWS Bill in 1907 and the Punishment of Incest Act in 1908, "one of the few grounds for which a woman could divorce her husband" until the category was abolished in 1923. Sybil Wolfram, "Eugenics and the Punishment of Incest Act 1908," *Criminal Law Review* (1983): 312. And even extramarital intercourse was understood to create affinity: "The first divorce secured by a woman, Mrs. Addison, in 1801, was for her husband's incestuous adultery with her sister, his sister-in-law. . . . Any further intercourse with her husband would have been incestuous." Wolfram, *In-Laws and Outlaws,* 28.

32. "A Woman of England," *The Women of England and Mr. Wortley's Marriages Bill: An Address to the Peers of the Realm* (London, 1850), 8.

33. [W. A. Beckett], *The Woman's Question and the Man's Answer; or, Reflections on the Social Consequences of Legalizing Marriage with a Deceased Wife's Sister* (London, 1859), 17.

34. Chadwick, *Report,* 192.

35. Ibid., 193.

36. Acton, *Prostitution,* 130, 209.

37. Wohl, *Eternal Slum,* 25, 42.

38. Koven, *Slumming,* 42.

39. Michael Mason, *The Making of Victorian Sexuality* (Oxford, 1994), 140.

40. *CHWC,* vol. 2, 139.

41. Ian Hacking, "The Making and Molding of Child Abuse," *Critical Inquiry* 17 (1991): 276–77.

42. Bivona and Henkle, *Imagination of Class,* 44. On the transformation of central London in this period, see Wohl, *Eternal Slum,* 26–27, and Gareth Stedman Jones, *Outcast London: A Study in the Relationship between Classes in Victorian Society* (Oxford, 1971), 159–78.

43. Alfred Henry Huth, *The Marriage of Near Kin, Considered with Respect to the Laws of Nations, the Results of Experience, and the Teachings of Biology* (London, 1875), 358, 308, emphasis in original.

44. Ann Laura Stoler, *Race and the Education of Desire: Foucault's "History of Sexuality" and the Colonial Order of Things* (Durham, 1995), 46, hereafter cited in the text; Claude Lévi-Strauss, *The Elementary Structures of Kinship,* rev. ed., trans. James Bell et al. (Boston, 1969), 46, 480.

45. Anthony Trollope, *The Way We Live Now,* ed. John Sutherland (Oxford, 1982), vol. 2, 263. I am most grateful to Anna Peak for alerting me to this passage.

46. Anita Levy, *Other Women: The Writing of Class, Race, and Gender, 1832–1898* (Princeton, 1991), 50.

47. *Hansard* 3 (Commons), vol. 195, col. 1299, 21 April 1869.

48. G. W. S. Russell, quoted in Nancy F. Anderson, "The 'Marriage with a Deceased Wife's Sister Bill' Controversy: Incest Anxiety and the Defense of Family Purity in Victorian England," *Journal of British Studies* 21:2 (1982): 79.

49. [John F. McLennan], "The Early History of Man," *North British Review, American Edition* 50 O.S. (1869): 278.

50. Jann, "Darwin and the Anthropologists," 298.

51. John F. McLennan, *Primitive Marriage: An Inquiry into the Origin of the Form of Capture in Marriage Ceremonies,* ed. Peter Riviere (Chicago, 1970), 69, 58; hereafter cited in the text.

52. McLennan, "Early History," 287.

53. Ibid.

54. *Hansard* 3 (Lords), vol. 214, col. 1902, 13 March 1873.

55. For the details of this position, see Jack Goody, *The Development of Family and Marriage in Europe* (Cambridge, 1983).

56. Vikki Bell, *Interrogating Incest: Feminism, Foucault, and the Law* (London, 1993), 97.

57. Judith Butler, *Bodies That Matter: On the Discursive Limits of "Sex"* (New York, 1993), x.

58. See Maureen Quilligan, *Incest and Agency in Elizabeth's England* (Philadelphia, 2005), 33–46.

59. Eve Kosofsky Sedgwick, *Tendencies* (Durham, 1993), 61. Sander Gilman observes that sibling incest "was a question that dominated the debates on incest . . . in

French culture from 1874 to 1886," being "a touchstone for the incest and inbreeding discussions of the late-nineteenth century and one of the often cited 'social problems' of that day," which perhaps makes it the more surprising that Foucault largely elides the intragenerational and limits his remarks on cross-generational incest to parents and children. Gilman, "Sibling Incest, Madness, and the 'Jews,' " *Social Research* 65 (1998): 401.

60. Stoler also identifies an archive of lecture materials in which Foucault emphasized the continuity between a seventeenth-century discourse of "the struggle between races" (e.g., Saxons, Normans, Celts) and the nineteenth-century discourse of class struggle. The lectures have now been published in English translation: Michel Foucault, *"Society Must Be Defended": Lectures at the Collège de France, 1975–76,* ed. Mauro Bertani and Alessandro Fontana, trans. David Macey (New York, 2003).

61. Here as elsewhere in this project, my point of view has also been shaped by Walter Benn Michaels, who writes of fiction by Cather, Hemingway, and Fitzgerald that "what's at stake in the desire to keep someone in the family is thus the sense that what is outside the family is also outside the race." Michaels, *Our America: Nativism, Modernism, and Pluralism* (Durham, 1995), 7–8. See also Werner Sollors, *Neither Black Nor White Yet Both: Thematic Explorations of Interracial Literature* (Cambridge, MA, 1997), 286–335.

62. Lévi-Strauss, *Elementary Structures,* 10.

63. Appeals to English liberty often appear in nineteenth-century materials concerning marriage prohibitions: MDWS advocates opposed the ban on the grounds that it constituted "an infringement of their natural liberty," "a gratuitous interference with individual conscience, as well as with the liberty of the subject," that encroaches on "what may be considered the first natural rights." *First Report* 10, 73, 97.

64. Pollak borrows the notion of nineteenth-century "incest anxiety" from Anderson, whose lack of a critical perspective on the Freudian model undermines the usefulness of her conclusions. See Anderson, "The 'Marriage with a Deceased Wife's Sister Bill' Controversy."

65. Gayle Rubin, "The Traffic in Women: Notes on the 'Political Economy' of Sex," in *Toward an Anthropology of Women,* ed. Rayna R. Reiter (New York, 1975), 157–210; Carolyn Dever, *Skeptical Feminism: Activist Theory, Activist Practice* (Minneapolis, 2004), 69.

66. Annette Weiner, *Inalienable Possessions: The Paradox of Keeping-While-Giving* (Berkeley, 1992), 67.

67. Sharon Marcus, *Between Women: Friendship, Desire, and Marriage in Victorian England* (Princeton, 2007), 13.

68. Kathy Alexis Psomiades, "Heterosexual Exchange and Other Victorian Fictions: *The Eustace Diamonds* and Victorian Anthropology," *Novel* 33 (1999): 111.

69. Jean Walton, *Fair Sex, Savage Dreams: Race, Psychoanalysis, Sexual Difference* (Durham, 2001), 10, emphasis in original.

70. Weiner writes, "Women are not merely a counter exchanged between brothers-in-law. When a woman marries, the full range of her reproductive powers is far too essential to be lost to her brother and the other members of her natal group. . . . Her other productive and reproductive roles—those usually omitted in kinship theory— remain clearly tied to the relations between herself and her brother" (*Inalienable*

Possessions 72). I am grateful to Kathy Alexis Psomiades for referring me to Weiner's work.

71. Psomiades, "Heterosexual Exchange," 93.

72. Adam Kuper, "The Rise and Fall of Maine's Patriarchal Society," in *The Victorian Achievement of Sir Henry Maine: A Centennial Reappraisal,* ed. Alan Diamond (Cambridge, 1991), 109.

73. Weiner, *Inalienable Possessions,* 151.

74. Leo Bersani, *A Future for Astyanax: Character and Desire in Literature* (Boston, 1976), 199, 202; J. Hillis Miller, *Fiction and Repetition: Seven English Novels* (Cambridge, MA, 1982), 64.

75. William R. Goetz, "Genealogy and Incest in *Wuthering Heights,*" *Studies in the Novel* 14 (1982): 363; Joseph Allen Boone, *Tradition Counter Tradition: Love and the Form of Fiction* (Chicago, 1987), 153.

76. Joseph A. Boone and Deborah E. Nord, "Brother and Sister: The Seductions of Siblinghood in Dickens, Eliot, and Brontë," *Western Humanities Review* 46 (1992): 178, emphasis in original.

77. Elsie B. Michie, *Outside the Pale: Cultural Exclusion, Gender Difference, and the Victorian Woman Writer* (Ithaca, 1993), 64; Susan Meyer, *Imperialism at Home: Race and Victorian Women's Fiction* (Ithaca, 1996), 111; Bersani, *Future for Astyanax,* 199, emphasis in original. Ivan Kreilkamp argues that "*species* seems as salient as race as a category by which to consider Brontë's depiction of [Heathcliff]," but also notes that "the anti-cruelty and antivivisection movements…were heavily indebted to the earlier abolitionist movement," making Brontë's "animalizing" of Heathcliff part of a broader discourse about the relations among (and between) humans and other creatures. "Petted Things:*Wuthering Heights* and the Animal," *Yale Journal of Criticism* 18 (2005): 98, 109n40.

78. Levy, *Other Women,* 87; Emily Brontë,*Wuthering Heights,* 4th ed., ed. Richard J. Dunn (New York, 2003), 29; hereafter cited in the text.

79. Levy, *Other Women,* 82. More broadly, Bruce Robbins reads several classic Victorian texts in which servants are identified with the children of the family from which they have been excluded. Robbins, *The Servant's Hand: English Fiction from Below* (Durham, 1993), 111, 139–49.

80. Sandra M. Gilbert and Susan Gubar note the parallel between Heathcliff's situation and Nelly's but add that she "is excluded from the family, specifically by being defined as its servant." Gilbert and Gubar,*The Madwoman in the Attic: The Woman Writer and the Nineteenth-Century Literary Imagination* (New Haven, 1979), 290.

81. Levy, *Other Women,* 87.

82. I am grateful to Deborah Denenholz Morse for the suggestion that giving Heathcliff the same name as the dead son installs him in the vacant place that Hindley had inherited.

83. Leonore Davidoff, "Where the Stranger Begins: The Question of Siblings in Historical Analysis," in *Worlds Between: Historical Perspectives on Gender and Class* (New York, 1995), 208, emphasis in original. "Friend" is one of Ellen and Catherine's preferred terms for Heathcliff, e.g., 42, 53, 64, 78.

84. Nancy Armstrong, *Fiction in the Age of Photography: The Legacy of British Realism* (Cambridge, MA, 1999), 173. For an alternative view of "breeding" in the text,

see Barbara Munson Goff, "Between Natural Theology and Natural Selection: Breeding the Human Animal in *Wuthering Heights,*" *Victorian Studies* 27 (1984): 494–502.

85. Bersani, *Future for Astyanax,* 199, 201, 221.

86. Terry Eagleton, *Heathcliff and the Great Hunger: Studies in Irish Culture* (London, 1995), 17–18.

87. Tess O'Toole, "Adoption and the 'Improvement of the Estate' in Trollope and Craik," in *Imagining Adoption: Essays on Literature and Culture,* ed. Marianne Novy (Ann Arbor, 2001), 17.

Chapter 2. "Cousins in Love, &c." in Jane Austen

1. Jane Austen, *Northanger Abbey,* ed. Marilyn Butler (London, 1995), 182; hereafter cited in the text.

2. Jane Austen, *Persuasion,* ed. John Davie (New York, 1980), 132; hereafter cited in the text.

3. Maaja Stewart, *Domestic Realities and Imperial Fictions: Jane Austen's Novels in Eighteenth-Century Contexts* (Athens, 1993), 44.

4. Jane Austen, *Pride and Prejudice,* ed. Donald Gray (New York, 1993), 57, 228; hereafter cited in the text.

5. Tony Tanner, *Adultery in the Novel: Contract and Transgression* (Baltimore, 1979), 81.

6. Tony Tanner, *Jane Austen* (Cambridge, MA, 1986), 105.

7. Clara Tuite, *Romantic Austen: Sexual Politics and the Literary Canon* (Cambridge, 2002), 10; hereafter cited in the text.

8. Nancy Armstrong, *Desire and Domestic Fiction: A Political History of the Novel* (New York, 1987), 51.

9. Randolph Trumbach, *The Rise of the Egalitarian Family* (New York, 1978), 19.

10. Jane Austen, *Sense and Sensibility,* ed. James Kinsley (Oxford, 1990), 178; hereafter cited in the text.

11. Ruth Perry, *Novel Relations,* 123; hereafter cited in the text.

12. For the phrase "endogamous economics," see Eileen Cleere, *Avuncularism: Capitalism, Patriarchy, and Nineteenth-Century English Culture* (Stanford, 2004), 33–75.

13. Glenda A. Hudson, *Sibling Love and Incest in Jane Austen's Fiction* (New York, 1999), 35; Tanner, *Jane Austen,* 148. Johanna M. Smith argues that marriage within the family is "a two-fold social strategy" for "protecting the family from contamination by strangers and for maintaining a hierarchical family structure against the forces of exogamous sexuality removing children from that structure." Smith, " 'My Only Sister Now': Incest in *Mansfield Park,*" *Studies in the Novel* 19 (1987): 3.

14. Claudia L. Johnson, *Jane Austen: Women, Politics, and the Novel* (Chicago, 1988), 96; hereafter cited in the text.

15. Key works include Moira Ferguson, "*Mansfield Park:* Slavery, Colonialism, and Gender," *Oxford Literary Review* 13 (1991): 118–39; Susan Fraiman, "Jane Austen and Edward Said: Gender, Culture, and Imperialism," *Critical Inquiry* 21 (1995): 805–21; Joseph Litvak, *Caught in the Act: Theatricality in the Nineteenth-Century English Novel* (Berkeley, 1992), 1–26; and Pollak, *Incest and the English Novel,* 162–99. The film adaptation of *Mansfield Park* (dir. Patricia Rozema, Miramax, 1999) offers

a very strong reading of slavery, especially in relationship to marriage, as the cause of Mansfield's sickness.

16. Austen's relationship to Burke has been a staple of critical discussion for almost four decades owing to the lasting influence of Alistair Duckworth, *The Improvement of the Estate: A Study of Jane Austen's Novels* (Baltimore, 1971).

17. Maureen Quilligan shows that for women, marrying within the family in the early modern period could be understood as a means of expanding opportunities: "When she remains untraded, for whatever reason, a woman is freer to choose her own desire actively." Quilligan, *Incest and Agency,* 35–36.

18. Sharon Marcus, *Between Women,* 31–32; hereafter cited in the text.

19. Jane Austen, *Mansfield Park,* ed. Claudia L. Johnson (New York, 1998), 161; hereafter cited in the text.

20. On the basis of this passage, Marianne Hirsch argues that "the entire novel constitutes an indictment of exogamy for women" and, more generally, that an "allegiance to 'brothers' shields nineteenth-century heroines from the perils of exogamy." Hirsch, *The Mother/Daughter Plot: Narrative, Psychoanalysis, Feminism* (Bloomington, 1989), 61.

21. Quoted in Virginia Woolf, "Jane Austen," *The Essays of Virginia Woolf, Volume II: 1912–1918,* ed. Andrew McNeillie (San Diego, 1990), 10.

22. Mary Poovey, *The Proper Lady and the Woman Writer: Ideology as Style in the Works of Mary Wollstonecraft, Mary Shelley, and Jane Austen* (Chicago, 1984), 221. For an alternative reading of this passage, see Leila S. May, "Jane Austen's 'Schemes of Sisterly Happiness,' " *Philological Quarterly* 81 (2002), esp. 333–34.

23. Randolph Trumbach, *Sex and the Gender Revolution, Volume One: Heterosexuality and the Third Gender in Enlightenment London* (Chicago, 1998), 344, 413.

24. Jane Austen, *Emma,* ed. David Lodge (London, 1971), 298. See also *Novel Relations,* 124.

25. On the latter point, see ibid., 32.

26. E. B. Pusey, *Marriage with a Deceased Wife's Sister Prohibited by Holy Scripture, as Understood by the Church for 1500 Years* (Oxford, 1849), 18.

27. As Marc Shell has written, "Belief in the difference between literal and figural kinship—in the possibility of knowing for sure who's who in the kinship system—is necessary to society if... obeisance to the taboo on incest is a precondition of the continuation of society, or of society as we know it." Shell, *Children of the Earth: Literature, Politics, and Nationhood* (New York, 1993), 4.

28. Trumbach, *Rise of the Egalitarian Family,* 19. Much of the historical material analyzed by Leonore Davidoff and Catherine Hall would also support this conclusion. See Davidoff and Hall, *Family Fortunes: Men and Women of the English Middle Class, 1780–1850* (Chicago, 1987).

29. Nelson, *Family Ties,* 142; see also 134–38.

30. On the U.S. context, see Martin Ottenheimer, *Forbidden Relatives: The American Myth of Cousin Marriage* (Urbana, 1996). As of this writing, Muslims in the United Kingdom who (allegedly) practice cousin-marriage are being stigmatized as a degenerate population, in a semantic slide from inbreeding to terrorism as comparable outrages against civilization. See Christopher Hitchens's essay on the bombings in London and Glasgow in July 2007, which quotes Michael O'Connor's interview with the novelist Nadeem Aslam. Neither Hitchens nor Aslam seems aware that

cousin-marriage has been perfectly legitimate in England for centuries. Hitchens, "Don't Mince Words," *Slate,* 2 July 2007; Aslam, "Writing Against Terror: Nadeem Aslam," *Three Monkeys Online,* July 2005.

31. Daniel Cottom, *The Civilized Imagination: A Study of Ann Radcliffe, Jane Austen, and Sir Walter Scott* (Cambridge, 1985), 105.

32. Cleere, *Avuncularism,* 34.

33. Cottom, *Civilized Imagination,* 98. Cottom proposes that "families are always the dominant characters in Austen's novels," as opposed to Paula Marantz Cohen, who describes *Mansfield Park* as "Jane Austen's one novel in which the life of the family takes precedence over the life of the individual." Cohen, *The Daughter's Dilemma: Family Process and the Nineteenth-Century Domestic Novel* (Ann Arbor, 1991), 59.

34. The most sustained study of Austen in anthropological terms is Richard Handler and Daniel Segal, *Jane Austen and the Fiction of Culture: An Essay on the Narration of Social Realities* (Tucson, 1990).

35. For more on the opening description of the Dashwood "settlement," see Margaret Anne Doody's excellent introduction to *Sense and Sensibility,* esp. viii–xii.

36. For a comparison of John Dashwood's "selfish neglect of family relations and the caprices of male inheritance" to contemporary practices of enclosure, and of enclosure to "the making of domestic isolation" that entails endogamous marriage, see Fraser Easton, "The Political Economy of *Mansfield Park:* Fanny Price and the Atlantic Working Class," *Textual Practice* 12 (1998): 458–88.

37. Compare Perry's point that "siblinghood of persons with the same father was the closest and most egalitarian of all agnatic relationships." *Novel Relations,* 109.

38. Isobel Armstrong, *Jane Austen: Sense and Sensibility* (Harmondsworth, U.K., 1994), 19. To my regret, I encountered Armstrong's extended consideration of "family" in the novel only as this chapter neared completion.

39. Tess O'Toole points out Mary's underlying objection to "the Hayter-Musgrove match," which is that it "is based not on considerations of family and estate integrity," with Charles and Henrietta being "cousins on the maternal side." O'Toole, "Reconfiguring the Family in *Persuasion,*" *Persuasions* 15 (1993): 203. On the issues discussed in this paragraph in regard to *Persuasion,* see Stewart, *Domestic Realities,* 88–89.

40. Isobel Armstrong, *Jane Austen,* 30. Leonore Davidoff argues that "the notion of a distinct 'blood relative'... seems to have been fully developed only at about the turn of the twentieth century"; moreover, "even as late as eighteenth-century England, just as the word *family* encompassed non-relatives, *friend* also referred to kin." Davidoff, "Where the Stranger Begins," 208.

41. Leila Silvana May, *Disorderly Sisters: Sibling Relations and Sororal Resistance in Nineteenth-Century British Literature* (Lewisburg, PA, 2001), 25.

42. Isobel Armstrong, *Jane Austen,* 30.

43. Amy Wolf, "Epistolarity, Narrative, and the Fallen Woman in *Mansfield Park,*" *Eighteenth-Century Fiction* 16 (2004): 269.

44. Valerie Sanders, *The Brother-Sister Culture in Nineteenth-Century Literature: From Austen to Woolf* (New York, 2002), 85.

45. Naomi Tadmor, *Family and Friends in Eighteenth-Century England: Household, Kinship, and Patronage* (Cambridge, 2001), 134, 139. Tadmor provides a fuller look

at how language "actually served to submerge the nuclear family in broader kinship relationships"; more generally, see Marcus, *Between Women,* 25–72.

46. Susan Sniader Lanser, "No Connections Subsequent: Jane Austen's World of Sisterhood," in *The Sister Bond: A Feminist View of a Timeless Connection,* ed. Toni A. H. McNaron (New York, 1985), 54. Thanks to Deborah Denenholz Morse for reminding me of this groundbreaking essay.

47. Originally appearing in the *London Review of Books,* Castle's essay has been reprinted as "Was Jane Austen Gay?" in *Boss Ladies, Watch Out! Essays on Women, Sex, and Writing* (New York, 2002), 128.

48. George E. Haggerty, *Unnatural Affections: Women and Fiction in the Later Eighteenth Century* (Bloomington, 1998), 84.

49. May, "Jane Austen's 'Schemes,'" 329, emphasis in original.

50. In my view, Henry and Maria's adulterous affair qualifies more nearly as incest in the contemporary legal and religious sense than any other incident in Austen's fiction, and Fanny's response surely indicates that she sees it in that light as well. Other critics who touch on the incestuous overtones of this event include Avrom Fleishman, *A Reading of "Mansfield Park": An Essay in Critical Synthesis* (Minneapolis, 1967), 65; Cohen, *Daughter's Dilemma,* 78; Hudson, *Sibling Love,* 46–47; Cleere, *Avuncularism,* 72–73.

51. D. A. Miller, *Narrative and Its Discontents: Problems of Closure in the Traditional Novel* (Princeton, 1981), 58, 59.

52. Litvak, *Caught in the Act,* 24.

53. Trumbach, *Rise of the Egalitarian Family,* 17, 19.

54. Ruth Bernard Yeazell, *Fictions of Modesty: Women and Courtship in the English Novel* (Chicago, 1991), 148.

55. George Levine, *Darwin and the Novelists: Patterns of Science in Victorian Fiction* (Chicago, 1988), 67, emphasis in original.

56. Cleere, *Avuncularism,* 49; Cohen, *Daughter's Dilemma,* 69. Cleere also recognizes that "Sir Thomas is resolute about the class division that must be erected and maintained between Fanny and her cousins" but goes on to claim that "his vanity prevents him from realizing that these intentions would seem to negate the conditions of his sister-in-law's prior argument." My sense is that the one set of intentions does not so much "negate" the other as asymmetrically position Fanny within the family and in relation to the marriage market.

57. Tuite connects Mary's question—"out" or "not"?—to "the incest taboo which structures the movement from a system of endogamy (being 'in') to exogamy (being 'out')." Note that "not out"—rather than "in"—is the term that Mary uses to describe Fanny's position; she is decidedly not contrasting endogamy with exogamy, merely glossing a distinction within the market for marriage that we now *call* "exogamous." Even within Mary's framework, one might marry "in," but only for the "right" reasons. *Romantic Austen,* 116.

58. Cohen, *Daughter's Dilemma,* 72.

59. Cleere, *Avuncularism,* 52, 57.

60. The key theoretical texts are Gayle Rubin, "Traffic in Women"; and Luce Irigaray, *This Sex Which Is Not One,* trans. Catherine Porter, with Carolyn Burke (Ithaca, 1985).

61. I owe this conclusion to Susan Morgan, who argues that "*Mansfield Park* insists that women, given all the forms of social and familial oppression that constrict them, given their personal forms of physical and emotional weakness, can yet make positive choices within those forms, can and must make their own lives." Morgan, *Sisters in Time: Imagining Gender in Nineteenth-Century British Fiction* (New York, 1989), 47.

Chapter 3. Husband, Wife, and Sister: Making and Unmaking the Early Victorian Family

1. E. M. Forster, *Marianne Thornton: A Domestic Biography, 1797–1887* (New York, 1956), 189; hereafter cited in the text.

2. Cassandra Leigh Austen, quoted in Deirdre Le Faye, *Jane Austen: A Family Record,* 2d ed. (Cambridge, 2004), 264. "When home from the Navy, [Charles] lived with his dead wife's sister respectably at her parents' house; but gossip focused on his behaviour with Harriet," which may have been a catalyst for their marriage in 1820. Park Honan, *Jane Austen: Her Life* (New York, 1987), 365.

3. Davidoff, "Where the Stranger Begins," 208.

4. "The first family" is an even more fluid construction than I indicate here, in that in addition to birth, fostered, and adoptive siblings, we should also consider siblings of the half blood (like the Dashwoods), with just one parent in common, who may or may not be construed as belonging to "one's own family." For example, Jack Wentworth tells his half-brother Frank in *The Perpetual Curate* (1864), only Gerald "and I are the original brood. You are all a set of interlopers, the rest of you," in being the children of a second wife. See Margaret Oliphant, *The Perpetual Curate* (Harmondsworth, U.K., 1987), 408. Whether half-siblings were related on the father's or mother's side would certainly make a difference in their status within the family in relation to inheritance practices and other privileges.

5. May, *Disorderly Sisters,* 29; hereafter cited in the text.

6. Elizabeth Rose Gruner, "Born and Made: Sisters, Brothers, and the Deceased Wife's Sister Bill," *Signs* 24 (1999): 423–47.

7. The historians of the family who have most shaped my thinking on this point include Davidoff and Hall, *Family Fortunes;* Lawrence Stone, *The Family, Sex and Marriage in England, 1500–1800* (New York, 1977); Tadmor, *Family and Friends;* and Trumbach, *Rise of the Egalitarian Family.* See also Nelson, *Family Ties,* published just as this book neared completion.

8. Michie, *Victorian Honeymoons,* 2; hereafter cited in the text.

9. Tanner, *Adultery in the Novel,* 5.

10. Margaret Morganroth Gullette, "The Puzzling Case of the Deceased Wife's Sister: Nineteenth-Century England Deals with a Second-Chance Plot," *Representations* 31 (1990): 146; Cynthia Fansler Behrman, "The Annual Blister: A Sidelight on Victorian Social and Parliamentary History," *Victorian Studies* 11 (1968): 494.

11. Karen Chase and Michael Levenson, *The Spectacle of Intimacy: A Public Life for the Victorian Family* (Princeton, 2000), 106. Chase and Levenson focus on the MDWS plot in relation to Dickens's life and writing, especially *David Copperfield.* For a queer revision of the second-choice plot in that novel in which the dying Dora bequeaths her husband to their best friend/virtual sister Agnes, see Marcus, *Between Women,* 88–91.

12. Helena Michie, *Sororophobia: Differences among Women in Literature and Culture* (New York, 1992), 24. Michie offers a concise list of the myriad ways in which sister-hood could be configured: "Are sisters reiterations of each other?... Competitors? Is the deceased sister primarily replaced as wife or mother or as both? Is one sister the most natural or the most unnatural replacement for another? Is marrying your sister's widower the ultimate act of betrayal or the ultimate act of loyalty to her memory? Are sisters too much the same (incest), or comfortingly similar (familial bliss)?"

13. [Beckett], *Woman's Question*, 10–11, emphasis in original.

14. Françoise Héritier, *Two Sisters and Their Mother: The Anthropology of Incest,* trans. Jeanine Herman (New York, 1999), 14.

15. Michie, *Sororophobia,* 24.

16. Such an arrangement had decided complications. When Leslie Stephen caught Anny kissing Richmond Ritchie, her much younger second cousin, in the drawing room, he put up a considerable fuss, subsequently referring to the event as "the catastrophe." *Sir Leslie Stephen's Mausoleum Book* (Oxford, 1977), 45. Noel Annan remarks both that "Anny's decision to marry Richmond Ritchie made [Les-lie and Julia's] marriage possible"—Anny being one of Julia Duckworth's clos-est friends—and that "Leslie resented Stella [Duckworth] leaving him as he had resented Anny's engagement." Annan, *Leslie Stephen,* 78, 116. For an even more vivid picture, see Henrietta Garnett, *Anny: A Life of Anne Isabella Thackeray Ritchie* (London, 2004), 185–226.

17. Matthew Arnold, *Friendship's Garland,* in *The Complete Prose Works of Mat-thew Arnold,* vol. 5, ed. R. H. Super (Ann Arbor, 1965), 315.

18. Compare Tess Durbeyfield's request to Angel Clare that he marry Liza-Lu in *Tess of the d'Urbervilles* (1891).

19. E. B. Pusey, *Marriage with a Deceased Wife's Sister,* 18.

20. Behrman, "Annual Blister," 485–86.

21. Gullette, "Puzzling Case," 160; Wolfram, *In-Laws and Outlaws,* 129.

22. "The Marriage Relation," *London Quarterly Review, American Edition* 85 (July and October 1849): 92.

23. Felicia Skene, *The Inheritance of Evil, Or, the Consequence of Marrying a Deceased Wife's Sister* (London, 1849), 96–97; hereafter cited in the text.

24. E. B. Pusey, *A Letter on the Proposed Change in the Laws Prohibiting Marriage between Those Near of Kin* (Oxford, 1842), 16–17.

25. Anderson, "The 'Marriage with a Deceased Wife's Sister Bill' Controversy," 74.

26. Ibid., 75.

27. Chase and Levenson, *Spectacle of Intimacy,* 114; Gullette, "Puzzling Case," 162.

28. Quoted in Chase and Levenson, *Spectacle of Intimacy,* 113.

29. *Hansard* 3 (Commons), vol. 106, col. 630, 20 June 1849.

30. "Marriage Relation," 92.

31. E. M. Forster, *Howards End,* ed. Oliver Stallybrass (London, 1973), 11.

32. "Marriage Relation," 92.

33. *Hansard* 3 (Lords), vol. 214, col. 1876, 13 March 1873. Wolfram observes that "his wife's sister did not inherit from a man who died intestate, and if a woman were left a legacy by her sister's husband, she paid the death duties customary for unrelated people"; cousins, by contrast, "paid at a reduced rate." Wolfram, *In-Laws and Outlaws,* 34.

34. Gullette, "Puzzling Case," 159. From a financial standpoint, of course, first-cousin marriage would often be not only acceptable but also desirable, as an interested mother in Margaret Oliphant's *Hester* (1883) points out to both her son and her niece in encouraging their marriage: "She asked her son how he could forget that if Catherine's money went out of the business it would make the most extraordinary difference? and she bade Catherine remember that it would be almost dishonest to enrich another family with money which the Vernons had toiled for." Oliphant, *Hester,* ed. Philip Davis and Brian Nellist (Oxford, 2003), 6.

35. [Abraham Hayward], *Summary of Objections to the Doctrine that a Marriage with the Sister of a Deceased Wife is Contrary to Law, Religion, or Morality* (London, 1839), 18, 19.

36. Ibid., 19.

37. Ibid.

38. [Beckett,] *Woman's Question,* 24; Richard A. Kaye, *The Flirt's Tragedy: Desire without End in Victorian and Edwardian Fiction* (Charlottesville, 2002), 86.

39. Oliphant, *Perpetual Curate,* 386–87.

40. Sarah Annes Brown, *Devoted Sisters: Representations of the Sister Relationship in Nineteenth-Century British and American Literature* (Aldershot, U.K., 2003), 106.

41. Harriet Martineau, *Deerbrook,* ed. Valerie Sanders (London, 2004), 139; hereafter cited in the text. See also Brown, *Devoted Sisters,* 130–31.

42. Ann Hobart writes, "though Hope marries a woman he does not love, we are not invited to question his integrity," a conclusion I would challenge on the basis of the passage cited here. Hobart, "Harriet Martineau's Political Economy of Everyday Life," *Victorian Studies* 37 (1994): 244.

43. In an otherwise thoughtful reading of the novel, Gruner asserts that Elizabeth's "jealousy is misplaced," discounting some of the warning notes that Skene strikes in the text. Gruner, "Born and Made," 430–33.

44. Relying on René Girard's theory of mediated or mimetic desire, May seeks to untangle the "thicket of rivalries and jealousies" that makes up the action of *Deerbrook.* Claiming that "Hester desires to *be*—to become—her rival," May imposes a competitive structure on the sister relation. My own reading of this passage and others emphasizes instead the way in which the second sister persistently figures the wife's unmet needs as she moves from her first to second family. See Girard, *Deceit, Desire, and the Novel: Self and Other in Literary Structure,* trans. Yvonne Freccero (Baltimore, 1965); May, *Disorderly Sisters,* 91, 92, emphasis in original.

45. Brown also makes this point. *Devoted Sisters,* 130.

46. Here as elsewhere in the novel, Skene was no doubt deliberately parodying the testimony presented in the *First Report* in which widowers routinely reported the deathbed words of their first wives as authorizing marriage to the second sister. In this particular instance, she was systematically undermining the authority of the presumed wishes and feelings of the dying wife, not only by revealing her inner thoughts, which Elizabeth is unable clearly to articulate, but also by demonstrating how her auditors twist what they hear to their own purposes.

47. Although the framework for my analysis differs from hers, May's work yet offers a noteworthy exception to the rule.

48. Sedgwick, *Tendencies,* 118; Haggerty, *Unnatural Affections,* 75. For an analysis of the homoerotic charge in a range of fictional representations, including Austen's novels, as well as in the MDWS debate, see Brown, *Devoted Sisters,* 135–51.

49. Martha Vicinus, *Intimate Friends: Women Who Loved Women, 1778–1928* (Chicago, 2004), 229.

50. For a brief reading of how "shared love" for Philip brings Margaret and Maria closer together "rather than driving them apart," see Marcus, *Between Women,* 84–85.

51. Hobart, "Harriet Martineau's Political Economy," 244.

52. Jennifer Yates, "A 'Habit of Speculation': Women, Gossip, and Publicity in Harriet Martineau's *Deerbrook,*" *Women's Writing* 9 (2002): 375.

53. As Valerie Sanders points out, Martineau's novel was "published only seven years after the 1832 Anatomy Act," passed in the aftermath of the Burke and Hare scandal, which serves as an explicit reference point for Hope's social ostracism. Sanders, *Reason over Passion: Harriet Martineau and the Victorian Novel* (New York, 1986), 75.

54. For further discussions of Mrs. Rowland's role as female gossip, see Hobart, "Harriet Martineau's Political Economy"; and Yates, "A 'Habit of Speculation.'"

55. Chase and Levenson, *Spectacle of Intimacy,* 108.

56. Quoted in Sanders, *Brother-Sister Culture,* 78. For an extended discussion of this essay, which appeared in the periodical *Once a Week* in 1862, see Diane M. Chambers, "Triangular Desire and the Sororal Bond: The 'Deceased Wife's Sister Bill,'" *Mosaic* 29:1 (1996): 31–32.

Chapter 4. Orphan Stories: Adoption and Affinity in Charlotte Brontë

1. Charlotte Brontë, *Shirley,* ed. Andrew and Judith Hook (Harmondsworth, U.K., 1974), 366; *Jane Eyre,* ed. Margaret Smith (Oxford, 1993), 475, both hereafter cited in the text.

2. [Henry Rogers], "Marriage with a Deceased Wife's Sister," *Edinburgh Review* 97 (April 1853): 329.

3. [Abraham Hayward], *Summary of Objections,* 22–23.

4. Dinah Mulock Craik, *Hannah* (London, 1871), 27.

5. Ibid., 296.

6. Henry Sumner Maine, *Ancient Law: Its Connection with the Early History of Society, and Its Relation to Modern Ideas* (Tucson, 1986), 26; hereafter cited in the text.

7. George K. Behlmer, *Friends of the Family: The English Home and Its Guardians, 1850–1940* (Stanford, 1998), 276.

8. Carolyn Dever, *Death and the Mother from Dickens to Freud: Victorian Fiction and the Anxiety of Origins* (Cambridge, 1998), 1.

9. Laura Peters, *Orphan Texts: Victorian Orphans, Culture, and Empire* (Manchester, 2000), 48.

10. Nancy Armstrong, *How Novels Think: The Limits of British Individualism from 1719–1900* (New York, 2005), 144.

11. "To amalgamate" implies the crossing of races also termed "miscegenation." Citing the earliest usage of the verb from 1802, the *OED* calls its definition figurative—"to unite together (classes, races, societies, ideas, etc.) so as to form a homogeneous or harmonious whole." How Maine would more specifically characterize the difference of the "men of alien descent" from Romans is a subject for speculation, but it does not seem that he thought of "race" in purely phenotypical terms; there may indeed be a self-consciously figurative element to his own usage.

12. Making contract the standard instrument of "progressive society," Maine remarked on the "Perpetual Tutelage" of wives to husbands in contemporary England as a sign of incomplete historical development: "The archaic principle of the barbarians has fixed the position of married women," with each husband exercising power that "had once belonged to his wife's male kindred." Maine, *Ancient Law,* 146, 152. Although contract has not always had a positive connotation in feminist theory, Marcus picks up on this strand of Maine's thinking to argue that it enabled contemporary reformers "to posit increasing equality and similarity between spouses as progress towards modernity," while Psomiades reads Maine as "redefining marriage as . . . a holdover from a world without the benefit of contract." Marcus, *Between Women,* 4; Psomiades, "Heterosexual Exchange," 101.

13. Although Psomiades claims that "in the kinship structure of agnation, . . . married women are seen as part of their husbands' families," my reading of Maine doesn't bear this out. "Heterosexual Exchange," 100. For Maine's discussion of the disabilities of married women, in ancient Rome and contemporary England, see *Ancient Law,* 142–54.

14. Levy, *Other Women,* 64; for a reading of this material, see Psomiades, "Heterosexual Exchange," 105–7, emphasis in original.

15. George W. Stocking Jr., *Victorian Anthropology* (New York, 1987), 203.

16. Psomiades, "Heterosexual Exchange," 100.

17. Lewis Henry Morgan, *Systems of Consanguinity and Affinity of the Human Family* (Lincoln, 1997), 470.

18. Penny Boumelha, *Charlotte Brontë* (Bloomington, 1990), 69; hereafter cited in the text.

19. Drew Lamonaca, *"We Are Three Sisters": Self and Family in the Writing of the Brontës* (Columbia, 2003), 69. Kristin Elizabeth Gager points out that "religious texts consistently invoke the metaphor of humans as 'adopted children' of God to elucidate the notion of the 'universal kinship' of humankind." Gager, *Blood Ties and Fictive Ties: Adoption and Family Life in Early Modern France* (Princeton, 1996), 13. On this point, see also Peters, *Orphan Texts,* 33–35, and Shell, *Children of the Earth.*

20. For more on what I call Brontë's "variegated view of maternal powerlessness," see the opening section of my essay, "Orphan Stories: Charlotte Brontë's Racial Fictions of Adoption," in *Other Mothers,* ed. Ellen Rosenman and Claudia Klaver (Columbus: Ohio State University Press, forthcoming).

21. Charlotte Brontë, "The African Queen's Lament," in *An Edition of the Early Writings of Charlotte Brontë: Volume II, Part I,* ed. Christine Alexander (Oxford, 1987–91), 3–6; hereafter cited in the text.

22. Charlotte Brontë, "The Green Dwarf," in *An Edition of the Early Writings of Charlotte Brontë,* ed. Alexander, 178; hereafter cited in the text.

23. Charlotte Brontë, "A Leaf from an Unopened Volume," in *An Edition of the Early Writings of Charlotte Brontë,* ed. Alexander, 326; hereafter cited in the text.

24. Firdous Azim, *The Colonial Rise of the Novel* (London, 1993), 126, emphasis in original; hereafter cited in the text.

25. Patricia Howe, "Fontane's 'Ellernklipp' and the Theme of Adoption," *Modern Language Review* 79 (1984): 128.

26. This, in brief, is the argument of Meyer's chapter on Charlotte Brontë's juvenilia. Meyer, *Imperialism at Home,* 29–59.

27. John Maynard, *Charlotte Brontë and Sexuality* (Cambridge, 1984), 49.

28. For discussions of the foundling plot in the Brontës' fiction, see Micael M. Clarke, "Brontë's *Jane Eyre* and the Grimms' Cinderella," *Studies in English Literature* 40 (2000): 695–710; and Rosemary Lovell-Smith, "Childhood and Adoption in Scott and the Writing of *Wuthering Heights*," *Scottish Literary Journal* 21 (1994): 24–31. Deborah Epstein Nord argues that both sisters' works "partake of a larger novelistic tradition of foundling or bastard plots, in which the hero of indeterminate or questionable origins discovers himself to be the (usually illegitimate) child of a well-born or aristocratic parent." Nord, "'Marks of Race': Gypsy Figures and Eccentric Femininity in Nineteenth-Century Women's Writing," *Victorian Studies* 41 (1998): 191.

29. For another reading of this story, see Meyer, *Imperialism at Home,* 52–56. Although Carl Plasa writes that "Zorayda believes herself to be the mixed-race child of a liaison between Quamina and a white woman," I have not found any textual evidence that supports this reading. Plasa, *Charlotte Brontë* (Houndmills, U.K., 2004), 6.

30. Azim emphasizes that Zorayda has comparatively more agency than does Quashia Quamina: "The lost site—the 'original' homeland—remains accessible to the white child, as the Angrian community draws her within its boundaries. But Quashia is truly homeless." Azim, *Colonial Rise,* 135.

31. For a reading of the eruption of Quashia Quamina into the Roe Head Journal passage that identifies Brontë with Quashia, see Meyer, *Imperialism at Home,* 41–47. In a letter inserted near the beginning of *Caroline Vernon* (ca. 1839), Quashia Quamina lays claim to this ward of Zamorna, who subsequently becomes her guardian's mistress. Charlotte Brontë, *Five Novelettes,* ed. Winifred Gérin (London, 1971), 282–84. Maynard points out that Caroline is also "half-sister to Zamorna's wife Mary," making her "Zamorna's undeceased wife's half-sister." Maynard, *Charlotte Brontë and Sexuality,* 61.

32. Overdetermined and undermotivated, the aversion between twin brothers foreshadows the antagonism between the Crimsworth brothers in *The Professor* (1857).

33. Plasa, *Charlotte Brontë,* 11.

34. George Eliot, *Silas Marner, The Weaver of Raveloe,* ed. Terence Cave (Oxford, 1996), 96.

35. Charlotte Brontë, "The Foundling," in *An Edition of the Early Writings of Charlotte Brontë,* ed. Alexander, 60.

36. Meyer, *Imperialism at Home,* 29.

37. Charlotte Brontë, *Villette,* ed. Margaret Smith and Herbert Rosengarten (Oxford, 1990), 179; hereafter cited in the text.

38. Elsewhere in her excellent monograph, Boumelha usefully locates the drama of the male orphan in *The Professor* in relation to the narratives of homeless girls and women that Brontë usually creates, arguing that his story deploys "tropes of plot victimage more commonly associated with female protagonists." Boumelha, *Charlotte Brontë,* 47.

39. Elizabeth Barrett Browning, *Aurora Leigh: A Poem* (Chicago, 1979), I:40.

40. Following Heather Glen, although looking at somewhat different aspects of Brontë's work, I emphasize the continuity rather than the break between the juvenilia and the adult writing: see Glen, *Charlotte Brontë: The Imagination in History* (Oxford, 2002), 5–32.

41. Suzanne Keen, *Victorian Renovations of the Novel: Narrative Annexes and the Boundaries of Representation* (Cambridge, 1998), 83.

42. As Cleere notes more generally, *Jane Eyre* "maps the heroine's struggle for individualism against the absent presence of neither fathers nor mothers, but three recently dead uncles." Cleere, *Avuncularism*, 5.

43. Maurianne Adams, "Family Disintegration and Creative Reintegration: The Case of Charlotte Brontë and *Jane Eyre,*" in *The Victorian Family: Structure and Stresses,* ed. Anthony S. Wohl (New York, 1978), 172, 173.

44. John Kucich, *Repression in Victorian Fiction: Charlotte Brontë, George Eliot, and Charles Dickens* (Berkeley, 1987), 112–13; Adams, "Family Disintegration," 169; James Buzard, *Disorienting Fiction: The Autoethnographic Work of Nineteenth-Century British Novels* (Princeton, 2005), 166, emphasis in original.

45. For an extended analysis of "the great disinheritance" of daughters owing to changing economic circumstances in the eighteenth century that concentrated transmissible wealth in the hands of eldest sons, see Perry, *Novel Relations,* 38–76.

46. Davidoff and Hall, *Family Fortunes,* passim.

47. Adams, "Family Disintegration," 169.

48. Nord, " 'Marks of Race,' " 196.

49. Adams, "Family Disintegration," 166.

50. Boone and Nord, "Brother and Sister," 166.

51. *Affinity* also has specific meanings in relation to the chemical sciences, which would repay further investigation.

52. Sanders, *Brother-Sister Culture,* 46.

53. Kucich, *Repression in Victorian Fiction,* 103.

54. Lucy obliquely refers here to the possibility of Paul marrying his goddaughter, Justine Marie, a prohibited marriage in the Catholic tradition, as godparent and godchild were understood to share affinity. But Paul himself appears to oppose the idea on other grounds: "Some of M. Emanuel's relations and connections would, indeed, it seems, have liked him to marry her, with a view to securing her fortune in the family; but to himself the scheme was repugnant, and the idea totally inadmissible" (*Villette* 612).

55. Sanders, *Brother-Sister Culture,* 95.

56. Bette London, *Writing Double: Women's Literary Partnerships* (Ithaca, 1999), 40.

57. Buzard, *Disorienting Fiction,* 170.

58. Kucich, *Repression in Victorian Fiction,* 39.

Chapter 5. Intercrossing, Interbreeding, and *The Mill on the Floss*

1. George Eliot, *The Mill on the Floss,* ed. Carol T. Christ (New York, 1994), 385; hereafter cited in the text.

2. Tanner, *Adultery in the Novel,* 72; William A. Cohen, *Sex Scandal: The Private Parts of Victorian Fiction* (Durham, 1996), 158.

3. See Richard Dellamora's brief reading of the story of Jonathan and David, which emphasizes not their kin tie, but their participation in "the covenant of friends," in the front matter of *Friendship's Bonds: Democracy and the Novel in Victorian England* (Philadelphia, 2004).

4. Cohen, *Sex Scandal,* 157; Gillian Beer, *George Eliot* (Bloomington, 1986), 94. On Eliot and the *Antigone,* see also May, *Disorderly Sisters,* 37–42; and, more broadly,

Gerhard Joseph, "The *Antigone* as Cultural Touchstone: Matthew Arnold, Hegel, George Eliot, Virginia Woolf, and Margaret Drabble," *PMLA* 96 (1981): 22–35.

5. I follow the practice of Rosemarie Bodenheimer in referring to the writer as Mary Ann Evans, Marian Evans, Marian Evans Lewes, Marian Lewes, or George Eliot depending on the context. Bodenheimer, *The Real Life of Mary Ann Evans: George Eliot, Her Letters and Fiction* (Ithaca, 1994).

6. Marian Evans Lewes, "To Barbara Bodichon," 21 December [1869], *The George Eliot Letters,* ed. Gordon S. Haight (New Haven, 1954–74), vol. 5, 74, emphasis in original.

7. Amy M. King, *Bloom: The Botanical Vernacular in the English Novel* (New York, 2003), 21.

8. Harriet Ritvo, *The Platypus and the Mermaid, and Other Figments of the Classifying Imagination* (Cambridge, MA, 1997), xiii.

9. Gillian Beer, *Darwin's Plots: Evolutionary Narrative in Darwin, George Eliot, and Nineteenth-Century Fiction,* 2d ed. (Cambridge, 2000), 28.

10. Ibid., esp. 74–83, 91–92, 156–58.

11. George Eliot, *Adam Bede,* ed. Carol A. Martin (Oxford, 2001), 146; hereafter cited in the text.

12. For a reading of this gap in Eliot's analysis, see my "Representing the Rural: The Critique of Loamshire in *Adam Bede,*" *Studies in the Novel* 20 (1988): 288–301. Nancy L. Paxton writes, "The causes of Hetty's selfishness are as mysterious as the origins of Dinah's altruism." Paxton, *George Eliot and Herbert Spencer: Feminism, Evolutionism, and the Reconstruction of Gender* (Princeton, 1991), 57; see also 45–48. Cleere's reading of the novel somewhat qualifies this conclusion: in her remarks on Hetty Sorrel's "paternal heritage," which entails "a history of economic distress," she aptly quotes old Mr. Poyser's attribution of Hetty's fall to the fact that she has "Sorrel's blood in her veins." Cleere, *Avuncularism,* 81–82.

13. Bodenheimer, *Real Life of Mary Ann Evans,* 77, emphasis in original.

14. Charles Darwin, *The Origin of Species by Means of Natural Selection; or, The Preservation of Favoured Races in the Struggle for Life,* ed. J. W. Burrow (Harmondsworth, U.K., 1968), 143, 147; hereafter cited in the text.

15. Jules Law, "Water Rights and the 'Crossing o' Breeds': Chiastic Exchange in *The Mill on the Floss,*" in *Rewriting the Victorians: Theory, History, and the Politics of Gender,* ed. Linda M. Shires (New York, 1992), 62; hereafter cited in the text.

16. Eliot, *Silas Marner,* 109.

17. Ritvo, *Platypus and the Mermaid,* 106, 107. This is just one of many examples of the prepotency ascribed to the male partner in reproductive matters. Another fascinating idea of the time concerned telegony, "almost universally believed by nineteenth-century breeders and fanciers and widely accepted within the zoological community," which "attributed to the 'previous sire'—usually understood as the father of a female's first child—the power of influencing her subsequent offspring." Ritvo, *Platypus and the Mermaid,* 107–8. Citing Ritvo, Gullette draws on this idea in her discussion of the MDWS debate, in which a woman's body "is imagined as something like a permanent container of the first male flesh she experiences." Gullette, "Puzzling Case," 162.

18. [George Henry Lewes], "Hereditary Influence, Animal and Human," *Westminster Review, American Edition* 66 O.S. (July 1856): 83, emphasis in original.

19. Charles Darwin, *The Descent of Man, and Selection in Relation to Sex* (London, 2004), 263; hereafter cited in the text. The theory of pangenesis posited "the existence of 'gemmules,' particles that were thrown off by all cells of the body and that circulated through the bodily fluids and eventually came to rest in the sexual organs, where they were combined into the sex cells.... Characters common to one sex might suddenly appear in the opposite sex." Cynthia Eagle Russett, *Sexual Science: The Victorian Construction of Womanhood* (Cambridge, MA, 1989), 65.

20. Robert M. Young, *Darwin's Metaphor: Nature's Place in Victorian Culture* (Cambridge, 1985), 113.

21. See Lucy's much later rebuttal of Mrs. Tulliver's classification of "brown skin" as not "respectable," when uncle Pullet refers both to Cowper's *The Task* and "The Nut-Brown Maid" in joining dark skin to madness (*MF* 310). Thanks to Deborah Denenholz Morse for reminding me of this passage.

22. For Maggie's identification with gypsies, which seems to be based in part on her own perception of herself as "dark," see Meyer, *Imperialism at Home*, 153–56; Alicia Carroll, *Dark Smiles: Race and Desire in George Eliot* (Athens, 2003), 41–50; and Deborah Epstein Nord, *Gypsies and the British Imagination, 1807–1930* (New York, 2006), 103–5.

23. Bob Jakin confides his concerns about the "lonely" Tom to Maggie, thinking he had "found out a soft place in him" when Tom "made a fuss" about getting a spaniel for Lucy. "A good deal moved by Bob's suggestion," Maggie nonetheless discounts it as "mere fancy": "the present of the dog meant nothing more than cousinship and gratitude" (*MF* 316). However Tom might feel about cousin Lucy, marrying the daughter of the boss would certainly advance his career.

24. Compare the anecdote from Eliot's "Recollections of the Scilly Isles and Jersey" (1857) in which a "Mr. Buckstone amused us by his contempt for curs—'O, I wouldn't have a cur—there's nothing to look at in a cur.'" *The Journals of George Eliot,* ed. Margaret Harris and Judith Johnson (Cambridge, 1998), 279.

25. For an extended reading of Matthew Arnold's reimagining of the English as a hybrid people, see my *Allegories of Union in Irish and English Writing, 1790–1870: Politics, History, and the Family from Edgeworth to Arnold* (Cambridge, 2000), 155–65.

26. George Levine, "Intelligence as Deception: *The Mill on the Floss,*" *PMLA* 80 (1965): 403.

27. Sally Shuttleworth, *George Eliot and Nineteenth-Century Science: The Make-Believe of a Beginning* (Cambridge, 1984), 57; U. C. Knoepflmacher, *George Eliot's Early Novels: The Limits of Realism* (Berkeley, 1968), 212, 213, 212.

28. Josephine McDonagh, "The Early Novels," in *The Cambridge Companion to George Eliot,* ed. George Levine (Cambridge, 2001), 47.

29. Nord, *Gypsies,* 112; Eliot quoted in Meyer, *Imperialism at Home,* 129.

30. Meyer, *Imperialism at Home,* 146. Examining breeding discourse largely in regard to the constitution of Maggie's "mixed" character, Meyer argues that "in Maggie's story Eliot also tells the story of the conflictual history of England, with particular reference to the contact between various racial groups." Because I look at breeding and crossing specifically in relation to contemporary discussions of animals and plants, I sense in Meyer's analysis a conflation of terms that are distinct in my own: for example, she identifies the term *breed* with *race,* which the wider scientific contexts in which such terms appear do not. Moreover, she fails to acknowledge fully

the extent to which contemporary racial discourses—and, at times, Eliot herself—problematized the concept of "fusion" in relation to races that would not "fuse" or mix well. Nevertheless, Meyer's emphasis on conflict and contact (as well as the lack thereof, in my analysis) between racialized groups highlights an important strand of Eliot's thinking about race and history.

31. As Sollors observes, "The zoological analogy with mules may…not have been the word's original, or exclusive, etymological source, but the term 'Mulatto' certainly did become intertwined with the animal that was a cross between two species." Sollors, *Neither Black Nor White,* 128.

32. Huth, *Marriage of Near Kin,* 332.

33. "The Marriage of Near Kin," *Westminster Review: American Edition* 104 O.S. (October 1875): 151.

34. Ritvo, *Platypus and the Mermaid,* 97; Robert J. C. Young, *Colonial Desire: Hybridity in Theory, Culture, and Race* (London, 1995), 16; see also Sollors, *Neither Black Nor White,* 129–35.

35. According to Robert J. C. Young, Herder, for example, regarded "colonization and racial mixture…as introducing a fatal heterogeneity," even though "the very progress of mankind comes as the result of diffusionism, or cultural mixing and communication." Gobineau, author of *An Essay on the Inequality of Human Races* (1853–55), similarly posited that the strong race must interbreed with the weaker if the weaker is to advance, yet the mixture itself brings on the decay of the stronger, characterizing "adulteration of blood" as "the basic cause of the fall of nations." Young, *Colonial Desire,* 41, 106.

36. Sollors, *Neither Black Nor White,* 134.

37. Lewes, "Hereditary Influence," 86. Lewes uses the word "intermarriage" differently from how we typically use that term today, and even from how Elizabeth Bennet uses it (see chapter 2), as a union "between members of *different* families, castes, tribes" (*OED*); this usage dates as far back as the seventeenth century. The first usage of "intermarriage" in the *OED* in precisely the opposite sense, the one Lewes follows—"marriage between persons [or interbreeding between animals] *nearly related*"—dates from the 1870s, although it appears much earlier, as in both the letter from Mary Ann Evans to John Sibree and the quotation from Tom Paine that follow in my text (all emphase added).

38. Lewes, "Hereditary Influence," 89.

39. Ibid., emphasis in original.

40. Ibid.

41. Ibid., 89–90.

42. George Eliot, "The Modern Hep! Hep! Hep!" in *Impressions of Theophrastus Such,* ed. Nancy Henry (Iowa City, 1994), 158.

43. Ibid., 160.

44. For a contemporary example of how such anxieties emerge in the context of Irish immigration to England at midcentury, see Corbett, *Allegories of Union,* 82–113. If an early letter is to be trusted, Mary Ann Evans was more sanguine about possibilities of fusion between some groups than others: "the repulsion between ["negroes"] and the other races seems too strong for fusion to take place to any great extent." "To John Sibree, Jr.," 11 February 1848, *The George Eliot Letters,* vol. 1, 246.

45. "To John Sibree, Jr.," 11 February 1848, *The George Eliot Letters,* vol. 1, 246.

46. Florence Nightingale, "Cassandra," Appendix I to Ray Strachey, *The Cause* (Port Washington, NY, 1969), 412.

47. Quoted in James B. Twitchell, *Forbidden Partners: The Incest Taboo in Modern Culture* (New York, 1987), 136. As in Lewes's reference to Jews, quoted above, Paine also identified Jewish exclusivity (rather than, say, Christian persecution) as a cause of their failure to mix. Sander Gilman argues that by the late nineteenth century, such thinking constructed "the Jews as an essentially 'ill' people and labeled the origins of that illness as incest/inbreeding," with "their refusal to marry beyond the inner group" taken as both symptom and cause of their degeneracy. Gilman, "Sibling Incest," 403.

48. Young, *Colonial Desire,* 13.

49. George Eliot, "The Natural History of German Life," in *Essays of George Eliot,* ed. Thomas Pinney (New York, 1963), 274.

50. Disraeli's Millbank remarks that "the real old families of this country are to be found among the peasantry." Hardy's Durbeyfields were ostensibly once D'Urbervilles. Benjamin Disraeli, *Coningsby; or, The New Generation,* ed. Thom Braun (Harmondsworth, U.K., 1983), 193.

51. Catherine Gallagher, *The Body Economic: Life, Death, and Sensation in Political Economy and the Victorian Novel* (Princeton, 2006), 173.

52. Quoted in Adrian Desmond and James Moore, *Darwin: The Life of a Tormented Evolutionist* (New York, 1991), 557, emphasis in original.

53. Charles Darwin, *On the Various Contrivances by which British and Foreign Orchids are Fertilised by Insects, and on the Good Effects of Intercrossing* (Stanfordville, NY, 1979), 359–60.

54. Charles Darwin, *The Variation of Animals and Plants under Domestication* (Brussels, 1969), vol. 2, 144; hereafter cited in the text.

55. For the first point, see Ottenheimer, *Forbidden Relatives,* 85–86; for the second, Adam Kuper, "Incest, Cousin Marriage, and the Origin of the Human Sciences in Nineteenth-Century England," *Past and Present* 174 (February 2002): 170n41.

56. For an overview of the whole issue, see Nancy F. Anderson, "Cousin Marriage in Victorian England," *Journal of Family History* 11 (1986): 285–301. For an example of the method on which the younger Darwin based his work, see Francis Galton, "On Blood-Relationship," *Proceedings of the Royal Society of London* 20 (1871–72): 394–402. Galton located the source of "large variation in individuals from their parents" as "a consequence of [the strict doctrine of heredity] wherever the breed is impure."

57. Kuper, "Incest," 172; see also Anderson, "Cousin Marriage," 295; and Ottenheimer, *Forbidden Relatives,* 86.

58. George H. Darwin, "Marriages between First Cousins in England and their Effects," *Journal of the Statistical Society of London* 38 (June 1875): 153.

59. Kuper, "Incest," 170.

60. See also George H. Darwin, "On Beneficial Restrictions to Liberty of Marriage," *Contemporary Review* 22 (1873): 412–26.

61. Jonathan Smith, "Darwin's Botany and Sensation Fiction," unpublished manuscript, 10–11. I am extremely grateful to Smith for sharing with me this work-in-progress. For his broader consideration of Darwin's botany, see *Charles Darwin and Victorian Visual Culture* (Cambridge, 2006), 137–78.

62. Anderson, "Cousin Marriage," 297.

63. William Adam, "Consanguinity in Marriage, Part I," *Fortnightly Review* 2 (November 1865): 727.

64. Desmond and Moore, *Darwin*, 447.

65. [G. W. Child], "Marriages of Consanguinity," *Westminster Review, American Edition* 80 O.S. (July 1863): 42; hereafter cited in the text.

66. Ritvo, *Platypus and the Mermaid*, 118, 119.

67. Harriet Ritvo, *The Animal Estate: The English and Other Creatures in the Victorian Age* (Cambridge, MA, 1987), 67.

68. Huth, *Marriage of Near Kin*, 254.

69. Gallagher explores the divergent interpretations of Malthusian thought through the distinction between Darwin's faith in and McLennan's skepticism about the human-animal analogy: "the Darwinian thinkers, including Darwin himself" and E. B. Tylor, "were reluctant to pursue the idea of any sharp discontinuity between animal and human adaptation. . . . They kept the focus on developmental continuities. Looking at sexual relations instead, McLennan immediately saw a developmental break—the incest taboo—which seemed to be a human universal without any animal analogues. Victorians did not doubt that this was a phenomenon limited to humans. . . . Yet its ubiquity in one form or another pointed toward a natural exigency." Gallagher, *Body Economic*, 164. If a taboo on incest was difficult to locate within the animal kingdom, a prohibition on miscegenation was not: as Ritvo writes, "works of natural history offered voluminous testimony to the desire of animals to avoid miscegenation, often citing a mutual repulsion between apparently similar creatures as persuasive evidence of specific difference." Ritvo, *Platypus and the Mermaid*, 89.

70. Kuper, "Incest," 175. For an overview of the disagreement among analysts of the origins of the incest taboo as to whether or not "an aversion to inbreeding had been 'selected for' in the course of natural selection," see Carl N. Degler, *In Search of Human Nature: The Decline and Revival of Darwinism in American Social Thought* (New York, 1991), 245–69. I thank Jen Cellio for the reference.

71. Beer, *Darwin's Plots*, 28, emphasis in original.

72. Levine, "Intelligence," 406.

73. Quoted in David Carroll, ed., *George Eliot: The Critical Heritage* (New York, 1971), 136.

74. Eliot's description of the Dodson adherence to custom also resonates with Paxton's analysis of how Marian Lewes depicted "the German peasant's devotion to custom" in "The Natural History of German Life": "the peasant's entrenchment in custom carries a negative valence precisely insofar as it is unreasoning, blind, and lacking in self-consciousness." Paxton, *George Eliot and Herbert Spencer*, 13–14.

75. Stocking, *Victorian Anthropology*, 235.

76. Emily Davies, "To Jane Crow," 21 August 1868, *Emily Davies: Collected Letters, 1861–1875*, ed. Ann B. Murphy and Deirdre Raftery (Charlottesville, 2004), 287; Daniel Cottom, *Social Figures: George Eliot, Social History, and Literary Representation* (Minneapolis, 1987), 53.

77. Bodenheimer, *Real Life*, 52; Cottom, *Social Figures*, 53.

78. Levine, "Intelligence," 403.

79. Quoted in David Carroll, *George Eliot*, 110.

80. Meyer, *Imperialism at Home,* 143; as she points out, the word *savage* recurs frequently during the second half of the novel. But Nancy Armstrong argues that Maggie, via her ongoing contrast with her cousin Lucy, is made to embody "an internal struggle between self-expression and self-discipline within a consequently complex and layered individual" in a move by which "masculine aggression"—a form of "savagery"—is relocated "in a female body where the threat it poses can be localized and contained." Armstrong, *How Novels Think,* 92, 93.

Chapter 6. Fictive Kinship and Natural Affinities in *Wives and Daughters*

1. Elizabeth Gaskell, *Wives and Daughters,* ed. Pam Morris (London, 1996), 41; hereafter cited in the text.

2. Mary Debrabant, "Birds, Bees, and Darwinian Survival Strategies in *Wives and Daughters," Gaskell Society Journal* 16 (2002): 17.

3. Louise Henson, "History, Science, and Social Change: Elizabeth Gaskell's 'Evolutionary' Narratives," *Gaskell Society Journal* 17 (2003): 27, 24. See also Leon Litvack, "Outposts of Empire: Scientific Discovery and Colonial Displacement in Gaskell's *Wives and Daughters," Review of English Studies* 55 (2004): 727–58.

4. As Linda K. Hughes and Michael Lund point out, Roger also "inherits" his mother's talent for mediation: "If Osborne perpetuates his mother's aesthetic and physical delicacy, Roger perpetuates her genius for comfort and conciliation." Hughes and Lund, *Victorian Publishing and Mrs. Gaskell's Work* (Charlottesville, 1999), 29.

5. Along these lines, Debrabant argues that Osborne's "'prohibited' offspring, the result of a mixed marriage, is, according to Darwinian logic, a likely source of vigour.... The child brings further potential for advantageous variation and diversity among the Hamley race." Debrabant, "Birds, Bees," 19.

6. Karen Boiko, "Reading and (Re)Writing Class: Elizabeth Gaskell's *Wives and Daughters," Victorian Literature and Culture* 33 (2005): 95, 96; Deirdre D'Albertis, *Dissembling Fictions: Elizabeth Gaskell and the Victorian Social Text* (New York, 1997), 142; Pam Morris, "Introduction," *Wives and Daughters,* xi.

7. While I would not claim that the unintended consequences of human sexual reproduction dominate the text in the way that they do in *The Mill on the Floss,* I do think that ideas about "chance, probability, and speculation" very much shape Gaskell's treatment of this strand of scientific discourse. D'Albertis, *Dissembling Fictions,* 137.

8. Jennifer Uglow, *Elizabeth Gaskell: A Habit of Stories* (New York, 1993), 25.

9. Yeazell, *Fictions of Modesty,* 199; hereafter cited in the text.

10. Here are the only two examples I've identified of "one-flesh" talk in the novel. When Mr. Gibson discovers that Mrs. Gibson has eavesdropped on his conversation with Dr. Nicholls and thus has learned something of Osborne's condition, he points to the damage she could do to his professional reputation: "Are not you and I one in all these respects?" (383). And Mrs. Gibson refers to Roger's becoming, after his engagement to her daughter, "as it were, my own flesh and blood" (427).

11. Sarah Franklin and Susan McKinnon, "New Directions in Kinship Study: A Core Concept Revisited," *Social Anthropology* 41 (April 2000): 277.

12. Hughes and Lund, *Victorian Publishing,* 26.

13. "To Anne Robson," [23 December 1841], letter 16 of *The Letters of Mrs. Gaskell,* ed. J. A. V. Chapple and Arthur Pollard (Cambridge, MA, 1967), 45, 46. On

the literary consequences of Gaskell's early loss of her mother, see Deanna L. Davis, "Feminist Critics and Literary Mothers: Daughters Reading Elizabeth Gaskell," *Signs* 17 (1992): 507–32.

14. For a reading of further connections between Gaskell's text and *Jane Eyre,* see Margaret Homans, *Bearing the Word: Language and Female Experience in Nineteenth-Century Women's Writing* (Chicago, 1986), 273–76; hereafter cited in the text. Leah Price argues that "the displacement of a character named after Jane Eyre by a character sharply contrasted to Jane Eyre"—Hyacinth Clare Kirkpatrick—"allows Gaskell to dissociate herself from a tradition" of governess representations. Price, "The *Life of Charlotte Brontë* and the Death of Miss Eyre," *Studies in English Literature* 35 (1995): 760.

15. Hilary M. Schor, *Scheherezade in the Marketplace: Elizabeth Gaskell and the Victorian Novel* (London, 1992), 189.

16. Emily Blair, *Virginia Woolf and the Nineteenth-Century Domestic Novel* (Albany, 2007), 86. See also Joellen Masters, "'Nothing More' and 'Nothing Definite': First Wives in Elizabeth Gaskell's *Wives and Daughters,*" *JNT: Journal of Narrative Theory* 34 (2004): 1–26.

17. See Elizabeth Langland, *Nobody's Angels: Middle-Class Women and Domestic Ideology in Victorian Culture* (Ithaca, 1995), 132–45.

18. In her psychobiography of Gaskell, Felicia Bonaparte argues that, herself "replaced" by a stepmother who bore two children, Gaskell invents a compensatory father-daughter fiction in which the "tie becomes so close, in fact, that it verges on the incestuous." Positing "an Electra complex at work in the feelings Gaskell imagines Molly having for her father," she identifies in Gaskell's fictional fathers "a reciprocal interest" in their daughters. Bonaparte, *The Gypsy-Bachelor of Manchester: The Life of Mrs. Gaskell's Demon* (Charlottesville, 1992), 57, 58.

19. Coral Lansbury, *Elizabeth Gaskell: The Novel of Social Crisis* (New York, 1975), 199; Langland, *Nobody's Angels,* 134.

20. Schor, *Scheherezade,* 188.

21. "Were it not for Gaskell's notorious casualness about the naming of her characters," Yeazell writes, "one would be tempted to find a direct allusion to Austen's heroine" in the name of the Hamleys' dead daughter; indeed, "Molly Gibson" is a name she had used before, in *Mary Barton* (1848), for Mary's putative rival for Jem Wilson's affection. "Direct" or not, however, the allusion to Fanny Price is highly meaningful for my analysis. Yeazell, *Fictions of Modesty,* 212.

22. For the connection to *Mansfield Park,* see also W. A. Craik, *Elizabeth Gaskell and the English Provincial Novel* (London, 1975), 202–4. Craik mentions but does not pursue Gaskell's allusions to *Jane Eyre* and *The Mill on the Floss.*

23. Langland, *Nobody's Angels,* 142–43.

24. Both Homans and Bonaparte read Molly's taking Fanny's place as an emblematic stage in what Homans calls the "death of the self." Homans, *Bearing the Word,* 255. As Bonaparte further argues, "'Mrs. Gaskell' required the marriage, but Gaskell's demon understood that to let Molly marry Roger was to acquiesce in her suicide." Bonaparte, *Gypsy-Bachelor,* 277. While I understand this skepticism, I do not share it.

25. For the elaboration of this argument, see Homans, *Bearing the Word,* 258, 269.

26. George Eliot, "Mr. Gilfil's Love Story," in *Scenes of Clerical Life,* ed. David Lodge (Harmondsworth, U.K., 1973), 152.

27. Marianne Novy, *Reading Adoption: Family and Difference in Fiction and Drama* (Ann Arbor, 2005), 125. Considering nineteenth-century novels, both Patricia Howe and Tess O'Toole have traced a discursive link between the practice of adoption and the languages of improvement. Howe, "Fontane's 'Ellernklipp'"; O'Toole, "Adoption."

28. Boiko, "Reading and (Re)Writing Class," 99.

29. Levine, *Darwin*, 114.

30. Beer, *Darwin's Plots*, 77.

31. See Langland, *Nobody's Angels*, 137–39.

32. On the role of secrecy in the novel, see Terence Wright, *Elizabeth Gaskell, "We Are Not Angels": Realism, Gender, Values* (New York, 1995), 46–53.

33. Margaret Oliphant, *Miss Marjoribanks* (London, 1969), 86.

34. When Mrs. Gibson retells the muffin anecdote later in the novel, she adds, "I don't think he ever got over the cold he caught that day" (*WD* 638), which has led some readers to claim she has all but killed her first husband.

35. "To George Smith," 3 May [1864], letter 550, *Letters of Mrs. Gaskell*, 731, emphasis added.

36. Ibid. Homans argues that "'Two Mothers' would be just as accurate a title for this final novel as *Wives and Daughters*, for while the actual title reflects the novel's overt thematic concern with the transformation of daughters into wives and with the multiplicity of wives... the earlier title exposes the hidden structure of the novel, the difference between two mothers, one living and one dead, which is also the difference between two kinds of signification." Homans, *Bearing the Word*, 251. My reading suggests that Gaskell might just as well have called it "Two Sisters."

37. I am grateful to Holly Forsythe Paul for this explanation: "Uncles and aunts 'à la mode Bretagne' are the first cousins of one's parents; nephews and nieces 'à la mode Bretagne' are the children of one's first cousins"; this is "not technically correct terminology, but a compromise that reflects generational relationships. So Cynthia isn't technically Molly's sister but their similar ages and the relationship of their parents leads to the fanciful coinage—a more intimate suggestion of kinship than 'stepsister' would offer (especially given fairy-tale conventions)." Paul, "A Sister 'à la mode de Bretagne' in Gaskell," *Victoria* 19th-Century British Culture and Society newsgroup, 19 May 2006.

38. For a cogent argument that it is reading that forms Molly's ideas about the desirable man, see Julia M. Wright, "'Growing Pains': Representing the Romantic in Gaskell's *Wives and Daughters*," in *Nervous Reactions: Victorian Recollections of Romanticism*, ed. Joel Faflak and Julia M. Wright (Albany, 2004), 174.

39. Brown, *Devoted Sisters*, 143; Amy K. Levin, *The Suppressed Sister: A Relationship in Novels by Nineteenth- and Twentieth-Century British Women* (Lewisburg, PA, 1992), 66.

40. Marcus does not discuss *Wives and Daughters* (or any of Gaskell's other writings), a curious omission since the concerns of the novel so clearly intersect with her central arguments.

41. As René Girard writes, "The impulse toward the object is ultimately an impulse toward the mediator." Levin also argues that Molly "desires (to be) Cynthia... and to be loved by Roger," while Brown suggests that Molly's agency in resolving the

conflict with Preston directly expresses her rivalry with (and likeness to) Cynthia. Girard, *Deceit, Desire,* 10; Levin, *Suppressed Sister,* 68; Brown, *Devoted Sisters,* 47–50.

42. Levin, *Suppressed Sister,* 67.

43. Debrabant, "Birds, Bees," 24.

44. Although she does not reference it, this along with Molly's other somewhat duplicitous uses of family language might be assimilated to Homans's argument as to how Molly comes to "participate for herself in…substitutive language" through interactions with the Kirkpatrick women. Homans, *Bearing the Word,* 269.

45. Bonaparte, *Gypsy-Bachelor,* 66.

46. For the phrase "maidenly modesty," see Elizabeth Gaskell, *Mary Barton: A Tale of Manchester Life,* ed. Macdonald Daly (London, 2003), 132.

Chapter 7. Virginia Woolf and Victorian "Incests"

1. "Old Bloomsbury," in *Moments of Being,* ed. Schulkind, 182.

2. Louise DeSalvo, *Virginia Woolf: The Impact of Childhood Sexual Abuse on Her Life and Work* (Boston, 1989). Thomas C. Caramagno convincingly argues, in contrast to DeSalvo, for a multilayered approach to understanding Woolf's experience of incestuous abuse. Caramagno, *The Flight of the Mind: Virginia Woolf's Art and Manic-Depressive Illness* (Berkeley, 1992).

3. I use the phrase "sexual abuse" to refer to unwanted or coerced sexual activity. In referring to Woolf's experiences, I use the phrase "incestuous sexual abuse." When working with historical materials that do not specify the relationship between abuser and abused, I use the phrase "(incestuous) sexual abuse" so as not to preclude the possibility of incest. I also use that phrase in the case of step-relations, even though sex between stepsiblings, for example, was not penalized by the Punishment of Incest Act in 1908 and thus did not constitute a legally punishable offense. For the theoretical and historical underpinnings of my approach, see Hacking, "Making and Molding"; Wilson, "'Not in This House'"; and Carol Smart, "A History of Ambivalence and Conflict in the Discursive Construction of the 'Child Victim' of Sexual Abuse," *Social and Legal Studies* 8 (1999): 391–409.

4. See especially Rosaria Champagne, *The Politics of Survivorship: Incest, Women's Literature, and Feminist Theory* (New York, 1996); and Kalí Tal, *Worlds of Hurt: Reading the Literatures of Trauma* (Cambridge, 1996). Janice Doane and Devon Hodges usefully critique Hacking's stance in *Telling Incest: Narratives of Dangerous Remembering from Stein to Sapphire* (Ann Arbor, 2001), 11–29. I am also indebted to the colleagues who have, over the years, substantially enriched my understanding of trauma: Vicki Smith, Tim Melley, Madelyn Detloff, and Elizabeth Swanson Goldberg.

5. Virginia Woolf, *The Voyage Out* (San Diego, n.d.), 216.

6. Christine Froula, *Virginia Woolf and the Bloomsbury Avant-Garde: War, Civilization, Modernity* (New York, 2005), 213; Virginia Woolf, 20 January 1931, *The Diary of Virginia Woolf,* ed. Anne Olivier Bell (San Diego, 1982), vol. 4, 6; *Three Guineas* (San Diego, 1968), 120, hereafter cited in the text; [28 July 1934], *Diary,* vol. 4, 233.

7. Lee, *Virginia Woolf,* 125, 136.

8. Diana L. Swanson, "An Antigone Complex? The Political Psychology of *The Years* and *Three Guineas,*" *Woolf Studies Annual* 3 (1997): 30–31.

9. Woolf, *Night and Day,* 379; 3 September 1928, *Diary,* vol. 3, 194. Nancy Ramsay also uses the latter phrase in *To the Lighthouse* (San Diego, 1981), 73; hereafter cited in the text.

10. This reading is necessarily speculative, as any reading would be: "Lack of evidence makes it impossible to assess whether Vanessa's love for Jack was passionate or merely fond." Frances Spalding, *Vanessa Bell* (London, 1983), 31.

11. Biographers agree that Virginia Stephen was ambivalent about both Stella Duckworth's marriage and Vanessa's subsequent relationship to Jack. Hermione Lee suggests that she was "infected by her father's feelings about the marriage." Lee, *Virginia Woolf,* 135. Mitchell Leaska argues that "when Virginia saw her sister getting so much of Jack's attention, she became jealous and resentful, first because that intimacy excluded her, but equally because with Stella's death Vanessa was becoming daily more a mother to her than a sister." Leaska, *Granite and Rainbow: The Hidden Life of Virginia Woolf* (New York, 1998), 83.

12. Lee provides a good account of the genesis of the memoir, which Julia Briggs describes as "stiff and Victorian, tailing off abruptly with the first threat of sexual scandal." Lee, *Virginia Woolf,* 228–31; Briggs, *Virginia Woolf: An Inner Life* (Orlando, 2005), 18.

13. Spalding suggests that "just as after Stella's death Vanessa had clung to her memory by growing closer to Jack, so now she gave her affection to Thoby's greatest friend." Alex Zwerdling describes Clive Bell, from Virginia's perspective, as "a virtual unknown, a potential threat, and a powerful rival." Leaska notes that the advent of a baby provided the impetus for Clive to flee toward Virginia, while Jane Dunn speculates that "the feeling which had driven [Virginia] in the nursery to break into the close relationship between Vanessa and Thoby" was repeated in her relationship to Clive. Spalding, *Vanessa Bell,* 60; Zwerdling, "Mastering the Memoir: Woolf and the Family Legacy," *Modernism/Modernity* 10 (2003): 173; Leaska, *Granite and Rainbow,* 131; Dunn, *A Very Close Conspiracy: Vanessa Bell and Virginia Woolf* (Boston, 1990), 109.

14. In her introduction to "Reminiscences," Schulkind attributes this perception to Quentin Bell but does not cite a print source for it. Woolf, "Reminiscences," in *Moments of Being,* ed. Schulkind, 26.

15. Froula, *Virginia Woolf,* 231, 242; for a fuller account of its symbolic meanings than I can offer here, see Froula, 242–51.

16. Virginia Woolf, "22 Hyde Park Gate," in *Moments of Being,* ed. Schulkind, 177.

17. Christopher Herbert, *Culture and Anomie: Ethnographic Imagination in the Nineteenth Century* (Chicago, 1991), 65.

18. Ibid., 66, 67.

19. Ibid., 65.

20. By decided contrast, here is the first sentence of Virginia Stephen's sketch of her father, quoted by his official biographer: "My impression as a child always was that my father was not very much older than we were." Frederic William Maitland, *The Life and Letters of Leslie Stephen* (London, 1907), 474.

21. Johannes Fabian, *Time and the Other: How Anthropology Makes Its Object* (New York, 1983).

22. Recent critics of modernism have begun to explore the anthropological dimensions of Woolf's thinking, albeit without reference to the discipline's Victorian past. See Jed Esty, *A Shrinking Island: Modernism and National Culture in England*

(Princeton, 2004), 85–107; and Carey Snyder, "Woolf's Ethnographic Modernism: Self-Nativizing in *The Voyage Out*," *Woolf Studies Annual* 10 (2004): 81–108.

23. *Gibbering* is a significantly sexualized word in Woolf's oeuvre: see both Rachel's dream in *The Voyage Out* (77) and the description of the man at the pillarbox in *The Pargiters: The Novel-Essay Portion of "The Years,"* ed. Mitchell Leaska (New York, 1977), 43; hereafter cited in the text. Further, the image of Leslie Stephen as lion recalls Mr. Hilbery's response at hearing the news of his daughter's engagement: "The extravagant, inconsiderate, uncivilized male, outraged somehow and gone bellowing to his lair with a roar which still sometimes reverberates in the most polished of drawing-rooms." Woolf, *Night and Day*, 500.

24. On Woolf's use of the phrase "heart of darkness," see Briggs, *Virginia Woolf*, 389–90.

25. Virginia Woolf, *The Years* (San Diego, n.d.), 10; hereafter cited in the text.

26. Joseph Conrad, *Heart of Darkness*, ed. Robert Kimbrough (New York, 1988), 14.

27. This scene of savagery at the dark heart of civilization also needs to be read from a postcolonial perspective: as Urmila Seshagiri argues, "even the most banal signifiers of English civility"—like the tea-table—"stem from centuries of racial exploitation" Seshagiri, "Orienting Virginia Woolf: Race, Aesthetics, and Politics in *To the Lighthouse*," *Modern Fiction Studies* 50 (2004): 69.

28. For a reading of the persistence of objects, through which "the past infiltrates the present," see Pamela L. Caughie, *Virginia Woolf and Postmodernism: Literature in Quest and Question of Itself* (Urbana, 1991), 102.

29. She also uses this term elsewhere: see 2 November 1932, *Diary*, vol. 4, 129. Froula reads Woolf's major problem with *The Pargiters* as involving "a crisis of verification": "If *The Pargiters* was to be a progressive and visionary history of the sexual life of women, how to document that history?" Froula, *Virginia Woolf*, 224.

30. For a groundbreaking discussion of "street love," see Susan M. Squier, *Virginia Woolf and London: The Sexual Politics of the City* (Chapel Hill, 1985), 142–53.

31. Vernon Lee [Violet Paget], *Miss Brown* (New York, 1978), 160, 197, 202, 160, 202; hereafter cited in the text. The narrative links incest among the brutish folk to the habitual sodomy of "their negligent and impure owner," as Koven describes Hamlin, whose "cottages are hotbeds of filth and sexual perversion, beset by incest rather than inversion." Koven, *Slumming*, 211.

32. As Wilson argues, "The effort to constitute bourgeois subjectivity as the successful suppression of natural animalism and passion by the intellectual and rational powers . . . laid the groundwork for middle-class fear and loathing of cultural 'others' who are supposed not to insist on (or not to the same degree) this hierarchy of forces within the subject." Wilson, " 'Not in This House,' " 48.

33. Caughie provides a very useful gloss on the status of conventions in Woolf's evolving thinking about *The Pargiters*, concluding that she could not "persist in the dichotomy of genuine feelings and false conventions that inspired the essay-novel divisions" and reframed her task as "exposing the seemingly natural as conventional and disclosing our tendency to accept certain conventions as natural and normative." Caughie, *Virginia Woolf and Postmodernism*, 99.

34. Some members of Woolf's circle also considered less volatile sexual material as unfit for her to name in print. "Can I mention erection?" she asked Maynard Keynes while writing Roger Fry's biography: "No you cant. I should mind your

saying it. Such revelations have to be in key with their time." "Is he right," Woolf wondered, "or only public school?" 6 January 1940, *Diary,* vol. 5, 256.

35. Sims, *"How the Poor Live" and "Horrible London,"* 118.

36. Jen Shelton, " 'Don't Say Such Foolish Things, Dear': Speaking Incest in *The Voyage Out,"* in *Incest and the Literary Imagination,* ed. Elizabeth Barnes (Gainesville, 2002), 240.

37. For use of the term *pargeting* to describe Woolf's critique of prohibitions on speech and her own method in *The Years,* see Leaska, *Granite and Rainbow,* 337–38.

38. Cohen, *Sex Scandal,* 1.

39. Smart, "History of Ambivalence," 406.

40. In a book she certainly did read, Beatrice Webb's *My Apprenticeship,* Woolf would have seen an example of suppressed evidence in an account of working-class life. Webb wrote that while she had gathered information about incest from the working women she encountered, she had chosen not to publish it in the 1880s. Her remarks exemplify the discourse of incest as a "savage" practice: "The fact that some of my workmates . . . could chaff each other about having babies by their fathers and brothers, was a gruesome example of the effect of debased social environment on personal character and family life, and therefore on racial progress. . . . To put it bluntly, sexual promiscuity, and even sexual perversion, are almost unavoidable among men and women of average character and intelligence crowded into the one-room tenement of slum areas." Beatrice Webb, *My Apprenticeship* (New York, 1926), 310n25.

41. Louise A. Jackson, *Child Sexual Abuse in Victorian England* (London, 2000), 55; hereafter cited in the text.

42. Cohen draws a comparable conclusion regarding the debate over public exposure of a sodomy scandal in 1870: "The issue here was . . . protection of the reading public from stories that might endanger it." Cohen, *Sex Scandal,* 91.

43. On this point, see Sheila Jeffreys, *The Spinster and Her Enemies: Feminism and Sexuality, 1880–1930* (London, 1985), 64–67.

44. Citing Quentin Bell, Lee asserts that the exhibitionist who appears in both *The Pargiters* and *The Years* was based on "a man who used to hang about Hyde Park Gate and expose himself to the children," which suggests another personal source for Woolf's representation of Rose's experience. Bell, *Virginia Woolf: A Biography* (San Diego, 1972), vol. 1, 35; Lee, *Virginia Woolf,* 123.

45. I use the phrase "familial sexual abuse" here since the range of relatives charged in these cases—fathers as well as stepfathers, uncles who may or may not be "blood relations" to their victims—exceeds the narrow scope of what came to be defined as "incest" in the Punishment of Incest Act of 1908. As Smart also observes, "There was no single term for this behaviour. . . . It was not conceptualized as abuse, and hence was not referred to as such until the 1970s." Smart, "History of Ambivalence," 393.

46. Roger Davidson, " 'This Pernicious Delusion': Law, Medicine, and Child Sexual Abuse in Early-Twentieth-Century Scotland," *Journal of the History of Sexuality* 10 (2001): 76.

47. Margot Gayle Backus, " 'Looking for that Dead Girl': Incest, Pornography, and the Capitalist Family Romance in *Nightwood, The Years,* and *Tar Baby,"* *American Imago* 51 (1994): 431.

48. "In the city today I was thinking of another book—about shopkeepers, & publicans, with low life scenes." 16 November 1931, *Diary,* vol. 4, 53. Grace Radin provides the most comprehensive view of the changes in the novel over time. Radin, *Virginia Woolf's "The Years": The Evolution of a Novel* (Knoxville, 1981).

49. By the "1891" section, Eleanor has followed the example of Octavia Hill, founder of the Charity Organization Society, in herself becoming a proprietor of housing for the poor. As Deborah Epstein Nord suggests, "the world of rent collecting and visiting the poor Jews of the East End which so attracts Eleanor Pargiter" conveys the experiences of a large group of socially conscious young women of the time. Nord, *Walking the Victorian Streets: Women, Representation, and the City* (Ithaca, 1995), 186; see also Lucy Bland, *Banishing the Beast: Sexuality and the Early Feminists* (New York, 1995), 95–123; and Koven, *Slumming,* 183–227. Yet another model for Eleanor's effort is Stella Duckworth herself, who "helped to set up a block of new buildings for the East End poor for which she had complete responsibility." Lee, *Virginia Woolf,* 121.

50. Deborah L. Parsons, *Streetwalking the Metropolis: Women, the City, and Modernity* (Oxford, 2000), 110.

51. All ellipses here are mine. As in the next sentence, I've emended Leaska's transcription of *The Pargiters,* which records Woolf's handwritten deletions and insertions, for ease of understanding. The full text of this brief passage in Leaska includes two significant but subsequently deleted phrases: Eleanor also says that she would "get to know the people" and devise "a better system" than slum living (*Pargiters* 23).

52. The various references to fighting cats in *The Years* indicate another instance of pargeting from Woolf's childhood, related in "A Sketch of the Past": "One night I lay awake horrified hearing, as I imagined, an obscene old man gasping and croaking and muttering senile indecencies—it was a cat, I was told afterwards; a cat's anguished love making" ("SP" 123).

53. Froula, *Virginia Woolf,* 238.

54. On this point, see DeSalvo, *Virginia Woolf,* 185–89; and Radin, *Virginia Woolf's "The Years,"* 23–25. The change of name from Bobby to Martin subtly references a brother-sister pair from the nineteenth-century tradition, the comparably squabbling Rose and Martin Yorke of Charlotte Brontë's *Shirley.*

55. Both Jane Marcus and Lee suggest that Rose is modeled on the composer Ethel Smyth, who had belonged to the Women's Social and Political Union (WSPU), the most militant wing of the suffrage movement, known for its violent tactics. Associating Rose with the WSPU rather than with suffrage groups that eschewed violence, Woolf also identified Rose with her father, the colonial military man. Marcus, *Virginia Woolf and the Languages of Patriarchy* (Bloomington, 1987), 51–52; Lee, *Virginia Woolf,* 581. As Sowon S. Park argues, "Woolf makes it clear that militant suffragism as practiced by Rose Pargiter is not on the side of human progress, but is rather a section in the continuum of violence that has fascism and militarism as its extreme." Park, "Suffrage and Virginia Woolf: 'The Mass Behind the Single Voice,'" *Review of English Studies* 56 (2005): 132.

56. In *The Pargiters,* Rose appears to conflate the "Red Indian game" with "her father's old stories of the Indian Mutiny" (*Pargiters* 42). In *The Years,* this episode is stripped of references to both Native Americans and the Sepoy Rebellion of 1857 but retains the detail of Colonel Pargiter's losing "two fingers of the right hand in the Mutiny" (*Years,* 13).

57. Shelton, " 'Don't Say,' " 229.

58. DeSalvo, *Virginia Woolf*, 30–31. Koven argues that "many elite men, for their part, were all too well aware of the intense emotional and physical bonds between boys and young men that bloomed in the hothouse atmosphere of all-male public schools and colleges": "Public schools, like casual wards and Oxford colleges, remained hotbeds of homosociability and homosexual experimentation." Koven, *Slumming*, 43, 84.

59. Regenia Gagnier, *Subjectivities: A History of Self-Representation in Britain, 1832–1920* (New York, 1991), 184, 185. For emerging anxieties about masturbation in the public schools, see J. R. de S. Honey, *Tom Brown's Universe: The Development of the Victorian Public School* (London, 1977), 167–96.

60. Manuscript evidence clearly indicates that Woolf conceived Rose as a lesbian: Radin refers to the "pattern of exclusion in which almost all the sexual material in *The Pargiters*" was excised from *The Years*. Radin, *Virginia Woolf's "The Years,"* 55. But see the early pages of the "1910" section, in which Rose stands looking out at the Thames, as a "buried feeling" emerges, recalling "how she had stood there on the night of a certain engagement, crying"; the narrator later remarks that she "had lived in many places, felt many passions, and done many things" (*Years* 161–62, 166). Ann Cvetkovich provides a useful starting point for thinking about and naming the relation between incest survivorship and lesbian identity: "As with lesbianism, so with incest: 'breaking the silence' is a queer process," with "queer" here signifying the "unpredictable connections between sexual abuse and its effects." Cvetkovich, *An Archive of Feelings: Trauma, Sexuality, and Lesbian Public Cultures* (Durham, 2003), 92, 90. My reading of the "queer scene" between Martin and Rose owes much to her theoretical analysis.

61. Judith Butler, *Antigone's Claim: Kinship between Life and Death* (New York, 2000), 24; hereafter cited in the text.

62. Mitchell A. Leaska, "Virginia Woolf, the Pargeter: A Reading of *The Years*," *Bulletin of the New York Public Library* 80 (1977): 204. More generally, Leaska reads Eleanor's relationship to her father as "emotional incest." *Granite and Rainbow*, 344–45.

63. Laura Moss Gottlieb, "*The Years:* A Feminist Novel," *Virginia Woolf: Centennial Essays*, ed. Elaine K. Ginsberg and Laura Moss Gottlieb (Troy, NY, 1983), 220.

64. Sophocles, *Antigone*, in *Sophocles I*, trans. Elizabeth Wyckoff (Chicago, 1954), ll. 917, 918.

65. Marcus, *Virginia Woolf*, 4. See also Liisa Saariluoma's related claim that "one social institution more than any other"—the family—"impedes a person from the realization of his or her real self." Saariluoma, "Virginia Woolf's *The Years:* Identity and Time in an Anti-Family Novel," *Orbis Litterarum* 54 [1999]: 287).

66. Marcus, *Virginia Woolf*, 39, emphasis in original.

67. Cf. Caughie's comment that "establishing a new order or the right relations necessitates exclusion, the very patriarchal or authoritarian gesture Woolf resists in *The Years*." Caughie, *Virginia Woolf and Postmodernism*, 107.

Conclusion

1. Sedgwick, *Tendencies*, 71, emphasis in original; hereafter cited in the text.

2. Yopie Prins extends and revises Sedgwick's framework to include "the tantular," implicitly contesting Sedgwick's fatalism about familialism. She concludes

the essay with a call to develop "another language of literary kinship" that speaks to "the various possibilities of female homoeroticism." Prins, "Greek Maenads, Victorian Spinsters," in *Victorian Sexual Dissidence,* ed. Richard Dellamora (Chicago, 1999), 72.

3. See, for example, her discussion of Charlotte Cushman's "matrilineal, adulterous, polygamous, homosexual household," in which one of her lovers married her adoptive son and nephew (*Between Women* 199).

4. See Michael Warner, *The Trouble with Normal: Sex, Politics, and the Ethics of Queer Life* (New York, 1999).

5. Briggs, *Virginia Woolf,* 310. For Woolf's rereading of the play, see Lee, *Virginia Woolf,* 631; and Brenda R. Silver, *Virginia Woolf's Reading Notebooks* (Princeton, 1983), 68, 314. The critics who best illuminate the ongoing use of the *Antigone* for Woolf's thinking and the specific references she makes to it in *The Years* include Joseph, "*Antigone*"; Swanson, "Antigone Complex?"; Clare Hanson, "Virginia Woolf in the House of Love: Compulsory Heterosexuality in *The Years,*" *Journal of Gender Studies* 6 (1997): 55–62; Froula, *Virginia Woolf,* 247–50; and Madelyn Detloff, " 'Tis Not My Nature to Join in Hating, but in Loving': Towards Survivable Public Mourning," in *Modernism and Mourning,* ed. Patricia Rae (Lewisburg, PA, 2007), 50–68.

6. Woolf, 6 April 1933, *Diary,* vol. 4, 149.

7. Froula, *Virginia Woolf,* 246.

8. For a useful consideration of the dialectical relationship between Ismene and Antigone, see Masako Hirai, *Sisters in Literature: Female Sexuality in "Antigone," "Middlemarch," "Howards End" and "Women in Love"* (New York, 1998), 25–40.

9. As Dever notes, "*To the Lighthouse* begins with a mother who is not only living but present"; the living mothers of *The Years,* however, are much less "present" in their children's lives than Mrs. Ramsay is in hers, even after her death. Dever, *Death and the Mother,* 203.

10. Woolf, 2 October 1934, *Diary,* vol. 4, 246. Lee notes the "nod to Elizabeth Gaskell." Lee, *Virginia Woolf,* 629.

11. In the Wyckoff translation that I use, this line reads, "I cannot share in hatred, but in love." *Antigone,* l. 523.

12. Eliot, "The Antigone and its Moral," in *Essays of George Eliot,* 262–63.

13. Detloff, " 'Tis Not My Nature,' " 53. Detloff takes Antigone as a figure for resistance and grieving in both Woolf's thinking and contemporary public life after 9/11.

14. *Antigone,* ll. 504–5; Eliot, *Middlemarch* (Oxford, 1996), 3.

❧ Bibliography

Acton, William. *Prostitution, Considered in its Moral, Social, & Sanitary Aspects, in London and Other Large Cities: with Proposals for the Mitigation and Prevention of its Attendant Evils.* 3d ed. Edited by Peter Fryer. Abridged and repr. New York: Praeger, 1968.

Adam, William. "Consanguinity in Marriage, Part I." *Fortnightly Review* 2 (November 1865): 710–30.

Adams, Maurianne. "Family Disintegration and Creative Reintegration: The Case of Charlotte Brontë and *Jane Eyre.*" In *The Victorian Family: Structure and Stresses,* edited by Anthony S. Wohl, 148–79. New York: St. Martin's Press, 1978.

Anderson, Nancy F. "Cousin Marriage in Victorian England." *Journal of Family History* 11 (1986): 285–301.

——. "The 'Marriage with a Deceased Wife's Sister Bill' Controversy: Incest Anxiety and the Defense of Family Purity in Victorian England." *Journal of British Studies* 21:2 (1982): 67–86.

Annan, Noel. *Leslie Stephen: The Godless Victorian.* London: Weidenfeld and Nicolson, 1984.

Armstrong, Isobel. *Jane Austen: Sense and Sensibility.* Harmondsworth, U.K.: Penguin, 1994.

Armstrong, Nancy. *Desire and Domestic Fiction: A Political History of the Novel.* New York: Oxford University Press, 1987.

——. *Fiction in the Age of Photography: The Legacy of British Realism.* Cambridge, MA: Harvard University Press, 1999.

——. *How Novels Think: The Limits of British Individualism from 1719–1900.* New York: Columbia University Press, 2005.

Arnold, Matthew. *"Culture and Anarchy" with "Friendship's Garland" and Some Literary Essays.* Vol. 5 of *The Complete Prose Works of Matthew Arnold,* edited by R. H. Super. Ann Arbor: University of Michigan Press, 1965.

Austen, Jane. *Emma.* Edited by David Lodge. London: Oxford University Press, 1971.

——. *Mansfield Park.* Edited by Claudia L. Johnson. New York: W. W. Norton, 1998.

——. *Northanger Abbey.* Edited by Marilyn Butler. London: Penguin, 1995.

——. *Persuasion.* Edited by John Davie. New York: Oxford University Press, 1980.

——. *Pride and Prejudice.* Edited by Donald Gray. New York: W. W. Norton, 1993.

——. *Sense and Sensibility.* Edited by James Kinsley. Oxford: Oxford University Press, 1990.

Azim, Firdous. *The Colonial Rise of the Novel.* London: Routledge, 1993.

Backus, Margot Gayle. "'Looking for that Dead Girl': Incest, Pornography, and the Capitalist Family Romance in *Nightwood, The Years,* and *Tar Baby.*" *American Imago* 51 (1994): 421–45.

Barrett Browning, Elizabeth. *Aurora Leigh: A Poem.* Chicago: Academy Chicago Publishers, 1979.

[Beckett, W. A.]. *The Woman's Question and the Man's Answer; or, Reflections on the Social Consequences of Legalizing Marriage with a Deceased Wife's Sister.* London, 1859.

Beer, Gillian. *Darwin's Plots: Evolutionary Narrative in Darwin, George Eliot, and Nineteenth-Century Fiction.* 2d ed. Cambridge: Cambridge University Press, 2000.

———. *George Eliot.* Bloomington: Indiana University Press, 1986.

Behlmer, George K. *Friends of the Family: The English Home and Its Guardians, 1850–1940.* Stanford: Stanford University Press, 1998.

Behrman, Cynthia Fansler. "The Annual Blister: A Sidelight on Victorian Social and Parliamentary History." *Victorian Studies* 11 (1968): 483–502.

Bell, Quentin. *Virginia Woolf: A Biography.* 2 vols. San Diego: Harcourt Brace Jovanovich, 1972.

Bell, Vikki. *Interrogating Incest: Feminism, Foucault, and the Law.* London: Routledge, 1993.

Beresford-Hope, Alexander James. *The Report of Her Majesty's Commission on the Laws of Marriage, Relative to Marriage with a Deceased Wife's Sister.* London, 1849.

Bersani, Leo. *A Future for Astyanax: Character and Desire in Literature.* Boston: Little, Brown, 1976.

Bivona, Daniel, and Roger B. Henkle. *The Imagination of Class: Masculinity and the Victorian Urban Poor.* Columbus: Ohio State University Press, 2006.

Blair, Emily. *Virginia Woolf and the Nineteenth-Century Domestic Novel.* Albany: State University of New York Press, 2007.

Bland, Lucy. *Banishing the Beast: Sexuality and the Early Feminists.* New York: New Press, 1995.

Bodenheimer, Rosemarie. *The Real Life of Mary Ann Evans: George Eliot, Her Letters and Fiction.* Ithaca: Cornell University Press, 1994.

Boiko, Karen. "Reading and (Re)writing Class: Elizabeth Gaskell's *Wives and Daughters.*" *Victorian Literature and Culture* 33 (2005): 85–106.

Bonaparte, Felicia. *The Gypsy-Bachelor of Manchester: The Life of Mrs. Gaskell's Demon.* Charlottesville: University Press of Virginia, 1992.

Boone, Joseph Allen. *Tradition Counter Tradition: Love and the Form of Fiction.* Chicago: University of Chicago Press, 1987.

Boone, Joseph Allen, and Deborah E. Nord. "Brother and Sister: The Seductions of Siblinghood in Dickens, Eliot, and Brontë." *Western Humanities Review* 46 (1992): 164–88.

Boumelha, Penny. *Charlotte Brontë.* Bloomington: Indiana University Press, 1990.

Briggs, Julia. *Virginia Woolf: An Inner Life.* Orlando: Harcourt, 2005.

Brontë, Charlotte. *An Edition of the Early Writings of Charlotte Brontë.* 3 vols. Edited by Christine Alexander. Oxford: Published for the Shakespeare Head Press by Basil Blackwell, 1987–91.

———. *Five Novelettes.* Edited by Winifred Gérin. London: Folio Press, 1971.

———. *Jane Eyre.* Edited by Margaret Smith. Oxford: Oxford University Press, 1993.

———. *The Letters of Charlotte Brontë, with a Selection of Letters by Family and Friends. Volume One: 1829–1847.* Edited by Margaret Smith. Oxford: Clarendon Press, 1995.

——. *Shirley.* Edited by Andrew and Judith Hook. Harmondsworth, U.K.: Penguin, 1974.

——. *Villette.* Edited by Margaret Smith and Herbert Rosengarten. Oxford: Oxford University Press, 1990.

Brontë, Emily. *Wuthering Heights.* 4th ed. Edited by Richard J. Dunn. New York: W. W. Norton, 2003.

Brown, Sarah Annes. *Devoted Sisters: Representations of the Sister Relationship in Nineteenth-Century British and American Literature.* Aldershot, U.K.: Ashgate Publishing, 2003.

Butler, Judith. *Antigone's Claim: Kinship between Life and Death.* New York: Columbia University Press, 2000.

——. *Bodies That Matter: On the Discursive Limits of "Sex."* New York: Routledge, 1993.

——. *Undoing Gender.* London: Routledge, 2004.

Buzard, James. *Disorienting Fiction: The Autoethnographic Work of Nineteenth-Century British Novels.* Princeton: Princeton University Press, 2005.

Caramagno, Thomas C. *The Flight of the Mind: Virginia Woolf's Art and Manic-Depressive Illness.* Berkeley: University of California Press, 1992.

Carroll, Alicia. *Dark Smiles: Race and Desire in George Eliot.* Athens: Ohio University Press, 2003.

Carroll, David, ed. *George Eliot: The Critical Heritage.* New York: Barnes and Noble, 1971.

Castle, Terry. "Was Jane Austen Gay?" In *Boss Ladies, Watch Out! Essays on Women, Sex, and Writing,* 125–36. New York: Routledge, 2002.

Caughie, Pamela L. *Virginia Woolf and Postmodernism: Literature in Quest and Question of Itself.* Urbana: University of Illinois Press, 1991.

Chadwick, Edwin. *Report on the Sanitary Condition of the Labouring Population of Great Britain.* Edited by M. W. Flinn. Edinburgh: Edinburgh University Press, 1965.

Chambers, Diane M. "Triangular Desire and the Sororal Bond: The 'Deceased Wife's Sister Bill.'" *Mosaic* 29:1 (1996): 19–36.

Champagne, Rosaria. *The Politics of Survivorship: Incest, Women's Literature, and Feminist Theory.* New York: New York University Press, 1996.

Chase, Karen, and Michael Levenson. *The Spectacle of Intimacy: A Public Life for the Victorian Family.* Princeton: Princeton University Press, 2000.

[Child, G. W.]. "Marriages of Consanguinity." *Westminster Review, American Edition* 80 O.S. (July 1863): 39–49.

Clarke, Micael M. "Brontë's *Jane Eyre* and the Grimms' Cinderella." *Studies in English Literature* 40 (2000): 695–710.

Cleere, Eileen. *Avuncularism: Capitalism, Patriarchy, and Nineteenth-Century English Culture.* Stanford: Stanford University Press, 2004.

Cohen, Paula Marantz. *The Daughter's Dilemma: Family Process and the Nineteenth-Century Domestic Novel.* Ann Arbor: University of Michigan Press, 1991.

Cohen, William A. *Sex Scandal: The Private Parts of Victorian Fiction.* Durham: Duke University Press, 1996.

Conrad, Joseph. *Heart of Darkness.* Edited by Robert Kimbrough. New York: W. W. Norton, 1988.

Corbett, Mary Jean. *Allegories of Union in Irish and English Writing, 1790–1870: Politics, History, and the Family from Edgeworth to Arnold*. Cambridge: Cambridge University Press, 2000.

———. "Orphan Stories and Maternal Legacies in Charlotte Brontë." *Other Mothers*. Edited by Ellen Rosenman and Claudia Klaver. Columbus: Ohio State University Press, forthcoming.

———. "Representing the Rural: The Critique of Loamshire in *Adam Bede*." *Studies in the Novel* 20 (1988): 288–301.

Cottom, Daniel. *The Civilized Imagination: A Study of Ann Radcliffe, Jane Austen, and Sir Walter Scott*. Cambridge: Cambridge University Press, 1985.

———. *Social Figures: George Eliot, Social History, and Literary Representation*. Minneapolis: University of Minnesota Press, 1987.

Craik, Dinah Mulock. *Hannah*. London, 1871.

Craik, W. A. *Elizabeth Gaskell and the English Provincial Novel*. London: Methuen, 1975.

Cvetkovich, Ann. *An Archive of Feelings: Trauma, Sexuality, and Lesbian Public Cultures*. Durham: Duke University Press, 2003.

D'Albertis, Deirdre. *Dissembling Fictions: Elizabeth Gaskell and the Victorian Social Text*. New York: St. Martin's Press, 1997.

Darwin, Charles. *The Descent of Man, and Selection in Relation to Sex*. London: Penguin, 2004.

———. *The Origin of Species by Means of Natural Selection; or, The Preservation of Favoured Races in the Struggle for Life*. Edited by J. W. Burrow. Harmondsworth, U.K.: Penguin, 1968.

———. *The Variation of Animals and Plants under Domestication*. 2 vols. Brussels: Culture et Civilisation, 1969.

———. *On the Various Contrivances by which British and Foreign Orchids are Fertilised by Insects, and on the Good Effects of Intercrossing*. Stanfordville, NY: Earl M. Coleman, 1979.

Darwin, George H. "On Beneficial Restrictions to Liberty of Marriage." *Contemporary Review* 22 (1873): 412–26.

———. "Marriages between First Cousins in England and Their Effects." *Journal of the Statistical Society of London* 38 (June 1875): 153–82.

Davidoff, Leonore. "Where the Stranger Begins: The Question of Siblings in Historical Analysis." In *Worlds Between: Historical Perspectives on Gender and Class*, 206–26. New York: Routledge, 1995.

———, and Catherine Hall. *Family Fortunes: Men and Women of the English Middle Class, 1780–1850*. Chicago: University of Chicago Press, 1987.

Davidson, Roger. "'This Pernicious Delusion': Law, Medicine, and Child Sexual Abuse in Early-Twentieth-Century Scotland." *Journal of the History of Sexuality* 10 (2001): 62–77.

Davies, Emily. *Emily Davies: Collected Letters, 1861–1875*. Edited by Ann B. Murphy and Deirdre Raftery. Charlottesville: University of Virginia Press, 2004.

Davis, Deanna L. "Feminist Critics and Literary Mothers: Daughters Reading Elizabeth Gaskell." *Signs* 17 (1992): 507–32.

Debrabant, Mary. "Birds, Bees, and Darwinian Survival Strategies in *Wives and Daughters*." *Gaskell Society Journal* 16 (2002): 14–29.

Degler, Carl N. *In Search of Human Nature: The Decline and Revival of Darwinism in American Social Thought.* New York: Oxford University Press, 1991.

Dellamora, Richard. *Friendship's Bonds: Democracy and the Novel in Victorian England.* Philadelphia: University of Pennsylvania Press, 2004.

DeSalvo, Louise. *Virginia Woolf: The Impact of Childhood Sexual Abuse on Her Life and Work.* Boston: Beacon Press, 1989.

Desmond, Adrian, and James Moore. *Darwin: The Life of a Tormented Evolutionist.* New York: W. W. Norton, 1991.

Detloff, Madelyn. " 'Tis Not my Nature to Join in Hating, but in Loving': Towards Survivable Public Mourning." In *Modernism and Mourning,* edited by Patricia Rae, 50–68. Lewisburg, PA: Bucknell University Press, 2007.

Dever, Carolyn. *Death and the Mother from Dickens to Freud: Victorian Fiction and the Anxiety of Origins.* Cambridge: Cambridge University Press, 1998.

——. *Skeptical Feminism: Activist Theory, Activist Practice.* Minneapolis: University of Minnesota Press, 2004.

Disraeli, Benjamin. *Coningsby; or, The New Generation.* Edited by Thom Braun. Harmondsworth, U.K.: Penguin, 1983.

——. *Sybil; or, The Two Nations.* Edited by Sheila M. Smith. Oxford: Oxford University Press, 1986.

Doane, Janice, and Devon Hodges. *Telling Incest: Narratives of Dangerous Remembering from Stein to Sapphire.* Ann Arbor: University of Michigan Press, 2001.

Duckworth, Alistair M. *The Improvement of the Estate: A Study of Jane Austen's Novels.* Baltimore: Johns Hopkins University Press, 1971.

Dunn, Jane. *A Very Close Conspiracy: Vanessa Bell and Virginia Woolf.* Boston: Little, Brown, 1990.

Eagleton, Terry. *Heathcliff and the Great Hunger: Studies in Irish Culture.* London: Verso, 1995.

Easton, Fraser. "The Political Economy of *Mansfield Park:* Fanny Price and the Atlantic Working Class." *Textual Practice* 12 (1998): 458–88.

Eliot, George. *Adam Bede.* Edited by Carol A. Martin. Oxford: Clarendon Press, 2001.

——. *The George Eliot Letters.* 9 vols. Edited by Gordon S. Haight. New Haven: Yale University Press, 1954–74.

——. *The Journals of George Eliot.* Edited by Margaret Harris and Judith Johnson. Cambridge: Cambridge University Press, 1998.

——. *Middlemarch.* Edited by David Carroll. Oxford: Oxford University Press, 1996.

——. *The Mill on the Floss.* Edited by Carol T. Christ. New York: W. W. Norton, 1994.

——. "The Modern Hep! Hep! Hep!" In *Impressions of Theophrastus Such,* edited by Nancy Henry, 143–65. Iowa City: University of Iowa Press, 1994.

——. "The Natural History of German Life." In *Essays of George Eliot,* edited by Thomas Pinney, 266–99. New York: Columbia University Press, 1963.

——. *Scenes of Clerical Life.* Edited by David Lodge. Harmondsworth, U.K.: Penguin, 1973.

——. *Silas Marner, The Weaver of Raveloe.* Edited by Terence Cave. Oxford: Oxford University Press, 1996.

Esty, Jed. *A Shrinking Island: Modernism and National Culture in England.* Princeton: Princeton University Press, 2004.

Fabian, Johannes. *Time and the Other: How Anthropology Makes Its Object.* New York: Columbia University Press, 1983.

Ferguson, Moira. "*Mansfield Park:* Slavery, Colonialism, and Gender." *Oxford Literary Review* 13 (1991): 118–39.

First Report of the Commissioners Appointed to Inquire into the State and Operation of the Law of Marriage as Relating to the Prohibited Degrees of Affinity, and to Marriages Solemnised Abroad or in the British Colonies. Rpt. Shannon: Irish University Press, 1969.

First Report of the Commissioners on the Housing of the Working Classes [England and Wales]. 2 vols. Rpt. Shannon: Irish University Press, 1970.

Fleishman, Avrom. *A Reading of "Mansfield Park": An Essay in Critical Synthesis.* Minneapolis: University of Minnesota Press, 1967.

Forster, E. M. *Howards End.* Edited by Oliver Stallybrass. London: Edward Arnold Publishers, 1973.

——. *Marianne Thornton: A Domestic Biography, 1797–1887.* New York: Harcourt, Brace, 1956.

Foucault, Michel. *The History of Sexuality. Volume I: An Introduction.* Translated by Robert Hurley. New York: Random House, 1978.

——. "Sexual Choice, Sexual Act: Foucault and Homosexuality." Interview with James O'Higgins. In *Politics, Philosophy, Culture: Interviews and Other Writings, 1977–1984,* edited by Lawrence D. Kritzman, translated by Alan Sheridan et al., 286–303. New York: Routledge, 1988.

——. "Society Must Be Defended": Lectures at the Collège de France, 1975–76. Edited by Mauro Bertani and Alessandro Fontana. Translated by David Macey. New York: Picador, 2003.

Fraiman, Susan. "Jane Austen and Edward Said: Gender, Culture, and Imperialism." *Critical Inquiry* 21 (1995): 805–21.

Franklin, Sarah, and Susan McKinnon. "New Directions in Kinship Study: A Core Concept Revisited." *Social Anthropology* 41 (2000): 275–79.

Froula, Christine. *Virginia Woolf and the Bloomsbury Avant-Garde: War, Civilization, Modernity.* New York: Columbia University Press, 2005.

Gager, Kristin Elizabeth. *Blood Ties and Fictive Ties: Adoption and Family Life in Early Modern France.* Princeton: Princeton University Press, 1996.

Gagnier, Regenia. *Subjectivities: A History of Self-Representation in Britain, 1832–1920.* New York: Oxford University Press, 1991.

Gallagher, Catherine. *The Body Economic: Life, Death, and Sensation in Political Economy and the Victorian Novel.* Princeton: Princeton University Press, 2006.

Galton, Francis. "On Blood-Relationship." *Proceedings of the Royal Society of London* 20 (1871–72): 394–402.

Garnett, Henrietta. *Anny: A Life of Anne Isabella Thackeray Ritchie.* London: Chatto and Windus, 2004.

Gaskell, Elizabeth. *The Letters of Mrs. Gaskell.* Edited by J. A. V. Chapple and Arthur Pollard. Cambridge, MA: Harvard University Press, 1967.

——. *Mary Barton: A Tale of Manchester Life.* Edited by Macdonald Daly. London: Penguin, 2003.

———. *Wives and Daughters.* Edited by Pam Morris. London: Penguin, 1996.

Gilbert, Sandra M., and Susan Gubar. *The Madwoman in the Attic: The Woman Writer and the Nineteenth-Century Literary Imagination.* New Haven: Yale University Press, 1979.

Gilman, Sander L. "Sibling Incest, Madness, and the 'Jews.' " *Social Research* 65 (1998): 401–33.

Girard, René. *Deceit, Desire, and the Novel: Self and Other in Literary Structure.* Translated by Yvonne Freccero. Baltimore: Johns Hopkins University Press, 1965.

Glen, Heather. *Charlotte Brontë: The Imagination in History.* Oxford: Oxford University Press, 2002.

Goetz, William R. "Genealogy and Incest in *Wuthering Heights.*" *Studies in the Novel* 14 (1982): 359–76.

Goff, Barbara Munson. "Between Natural Theology and Natural Selection: Breeding the Human Animal in *Wuthering Heights.*" *Victorian Studies* 27 (1984): 477–508.

Goody, Jack. *The Development of Family and Marriage in Europe.* Cambridge: Cambridge University Press, 1983.

Gottlieb, Laura Moss. "*The Years:* A Feminist Novel." In *Virginia Woolf: Centennial Essays,* edited by Elaine K. Ginsberg and Laura Moss Gottlieb, 215–29. Troy, NY: Whitson, 1983.

Gruner, Elizabeth Rose. "Born and Made: Sisters, Brothers, and the Deceased Wife's Sister Bill." *Signs* 24 (1999): 423–47.

Gullette, Margaret Morganroth. "The Puzzling Case of the Deceased Wife's Sister: Nineteenth-Century England Deals with a Second-Chance Plot." *Representations* 31 (1990): 142–66.

Hacking, Ian. "The Making and Molding of Child Abuse." *Critical Inquiry* 17 (1991): 253–88.

Haggerty, George E. *Unnatural Affections: Women and Fiction in the Later Eighteenth Century.* Bloomington: Indiana University Press, 1998.

Handler, Richard, and Daniel Segal. *Jane Austen and the Fiction of Culture: An Essay on the Narration of Social Realities.* Tucson: University of Arizona Press, 1990.

Hanson, Clare. "Virginia Woolf in the House of Love: Compulsory Heterosexuality in *The Years.*" *Journal of Gender Studies* 6 (1997): 55–62.

Harrison, Kathryn. *The Kiss: A Memoir.* New York: Random House, 1997.

[Hayward, Abraham]. *Summary of Objections to the Doctrine that a Marriage with the Sister of a Deceased Wife is Contrary to Law, Religion, or Morality.* London, 1839.

Henson, Louise. "History, Science, and Social Change: Elizabeth Gaskell's 'Evolutionary' Narratives." *Gaskell Society Journal* 17 (2003): 12–33.

Herbert, Christopher. *Culture and Anomie: Ethnographic Imagination in the Nineteenth Century.* Chicago: University of Chicago Press, 1991.

Héritier, Françoise. *Two Sisters and Their Mother: The Anthropology of Incest.* Translated by Jeanine Herman. New York: Zone Books, 1999.

Herman, Judith Lewis, with Lisa Hirschman. *Father-Daughter Incest.* Cambridge, MA: Harvard University Press, 1981.

Hirai, Masako. *Sisters in Literature: Female Sexuality in "Antigone," "Middlemarch," "Howards End" and "Women in Love."* New York: St. Martin's Press, 1998.

Hirsch, Marianne. *The Mother/Daughter Plot: Narrative, Psychoanalysis, Feminism.* Bloomington: Indiana University Press, 1989.

Hitchens, Christopher. "Don't Mince Words." *Slate,* 2 July 2007. http://slate.com/id/2169592/, accessed 6 March 2008.

Hobart, Ann. "Harriet Martineau's Political Economy of Everyday Life." *Victorian Studies* 37 (1994): 223–51.

Hollingshead, John. *Ragged London in 1861.* Rpt. New York: Garland Publishing, 1985.

Homans, Margaret. *Bearing the Word: Language and Female Experience in Nineteenth-Century Women's Writing.* Chicago: University of Chicago Press, 1986.

Honan, Park. *Jane Austen: Her Life.* New York: St. Martin's Press, 1987.

Honey, J. R. de S. *Tom Brown's Universe: The Development of the Victorian Public School.* London: Millington Books, 1977.

Howe, Patricia. "Fontane's 'Ellernklipp' and the Theme of Adoption." *Modern Language Review* 79 (1984): 114–30.

Hudson, Glenda A. *Sibling Love and Incest in Jane Austen's Fiction.* New York: St. Martin's Press, 1999.

Hughes, Linda K., and Michael Lund. *Victorian Publishing and Mrs. Gaskell's Work.* Charlottesville: University Press of Virginia, 1999.

Huth, Alfred Henry. *The Marriage of Near Kin, Considered with Respect to the Laws of Nations, the Results of Experience, and the Teachings of Biology.* London, 1875.

Irigaray, Luce. *This Sex Which Is Not One.* Translated by Catherine Porter, with Carolyn Burke. Ithaca: Cornell University Press, 1985.

Jackson, Louise A. *Child Sexual Abuse in Victorian England.* London: Routledge, 2000.

Jann, Rosemary. "Darwin and the Anthropologists: Sexual Selection and its Discontents." *Victorian Studies* 37 (1994): 287–306.

Jeffreys, Sheila. *The Spinster and Her Enemies: Feminism and Sexuality, 1880–1930.* London: Pandora Press, 1985.

Johnson, Claudia L. *Jane Austen: Women, Politics, and the Novel.* Chicago: University of Chicago Press, 1988.

Jones, Gareth Stedman. *Outcast London: A Study in the Relationship between Classes in Victorian Society.* Oxford: Clarendon Press, 1971.

Joseph, Gerhard. "The *Antigone* as Cultural Touchstone: Matthew Arnold, Hegel, George Eliot, Virginia Woolf, and Margaret Drabble." *PMLA* 96 (1981): 22–35.

Kaye, Richard A. *The Flirt's Tragedy: Desire without End in Victorian and Edwardian Fiction.* Charlottesville: University Press of Virginia, 2002.

Keen, Suzanne. *Victorian Renovations of the Novel: Narrative Annexes and the Boundaries of Representation.* Cambridge: Cambridge University Press, 1998.

King, Amy M. *Bloom: The Botanical Vernacular in the English Novel.* New York: Oxford University Press, 2003.

Knoepflmacher, U. C. *George Eliot's Early Novels: The Limits of Realism.* Berkeley: University of California Press, 1968.

Koven, Seth. *Slumming: Sexual and Social Politics in Victorian London.* Princeton: Princeton University Press, 2004.

Kreilkamp, Ivan. "Petted Things: *Wuthering Heights* and the Animal." *Yale Journal of Criticism* 18 (2005): 87–110.

Kucich, John. *Repression in Victorian Fiction: Charlotte Brontë, George Eliot, and Charles Dickens.* Berkeley: University of California Press, 1987.

Kuper, Adam. "Incest, Cousin Marriage, and the Origin of the Human Sciences in Nineteenth-Century England." *Past and Present* 174 (2002): 158–83.

——. "The Rise and Fall of Maine's Patriarchal Society." In *The Victorian Achievement of Sir Henry Maine: A Centennial Reappraisal,* edited by Alan Diamond, 99–110. Cambridge: Cambridge University Press, 1991.

Lamonaca, Drew. *"We Are Three Sisters": Self and Family in the Writing of the Brontës.* Columbia: University of Missouri Press, 2003.

Langland, Elizabeth. *Nobody's Angels: Middle-Class Women and Domestic Ideology in Victorian Culture.* Ithaca: Cornell University Press, 1995.

Lansbury, Coral. *Elizabeth Gaskell: The Novel of Social Crisis.* New York: Harper and Row, 1975.

Lanser, Susan Sniader. "No Connections Subsequent: Jane Austen's World of Sisterhood." In *The Sister Bond: A Feminist View of a Timeless Connection,* edited by Toni A. H. McNaron, 53–67. New York: Pergamon Press, 1985.

Law, Jules. "Water Rights and the 'Crossing o' Breeds': Chiastic Exchange in *The Mill on the Floss.*" In *Rewriting the Victorians: Theory, History, and the Politics of Gender,* edited by Linda M. Shires, 52–69. New York: Routledge, 1992.

Leaska, Mitchell. *Granite and Rainbow: The Hidden Life of Virginia Woolf.* New York: Farrar Straus Giroux, 1998.

——. "Virginia Woolf, the Pargeter: A Reading of *The Years.*" *Bulletin of the New York Public Library* 80 (1977): 172–210.

Lee, Hermione. *Virginia Woolf.* New York: Alfred A. Knopf, 1997.

Lee, Vernon [Violet Paget]. *Miss Brown.* Rpt. New York: Garland Publishing, 1978.

Le Faye, Deirdre. *Jane Austen: A Family Record.* 2d ed. Cambridge: Cambridge University Press, 2004.

Lévi-Strauss, Claude. *The Elementary Structures of Kinship.* Rev. ed. Translated by James Bell et al. Boston: Beacon Press, 1969.

Levin, Amy K. *The Suppressed Sister: A Relationship in Novels by Nineteenth- and Twentieth-Century British Women.* Lewisburg, PA: Bucknell University Press, 1992.

Levine, George. *Darwin and the Novelists: Patterns of Science in Victorian Fiction.* Chicago: University of Chicago Press, 1988.

——. "Intelligence as Deception: *The Mill on the Floss.*" *PMLA* 80 (1965): 402–9.

Levy, Anita. *Other Women: The Writing of Class, Race, and Gender, 1832–1898.* Princeton: Princeton University Press, 1991.

[Lewes, George Henry]. "Hereditary Influence, Animal and Human." *Westminster Review, American Edition* 66 O.S. (July 1856): 75–90.

Litvack, Leon. "Outposts of Empire: Scientific Discovery and Colonial Displacement in Gaskell's *Wives and Daughters.*" *Review of English Studies* 55 (2004): 727–58.

Litvak, Joseph. *Caught in the Act: Theatricality in the Nineteenth-Century English Novel.* Berkeley: University of California Press, 1992.

London, Bette. *Writing Double: Women's Literary Partnerships.* Ithaca: Cornell University Press, 1999.

Lovell-Smith, Rosemary. "Childhood and Adoption in Scott and the Writing of *Wuthering Heights.*" *Scottish Literary Journal* 21 (1994): 24–31.

Maine, Henry Sumner. *Ancient Law: Its Connection with the Early History of Society, and Its Relation to Modern Ideas.* Tucson: University of Arizona Press, 1986.

Maitland, Frederic William. *The Life and Letters of Leslie Stephen*. London: Duckworth & Co., 1907.

Mansfield Park. Dir. Patricia Rozema. Miramax, 1999.

Marcus, Jane. *Virginia Woolf and the Languages of Patriarchy*. Bloomington: Indiana University Press, 1987.

Marcus, Sharon. *Between Women: Friendship, Desire, and Marriage in Victorian England*. Princeton: Princeton University Press, 2007.

"The Marriage of Near Kin." *The Westminster Review: American Edition* 104 O.S. (October 1875): 147–55.

"The Marriage Relation." *London Quarterly Review, American Edition* 85 (July and October 1849): 84–98.

Martineau, Harriet. *Deerbrook*. Edited by Valerie Sanders. London: Penguin, 2004.

Mason, Michael. *The Making of Victorian Sexuality*. Oxford: Oxford University Press, 1994.

Masters, Joellen. " 'Nothing More' and 'Nothing Definite': First Wives in Elizabeth Gaskell's *Wives and Daughters* (1866)." *JNT: Journal of Narrative Theory* 34 (2004): 1–26.

May, Leila S. "Jane Austen's 'Schemes of Sisterly Happiness.' " *Philological Quarterly* 81 (2002): 327–58.

——. *Disorderly Sisters: Sibling Relations and Sororal Resistance in Nineteenth-Century British Literature*. Lewisburg, PA: Bucknell University Press, 2001.

Mayhew, Henry. *London Labour and the London Poor*. 4 vols. Edited by John D. Rosenberg. New York: Dover Publications, 1968.

Maynard, John. *Charlotte Brontë and Sexuality*. Cambridge: Cambridge University Press, 1984.

McDonagh, Josephine. "The Early Novels." In *The Cambridge Companion to George Eliot,* edited by George Levine, 38–56. Cambridge: Cambridge University Press, 2001.

[McLennan, John F.]. "The Early History of Man." *North British Review, American Edition* 50 O.S. (July 1869): 272–90.

——. *Primitive Marriage: An Inquiry into the Origin of the Form of Capture in Marriage Ceremonies*. Edited by Peter Riviere. Chicago: University of Chicago Press, 1970.

Mearns, Andrew. *The Bitter Cry of Outcast London*. Edited by Anthony S. Wohl. Leicester: Leicester University Press, 1970.

Meyer, Susan. *Imperialism at Home: Race and Victorian Women's Fiction*. Ithaca: Cornell University Press, 1996.

Michaels, Walter Benn. *Our America: Nativism, Modernism, and Pluralism*. Durham: Duke University Press, 1995.

Michie, Elsie B. *Outside the Pale: Cultural Exclusion, Gender Difference, and the Victorian Woman Writer*. Ithaca: Cornell University Press, 1993.

Michie, Helena. *Sororophobia: Differences among Women in Literature and Culture*. New York: Oxford University Press, 1992.

——. *Victorian Honeymoons: Journeys to the Conjugal*. Cambridge: Cambridge University Press, 2006.

Miller, D. A. *Narrative and Its Discontents: Problems of Closure in the Traditional Novel*. Princeton: Princeton University Press, 1981.

Miller, J. Hillis. *Fiction and Repetition: Seven English Novels.* Cambridge, MA: Harvard University Press, 1982.

Morgan, Lewis Henry. *Systems of Consanguinity and Affinity of the Human Family.* Rpt. Lincoln: University of Nebraska Press, 1997.

Morgan, Susan. *Sisters in Time: Imagining Gender in Nineteenth-Century British Fiction.* New York: Oxford University Press, 1989.

Morris, Polly. "Incest or Survival Strategy? Plebeian Marriage within the Prohibited Degrees in Somerset, 1730–1835." In *Forbidden History: The State, Society, and the Regulation of Sexuality in Modern Europe,* edited by John C. Fout, 139–69. Chicago: University of Chicago Press, 1992.

Nelson, Claudia. *Family Ties in Victorian England.* Westport, CT: Praeger, 2007.

Nightingale, Florence. "Cassandra." Appendix I to Ray Strachey, *The Cause.* Rpt. Port Washington, NY: Kennikat Press, 1969. 395–418.

Nord, Deborah Epstein. *Gypsies and the British Imagination, 1807–1930.* New York: Columbia University Press, 2006.

——. "'Marks of Race': Gypsy Figures and Eccentric Femininity in Nineteenth-Century Women's Writing." *Victorian Studies* 41 (1998): 189–210.

——. *Walking the Victorian Streets: Women, Representation, and the City.* Ithaca: Cornell University Press, 1995.

Novy, Marianne. *Reading Adoption: Family and Difference in Fiction and Drama.* Ann Arbor: University of Michigan Press, 2005.

O'Connor, Michael. "Writing Against Terror: Nadeem Aslam." *Three Monkeys Online.* July 2005. www.threemonkeysonline.com/three mon article_nadeem_aslam_interview.htm, accessed 6 March 2008.

Oliphant, Margaret. *Hester.* Edited by Philip Davis and Brian Nellist. Oxford: Oxford University Press, 2003.

——. *Miss Marjoribanks.* London: Chatto and Windus, 1969.

——. *The Perpetual Curate.* Harmondsworth, U.K.: Penguin/Virago, 1987.

O'Toole, Tess. "Adoption and the 'Improvement of the Estate' in Trollope and Craik." In *Imagining Adoption: Essays on Literature and Culture,* edited by Marianne Novy, 17–33. Ann Arbor: University of Michigan Press, 2001.

——. "Reconfiguring the Family in *Persuasion.*" *Persuasions* 15 (1993): 200–206.

Ottenheimer, Martin. *Forbidden Relatives: The American Myth of Cousin Marriage.* Urbana: University of Illinois Press, 1996.

Park, Sowon S. "Suffrage and Virginia Woolf: 'The Mass Behind the Single Voice.'" *Review of English Studies* 56 (2005): 119–34.

Parsons, Deborah L. *Streetwalking the Metropolis: Women, the City, and Modernity.* Oxford: Oxford University Press, 2000.

Paul, Holly Forsythe. "A Sister 'a la mode de Bretagne' in Gaskell." *Victoria* 19th-Century British Culture and Society newsgroup, 19 May 2006. https://listserv.indiana.edu/cgi-bin/wa-iub.exe?A0=VICTORIA, accessed 6 March 2008.

Paxton, Nancy L. *George Eliot and Herbert Spencer: Feminism, Evolutionism, and the Reconstruction of Gender.* Princeton: Princeton University Press, 1991.

Perry, Ruth. *Novel Relations: The Transformation of Kinship in English Literature and Culture, 1748–1818.* Cambridge: Cambridge University Press, 2004.

Peters, Laura. *Orphan Texts: Victorian Orphans, Culture, and Empire.* Manchester: Manchester University Press, 2000.

Plasa, Carl. *Charlotte Brontë.* Houndmills, U.K.: Palgrave Macmillan, 2004.

Pollak, Ellen. *Incest and the English Novel, 1684–1814.* Baltimore: Johns Hopkins University Press, 2003.

Poovey, Mary. *The Proper Lady and the Woman Writer: Ideology as Style in the Works of Mary Wollstonecraft, Mary Shelley, and Jane Austen.* Chicago: University of Chicago Press, 1984.

Price, Leah. "The *Life of Charlotte Brontë* and the Death of Miss Eyre." *Studies in English Literature* 35 (1995): 757–68.

Prins, Yopie. "Greek Maenads, Victorian Spinsters." In *Victorian Sexual Dissidence,* edited by Richard Dellamora, 43–81. Chicago: University of Chicago Press, 1999.

Psomiades, Kathy Alexis. "Heterosexual Exchange and Other Victorian Fictions: *The Eustace Diamonds* and Victorian Anthropology." *Novel* 33 (1999): 93–118.

Pusey, E. B. *A Letter on the Proposed Change in the Laws Prohibiting Marriage between Those Near of Kin.* Oxford, 1842.

——. *Marriage with a Deceased Wife's Sister Prohibited by Holy Scripture, as Understood by the Church for 1500 Years.* Oxford, 1849.

Quilligan, Maureen. *Incest and Agency in Elizabeth's England.* Philadelphia: University of Pennsylvania Press, 2005.

Radin, Grace. *Virginia Woolf's "The Years": The Evolution of a Novel.* Knoxville: University of Tennessee Press, 1981.

Ritvo, Harriet. *The Animal Estate: The English and Other Creatures in the Victorian Age.* Cambridge, MA: Harvard University Press, 1987.

——. *The Platypus and the Mermaid, and Other Figments of the Classifying Imagination.* Cambridge, MA: Harvard University Press, 1997.

Robbins, Bruce. *The Servant's Hand: English Fiction from Below.* Durham: Duke University Press, 1993.

[Rogers, Henry]. "Marriage with a Deceased Wife's Sister." *Edinburgh Review* 97 (April 1853): 315–41.

Rubin, Gayle. "The Traffic in Women: Notes on the 'Political Economy' of Sex." In *Toward an Anthropology of Women,* edited by Rayna R. Reiter, 157–210. New York: Monthly Review Press, 1975.

Russett, Cynthia Eagle. *Sexual Science: The Victorian Construction of Womanhood.* Cambridge, MA: Harvard University Press, 1989.

Saariluoma, Liisa. "Virginia Woolf's *The Years:* Identity and Time in an Anti-Family Novel." *Orbis Litterarum* 54 (1999): 276–300.

Sanders, Valerie. *The Brother-Sister Culture in Nineteenth-Century Literature: From Austen to Woolf.* New York: Palgrave, 2002.

——. *Reason over Passion: Harriet Martineau and the Victorian Novel.* New York: St. Martin's Press, 1986.

Schor, Hilary M. *Scheherezade in the Marketplace: Elizabeth Gaskell and the Victorian Novel.* London: Oxford University Press, 1992.

Sedgwick, Eve Kosofsky. *Tendencies.* Durham: Duke University Press, 1993.

Seshagiri, Urmila. "Orienting Virginia Woolf: Race, Aesthetics, and Politics in *To the Lighthouse.*" *Modern Fiction Studies* 50 (2004): 58–84.

Shell, Marc. *Children of the Earth: Literature, Politics, and Nationhood.* New York: Oxford University Press, 1993.

Shelton, Jen. "'Don't Say Such Foolish Things, Dear': Speaking Incest in *The Voyage Out*." In *Incest and the Literary Imagination*, edited by Elizabeth Barnes, 224–48. Gainesville: University Press of Florida, 2002.

Shuttleworth, Sally. *George Eliot and Nineteenth-Century Science: The Make-Believe of a Beginning*. Cambridge: Cambridge University Press, 1984.

Silver, Brenda R. *Virginia Woolf's Reading Notebooks*. Princeton: Princeton University Press, 1983.

Sims, George R. *"How the Poor Live" and "Horrible London."* 1889. Rpt. New York: Garland Publishing, Inc., 1984.

Skene, Felicia. *The Inheritance of Evil, Or, the Consequence of Marrying a Deceased Wife's Sister.* London, 1849. *Victorian Women Writers Project.* Edited by Perry Willett. 11 March 1997. Indiana University. www.indiana.edu/~letrs/vwwp/skene/evil.html, accessed 6 March 2008.

Smart, Carol. "A History of Ambivalence and Conflict in the Discursive Construction of the 'Child Victim' of Sexual Abuse." *Social and Legal Studies* 8 (1999): 391–409.

Smith, Johanna M. "'My Only Sister Now': Incest in *Mansfield Park*." *Studies in the Novel* 19 (1987): 1–15.

Smith, Jonathan. *Charles Darwin and Victorian Visual Culture*. Cambridge: Cambridge University Press, 2006.

——. "Darwin's Botany and Sensation Fiction." Unpublished manuscript.

Snyder, Carey. "Woolf's Ethnographic Modernism: Self-Nativizing in *The Voyage Out*." *Woolf Studies Annual* 10 (2004): 81–108.

Sollors, Werner. *Neither Black Nor White Yet Both: Thematic Explorations of Interracial Literature.* Cambridge, MA: Harvard University Press, 1997.

Sophocles. *Sophocles I.* Translated by Elizabeth Wyckoff. Chicago: University of Chicago Press, 1954.

Spalding, Frances. *Vanessa Bell*. London: Weidenfeld and Nicolson, 1983.

Squier, Susan M. *Virginia Woolf and London: The Sexual Politics of the City*. Chapel Hill: University of North Carolina Press, 1985.

Stephen, Leslie. *Sir Leslie Stephen's Mausoleum Book*. Oxford: Clarendon Press, 1977.

Stewart, Maaja. *Domestic Realities and Imperial Fictions: Jane Austen's Novels in Eighteenth-Century Contexts.* Athens: University of Georgia Press, 1993.

Stocking, George W., Jr. *Victorian Anthropology.* New York: Free Press, 1987.

Stoler, Ann Laura. *Race and the Education of Desire: Foucault's "History of Sexuality" and the Colonial Order of Things.* Durham: Duke University Press, 1995.

Stone, Lawrence. *The Family, Sex, and Marriage in England, 1500–1800.* New York: Harper and Row, 1977.

Swanson, Diana L. "An Antigone Complex? The Political Psychology of *The Years* and *Three Guineas*." *Woolf Studies Annual* 3 (1997): 28–44.

Tadmor, Naomi. *Family and Friends in Eighteenth-Century England: Household, Kinship, and Patronage.* Cambridge: Cambridge University Press, 2001.

Tal, Kalí. *Worlds of Hurt: Reading the Literatures of Trauma.* Cambridge: Cambridge University Press, 1996.

Tanner, Tony. *Adultery in the Novel: Contract and Transgression.* Baltimore: Johns Hopkins University Press, 1979.

——. *Jane Austen.* Cambridge, MA: Harvard University Press, 1986.

Tennyson, Alfred Lord. *The Poems of Tennyson*. 3d ed. 3 vols. Edited by Christopher Ricks. Berkeley: University of California Press, 1987.

Trollope, Anthony. *The Way We Live Now.* 2 vols. Edited by John Sutherland. Oxford: Oxford University Press, 1982.

Trumbach, Randolph. *The Rise of the Egalitarian Family.* New York: Academic Press, 1978.

——. *Sex and the Gender Revolution. Volume One: Heterosexuality and the Third Gender in Enlightenment London.* Chicago: University of Chicago Press, 1998.

Tuite, Clara. *Romantic Austen: Sexual Politics and the Literary Canon.* Cambridge: Cambridge University Press, 2002.

Twitchell, James B. *Forbidden Partners: The Incest Taboo in Modern Culture.* New York: Columbia University Press, 1987.

Uglow, Jennifer. *Elizabeth Gaskell: A Habit of Stories.* New York: Farrar Straus Giroux, 1993.

United Kingdom, *Hansard Parliamentary Debates,* 3d and 4th ser.

Vicinus, Martha. *Intimate Friends: Women Who Loved Women, 1778–1928.* Chicago: University of Chicago Press, 2004.

Walkowitz, Judith R. *City of Dreadful Delight: Narratives of Sexual Danger in Late-Victorian London.* Chicago: University of Chicago Press, 1992.

Walton, Jean. *Fair Sex, Savage Dreams: Race, Psychoanalysis, Sexual Difference.* Durham: Duke University Press, 2001.

Warner, Michael. *The Trouble with Normal: Sex, Politics, and the Ethics of Queer Life.* New York: Free Press, 1999.

Webb, Beatrice. *My Apprenticeship.* New York: Longmans, Green, 1926.

Weiner, Annette. *Inalienable Possessions: The Paradox of Keeping-While-Giving.* Berkeley: University of California Press, 1992.

Wilson, Elizabeth. "'Not in This House': Incest, Denial, and Doubt in the White Middle Class Family." *Yale Journal of Criticism* 8 (1995): 35–58.

Wohl, Anthony S. *The Eternal Slum: Housing and Social Policy in Victorian London.* Montreal: McGill-Queen's University Press, 1977.

Wolf, Amy. "Epistolarity, Narrative, and the Fallen Woman in *Mansfield Park*." *Eighteenth-Century Fiction* 16 (2004): 265–85.

Wolfram, Sybil. "Eugenics and the Punishment of Incest Act 1908." *Criminal Law Review* (1983): 308–16.

——. *In-Laws and Outlaws: Kinship and Marriage in England.* London: Croom Helm, 1987.

"A Woman of England." *The Women of England and Mr. Wortley's Marriages Bill: An Address to the Peers of the Realm.* London, 1850.

Wood, William Page. *A Vindication of Law Prohibiting Marriage with a Deceased Wife's Sister, I. On social principles: II. On Scripture principles: in two letters addressed to the Dean of Westminster.* London, 1861.

Woolf, Virginia. *The Diary of Virginia Woolf.* 5 vols. Edited by Anne Olivier Bell, with Andrew McNeillie. San Diego: Harvest/HBJ, 1977–84.

——. "Jane Austen." *The Essays of Virginia Woolf. Volume II: 1912–1918.* Edited by Andrew McNeillie. San Diego: Harvest/HBJ, 1990. 9–16.

——. *The Letters of Virginia Woolf.* 6 vols. Edited by Nigel Nicolson and Joanne Trautmann. New York: Harcourt Brace Jovanovich, 1975–80.

——. *Moments of Being: A Collection of Autobiographical Writing.* Edited by Jeanne Schulkind. San Diego: Harcourt, 1985.

——. *Mrs. Dalloway.* San Diego: Harcourt Brace, 1981.

——. *Night and Day.* San Diego: Harcourt Brace Jovanovich, 1973.

——. *The Pargiters: The Novel-Essay Portion of "The Years."* Edited by Mitchell A. Leaska. New York: Harcourt Brace Jovanovich, 1977.

——. *Three Guineas.* San Diego: Harcourt Brace Jovanovich, 1968.

——. *To the Lighthouse.* San Diego: Harcourt Brace Jovanovich, 1981.

——. *The Voyage Out.* San Diego: Harcourt Brace Jovanovich, n.d.

——. *The Years.* San Diego: Harcourt Brace Jovanovich, n.d.

Wright, Julia M. "'Growing Pains': Representing the Romantic in Gaskell's *Wives and Daughters.*" In *Nervous Reactions: Victorian Recollections of Romanticism,* edited by Joel Faflak and Julia M. Wright, 163–85. Albany: State University of New York Press, 2004.

Wright, Terence. *Elizabeth Gaskell, "We Are Not Angels": Realism, Gender, Values.* New York: St. Martin's Press, 1995.

Yates, Jennifer. "A 'Habit of Speculation': Women, Gossip, and Publicity in Harriet Martineau's *Deerbrook.*" *Women's Writing* 9 (2002): 369–78.

Yeazell, Ruth Bernard. *Fictions of Modesty: Women and Courtship in the English Novel.* Chicago: University of Chicago Press, 1991.

Young, Robert J. C. *Colonial Desire: Hybridity in Theory, Culture, and Race.* London: Routledge, 1995.

Young, Robert M. *Darwin's Metaphor: Nature's Place in Victorian Culture.* Cambridge: Cambridge University Press, 1985.

Zwerdling, Alex. "Mastering the Memoir: Woolf and the Family Legacy." *Modernism/Modernity* 10 (2003): 165–88.

❧ INDEX

Acton, William, 7, 11
Adams, Maurianne, 107
adoption: as an analogue to marriage, x, 89, 92, 110; anthropological fictions of, xi, 87–92; in Brontë's juvenilia, x–xi, 93–96, 157; as a colonizing practice, 95–96, 99; and concepts of affinity, 87, 89; and family membership, x, 21, 26–27, 60, 87–88, 96, 204, 205; as fictive kinship in *Wives and Daughters,* 147, 153, 154, 156–58, 172; as grafting or hybridization, 157, 158; as a homosocial practice, 89–91; in *Jane Eyre,* 88–89, 103, 106; legal, 88, 205; in *Mansfield Park,* 50, 67; in "Mr. Gilfil's Love Story," 157; as trope of difference, 26, 67, 91; in *Wuthering Heights,* ix, 25–28
adoptive kin, 8, 21, 60; in the Brontë juvenilia, 96–97; in *Jane Eyre,* 88–89, 106–7; in *Wives and Daughters,* 155–56; in *Wuthering Heights,* 25–26
adultery, 48, 49. *See also* incestuous adultery
affinal kin, x, 4, 8, 39–40, 44, 47, 59, 85. *See also* wife's sister
affinal marriage, vii, x, 4, 8–11, 17, 19–20, 38–39, 45–46, 87, 147
affinity, x, xii, 116, 204, 205; and consanguinity, 39, 67, 85, 86, 89, 108; as created by marriage, 39, 43–44, 59, 64–68, 85, 86–87, 104–5, 159, 167; definitions of, 4, 27, 64, 87, 111, 226n51; as inclination or attraction, 87–89, 108, 109–10, 156, 158; prohibited degrees of, 73; spiritual, xi, 27, 28, 128–29, 158, 226n54. *See also* "one flesh" *and* family membership
agnatic kinship, 90–92, 98–99, 104, 108
analogy, 117, 147; in *Adam Bede,* 118–19; between adoption and marriage, 92, 110; as agent of fictive kinship in *Wives and Daughters,* xii, 60, 147, 156, 158–59, 172, 207; between animal and human

breeding, 137–38; between animals and humans, 117–18, 126, 137; between consanguineal and affinal kin, 66, 85; in *The Mill on the Floss,* 119–20, 140–42; between plants and humans, 117–18, 135, 137
Anderson, Nancy F., 65, 135, 214n64
Angel in the House, The (Patmore), 68
animal breeding, ix, 117, 119–120, 124–25, 130, 137–38; in *The Mill on the Floss,* 126–27
Antigone (Sophocles), 116, 196, 199, 206–8, 241n5
Armstrong, Isobel, 44
Armstrong, Nancy, 27, 33, 36, 88, 232n80
Arnold, Matthew, 14, 64, 228n25
Aurora Leigh (Barrett Browning), viii, 103
Austen, Jane, vii, ix–x, xii, 6, 29, 38, 55–56, 58–59, 81, 147, 205, 207; *Emma,* 31–2, 36, 39, 40; *Mansfield Park,* x, xii, 19, 34, 35–41, 45–56, 59–60, 83, 107, 109, 115, 148, 153–55, 156, 159, 169–70; *Northanger Abbey,* 30–32, 45–6, 79; *Persuasion,* 31, 32, 43, 44; *Pride and Prejudice,* 32–4, 35, 36, 38, 39, 45–46, 56, 68, 109; *Sense and Sensibility,* 34–35, 36, 39, 40, 41–45, 49, 51, 56, 74, 104, 109
Azim, Firdous, 95, 96, 100, 106, 225n30

Backus, Margot Gayle, 191
Barrett Browning, Elizabeth, viii, 103, 208
Beer, Gillian, 116, 117, 139, 158
Behrman, Cynthia Fansler, 61
Bell, Clive, 179–80, 236n13
Bell, Vanessa Stephen, 1–4, 177–78, 179–80, 181, 183–84, 211n4, 236nn10–11, 236n13
Bell, Vikki, 17
Bersani, Leo, 24–25, 28
bigamy, 103, 106

259

biological kinship, xi, xii, 5, 8, 24, 25, 26, 28, 38–39, 44, 55, 59, 87–91, 108–9, 116, 117, 148, 165, 202, 207. *See also* consanguineal kin
birth family. *See* first family
Bitter Cry of Outcast London, The (Mearns), 6, 188
Bivona, Daniel, 6
Blair, Emily, 150
blended family, 176; in *Wives and Daughters,* xii, 146–47, 153, 159, 163, 165
Bodenheimer, Rosemarie, 119, 141
Bodichon, Barbara, 117
Boiko, Karen, 146, 158
Bonaparte, Felicia, 168, 233n18
Boone, Joseph Allen, 25, 110, 111
Boumelha, Penny, 93, 101, 102, 105, 225n38
Braddon, Mary Elizabeth, viii
Briggs, Julia, 185
Brontë, Branwell, 96
Brontë, Charlotte, vii, ix, x–xi, xii, 85, 116, 117, 147, 157, 158, 179, 205, 206, 208; "The African Queen's Lament," 93–95; *Caroline Vernon,* 97; "The Foundling," 100; "The Green Dwarf," 93, 96; *Jane Eyre,* xi, 86, 88–89, 92–93, 94–96, 97, 101, 103–10, 112, 113–14; "A Leaf from an Unopened Volume," 95, 97–101; *The Professor,* 225nn32, 38; "Roe Head Journal," 97; *Shirley,* 86, 103, 239n54, 114; *Villette,* xi, 89, 95–96, 101–3, 110–14
Brontë, Emily, ix, 147, 205, 206; *Wuthering Heights,* ix, 5, 24–29, 48, 88, 94, 97, 109, 114, 115, 145
Brown, Sarah Annes, 68, 180
Butler, Judith, 4, 13, 17, 21, 22, 147, 199, 202–3, 205–6
Buzard, James, 107, 114

Castle, Terry, 46
Census Act (1871), 136
Chase, Karen, 61, 65, 69
Child, G. W., 137
Cleere, Eileen, 41, 219n56, 226n42, 227n12
cognatic kinship, 91
Cohen, Paula Marantz, 51, 218n33
Cohen, William A., 115–16, 189, 238n42
Collins, Wilkie, viii
Comte, Auguste, 130, 131, 142
conjugal family. *See* second family
conjugality, viii, x, 61, 70, 80, 81, 83, 85
Conrad, Joseph, 185
consanguineal kin, 40, 59, 81, 84–85

consanguineous marriage. *See* cousin-marriage
consanguinity, 36, 85, 89, 104, 147, 205; and affinity, 39, 67, 81, 85, 86–87, 89, 108; defined, 4, 64. *See also* first family
contract model of marriage, 66, 224n12
Cooper, Anthony Ashley, 7th earl of Shaftesbury, 6–7
Cottom, Daniel, 41, 141, 142
cousin-marriage, vii, 13, 17, 22, 24, 27, 34, 40, 59–60, 67, 132; in Austen, ix–x, 19, 32–37, 43, 49–50, 135–36; in C. Brontë, xi, 99, 109–10; as conservative practice, 35–37, 49–50; as economic strategy, 34–35, 109; impact on offspring of, 13, 86–87, 110, 133–34, 136–38; as "inbreeding," 28, 132, 217–18n30; as incestuous, 35–36, 40–41; and marriage with a deceased wife's sister, 13, 24, 67, 84–85, 86–87, 117–18, 136; among the middle classes, 13; in *Wuthering Heights,* 27–28
Craik, Dinah Mulock, viii, 87
Criminal Law Amendment Act (1885), 189

D'Albertis, Deirdre, 146
Dallas, E. S., 140
Darwin, Charles, xi, 15, 68, 116–18, 129–30, 134–41, 145, 158, 231n69; *The Descent of Man,* 123–25, 134, 135–36; *The Origin of Species,* 120, 134; *The Variation of Animals and Plants under Domestication,* 135, 137–39; *On the Various Contrivances,* 134–35, 136, 137
Darwin, George, 135–36
Davidoff, Leonore, 26, 59, 108, 217n28, 218n40
Davidson, Roger, 191
Davies, Emily, 141
Dealtry, Emily, 57, 59, 75, 82, 84, 206
Debrabant, Mary, 145
Deceased Wife's Sister Marriage Act (1907), 2, 4, 58, 66, 177
deployments of alliance and sexuality, 5, 16–19, 24, 84, 110
DeSalvo, Louise, 175
Detloff, Madelyn, 208, 241n13
Dever, Carolyn, 21, 88, 220n11, 241n9
Dickens, Charles, viii, 69, 88
Disraeli, Benjamin: *Sybil,* 7; *Coningsby,* 133
divorce, 66, 146
Duckworth, George, 1–4, 174–75, 177–78, 180, 181–85, 211n2
Duckworth, Gerald, 175, 183–86

Early History of Man (Tylor), 138
Eliot, George, vii, ix, xi, 27, 29, 116–18, 119,
    123, 127–28, 130–32, 134, 141, 142, 144,
    147, 157, 184, 205, 207, 208–9; *Adam
    Bede,* 118–19; "The *Antigone* and Its
    Moral," 208; *Daniel Deronda,* 116, 132;
    Felix Holt, 116; *Middlemarch,* 79, 116,
    208; *The Mill on the Floss,* xi, 115, 116,
    117, 118–29, 134, 140–43, 144, 146, 208,
    232n7, 233n22; "Mr. Gilfil's Love Story,"
    157; "The Modern Hep! Hep! Hep!" 131;
    "The Natural History of German Life,"
    130, 132–34; *Silas Marner,* 99, 122, 157;
    The Spanish Gypsy, 128–29
endogamy, ix, x, 23, 26, 37, 55–56, 134; and
    the *Antigone,* 206; and affinal marriage,
    83; as a class/race formation; ix; 13–14,
    22–24, 145; and cousin-marriage, 27,
    34, 41; and exchange, 20–24; and
    "interbreeding," xi, 14, 15, 20, 118,
    130–40, 141
Esty, Jed, 236–37n22
eugenics, 110
exogamy, 4, 13–14, 26, 27, 49–50, 53,
    116; and cousin-marriage, 27, 33; and
    exchange, 20–24; and the heterosexual
    marriage plot, x, 22, 33, 36–37, 49, 55–56,
    83, 206–7; and "intercrossing," xi, 27, 118,
    120, 126, 130, 133–34, 135–36, 138–39

Fabian, Johannes, 184
family membership, 87–88, 95–96; as an
    effect of affinity, xii, 27, 39–40, 43–44,
    59–60, 64–65, 88–89, 107–8, 156, 207;
    as an effect of biology, 28, 29, 39, 44,
    59–60, 64–65, 88–89, 90–92; in *Jane Eyre,*
    103–7; and language, 45–47, 156; and
    marital choice, 5, 38–45, 65; performative
    dimension of, 147–48, 157–60; racialized
    basis for, xi, 23, 24–29. *See also* adoption
first family, viii–ix, x, 35, 37–40, 47, 59–60,
    63, 65, 67, 81, 84, 85, 153, 162, 203, 208;
    in *Deerbrook,* 72; in *Jane Eyre,* 103–4, 110,
    112; in *The Mill on the Floss,* 121–22, 142;
    in relationship to second family, x, 65–67,
    85, 103–4, 105–6, 115–16, 149, 165,
    176, 177
first marriage, 9, 27, 42, 61, 65, 68, 149, 204
first wife, 9, 27, 57, 83, 58, 61, 63–64, 67,
    68, 82, 83, 152, 162, 178. *See also* first
    marriage *and* first family
Forster, E. M., 62; *Howards End,* 66, 82;
    Marianne Thornton, 57–8
Foster, Thomas Campbell, 10–11

Franklin, Sarah, 147–48
friends: as a kin term, 26, 32, 46
friendship, 46, 52, 60
Friendship's Garland (Arnold), 64
Froula, Christine, 176, 181

Gagnier, Regenia, 196
Gallagher, Catherine, 133, 231n69
Galton, Francis, 130, 133, 135
Gaskell, Elizabeth, viii, ix, 29; *Mary Barton,*
    235n46; *Wives and Daughters,* xi–xii, 60,
    144–47, 148–156, 157–58, 159–73, 207
Giaour, The (Byron), 63, 171
Girard, René, 165
Gladstone, William, 65
Goetz, William R., 25
Greenwood, Frederick, 145
Gruner, Elizabeth Rose, 60
Gullette, Margaret Morganroth, 61, 65

Hacking, Ian, 12
Haggerty George E., 46, 74
Hale, William Hale, 65
Hall, Catherine, 108
Hall, Radclyffe, 188
Hannah (Craik), 87
Hardy, Thomas, viii, 133
Hemyng, Bracebridge, 8–9, 10, 11
Henkle, Roger B., 6
Henson, Louise, 145
Herbert, Christopher, 183
Héritier, Françoise, 63
Hills, Jack, 1–3, 4, 177–78, 179–81
Hills, Stella Duckworth, 1, 2, 175, 176,
    178–81, 182, 184, 186, 239n49
History of Sexuality, The (Foucault), 5, 12–13,
    16–19, 24, 110, 193, 213–14n59
Homans, Margaret, 150, 154, 155, 160,
    169, 172
Horrible London (Sims), 188
Howe, Patricia, 95
Hughes, Linda K., 148
human biological reproduction, xi, 91,
    117–18, 125–26, 128–29, 137, 143, 205–6;
    interbreeding and, 14–15, 20, 118, 120,
    131–32, 135, 137–39; intercrossing and,
    13, 14, 27–28, 118, 119–20, 123, 125–26,
    129–30, 133–35, 137, 140, 142. *See also*
    miscegenation
Huth, Alfred Henry, 13, 29

incest, vii, ix; affinal, 4, 9, 59, 64, 67–68, 76,
    181; anxiety about, 20; consanguineal, 4,
    64; and cousin-marriage, 13, 67;

incest *(continued)*
heterosexual, 12, 18; homosexual, 65; incitement to, 19, 24; instinctual aversion to, 15; intergenerational, 17–18, 206; lack of criminal penalties for, 4, 6; as limited to "biological" relations, 4, 8; in *Mansfield Park,* 35–37, 40–41; and miscegenation, xi, 13–14, 19–20, 25; and the middle classes, 1–2, 5, 7, 9, 13, 18, 24; in *The Mill on the Floss,* 115–16; prohibitions on, ix, 16–17; as a racialized formation, 13, 18–19, 23, 24; as a "savage" practice, vii, xii, 5, 6, 13–17, 187–88, 238n40; sibling, 25, 115–16, 213–14n59; and trauma, xii, 175; in *Wives and Daughters,* 151–52, 172–73; and the working classes, 5–8, 9, 11–15, 192; in *Wuthering Heights,* 25. *See also* incestuous sexual abuse, marriage with a deceased wife's sister, *and* endogamy
incest taboo, 13–14, 17–18, 20–21, 49, 55–56, 69, 139, 206, 217n27; 231n69; among apes, 138–39
incestuous adultery, 11, 34, 49, 65, 67
incestuous sexual abuse, 4–5, 175, 185–87, 188–91, 192, 235n3. *See also* sexual abuse
in-laws. *See* affinal kin
interbreeding. *See* endogamy
intercrossing. *See* exogamy

Jackson, Louise A., 189–91
Jann, Rosemary, 6
Johnson, Claudia L., 35–36, 37, 54, 55
Joyce, James, 188

King, Amy M., 117
Knoepflmacher, U. C., 128
Koven, Seth, 8
Kreilkamp, Ivan, 215n77
Kucich, John, 107, 111, 114
Kuper, Adam, 23

Lamonaca, Drew, 93
Langland, Elizabeth, 151, 160
Lansbury, Coral, 151
Lanser, Susan Sniader, 46
Law, Jules, 121, 122, 128–29
Lawrence, D. H., 188, 207
Leaska, Mitchell, 199
Lee, Hermione, 176
Levenson, Michael, 61, 65, 69
Levin, Amy K., 164, 166
Levine, George, 128, 158
Lévi-Strauss, Claude, 13, 19, 22, 205
Levy, Anita, 14, 91

Lewes, George Henry, xi, 116, 118, 123, 129, 130–31, 132, 133, 142
London, Bette, 113
London Labour and the London Poor (Mayhew), 8
Lubbock, Sir John, 135–36
Lund, Michael, 148

Maine, Henry, 95, 159, 223n11, 224n13; *Ancient Law,* 61, 87–88, 89–92, 157–58, 224n12
Marriage of Near Kin, The (Huth), 13, 29
Martineau, Harriet, viii, 83–84; *Deerbrook,* x, xii, 61, 69–70, 71–72, 74, 75–80, 83, 84, 156, 162, 165, 176
Marcus, Jane, 200
Marcus, Sharon, 21–22, 37, 46, 74, 89, 204
marriage with a deceased husband's brother, 17, 65
marriage with a deceased wife's sister (MDWS), x, xii, 5, 7–8, 16, 22, 24, 39–40, 57–59, 60–62, 73, 74, 75, 79, 91, 149, 158, 161; arguments against, 3, 11, 64–65, 67, 86; arguments for, 3, 8, 22, 62–64, 68, 82–83, 86–87, 214n63; and cousin-marriage, 67, 84–85, 86–87, 117, 136; Martineau on, 83–84; and middle-class male prerogative, 9–11, 61; among the middle classes, 8–11, 13; prohibitions on, x, 2–3, 7–9, 14, 17, 24; as prostitution, 8–10, 11; in "Reminiscences," 177–79; in "A Sketch of the Past," 180–81; among the working classes, 8–11. *See also* affinity
marriage plot, vii, x, 33–37, 41, 49, 51, 55, 61, 88; cross-class, 33–34, 36. *See also* endogamy *and* exogamy
Mason, Michael, 12
Matrimonial Causes Act (1857), 4, 64
May, Leila Silvana, 60
McDonagh, Josephine, 128
McKinnon, Susan, 147–48
McLennan, John F., 14, 15–16, 138, 231n69; *Primitive Marriage,* 15, 23–24, 89, 91–92, 93
Meyer, Susan, 25, 95, 129
Michie, Elsie B., 25
Michie, Helena, viii, 61, 204
Miller, D. A., 49
Miller, J. Hillis, 25
miscegenation, 27–28, 97–100, 129–30, 223n11, 231n69; anxiety about, 20; incest and, xi, 13–14, 19–20, 25; as "intercrossing," 130–31. *See also* exogamy

Miss Brown (Lee), 187–88

Mitford, Mary Russell, 38

monogamous marriage, 21, 89, 91, 92; as sign of civilization, 14–17

Morgan, Lewis Henry, 92

Morris, Pam, 146

Morris, Polly, 7

My Apprenticeship (Webb), 238n40

natural selection, 125, 138–39, 141

Nightingale, Florence, 132

Nord, Deborah Epstein, 25, 109, 110–11, 128–29

Novy, Marianne, 157

Oliphant, Margaret, viii; *Hester,* 222n34; *Miss Marjoribanks,* 161; *The Perpetual Curate,* 68, 220n4

"one flesh," 9, 64–65, 67, 69, 71, 80, 147, 204. *See also* affinal marriage *and* marriage with a deceased wife's sister

Ottenheimer, Martin, 135

Paine, Thomas, 132

pangenesis, 123

Perry, Ruth, viii; 34, 37, 42, 49–50, 81–82, 83, 84–85

Peters, Laura, 88

Pollak, Ellen, 5, 16, 19–21, 48, 55

polyandry, 91

Poovey, Mary, 38

pornography, 17

primitive promiscuity, 14–16, 91

primogeniture, 42

Psomiades, Kathy Alexis, 22, 23, 92, 224n12–13

psychoanalysis, 18

Punishment of Incest Act (1908), 3–4, 212n31

Pusey, Edward, 64–65, 66

remarriage. *See* second marriage

Report on the Sanitary Condition of the Labouring Population of Great Britain (Chadwick), 7, 11–12

Ritvo, Harriet, 117, 123, 138

Robbins, Bruce, 215n79

Rogers, Henry, 86

Royal Commission on the Housing of the Working Classes, 6

Royal Commission on Prohibited Degrees of Affinity, 10, 63, 66, 67, 80, 82, 171

Rubin, Gayle, 21

Sanders, Valerie, 46, 111

Schneider, David, 147

Schor, Hilary M., 150, 151, 172

second family, viii, 25, 40, 56, 60–61, 65, 70–71, 83, 110, 116, 136, 176; in Austen's fiction, x, 34, 41–43, 46–47, 56, 60, 61, 68, 81–83, 85; in *Deerbrook,* 70–71, 75–78; in *The Inheritance of Evil,* 70–71, 74; in *Jane Eyre,* 103–4, 110, 112; in *The Mill on the Floss,* 121–22; in relationship to first family, x, 65–67, 85, 105–6; in *Wives and Daughters,* 146, in *Wuthering Heights,* 25. *See also* conjugality

second marriage, 5, 9, 61, 82, 176, 204; impact of first marriage on, 65–66; in *Wives and Daughters,* xii, 146, 148–52, 153, 155, 159, 162, 165, 166, 168. *See also* marriage with a deceased wife's sister

second wife, x, 20, 27, 62, 65; in *Wives and Daughters,* 151–52, 161–62. *See also* second marriage *and* wife's sister

Sedgwick, Eve Kosofsky, 17–18, 74, 201–2, 203–6

sexual abuse, xii, 175, 186–87, 188–91, 194–95, 196, 235n3, 238n45

sexual selection, 68, 124–25

Shuttleworth, Sally, 128

sibling terminology, 25, 39, 44–47, 60, 89, 110–13, 147, 156

siblingship, ix, xii, 18, 21, 24, 25–26, 38–39, 40, 50, 54, 59–61, 64–68, 85, 103, 113–14, 146, 164, 177

sisters, xii, 45–47, 60, 62, 63, 74–75; by birth, 47, 50, 60, 66, 67; desire between, 74–75, 164–65; jealousy or rivalry between, 61–62, 71–72, 74, 163, 179–80; by marriage, 4, 8, 9, 39, 44–47, 60; in the second family, x, 2, 58, 69–70, 72, 79–80, 83–85, 170. *See also* wife's sister

Skene, Felicia, viii, 76, 176; *The Inheritance of Evil,* x, 61, 64–65, 69, 70–71, 72–74, 75, 79, 80, 162

Smart, Carol, 189

Smith, Jonathan, 136

Snyder, Carey, 237n22

sodomy, 237n31, 238n42

Sollors, Werner, 130

Spencer, Herbert, 130, 131, 133, 142, 183

Stephen, Julia, 178

Stephen, Laura, 63, 183

Stephen, Leslie, 63, 176, 178, 179, 180, 184–85

Stephen, Minny Thackeray, 63

Stephen, Thoby, 180

step-relations, 8, 235n3; as strangers, 153, 159; in *Sense and Sensibility*, 41, 43; in *Wives and Daughters*, xii, 146, 149, 152, 153, 155, 157, 159–61, 163–65, 171, 172. *See also* blended family
Stocking, George W., Jr., 140
Stoler, Ann Laura, 13, 17, 18–19
strangers, 31–32, 35–36, 37, 44–45, 56, 88, 90–92; molestation by, xii, 189–91; risks of second marriage to, 22, 35, 40, 82–83; transformation into kin, 43–48, 110, 146–47, 204
Swanson, Diana L., 177
Symonds, John Addington, 204

Tadmor, Naomi, 46
Tanner, Tony, 33, 35, 36, 61, 115
Tess of the d'Urbervilles (Hardy), 133, 221n18
Thackeray, Anny, 63, 178
Thornton, Henry, 57–9, 75, 82, 84
Thornton, Marianne, 57–60, 65, 82, 84, 206
Trollope, Anthony, viii; *The Way We Live Now,* 13, 19
Trumbach, Randolph, 39, 49
Tuite, Clara, 33–34, 41, 50

Uglow, Jennifer, 146

Vicinus, Martha, 74

Walkowitz, Judith R., 7
Walton, Jean, 22
Weiner, Annette, 21, 22, 24
wife's sister, 9, 11, 20, 22, 27, 58, 61, 62–64, 66–67, 68–69, 71, 75, 79, 85, 170; as stepmother, 58–59, 63, 73, 82; preferable to a stranger, x, 82–83
Wilson, Elizabeth, 5–6
Wohl, Anthony, 11–12
Wolf, Amy, 45
Wolfram, Sybil, 4
Woolf, Virginia, viii, ix, xii–xiii, 3, 6, 116, 189, 206–7; "22 Hyde Park Gate," 3, 181; *Mrs. Dalloway,* 3; *Night and Day,* 3, 177; *The Pargiters,* xii, 177, 187–88, 190, 191, 192–96; "Reminiscences," 1–3, 177–81; "A Sketch of the Past," 174–75, 180–87, 191; *Three Guineas,* 176–77, 182, 186, 208–9; *To the Lighthouse,* 178, 179; *The Voyage Out,* 3, 176; *The Years,* xii–xiii, 176, 177, 179, 185, 188, 191–94, 196–200
working-class housing, 11–12; overcrowding as cause of incest in, 6–8, 11–12, 238n40

Yeazell, Ruth Bernard, 147, 148, 151, 152, 153–54
Young, Robert J. C., 129